Archaeologies of Indigenous Presence

UNIVERSITY PRESS OF FLORIDA

Florida A&M University, Tallahassee
Florida Atlantic University, Boca Raton
Florida Gulf Coast University, Ft. Myers
Florida International University, Miami
Florida State University, Tallahassee
New College of Florida, Sarasota
University of Central Florida, Orlando
University of Florida, Gainesville
University of North Florida, Jacksonville
University of South Florida, Tampa
University of West Florida, Pensacola

ARCHAEOLOGIES OF
INDIGENOUS PRESENCE

Edited by Tsim D. Schneider and Lee M. Panich

UNIVERSITY PRESS OF FLORIDA

Gainesville / Tallahassee / Tampa / Boca Raton

Pensacola / Orlando / Miami / Jacksonville / Ft. Myers / Sarasota

Production of this book was funded in part by a grant from
the Office of the Provost at Santa Clara University.

First cloth printing, 2022
First paperback printing, 2023

28 27 26 25 24 23   6 5 4 3 2 1

Library of Congress Cataloging-in-Publication Data
Names: Schneider, Tsim D., 1979– editor. | Panich, Lee M., 1978– editor.
Title: Archaeologies of indigenous presence / edited by Tsim D. Schneider and Lee M. Panich
Description: Gainesville : University Press of Florida, [2022] | Includes
bibliographical references and index.
Identifiers: LCCN 2021027216 (print) | LCCN 2021027217 (ebook) | ISBN
9780813069159 (hardback) | ISBN 9780813070001 (pdf) | ISBN 9780813080185 (pbk.)
Subjects: LCSH: Indigenous peoples—North America—Antiquities. | Indians
of North America—Antiquities. | Indians of North America—History. |
BISAC: SOCIAL SCIENCE / Indigenous Studies | SOCIAL SCIENCE / Archaeology
Classification: LCC E61 .A718 2022 (print) | LCC E61 (ebook) | DDC 970.01—dc23
LC record available at https://lccn.loc.gov/2021027216
LC ebook record available at https://lccn.loc.gov/2021027217

The University Press of Florida is the scholarly publishing agency for the State University System
of Florida, comprising Florida A&M University, Florida Atlantic University, Florida Gulf Coast
University, Florida International University, Florida State University, New College of Florida,
University of Central Florida, University of Florida, University of North Florida, University
of South Florida, and University of West Florida.

University Press of Florida
2046 NE Waldo Road
Suite 2100
Gainesville, FL 32609
http://upress.ufl.edu

Contents

Part II. Conceptual and Practical Advances

Figures

Tables

Acknowledgments

We owe a debt of gratitude to many people, all of whom worked against the backdrop of the COVID-19 pandemic, wildfires, hurricanes, and political turmoil to keep this project on track. We appreciate their patience and flexibility. The contributors to the volume all deserve heartfelt thanks for producing their engaging chapters under these trying circumstances. The collected chapters and the book as a whole were improved by the insightful and constructive reviews Charles Cobb and Rae Gould provided. We thank Heather Law Pezzarossi and James Snead for sharing their insights into the issues explored here in a previous forum. Ka'ila Farrell-Smith generously shared her artwork (a collaboration with Judith Baumann) for the book cover; it is a powerful and beautiful statement of Indigenous presence. We also thank the staff of the University Press of Florida, particularly Meredith Babb, Mary Puckett, and Marthe Walters, who along with Kate Babbitt ensured a seamless editorial and production process.

Our ideas on the subject of Indigenous presence in archaeology continue to be inspired by our work and conversations with Tribal communities in California, including the Federated Indians of Graton Rancheria, the Amah Mutsun Tribal Band, the Muwekma Ohlone Tribe, the Ohlone Indian Tribe, and the Paipai Indian community of Baja California, Mexico. We acknowledge that considerable work must still be done to attain a decolonized archaeology centered on the goals and interests of Indigenous communities. As one further step in the right direction, however, we are inspired and heartened that the chapters presented here include the perspectives from several Indigenous scholars, Tribal staff, and academic and CRM partners from across North America.

Lastly, we thank our families for their love and support in such a disruptive year.

1

Introduction

Archaeology, Unknowing, and the Recognition of Indigenous Presence in Post-1492 North America

LEE M. PANICH AND TSIM D. SCHNEIDER

The past three decades have seen important developments in archaeological studies of colonial encounters, which have shifted from a focus on the negative impacts of colonialism for Indigenous societies—disease, violence, cultural suppression—to more nuanced and collaborative explorations of how Native people made do despite the pressures of the times. This volume aims to take the conversation one step further by identifying and countering archaeological practices that range from field recording to higher-level interpretations that continue to support narratives of cultural loss among North America's Native groups. The contributors to this volume, which include several Native scholars and Tribal resource managers, examine different ways that archaeologists can center long-term Indigenous presence in the practice of fieldwork, laboratory analysis, scholarly communication, and public interpretation.

At the outset, we want to acknowledge the great strides archaeologists have made to grapple more fully with the effects of colonialism and the continued persistence of Indigenous peoples throughout the world. The archaeology of postcontact North America, in particular, has advanced in many important ways as non-Native researchers and Indigenous communities have increasingly worked together to address decades of scientific colonialism (Kerber 2006; Lippert 1997; McGuire 1992; Watkins 2005; Zimmerman 1997). Yet even as these relationships evolve, the archaeological toolkit for documenting and interpreting the full range of Indigenous experiences in the centuries since the arrival of Europeans remains underdeveloped. In an era of increasing conceptual, geospatial, and analytical sophistication, the archaeological investigation of postcontact Native presence is often limited to times and places where archaeologists expect to find Native people—sites such as forts, missions, and reservations—or reflected by a limited range of index artifacts that perpetuate essentialist understandings of Indigenous identity and cultural practices (Lightfoot 2006; Rubertone 2012; Silliman 2010). These frameworks hinder deeper discussions about Indigenous social networks, cultural perseverance, or long-term connections to homelands. We have a garage full of increasingly powerful tools and technologies for conducting the archaeology of postcontact North America, but when we peer into the proverbial dig kit we see only a worn Marshalltown trowel.

In this introductory chapter, we examine the reasons why North American archaeology still struggles to identify and interpret Native sites dating to the sixteenth century onward and what we might do to improve practices. As discussed in the first section, we see the discipline of archaeology as part of a dominant society that has a long history of simultaneously questioning Indigenous authenticity and maintaining ignorance about continued Native presence. While these ideological foundations pose significant obstacles to the work of centering Native histories in the study of the postcontact Americas, a wide array of scholars and Tribal communities are pointing the way forward. In the second section, we provide an overview of what we see as some of the key remedies to several major conceptual and practical challenges identified in the contributions to this book and in the broader literature on the historical archaeology of Native Americans (Figure 1.1). We close by introducing the organization of this book and framing the contributions within broader structures of unknowing in archaeology and society at large.

Historical Legacies: Authenticity and Unknowing

In popular consciousness, Native Americans—like Indigenous peoples elsewhere—often occupy a space outside of time. They are seen as passive relics who are incapable of change and are in possession of cultures that are incompatible with modernity (Cipolla 2013; Deloria 2004; McGuire 1992; Raibmon 2005). This mythology limits what scholars and the public alike consider to be

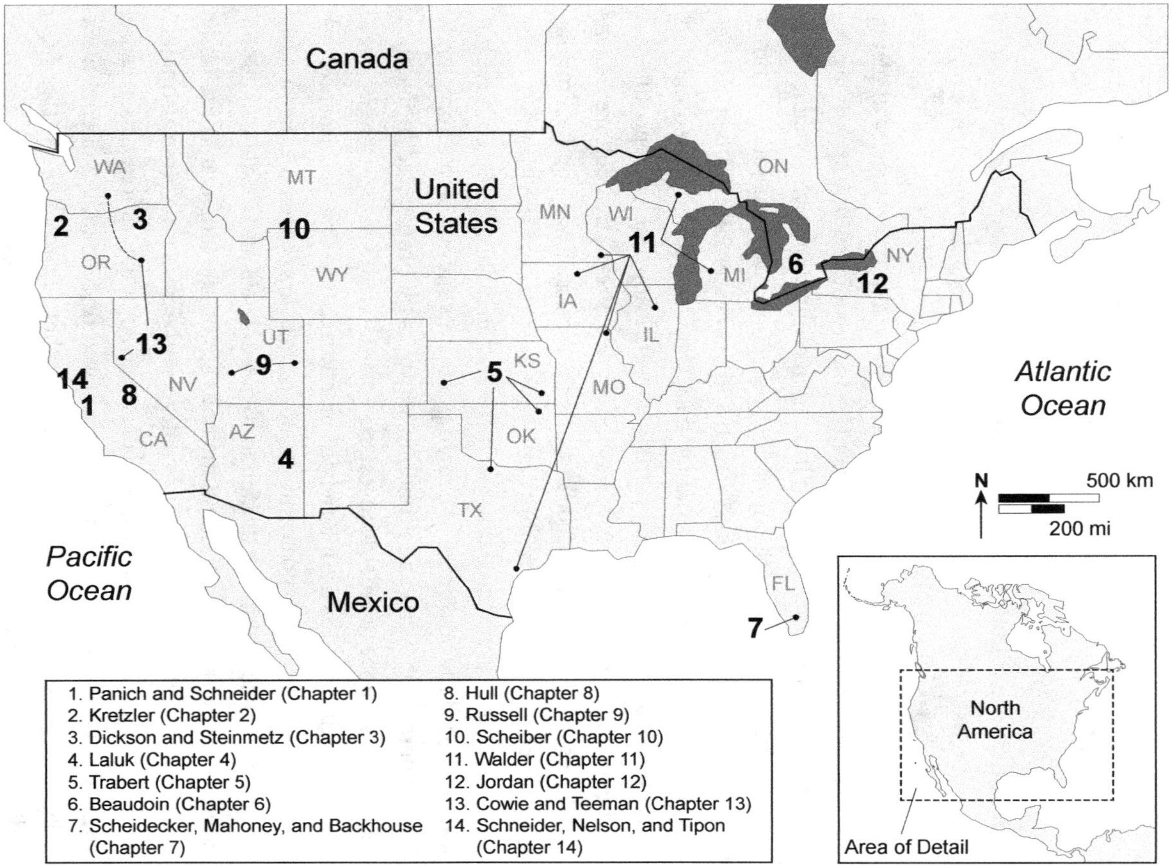

Figure 1.1. Case study locations featured in this volume.

"authentic" Native lifeways to traditions that existed before the arrival of Europeans. Accordingly, any deviation from that normative baseline is seen as externally induced change and thus inauthentic. Such assumptions are baked into the very fabric of anthropology, as evidenced by the "salvage ethnography" of the late nineteenth and early twentieth centuries (Bruchac 2018). Formidable figures such as Alfred Kroeber dismissed the lifeways of Native people living at the time in the search for supposedly pure and uncontaminated Indigenous culture (Lightfoot 2005).

Assumptions about Indigenous authenticity have myriad ramifications for how archaeologists understand and document long-term presence on the landscape. Sites where Native people lived and worked are typically identified by certain types of projectile points, pottery styles, and species of plants and animals that stand in for "authentic" Indigenous cultural practices. As we have argued elsewhere, a major limitation of this approach is that it effectively conflates identity with chronology, coupling Native histories to times before the arrival of Europeans (Panich and Schneider 2019). When archaeologists have considered postcontact sites, they have long focused on sites such as missions and forts where outsiders were known to have encountered "authentic" Indians and where it was therefore expected that culture change could be successfully measured. In this way, the essentialist underpinnings of early acculturation frameworks not only underscored the idea that colonial institutions represented the final instantiation of Indigenous cultures but also foreclosed the possibility of contemporaneous sites in Native homelands and the persistent social and economic networks that connected Indigenous people across those broader landscapes.

When archaeologists use interrelated practices that favor a mythical precontact past at the expense of postcontact realities, they inadvertently create a position of ignorance within the discipline—what Schaefli and Godlewska (2014, 299) call "an outcome of structural methods of not-knowing that, consciously or not, perpetuate the status quo, privilege, and domination" (see also Sullivan and Tuana 2007). Within the field of archaeology, ignorance exists because we have collectively, if tacitly, accepted a flawed understanding of continued Indigenous presence in North America and other settler contexts. This state of disciplinary ignorance, in turn, is used to justify access to and control over Indigenous heritage and to discount community concerns about archaeological research (Cipolla 2013; Custer 2018; Lippert 2021; Schneider and Hayes 2020).

Ignorance, in this sense, is a form of "colonial unknowing [that] manifests in ways that foreclose upon future possibilities." In such a context, "decolonization is named as either impossible or unreasonable" (Vimalassery et al. 2016).

Such unknowing supports the structure of settler colonialism, which takes as its central logic the elimination of Indigenous peoples, through violence, removal, or—as in this case—scholarship (Wolfe 1999, 2006). Indeed, the same ignorance that exists in archaeology characterizes much of the public sphere, including newspaper stories, museum exhibits, and school curricula where the sovereignty of contemporary Tribal groups is often questioned on the basis of cultural essentialism and misunderstandings about the continued presence of Native people throughout various colonial regimes (Schneider 2019). Since the inception of the discipline of American archaeology, the dominant society has mobilized it to "bury Native history." As O'Brien (2010) discusses for New England, archaeology allowed settlers to ignore living Native Americans by locating them physically in the ground and therefore in the past. When scholars and popular audiences did look to the evidence from the colonial period, what they saw was loss of authenticity. Archaeology has thus contributed to the myth of the vanishing Indian, or what Wilcox (2009) has aptly called "terminal narratives."

These inherited challenges in North American archaeology are both diffused and perpetuated across various sectors, including academic archaeology and cultural resource management (CRM). But these obstacles are not insurmountable. Indigenous and community-based participatory forms of archaeological research, for example, reflect positive steps toward decolonizing the field and dismantling harmful narratives of Indigenous cultural loss and disappearance (Atalay 2006; Cowie et al. 2019; Gould et al. 2020; Marek-Martinez 2021). Relevance, responsibility, and reciprocity must not be confined to the research endeavor alone, however. The widespread, or epistemic, saturation of such narrative tropes may require additional "undisciplining" efforts and structural transformations in our colleges, universities, and civic domains (Schneider and Hayes 2020; see Flewellen et al. 2021 for similar arguments about how to dismantle antiblackness in archaeology).

Inspiration may also be found in recent calls for an explicitly pragmatic approach to archaeology, which is defined by a concern for the effects of archaeological research in the world (Preucel and Mrozowski 2010). As applied to the archaeology of the post-1492 Americas, a primary organizing principle involves documenting Indigenous presence at a range of geographical locations and temporal contexts and working with Tribal communities to disseminate that information beyond the walls of academia and CRM. This type of research helps counter terminal narratives, undo historical silences, and where appropriate can provide evidence for Tribes' ongoing cases for federal recognition or restoration (Mrozowski 2012). This is the approach we take in this book. Pragmatism also rests upon self-reflection. We suggest that the act of identifying and understanding the colonial "obstinacies of unknowing" (Vimalassery et al. 2016) that undergird American archaeology can help recalibrate and enhance archaeological methods and analytical techniques used to fathom Indigenous peoples' deep and continued presence in North America. In the following sections, we offer some suggestions—guided by the contributions to this volume—that may help us in the goal of more fully centering postcontact Indigenous histories.

Conceptual and Practical Advances

Reimagining Colonial Time and Space

TERMINOLOGY

One of the clearest and perhaps most critical advances in archaeology during the past three decades has been the move away from the pejorative and limiting concept of prehistory in the archaeology of Indigenous peoples (Lightfoot 1995; Scheiber and Mitchell 2010; Oland et al. 2012; Schmidt and Mrozowski 2013). By breaking the barrier created by the arbitrary distinction between prehistory and the historical period, we can more easily trace the "changing continuities" that constitute dynamic cultural traditions (Ferris 2009). However, those of us studying more recent times are left with few good alternatives for temporal precision. In academic writing, many archaeologists—ourselves included—use the slightly less problematic shorthand of precontact and postcontact. Yet many official archaeological recording systems still rely on the prehistoric-historic dichotomy or the ambiguous triad of prehistoric, protohistoric, and historic (Panich and Schneider 2019). One way forward is to reframe site chronologies in calendar years. This intervention breaks the link between chronology and identity and invites archaeologists to justify how and why ethnicities are assigned to site occupants (Beaudoin, this volume).

Recent scholarship also examines how archaeologists refer to the processes that unfolded during and after the arrival of Europeans. Silliman (2005), for example, artfully dismantles the phrase "culture contact" for its emphasis on early encounters and its lack of attention to issues of power. While he argues that the term colonialism better captures the issues surrounding most instances of Indigenous peoples' interactions with newcomers, others have maintained the need to carve out space for distinct historical processes. For example, Trabert (2018, this volume) suggests that the concept of pericolonialism more accurately reflects certain instances in which Native people maintained autonomy outside of colonial systems. Others prefer "cultural entanglement" over colonialism, given that it covers a broader array of historical contexts, including those in which Indigenous groups held the upper hand (Beaudoin 2019; Jordan 2014). In fact, Mitchell and Scheiber (2010) argue that the continued focus on colonialism itself, as opposed to Indigenous autonomy, is a stubborn remnant of centuries-old colonial discourses. Lastly, we must critically assess our usage of terms such as "abandoned" that gave cover to colonial land grabs in the past and that continue to obscure Indigenous presence today (Church et al. 2019).

Other shifts in terminology may be generated through collaborative approaches with living communities (Cowie and Teeman, this volume). As several chapters in this volume explore, archaeological time—including but not limited to the concept of prehistory—does not mesh with the way Native peoples see their own pasts. Collaboration may lead to still further self-reflection and refinements in the decisions we make. This includes how we describe what we do and the things we find, practices that may need updating to demonstrate more complete connections between communities and their histories, even in the recent past. For example, Kretzler (this volume) describes the use of the term "belongings" instead of artifacts, an intervention that stems from collaborative approaches with the Confederated Tribes of Grand Ronde. Kretzler states that "belongings are proof of presence, not absence."

TEMPORAL RANGE

At the same time that archaeologists have deemphasized the "divide" between prehistoric and historic time by extending archaeological approaches to Native-lived colonialism into the ancient past, many have also extended their temporal scope forward. These approaches move beyond the early colonial forts, missions, and mercantile outposts to consider how Native people dealt with the expanded scope of sustained colonialism (Frink 2016; Lightfoot and Gonzalez 2018; Scheiber and Burnett 2020). In many North American contexts, this temporal range largely maps onto the settler colonial states of the United States and Canada, opening up new avenues for research into how Native people negotiated still other insidious forms of colonialism. This work, however, is not without risks. As Cowie and Teeman (this volume) argue, researching past traumas, such as the afterlife of the Native American boarding school and removal experiences, requires adequate space for healing among community partners.

In histories of the recent past, the use of terms such as "American period" continues to foreground colonial systems rather than Native people. In contrast, a focus on presence may require archaeologists to approach temporalizations from a slightly different perspective. As Liebmann (2012) discusses for the Pueblo Southwest, referring to times after the arrival of Euro-Americans as the "historic period" does a disservice to the Indigenous nations who persisted despite successive waves of colonial encroachment. He argues that the existing Pecos Classification should be expanded forward in time to include a Pueblo VI period covering 1848 to the present. This call corresponds to the suggestion that calendrical dates may offer a less biased way of recording sites that date to relatively recent times and therefore a way around essentialist assumptions that continue to locate Native people solely in the precontact past (Holland-Lulewicz et al. 2020; Panich and Schneider 2019; Scheiber and Finley 2012).

The types of sites and materials Native people used after the arrival of Europeans vary considerably. Many ancient sites continued to have profound importance to Native communities well into the late nineteenth and early twentieth centuries, as exemplified by the use of long-standing sites as locations for the Ghost Dance in Nevada (Carroll et al. 2004). Yet, as several chapters in this volume discuss, archaeologists must also be attentive to more recent sites that may not differ substantially from those of Euro-American settlers. Some may relate to labor, including places where Native people were present but primarily used tools and other objects introduced by colonists (Silliman 2010). In other instances, however, Native people may have used mass-produced material culture as a way of securing or maintaining social status or simply because they wanted to (Moore 2020; Watkins 2017; Yellowhorn 2015). These materials and the sites where they were deposited are a complex rejoinder to the trope of authenticity and are crucial for the archaeological study of Indigenous presence.

Geographic Scope

Archaeologists have expanded their geographic focus to include a broader landscape beyond the most visible and enduring colonial institutions (Cobb 2019; Panich and Schneider 2015; Scheiber and Finley 2012; Trabert 2018). One by-product of the early focus on missions, forts, and related sites is that when researching these key colonial establishments, archaeologists and other scholars often lost sight of the rich Native homelands that existed contemporaneously. These were the lands that colonial enterprises operated in, that sustained the Indigenous economies and trade routes that persisted and often percolated though colonial ones, and that supplied the Indigenous labor and know-how that colonialism depended on. As Jordan (this volume) demonstrates, the traditional approach to colonial-era sites produces the same kind of bias as judgmental sampling: the focus on the largest and most visible sites blinds us to smaller locales and the array of decisions Native people made to negotiate the past five centuries. Archaeologists and resource managers must be attentive to sites that are small, that are located in unexpected places, or that lack obvious physical evidence of postcontact use (Laluk, this volume; Scheidecker et al., this volume).

This move away from colonial institutions also helps counter the image of Native people as stuck in carceral, or prison-like, situations in which they had no room to exercise agency or autonomy. A classic example is the Spanish colonial mission system of the North American borderlands. In California, archaeologists have examined mission assemblages for links to external networks through studies of obsidian and beads and have investigated a range of sites outside missions. Some were nearby refuge sites where Native people came together, perhaps clandestinely, for sustenance and community, while others were autonomous population centers that openly challenged colonial domination (Acebo 2020; Bernard and Robinson 2018; Panich and Schneider 2015; Schneider 2015; and see Hull this volume). Native people were not confined by later reservations, either. As detailed by multiple chapters in this volume, many who lived in what is today Oregon and Washington continued to access traditional gathering and fishing areas and to work in the agricultural sector, although recorded archaeological sites related to these pursuits are rare (Kretzler, this volume; Dickson and Steinmetz, this volume).

In other cases, archaeology can help us understand broader Indigenous landscapes that existed both before broad-scale settler incursion and those that date to relatively recent times. For example, Walder (this volume) uses the chemical analysis of glass beads to explore the far-reaching Indigenous trade networks that connected communities in the midcontinent during the seventeenth century. Here, analytical techniques that have often been the purview of precontact archaeology can help us better understand the scope of post-1492 Indigenous landscapes. Similarly, Jordan (this volume) makes the case that sixteenth-century Haudenosaunee settlements included a wider range of site types than previously considered, reflecting a period of autonomy from colonial domination (see also Jordan 2008). Conversely, Native people were present in burgeoning urban areas of the nineteenth century, sometimes working for others but sometimes for themselves (Rubertone 2017). As Law Pezzarossi (2020, 125) demonstrates through a careful consideration of how generations of Nipmuc people continued to dwell in their ancestral landscape even as settler New England grew up around them, archaeology can illuminate "the different ways people occupy a place, to make it their own and continue to reside upon it regardless of ownership."

An Archaeology of Presence

SITE RECORDING PRACTICES

A key insight in many chapters in this volume is that traditional archaeological field identification and recording practices often overlook sites related to post-1492 Indigenous presence, a pattern that can introduce significant biases in regional databases and interpretation (Beaudoin 2016; Panich and Schneider 2019). This is especially true in areas where site recording practices rely on archaeologists to assign an ethnic or cultural affiliation to sites, frequently without explicit guidance on how to make such determinations. In our experience, too often these decisions boil down to training and to essentialist assumptions about what constitutes Indigenous or Euro-American material culture. Items such as projectile points easily stand in for Native occupation while mass-produced ceramics, glass, and metal signify the presence of Euro-Americans. The fact that a site has "historic" materials does not preclude Indigenous presence (e.g., Dickson and Steinmetz, this volume). Conversely, identifying all imported or mass-produced goods as "European" does an equal disservice to potential archaeological studies of what it meant to be European in a settler colonial context (Beaudoin 2019).

Part of the challenge, particularly in CRM, is that archaeologists may not expect to find Indigenous sites dating to more recent times and they are not always prepared to identify those that do. The project-driven nature of CRM work means that archaeologists are forced to make decisions in the field about whether a particular site can be connected to postcontact Indigenous histories instead of selecting a specific site based on background research (as one might do in an academic setting). For many CRM projects, archaeologists must rely on project or regionally specific background documents to help determine a site's temporal placement, ethnic/cultural affiliation, and, ultimately, its significance under the law (Beaudoin, this volume; Dickson and Steinmetz, this volume). These documents often provide meticulously detailed accounts of precontact culture histories that abruptly shift focus away from Native people in the early colonial period, a trend that is only recently starting to change (Byrd et al. 2017; Panich and Schneider 2019). As archaeology moves to see Native people in "unexpected times and unexpected places" (Rubertone 2012), we will do well to reforge our institutional boilerplate to acknowledge that they have been there all along.

Other challenges are more practical. Native people were present at various places on the landscape, ranging from sites they initially inhabited in precontact times to sites that contain only mass-produced materials. Hull (this volume; see also Hull 2009) offers a wealth of advice drawn from her decades of experience in California's Sierra Nevada about how we may better recognize post-1492 Indigenous sites. She stresses multiple lines of evidence, including a pre-fieldwork review of the textual and visual record and attention to post-fieldwork analyses such as radiocarbon and obsidian hydration dating. Her approach meshes well with recent suggestions that archaeologists should move beyond a reliance solely on index artifacts to include chronometric dates, the documentary record, and close collaboration with living communities wherever possible (Birch et al. 2020; Holland-Lulewicz et al. 2020; Panich and Schneider 2019). As Dickson and Steinmetz (this volume) and Russell (this volume) further demonstrate, closer inspection of the places and materials that typically contribute to the "history" of places and entire regions can blur the lines that simultaneously constrain and isolate Native histories to particular time periods (e.g., prehistory) and spaces (e.g., reservations).

PUBLIC MEMORY

Archaeologists are also increasingly involved in collaborative efforts to communicate and commemorate Indigenous persistence in the public sphere. This work involves deconstructing how public memory operates and building alternative narratives—often referred to as "counter-memory"—that help reinsert Native people into the contemporary landscape (Hart 2019; Hayes 2019; Kryder-Reid 2016; McAnany 2016; Van Dyke 2019; and see Flewellen et al. 2021). As we observed in Marin County, California, not long ago, our archaeological and historical research on the lives and experiences of Indigenous peoples who labored at a coastal trading post in the decades after destructive Catholic missions ceased operating (ca. 1830s to 1870s) exposed large gaps in scholarly knowledge of resilient Native communities that countered the terminal narratives of anthropologists (Schneider and Panich 2019; Panich et al. 2021). In response to an impromptu discussion about the importance of our research for the Native American community who approved and permitted the project, one local resident said, "I didn't know there was a Tribe still around." This comment reveals the kinds of engrained silences that endure in conventional wisdom beyond the academy.

The erasure of Indigenous people includes naming practices; Euro-Americans renamed places and landmarks across the North American continent to make the landscape legible to themselves and to connect it to their own histories and sensibilities. As Bauer (2016), a citizen of Round Valley Indian Tribes and professor of history, explores for California, the practice of renaming expunged Native sovereignty over the land and the historical processes that undergirded that relationship and authority (see also Scheiber, this volume). "Creators," Bauer (2016, 28) writes, "made the world for a certain People and a unique People for a specific place." In other cases, Europeans even appropriated Indigenous sites as their own, effectively building mythologies of historical precedence (Trabert, this volume). When Native names are present, they often continue to essentialize Indigenous people—for example, applying Native names to nature preserves while buildings, streets, and cities continue to commemorate colonists and other newcomers. These practices relegate Native people to a time before Europeans, obscuring their continued presence in their homelands (Field et al. 2013; Schneider 2019). Archaeology directed at understanding Native presence can help expose silenced histories of people and communities that have been there all along. This work might encourage reassessments of inaccurate or appropriative place-names and critical and creative re-readings of documents, photographs, and other archives that have contributed to epistemic erasures.

On college campuses, ongoing debates about the complicity of universities in institutionalized, race-based slavery have recently spilled over into examinations of how US higher education has profited from and continues to ignore the ongoing structures of settler colonialism (Clarke and Fine 2010; Lee and Ahtone 2020; Nash 2019). While archaeologists have not been on the front lines of such efforts, they create excellent opportunities to make Indigenous presence an active part of archaeological pedagogy. Given that all North American institutions of higher education are located on Native land and that most have at least some associated archaeological deposits, campus-based archaeologists have opportunities to engage students in exploring how their own institutions relate to Tribal communities past and present. For example, at Santa Clara University in California, Panich and colleagues have embarked on collaborative a project with local Ohlone Tribal groups. This work harnesses students' interest in archaeological topics and encourages people to rethink the existing heritage discourse on campus, which has to date focused on the Spanish colonial mission of Santa Clara de Asís rather than the thousands of Native people who lived and worked there from the 1770s into the 1840s (Kroot and Panich 2020; Lueck and Panich 2020). While not all campuses will have the same archaeological histories, they all have the capacity to engage students in the examination of how their schools choose to acknowledge or ignore long-term Indigenous presence.

COLLABORATION

Collaborative approaches have made great strides in archaeology in recent decades, to the point where it is now axiomatic that archaeological research into postcontact Indigenous sites will involve or even be led by Tribal communities or their members (Jordan 2016, 62–63). What this looks like in practice necessarily varies from project to project, but those rooted in the frameworks of Indigenous archaeology and community-based participatory research are well suited to examine Native histories within the ongoing structures of settler colonialism (Gonzalez et al. 2018; see also Schneider et al., this volume).

One obvious benefit of working with communities is gaining an understanding of the cultural relevance of different locales on the landscape. This includes the need to problematize the places that archaeologists consider to be sites dating to times after the arrival of Europeans. As a host of examples in this volume and elsewhere demonstrate, the physicality of places and the materials earlier inhabitants left behind, either incidentally or intentionally, continue to shape the historical consciousness of future generations. This observation calls into question archaeological concepts of abandonment and reminds us that even sites that may not show physical use in recent times likely still hold cultural importance (Bernstein and Ortman 2020; Duwe 2020; Nelson 2019; Scheiber, this volume; Scheidecker et al., this volume). In other cases, traditional archaeological understandings of what constitutes a "site" may not fully reflect how Native people engage with landscapes and culturally significant places, past and present (Laluk, this volume). Taken together, these points may complicate—but will also enrich—efforts to more fully account for Indigenous presence in the past 500 years.

Encouragingly, these perspectives are being passed on to the next generation of archaeologists through an increasing number of Tribally led and collaborative field schools (e.g., Cipolla and Quinn 2016; Cowie et al. 2019; Gonzalez et al. 2006; Gonzalez and Edwards 2020; Silliman 2008). These projects put Indigenous presence front and center for students, decentering Native communities as the *object* of study and instead modeling research practices that acknowledge Tribes as living entities with their own rights, interests, and epistemologies. Collaborative field schools are especially important, given the trend toward narrowly focused technical training for CRM careers, often at the expense of the slower, less linear path of learning to work respectfully with descendant communities. Yet another critical point here is that community input should not be relegated to the process of doing archaeology but must also include collaborative approaches to interpretation and dissemination of results (Jordan 2016, 73–74). Two recent edited volumes—one focused on long-term Nipmuc landscapes in the Northeast and the other on the Stewart Indian School in Nevada—highlight how these partnerships can grow from field schools through to fully collaborative scholarly works (Cowie et al. 2019; Gould et al. 2020; and see Cowie and Teeman, this volume).

Several chapters in this volume describe promising developments in cultural resource and heritage management in the United States and Canada (Beaudoin, this volume; Cowie and Teeman, this volume; Dickson and Steinmetz, this volume; Russell, this volume; Scheidecker et al., this volume). These examples resonate with wider trends such as Indigenous-run CRM, opened and balanced decision-making powers, novel funding streams, enhanced training and capacity-building opportunities for Tribes, and archaeological practitioners who move back and forth between academic and compliance work (e.g., Lyons 2013, 138–141; Martindale and Lyons 2014; see also Schneider et al., this volume). In light of these developments and as more Native people seek training and find employment in academic and compliance archaeology, collaboration with Tribes in CRM will grow to include not just more construction monitors who have training in the methods and techniques of archaeology but also people who make the key transition into the realms of consultation and report writing. Collaboration in CRM might grow to include co-authored research designs. As collaborative partnerships solidify, compliance reports might also benefit from Tribal members with traditional cultural and ecological knowledge and, increasingly, knowledge of how their epistemology can expand the quality, depth, and accuracy of archaeological knowledge.

Reading This Book

This volume seeks to counter continued patterns of unknowing in archaeology and beyond. In so doing, we see certain parallels in current events. This book initially came together against the backdrop of the Society for American Archaeology's mishandling of sexual misconduct cases and further revelations about the pervasive abuse many in our discipline have suffered (see, for example, Voss 2021). As the contributors prepared their chapters for the peer review process, the world was rocked by the COVID-19 crisis, and as we penned this introduction, the murders of George Floyd and Breonna Taylor laid bare, once again, the systemic violence police perpetrate against Black Americans. All of these seemingly disparate developments are attributable to the "obstinacies of unknowing" that Vimalassery et al.

(2016) describe: the willful ignorance of sexual misconduct in archaeology, the purposeful lack of a coordinated approach to COVID-19 testing in the United States under the Trump administration, and the centuries-long unwillingness of those in the dominant society to acknowledge the simple fact that Black lives matter.

For Native people, these crises echo historical amnesia in both archaeology and in settler society more broadly. Gatekeeping in the form of recent rearguard resistance to repatriation has been a particularly disheartening reminder about scholarly ignorance of Indigenous presence and basic human rights. But such attitudes are part of larger patterns of land theft and the ongoing disregard that the governments of the United States and Canada have for Indigenous sovereignty. From Standing Rock to Wet'suwet'en First Nation to Donald Trump's cherished wall along the US-Mexico border, Tribal nations have steadfastly asserted their sovereignty despite the attempts of governments to ignore it. As Schneider and colleagues (this volume) make clear, Tribal communities have been here all along and they are not going anywhere. However, there are very real risks in exposing these histories simply for the sake of knowing (Schneider and Hayes 2020). The "co-presence" or entanglement of people, places, objects, and experiences requires enormous caution about even the most routine field practices (e.g., collecting materials) that might "*risk disrupting the very fabric of the universe*" (Cowie and Teeman, this volume, emphasis in the original). In these heavy times, the contributors hope that this collection can be one step forward on the path toward an archaeological practice that takes these lessons to heart.

The contributed chapters are organized into two main sections, one focused on conceptual approaches to Native presence and the other on methodological approaches. The first section considers how the very concepts we use—such as the common triad of prehistory, protohistory, and history—continue to limit where and when archaeologists expect to find evidence of Indigenous people at sites that postdate 1492. The second section moves the discussion to the field and the laboratory, highlighting various ways archaeologists across the continent are using the material and documentary record to center long-term Indigenous histories and restore Native presence to a wide variety of archaeological places. A concluding chapter by Schneider, Nelson, and Tipon discusses common themes identified in the case studies included in this volume and explores areas of overlap and possibilities for further work in the archaeology of Native presence. As archaeologists and citizens of the Federated Indians of Graton Rancheria, Schneider, Nelson, and Tipon also provide a reflection on the theme of presence as it relates to their efforts to challenge and enhance archaeological study done in their ancestral lands.

References Cited

Acebo, Nathan Patrick. 2020. Re-Assembling Radical Indigenous Autonomy in the Alta California Hinterlands: Survivance at Puhú. PhD diss., Stanford University.

Atalay, Sonya. 2006. Indigenous Archaeology as Decolonizing Practice. *American Indian Quarterly* 30(3 & 4): 280–310.

Bauer, William J., Jr. 2016. *California Through Native Eyes: Reclaiming History.* Seattle: University of Washington Press.

Beaudoin, Matthew A. 2016. Archaeologists Colonizing Canada: The Effects of Unquestioned Categories. *Archaeologies: Journal of the World Archaeological Congress* 12: 7–37.

———. 2019. *Challenging Colonial Narratives: Nineteenth-Century Great Lakes Archaeology.* Tucson: University of Arizona Press.

Bernard, Julienne, and David W. Robinson. 2018. Contingent Communities in a Region of Refuge. In *Forging Communities in Colonial Alta California,* edited by Kathleen L. Hull and John G. Douglass, 113–132. Tucson: University of Arizona Press.

Bernstein, Bruce, and Scott G. Ortman. 2020. From Collaboration to Partnership at Pojoaque, New Mexico. *Advances in Archaeological Practice* 8(2): 95–110.

Birch, Jennifer, Sturt W. Manning, Samantha Sanft, and Megan Anne Conger. 2020. Refined Radiocarbon Chronologies for Northern Iroquoian Site Sequences: Implications for Coalescence, Conflict, and the Reception of European Goods. *American Antiquity* 86(1): 61–89.

Bruchac, Margaret M. 2018. *Savage Kin: Indigenous Informants and American Anthropologists.* Tucson: University of Arizona Press.

Byrd, Brian F., Adrian R. Whitaker, Patricia J. Mikkelsen, and Jeffrey S. Rosenthal. 2017. San Francisco Bay-Delta Regional Context and Research Design for Native American Archaeological Resources, Caltrans District 4. Unpublished report. California Department of Transportation, Oakland.

Carroll, Alex K., M. Nieves Zedeño, and Richard W. Stoffle. 2004. Landscapes of the Ghost Dance: A Cartography of Numic Ritual. *Journal of Archaeological Method and Theory* 11(2): 127–156.

Church, Minette C., Jason Yaeger, and Christine A. Kray. 2019. Re-Centering the Narrative: British Colonial Memory and the San Pedro Maya. In *Archaeologies of the British in Latin America,* edited by Charles E. Orser, Jr., 73–97. Cham: Springer.

Cipolla, Craig N. 2013. Native American Historical Archaeology and the Trope of Authenticity. *Historical Archaeology* 47(3): 12–22.

Cipolla, Craig N., and James Quinn. 2016. Field School Archaeology the Mohegan Way: Reflections on Twenty Years of Community-Based Research and Teaching. *Journal of Community Archaeology & Heritage* 3(2): 118–134.

Clarke, Max, and Gary Alan Fine. 2010. "A" For Apology: Slavery and the Collegiate Discourses of Remembrance—The Cases of Brown University and the University of Alabama. *History and Memory* 22(1): 81–112.

Cobb, Charles R. 2019. *The Archaeology of Southeastern Native American Landscapes of the Colonial Era.* Gainesville: University Press of Florida.

Cowie, Sarah E., Diane L. Teeman, and Christopher C. LeBlanc, eds. 2019. *Collaborative Archaeology at Stewart Indian School.* Reno: University of Nevada Press.

Custer, Jay F. 2018. A Postcolonial Perspective on Contact Period Archaeology. In *Middle Atlantic Prehistory: Foundations and Practice,* edited by Heather A. Wholey and Carole L. Nash, 325–370. Lanham, MD: Rowman & Littlefield.

Deloria, Phillip J. 2004 *Indians in Unexpected Places.* Lawrence: University Press of Kansas.

Duwe, Samuel. 2020. *Tewa Worlds: An Archaeological History of Being and Becoming in the Pueblo Southwest.* Tucson: University of Arizona Press.

Ferris, Neal. 2009. *The Archaeology of Native-Lived Colonialism: Challenging History in the Great Lakes.* Tucson: University of Arizona Press.

Field, Les W., Alan Leventhal, and Rosemary Cambra. 2013. Mapping Erasure: The Power of Nominative Cartography in the Past and Present of the Muwekma Ohlones of the San Francisco Bay Area. In *Recognition, Sovereignty Struggles, and Indigenous Rights in the United States: A Sourcebook,* edited by Amy E. Den Ouden and Jean M. O'Brien, 287–309. Chapel Hill: University of North Carolina Press.

Flewellen, Ayana Omilade, Justin P. Dunnavant, Alicia Odewale, Alexandra Jones, Tsione Wolde-Michael, Zoë Crossland, and Maria Franklin. 2021. "The Future of Archaeology Is Antiracist": Archaeology in the Time of Black Lives Matter. *American Antiquity* 86(2): 224–243.

Frink, Liam. 2016. *A Tale of Three Villages: Indigenous-Colonial Interactions in Southwestern Alaska, 1740-1950.* Tucson: University of Arizona Press.

Gonzalez, Sara L., and Briece Edwards. 2020. The Intersection of Indigenous Thought and Archaeological Practice: The Field Methods in Indigenous Archaeology Field School. *Journal of Community Archaeology & Heritage* 7(3): 1–16.

Gonzalez, Sara L., Ian Kretzler, and Briece Edwards. 2018 Imagining Indigenous and Archaeological Futures; Building Capacity with the Confederated Tribes of Grand Ronde. *Archaeologies: Journal of the World Archaeological Congress* 14(1): 85–114.

Gonzalez, Sara L., Darren Modzelewski, Lee M. Panich, and Tsim D. Schneider. 2006. Archaeology for the Seventh Generation. *American Indian Quarterly* 30(3&4): 388–415.

Gould, D. Rae, Holly Herbster, Heather Law Pezzarossi, and Stephen A. Mrozowski. 2020. *Historical Archaeology and Indigenous Collaboration: Discovering Histories That Have Futures.* Gainesville: University Press of Florida.

Hart, Siobhan M. 2019. *Colonialism, Community, and Heritage in Native New England.* Gainesville: University Press of Florida.

Hayes, Katherine. 2019. Conflicts in Memory and Heritage: Dakota Perspectives on Historic Fort Snelling, Minnesota. In *The Sound of Silence: Indigenous Perspectives on the Historical Archaeology of Colonialism,* edited by Tiina Äikäs and Anna-Kaisa Salmi, 162–181. New York: Berghahn.

Holland-Lulewicz, Jacob, Victor D. Thompson, James Wettstaed, and Mark Williams. 2020. Enduring Traditions and the (Im)materiality of Early Colonial Encounters in the Southeastern United States. *American Antiquity* 85(4): 694–714.

Hull, Kathleen L. 2009. *Pestilence and Persistence: Yosemite Indian Demography and Culture in Colonial California*. University of California Press, Berkeley.

Jordan, Kurt A. 2008. *The Seneca Restoration, 1715–1754: An Iroquois Local Political Economy*. Gainesville: University Press of Florida.

———. 2014. Pruning Colonialism: Vantage Point, Local Political Economy, and Cultural Entanglement in the Archaeology of Post-1415 Indigenous Peoples. In *Rethinking Colonial Pasts through Archaeology*, edited by Neal Ferris, Rodney Harrison, and Michael V. Wilcox, 103–120. Oxford: Oxford University Press.

———. 2016. Categories in Motion: Emerging Perspectives in the Archaeology of Postcolumbian Indigenous Communities. *Historical Archaeology* 50(3): 62–80.

Kerber, Jordan E., ed. 2006. *Cross-Cultural Collaboration: Native Peoples and Archaeology in the Northeastern United States*. Lincoln: University of Nebraska Press.

Kroot, Matthew V., and Lee M. Panich. 2020. Students Are Stakeholders in On-Campus Archaeology. *Advances in Archaeological Practice* 8(2): 134–150.

Kryder-Reid, Elizabeth. 2016. *California Mission Landscapes: Race, Memory, and the Politics of Heritage*. Minneapolis: University of Minnesota Press.

Law Pezzarossi, Heather. 2020. Movement and the Nipmuc Landscape: The Legacy of Sarah "Boston" Philips. In *Historical Archaeology and Indigenous Collaboration: Discovering Histories That Have Futures*, edited by Gould, D. Rae, Holly Herbster, Heather Law Pezzarossi, and Stephen A. Mrozowski, 125–148. Gainesville: University Press of Florida.

Lee, Robert, and Tristan Ahtone. 2020. Land-Grab Universities: Expropriated Indigenous Land Is the Foundation of the Land-Grant University. *High Country News*, March 30.

Liebmann, Matthew. 2012. The Rest Is History: Devaluing the Recent Past in the Archaeology of the Pueblo Southwest. In *Decolonizing Indigenous Histories*, edited by Maxine Oland, Siobahn M. Hart, and Liam Frink, 19–44. Tucson: University of Arizona Press.

Lightfoot, Kent G. 1995. Culture Contact Studies: Redefining the Relationship between Prehistoric and Historical Archaeology. *American Antiquity* 60(2): 199–217.

———. 2005. *Indians, Missionaries, and Merchants: The Legacy of Colonial Encounters on the California Frontiers*. Berkeley: University of California Press.

———. 2006. Missions, Furs, Gold and Manifest Destiny: Rethinking an Archaeology of Colonialism for Western North America. In *Historical Archaeology*, edited by Martin Hall and Stephen W. Silliman, 272–292. Oxford: Blackwell.

Lightfoot, Kent G., and Sara L. Gonzalez. 2018. The Study of Sustained Colonialism: An Example from the Kashaya Pomo Homeland in Northern California. *American Antiquity* 83(3): 427–443.

Lippert, Dorothy. 1997. In Front of the Mirror: Native Americans and Academic Archaeology. In *Native Americans and Archaeologists: Stepping Stones to Common Ground*, edited by Nina Swidler, Kurt E. Dongoske, Roger Anyon, and Alan S. Downer, 120–128. Walnut Creek, CA: AltaMira Press.

———. 2021. The Limits of Repatriation's Decolonizing Abilities. In *Routledge Handbook of the Archaeology of Indigenous-Colonial Interaction in the Americas*, edited by Lee M. Panich and Sara L. Gonzalez, 516–523. New York: Routledge.

Lueck, Amy, and Lee Panich. 2020. Representing Indigenous Histories Using XR Technologies in the Classroom. *Journal of Interactive Technology and Pedagogy* 17. https://jitp.commons.gc.cuny.edu/representing-indigenous-histories-using-xr-technologies-in-the-classroom/.

Lyons, Natasha. 2013. *Where the Wind Blows Us: Practicing Critical Community Archaeology in the Canadian North*. Tucson: University of Arizona Press.

Marek-Martinez, Ora V. 2021. Indigenous Archaeological Approaches and the Refusal of Colonialism in Archaeology. In *Routledge Handbook of the Archaeology of Indigenous-Colonial Interaction in the Americas*, edited by Lee M. Panich and Sara L. Gonzalez, 503–515. New York: Routledge.

Martindale, Andrew, and Natasha Lyons, eds. 2014. Special Section: Community-Oriented Archaeology. *Canadian Journal of Archaeology* 38: 425–433.

McAnany, Patricia A. 2016. *Maya Cultural Heritage: How Archaeologists and Indigenous Communities Engage the Past*. Lanham, MD: Rowman and Littlefield.

McGuire, Randall H. 1992. Archaeology and the First Americans. *American Anthropologist* 94(4): 816–836.

Mitchell, Mark D., and Laura L. Scheiber. 2010. Crossing Divides: Archaeology as Long-Term History. In *Across a Great Divide: Continuity and Change in Native North American Societies, 1400–1900*, edited by Laura L. Scheiber and Mark D. Mitchell, 1–22. Amerind Studies in Archaeology. Tucson: University of Arizona Press.

Moore, Summer. 2020. Foreign Objects in Colonial-Era Hawaiian Sites: Change and Continuity in Nineteenth-Century Nuʻalolo Kai, Kauaʻi Island. *Journal of the Polynesian Society* 129(2): 193–326.

Mrozowski, Stephen A. 2012. Pragmatism and the Relevancy of Archaeology for Contemporary Society. In *Archaeology in Society: Its Relevance in the Modern World*, edited by Marcy Rockman and Joe Flatman, 239–256. Springer, New York.

Nash, Margaret A. 2019. Entangled Pasts: Land-Grant Colleges and American Indian Dispossession. *History of Education Quarterly* 59(4): 437–467.

Nelson, Peter A. 2019. Indigenous Refusal of Settler colonialism in Nineteenth-Century Central California: A Case from the Tolay Valley, Sonoma County. In *Indigenous Persistence in the Colonized Americas: Material and Documentary Perspectives on Entanglement*, edited by Heather Law Pezzarossi and Russell N. Sheptak, 169–185. Albuquerque: University of New Mexico Press.

O'Brien, Jean M. 2010. *Firsting and Lasting: Writing Indians Out of Existence in New England*. Minneapolis: University of Minnesota Press.

Oland, Maxine, Siobhan M. Hart, and Liam Frink, eds. 2012. *Decolonizing Indigenous Histories: Exploring Prehistoric/Colonial Transitions in Archaeology*. Tucson: University of Arizona Press.

Panich, Lee M., and Tsim D. Schneider. 2015. Expanding Mission Archaeology: A Landscape Approach to Indigenous Autonomy in Colonial California. *Journal of Anthropological Archaeology* 40: 48–58.

———. 2019. Categorical Denial: Evaluating Post-1492 Indigenous Erasure in the Paper Trail of American Archaeology. *American Antiquity* 84(4): 651–668.

Panich, Lee M., GeorgeAnn DeAntoni, and Tsim D. Schneider. 2021. "By the Aid of His Indians": Native Negotiations of Settler Colonialism in Marin County, California, 1840–1870. *International Journal of Historical Archaeology* 25: 92–115.

Preucel, Robert W., and Stephen A. Mrozowski, eds. 2010. *Contemporary Archaeology in Theory: The New Pragmatism*. New York: Wiley-Blackwell.

Raibmon, Paige. 2005. *Authentic Indians: Episodes of Encounter from the Late-Nineteenth Century Northwest Coast*. Durham, NC: Duke University Press.

Rubertone, Patricia E. 2012. Archaeologies of Colonialism in Unexpected Times and Unexpected Places. In *Decolonizing Indigenous Histories: Exploring Prehistoric/Colonial Transitions in Archaeology,* edited by Maxine Oland, Siobhan M. Hart, and Liam Frink, 267–281. Tucson: University of Arizona Press.

———. 2017. Archaeologies of Native Production and Marketing in 19th-Century New England. In *Foreign Objects: Rethinking Indigenous Consumption in American Archaeology,* edited by Craig N. Cipolla, 204–221. Tucson: University of Arizona Press.

Schaefli, Laura, and Anne Godlewska. 2014. Social Ignorance and Indigenous Exclusion: Public Voices in the Province of Quebec, Canada. *Settler Colonial Studies* 4(3): 227–244.

Scheiber, Laura L., and Katherine L. Burnett. 2020. Writing Histories at Êngkahonovita Ogwêvi: Multicultural Entanglement at Red Canyon, Wyoming. *Antiquity* 94(378): 1592–1613.

Scheiber, Laura L., and Judson Byrd Finley. 2012. Situating (Proto) History on the Northwestern Plains and Rocky Mountains. In *Handbook of North American Archaeology,* edited by Timothy R. Pauketat, 347–358. Oxford: Oxford University Press.

Scheiber, Laura L. and Mark D. Mitchell. 2010. *Across a Great Divide: Continuity and Change in Native North American Societies, 1400-1900.* Tucson: University of Arizona Press.

Schneider, Tsim D. 2015. Placing Refuge and the Archaeology of Indigenous Hinterlands in Colonial California. *American Antiquity* 80: 695–713.

———. 2019. Heritage In-Between: Seeing Native Histories in Colonial California. *The Public Historian* 41(1): 51–63.

Schneider, Tsim D., and Katherine Hayes. 2020. Epistemic Colonialism: Is It Possible to Decolonize Archaeology? *American Indian Quarterly* 44(2): 127–148.

Schneider, Tsim D., and Lee M. Panich. 2019. Landscapes of Refuge and Resiliency: Native Californian Persistence at Tomales Bay, California, 1770s–1870s. *Ethnohistory* 66(1): 21–47.

Schmidt, Peter R., and Stephen A. Mrozowski, eds. 2013. *The Death of Prehistory.* Oxford: Oxford University Press.

Silliman, Stephen W. 2005. Culture Contact or Colonialism? Challenges in the Archaeology of Native North America. *American Antiquity* 70(1): 55–74.

———. 2010. Indigenous Traces in Colonial Spaces: Archaeologies of Ambiguity, Origin, and Practice. *Journal of Social Archaeology* 10(1): 28–58.

Silliman, Stephen W., ed. 2008. *Collaborating at the Trowel's Edge: Teaching and Learning in Indigenous Archaeology.* Tucson: University of Arizona Press.

Sullivan, Shannon, and Nancy Tuana, eds. 2007. *Race and Epistemologies of Ignorance.* Albany: State University of New York Press.

Trabert, Sarah. 2018. Reframing the Protohistoric Period and the (Peri)Colonial Process for the North American Central Plains. *World Archaeology* 50(5): 820–834.

Van Dyke, Ruth M. 2019. Archaeology and Social Memory. *Annual Review of Anthropology* 48: 207–225.

Vimalassery, Manu, Juliana Hu Pegues, and Alyosha Goldstein. 2016. On Colonial Unknowing. *Theory & Event* 19(4).

Voss, Barbara L. 2021. Documenting Cultures of Harassment in Archaeology: A Review and Analysis of Quantitative and Qualitative Research Studies. *American Antiquity* 86(2): 244–260.

Watkins, Joe. 2005. Through Wary Eyes: Indigenous Perspectives on Archaeology. *Annual Review of Anthropology* 34: 429–449.

————2017. Can We Separate the "Indian" from the "American" in the Historical Archaeology of the American Indian? In *Historical Archaeology through a Western Lens,* edited by Mark Warner and Margaret Purser, 113–137. Lincoln: University of Nebraska Press and Society for Historical Archaeology.

Wilcox, Michael V. 2009. *The Pueblo Revolt and the Mythology of Conquest: An Indigenous Archaeology of Contact.* Berkeley: University of California Press.

Wolfe, Patrick. 1999. *Settler Colonialism and the Transformation of Anthropology: The Politics and Poetics of an Ethnographic Event.* London: Cassell.

————. 2006. Settler Colonialism and the Elimination of the Native. *Journal of Genocide Research* 8(4): 387–409.

Yellowhorn, Eldon. 2015. Just Methods, No Madness: Historical Archaeology on the Piikani First Nation. In *Ethics and Archaeological Praxis,* edited by Cristóbal Gnecco and Dorothy Lippert, 245–256. New York: Springer.

Zimmerman, Larry J. 1997. Remythologizing the Relationship between Indians and Archaeologists. In *Native Americans and Archaeologists: Stepping Stones to Common Ground,* edited by Nina Swidler, Kurt E. Dongoske, Roger Anyon, and Alan S. Downer, 44–56. Walnut Creek, CA: AltaMira Press.

HISTORICAL LEGACIES

Authenticity and Unknowing

2

"I Can Tell It Always"

Confronting Expectations of Native Disappearance through Collaborative Research

IAN KRETZLER

The parallel projects of Indigenous archaeologies and archaeologies of co-lonialism have cast a spotlight on the practice of archaeology. Aided by the knowledge and insight of Indigenous communities, archaeologists have shown that the discipline's interpretive and methodological conventions are partly responsible for the relative absence of historical accounts that give full weight to Indigenous peoples' long-term presence and persistence in colonial settings (Beaudoin 2016; Dickson and Steinmetz this volume; Liebmann 2012; Panich and Schneider 2019). Given that these conventions developed along-side and were influenced by European and US colonial projects (McGuire 1992; McNiven and Russell 2005; Rubertone 2000; Trigger 1980), archaeolo-gies of colonialism are as much investigations of the material manifestations of colonial spaces and policies as they are forms of disciplinary self-reflection. The success of collaborative approaches that integrate diverse epistemologies (Atalay 2006; Martindale and Nicholas 2014), employ culturally contextual-ized field strategies (Gonzalez 2016; Laluk, this volume; Two Bears 2008), and speak to the pasts, presents, and futures of Indigenous communities (Atalay et al. 2014; Gonzalez and Edwards 2020; Gould et al. 2020; Lyons 2013) dem-onstrate that the paths toward comprehensive understandings of colonialism and a more engaged, ethical, and accountable archaeology are intertwined.

Of course, the process of disentangling archaeology from its colonial origins is incomplete. In this chapter, I explore one enduring aspect of US settler colonialism: the presumed physical or cultural disappearance of Native peoples in the wake of settler incursion. During the nineteenth century, Native disappearance emerged as a highly anticipated outcome of westward expansion and the nascent federal reservation system. Following Deloria (2004, 4), I see Native disappearance as an expectation, one of the "products and the tools of domination" that influenced, motivated, and justified the actions of settlers, policy makers, and contemporary social scientists (including archaeologists). That Native peoples were or were soon to be extinct or assimilated is a constant in federal discourse during the nineteenth century. Nearly two centuries later, Native disappearance remains foundational to popular histories of national "progress" (Lewis 2014).

Archaeologists have examined the role Native disappearance and other expectations play in shaping scholars' approaches to the study of postcontact Native histories (e.g., Rubertone 2012). Building on this work, I discuss the implementation and results of two community-based projects developed in partnership with the Confederated Tribes of Grand Ronde Historic Preservation Office (Grand Ronde HPO). Since 2014, I have worked in partnership with Grand Ronde historic preservation staff and Tribal members to explore the nineteenth- and early twentieth-century history of the Grand Ronde Reservation in northwestern Oregon (Figure 2.1). Our research has focused on identifying expectations of Grand Ronde disappearance in archival documents and archaeological practice. We have countered these expectations first by drawing on community knowledge to complicate the federal government's "terminal narratives" (Wilcox 2009) and second by developing archaeological research methods grounded not in the presumption of absence but in the distinctive, enduring presence of the Grand Ronde community—what we understand as survivance (Vizenor 1999, 2009). We have used a suite of low-impact and minimally invasive field techniques, rethought basic terminology—for example, we referred to objects as "belongings" rather than "artifacts"—and followed Grand Ronde cultural protocols when interacting with places of historical significance. This uniquely Grand Ronde archaeology brought new detail to the stories of survivance at the Tribe's Uyxat Powwow Grounds, a deeply meaningful landscape that has been central to Tribal history over the past 150 years.

Collaboration with the Grand Ronde HPO has resulted in a research program that leaves space for—and expects—the unexpected. In the seven decades after the forced removal of western Oregon Native peoples to Grand

Ronde, the reservation community maintained relationships within and between extended families and with their ancestral homelands. In doing so, they undermined the assimilationist agenda fundamental to US settler colonialism, demonstrating that the anticipated disappearance of Grand Ronde people would not come to pass.

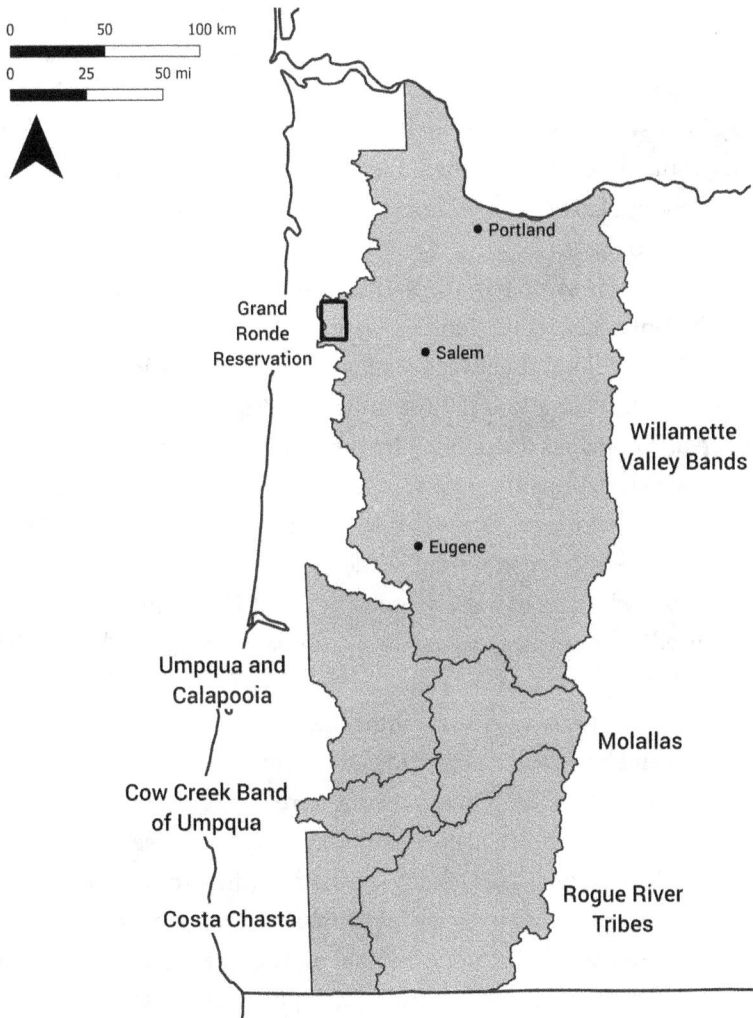

Figure 2.1. Map of western Oregon showing the original boundaries of the Grand Ronde Reservation and ceded lands of the Confederated Tribes of Grand Ronde.

Expecting the Unexpected in Archaeologies of Colonialism

In *Indians in Unexpected Places*, Deloria (2004) traces representations of Native peoples in early twentieth-century film, music, advertising, photography, and sports. These forms of early mass media cast Native peoples in diverse, though often contradictory, roles. They were portrayed as intractably violent savages but also pacified remnants of a fallen race, culturally stagnant peoples who were nevertheless capable of progress, racialized Others and near equals. Deloria argues that these representations trafficked not in mere stereotypes but in expectations. Expectations bundle ideology and discourse into "dense economies of meaning, representation, and act" (Deloria 2004, 11). They served as vehicles for engaging with a range of Native alterities while reiterating hierarchies of the settler state. Expectations assuaged settler anxieties about Native peoples' uncertain position in a post-frontier, early modern United States.

During this same period, Native actors, performers, and composers forwarded nuanced depictions of Native communities and experiences that operated within and between settler expectations. Deloria argues that these counter-representations may be understood as either anomalies or the unexpected. Anomalies are defined by the expectations from which they depart. They are deviations from how an individual should behave. Indeed, settlers responded with confusion, humor, and unease when presented with Native people as heroic, technologically adept, or culturally sophisticated. These responses, Deloria contends, demonstrate that Native images and stories that departed from settlers' expectations ultimately reinforced them. They were exceptions that proved the rule.

For Native participants and audiences, however, these counter-representations would have been compelling and eminently intelligible. Native creators and consumers of early mass media were motivated by culturally situated logics and the complex historical entanglements between their communities and settler colonialism. Deloria shows that when these motivations occupy the center rather than the margins of analysis, Native history becomes replete with the unexpected. Unlike anomalies, the unexpected resists categorization. It challenges existing systems of expectation by drawing on surprising (at least within the context of dominant expectations) links between Native people and a variety of spaces, objects, and activities. Deloria's work pushes scholars to reflect on the frames they place around the study of postcontact Native history. Do these frames come with implicit or explicit expectations that reproduce settler colonial narratives about Native people? In what ways do these expectations render the unexpected invisible? How might expectations be expanded, reformulated, or dismissed entirely in order to broaden the types of stories told about postcontact Native history? How might this process leave scholars expecting the unexpected?

Deloria's discussion can be applied to other aspects of postcontact Native history, none more so than the federal government's relationship with Native peoples. The expectation of Native disappearance occupied a prominent position in the nation's expansionist policies. In the decades after the Revolutionary War, federal officials intensified British practices of buying or seizing Native land and forcibly removing its inhabitants to locations west of settler towns. This approach culminated with the lethal mass deportations of the 1830s, which affected Native communities across the Southeast and the Old Northwest (Black 2015).

During the middle decades of the nineteenth century, the mass migration of settlers to California and Oregon Territory precluded even nominal separation between Native and settler societies. With physical exclusion increasingly impossible, policy makers forwarded a constellation of assimilationist programs that promised the cultural elimination of Native peoples. Legislators and Bureau of Indian Affairs officials lobbied for assimilation as a more politically palatable route toward Native disappearance. Yet when push to came to shove, any method of making Native peoples disappear—even extermination-minded violence—was a suitable alternative (Whaley 2016). Whatever approach the government took, federal officials expected the same result. As Oregon's Superintendent of Indian Affairs Edward Geary (1859, 384) put it, "[extinction] in the natural and unrestrained operation of the laws of progress, is the impending destiny of the tribes. . . . The alternative is civilization or annihilation."

Recent theorizations emphasize the centrality of Native disappearance to the settler colonial project (Cavanagh and Veracini 2017). Unlike external colonialism—for example, British India or French Algeria—which depends on the perpetuation of unequal power relations between colonizer and colonized, settler colonialism conceals and seeks to extinguish colonial relations. It attempts to "covers its tracks" (Veracini 2011, 3) and ultimately transition the *settler* state into a *settled* state. In the United States, this process has unfolded via military campaigns and treaties that secured settlers' access to Native lands and resources. It has been advanced by Manifest Destiny and other popular narratives that cast national expansion as progressive and inevitable. And it has relied on the erasure of Native peoples in an effort to neutralize those who were (and are) uniquely able to expose the settler state's violent origins and contingent hegemony.

Archaeology has not been isolated from expectations of Native disappearance. Setting aside the discipline's nineteenth-century history, which is rife with examples of scholars who minimized Native peoples' accomplishments and ties to their ancestral landscapes, for much of the twentieth century, archaeologists treated US and European colonial intrusion as temporal benchmarks that signaled the end of "authentic" Native lifeways (Rubertone 2000). Today, the decades surrounding "contact," to say nothing of the continent's "prehistory," continue to attract disproportionate scholarly interest. The relative paucity of research on Native experiences in the centuries after contact implies that Native people were (and are) fundamentally diminished as a result of colonialism (Lightfoot and Gonzalez 2018). As others have made clear (e.g., Beaudoin 2016; Panich and Schneider 2019), archaeologists' taken-for-granted methodological and interpretive practices also reflect and reproduce the expectation of Native disappearance.

How might archaeologists dislodge expectations of Native disappearance from their work? The answer, I believe, is twofold. First, following Deloria, archaeologists must place enduring Native presence, or survivance, at the center of their analyses. When viewed through a survivance lens, Native cultural practice transcends reductive interpretive dichotomies such as change versus continuity and becomes a dynamic process of making anew, a process in which practice, relationships, and landscapes helped Native peoples survive and thrive amid the state's attempts to eliminate them. This approach does not minimize struggle or hardship but challenges scholars to rethink the standard formula that oppression leads to inauthenticity and decline. It begins from a place of historical possibility whereby the material traces of Native presence may be investigated free of (or at least less encumbered by) archaeologists' expectations. This interpretive flexibility primes scholars to expect the unexpected.

Second, collaboration with Native communities is critical. Archaeologists would do well to remember that Native people have studied, resisted, and circumvented the US settler colonial project for centuries. These long-term histories continue to shape the efforts of Tribes to contest settler colonialism's legacies (see Cowie and Teeman this volume; Dickson and Steinmetz this volume; Estes 2019). Meaningful engagement with Native knowledge and lived experience may, among other things, expose archaeologists to other "realities" concealed by their ethnocentric assumptions (Martindale and Nicholas 2014). As I discuss below, research with the Grand Ronde HPO did not focus on whether Tribal members' insights were relevant to the study of reservation history—there was no question that they were—but on whether archaeological research could adequately incorporate those insights.

Shadows of Survivance within the Colonial Archive

In 2014, Grand Ronde historic preservation staff developed the Grand Ronde Land Tenure Project (GRLTP). The goal of the project was to trace land use and ownership on the Grand Ronde Reservation in the decades after its establishment in 1856. Access to and control over Native land, settler colonialism's "irreducible element" (Wolfe 2006, 388), guided state actions in western Oregon before and after the creation of the reservation system. HPO staff knew, for instance, that the implementation of the General Allotment Act of 1887 (commonly referred to as the Dawes Act) led to the near-total dissolution of individual land ownership among Tribal members during the early twentieth century. Yet they were unsure about the pace of dispossession across space and time and, as importantly, the strategies the reservation community used to maintain relationships within and between extended families in the absence of formal legal title. To shed light on these questions, HPO staff proposed archival research and GIS analysis to identify and visualize spatial information on reservation maps and in land records and related documents. They contracted me to carry out the bulk of this work (Kretzler 2017).

In order to realize the HPO's vision for the GRLTP, I refined my approach to engaging with Grand Ronde's archival record. The overwhelming majority of historical documents, ethnographies, maps, and photographs concerning Grand Ronde history were authored by non-Grand Ronde individuals, most commonly reservation agents and other federal officials who were invested in the reservation's assimilationist mission. I could not accept these datasets at face value; instead, I had to examine them as part of a colonial archive (Stoler 2002; Zeitlyn 2012). Colonial archives operate as both repositories of ideologically and culturally situated representations of Indigenous subjects and as sites of knowledge production whereby the creation, curation, and dissemination of state-sanctioned information sustained colonial projects. At Grand Ronde and elsewhere, federal officials not only presented Native lifeways in the context of their presumed disappearance, they also crafted justifications for current and future assimilationist policies. As Wylie (1995, 260) writes: "The theses of extinction, abandonment, and assimilation became self-fulfilling colonial ambitions."

Grand Ronde's loss of federal recognition under the 1954 Western Oregon Indian Termination Act provides an example of the colonial archive in action. In the years after the reservation's founding, agents extolled the community's adoption of settler goods and rapid construction of settler-style homes. Agent Sinnott (1873, 321) went so far as to claim that "the Indians here are far in advance of any other tribes of the Pacific coast." Agents clarified that such pronouncements were not exaggeration but were grounded in (self-appointed) expertise. At the Siletz Reservation west of Grand Ronde, Agent Wadsworth (1885, 167) offered a widely shared sentiment: "No one can understand as well as we that are constantly with this people when, where, and how they improve. I can tell it always."

Agents' confidence in the reservation system (and in themselves) inspired additional federal action. In 1889, federal officials included Grand Ronde in the first group of reservations to be selected for allotment under the Dawes Act. The architects of the allotment program believed that it would transform Native peoples into sedentary, yeomen farmers. The act divided reservations into individually owned tracts, or allotments, that were to be held in trust for twenty-five years, after which allottees would receive fee simple title and citizenship. Lawmakers reasoned that allotments, which ranged in size from 40 to 160 acres, were all that was required to develop self-sustaining agricultural economies. Thus, unallotted, or "surplus," lands had no long-term value for reservation communities and could be made available to settlers for purchase. Some Native people prospered under allotment. Many more were placed on paths that led to landlessness. Forced fee patenting—a practice in which agents awarded land patents to allottees without their knowledge or against their wishes—combined with economic hardship left allottees with little choice but to sell. By the time the program was halted in 1934, 118 reservations had been allotted. Over four decades, approximately 60 percent of Native land nationwide—including more than 95 percent of the Grand Ronde Reservation—passed into settler ownership (Kretzler 2017).

The impact of allotment at Grand Ronde was felt beyond dispossession. In the 1950s, as legislators and Bureau of Indian Affairs officials debated the merits of termination, a policy that would end the federal government's recognition of Tribes in an effort to encourage assimilation, they celebrated the absence of trust land as a mark of progress. The director of the Portland office of the Bureau of Indian Affairs, E. Morgan Pryse (1954, 142), testified before Congress that those at Grand Ronde "attest a degree of acculturation which provides little, if any, evidence to distinguish or identify [them as] Indians." He made no mention of the circumstances under which settlers had come to own reservation land. No Tribal members testified.

For over a century, a parade of federal officials who believed that they could "tell it always" manufactured an image of Grand Ronde that bore a questionable resemblance to the lifeways or experiences of the reservation community. The inner workings of settler colonialism can be found in agent reports, land surveys, and records of congressional hearings. Within these datasets, evidence of Grand Ronde disappearance justified the reservation system, which in turn bolstered the state's pursuit of assimilation. This recursive relationship between observation and policy peaked in 1954, when, thanks in part to Pryse's testimony, Congress moved to declare western Oregon a settled colony. Under the Western Oregon Indian Termination Act, the federal government no longer recognized the Confederated Tribes of Grand Ronde. In subsequent years, Bureau of Indian Affairs officials disposed of 597 acres of Tribal land and awarded fee patents to remaining allottees. By the time the termination process concluded, the Tribe retained only its 2.5-acre cemetery. The act also stripped Grand Ronde's neighbors at Siletz and all other western Oregon Native peoples of federal recognition.

The Grand Ronde community endured three decades of termination until the tireless activism of Tribal members brought a restoration bill before Congress. In her remarks before the House Interior and Insular Affairs Committee, Kathryn Harrison, vice chair of the Tribal Council, interrupted more than a century of colonial discourse: "I bring you greetings from my People: descendants of a People who began our passage through Oregon's unwritten history 127 years ago. How fortunate we are that they persisted so we, who came after them, could be here" (Olson 2005, 115). In 1983, Congress restored the Confederated Tribes of Grand Ronde. Five years later, the Tribe received over 9,000 acres of the original reservation.

The history of termination remains close to the surface for many Tribal members. HPO staff are sensitive to the colonial archive's ability to misrepresent Tribal lifeways and threaten Tribal sovereignty. My charge for the GRLTP was to sift through the archive's "simulated realities of tribal cultures" (Vizenor 1999, 23–24) for evidence that complicated its expectation of Grand Ronde disappearance. This evidence was to be found, if it existed at all, in subtext, between the lines, and in the offhand remarks of agents and other officials. According to Lopenzina (2010, 210), even if the "past lives of Native peoples flicker like shadows" within the archive, "a shadow may still form an impression, may still inform the manner by which we judge space and distance" (see also Vizenor 1999, 63–106).

To identify these archival shadows, I had to calibrate my eyes to see beyond settler expectations. This process unfolded over phone calls, working lunches, and email threads, as HPO staff, particularly Briece Edwards and David Harrelson, introduced me to accounts of Grand Ronde history rooted in the experiences of Tribal members. These stories served as spotlights. When directed at the colonial archive, the motivations and biases that pervaded federal observations and writings stood out more clearly, as did the shadows of Grand Ronde survivance.

The GRLTP revealed that the Grand Ronde community shaped the reservation into a distinctively Native space. In the mid-1850s, approximately 2,000 Native people from across western Oregon were forcibly removed to the reservation. The years that followed brought considerable hardship. Grand Ronde's unproductive soils never supported a robust agricultural economy, and the federal government repeatedly failed to deliver treaty-stipulated funds and supplies. Illness and malnourishment were endemic.

Even against this backdrop, the reservation community established a network of settlements that reinforced culturally salient relationships. Early reservation settlements consisted of groups of extended families with shared linguistic traditions, resource-gathering areas, and cultural practices. Agents understood these groups as "bands" or "tribes." These settlements provided a modicum of familiarity on an unfamiliar landscape. They also facilitated the continuation of intergroup relationships that had long shaped trade, politics, kinship, and cultural exchange. Individuals and families maintained connections to specific places, practices, and identities that distinguished them as Umpqua, Molalla, Rogue River, Kalapuya, or Shasta (e.g., Schrock and Zenk 2017). Settlement distribution accomplished similar work. People lived among members of their extended family and in the same relative location to their historical neighbors. Columbia River and Willamette Valley groups from northwestern Oregon lived north of the reservation's South Yamhill River, Umpqua and Rogue River Valley groups from central and southwestern Oregon lived south of the river, and Molalla groups from the foothills of the Cascades lived along the reservation's eastern boundary. In effect, the community transformed Grand Ronde into a microcosm of the pre-reservation cultural landscape.

This settlement pattern continued into the allotment period. As part of my work for the GRLTP, I digitized allotment records and recorded each allottee's "tribal" affiliation. Although Grand Ronde families maintained diverse affiliations that spanned the discrete "bands" and "tribes" agents described, allotment records provide only a single affiliation for each allottee. To resolve this issue, HPO staff and I corrected and expanded affiliation data using community histories and genealogical records. We identified cultural/linguistic groups and broad geographic interaction groups that accounted for methods of exchange, movement, and association in pre-reservation periods (see also Kretzler 2017; Zenk 1984). We reclassified affiliation information for each allottee and found that Grand Ronde allotments were not randomly distributed but were clustered by cultural/linguistic group and especially by geographic interaction group. Individuals selected land near members of their extended family and/or near those with similar linguistic and cultural practices and geographic connections. Those with historical ties to northwestern and southwestern Oregon continued to live north and south of the South Yamhill River, respectively.

Some reservation communities, for instance Grand Ronde's neighbors at Siletz, pushed for allotment, hoping that removing federal oversight and transferring land title into the hands of residents would provide long-term security (Wilkinson 2010, 220–223). At Grand Ronde, the beginnings of such a self-determined land policy were on full display. The community successfully imported—one could say assimilated—a settler colonial policy into existing paradigms about where and near whom it was appropriate to live. Although this strategy later faltered as allotment morphed into a tool of dispossession (Kretzler 2017), the reservation community nevertheless left an enduring mark—an unmistakable shadow of survivance—in the colonial archive.

The GRLTP also set the stage for archaeological investigation. The maps and land records consulted over the course of the project supplied a wealth of information about the location and nature of reservation settlements. HPO staff expressed an interest in using this information to assess whether the community paired their settlement system with practices that fostered self-determination at the household scale. They selected a seven-acre parcel in the southwestern corner of the Uyxat Powwow Grounds as an appropriate place for exploring this question.

The Uyxat Powwow Grounds

The Uyxat Powwow Grounds is a landscape of dense historical and contemporary significance. Following removal, Molalla families established a settlement on the grounds. This location afforded access to nearby Cosper Creek and much of the reservation's (comparatively) arable land. It was also actively surveilled by the military garrison at Fort Yamhill, located atop a nearby hill. During the first decade of the reservation, the fort operated as a prison for those caught leaving Grand Ronde without approval. During the implementation of the Dawes Act, the southwestern portion of the powwow grounds became part of James Foster's 153-acre allotment. Foster's ancestry—Clackamas Chinook and Native Hawaiian—speaks to the diverse encounters in early colonial Oregon, particularly around Fort Vancouver (Wilson 2018). Consistent with patterns across the reservation, Foster selected land near allottees with Chinookan ancestry.

In 1910, Foster sold a seven-acre portion of his allotment to Joseph Teabo. Teabo did not live at Grand Ronde but served as an administrator at Chemawa Indian School in Salem, where he had been a student. Records do not comment on his interest in the land, although the notes of Oliver Applegate are suggestive. Applegate conducted interviews with reservation residents over a two-month period in 1905 to determine individuals' eligibility for proceeds resulting from the sale of Grand Ronde's "surplus" lands. John Wacheno stated that when Agent Collins arrived to implement the Dawes Act, Edward Teabo, Joseph's brother, was fishing along the Columbia River. After he returned, Foster went with Edward to inquire about additional allotments. They were told that none would be awarded (Applegate 1905, 53–55).

After seeing Edward excluded from the allotment process, Foster may have sold part of his holdings to Joseph to provide a place for his brother to live or work during his time on the reservation. Alternatively, Joseph may have purchased the property in order to be near relations and away from Salem and Chemawa. In either case, this chain of title suggests that the use of private property ownership to strengthen relationships within and between families continued well after the initial allotment process.

After Joseph died, his widow Dolly sold the property to settler farmer Walter Werth in 1923. Over the next several decades, it passed through several settler owners. Native residents of Grand Ronde disappeared from the official record, although they may have remained on the property. According to Werth's grandson, Grand Ronde families frequently resided on settler-owned lands under various formal and informal arrangements (Dennis Werth, personal communication 2019). Similar practices occurred at Siletz (Wilkinson 2010, 227).

The property was used as cropland and remained largely devoid of structures into the twenty-first century. Grand Ronde purchased the property in 2006 as part of land consolidation efforts within the original boundaries of the reservation, reversing the tide of dispossession set in motion by allotment over a century earlier. It is now part of the Uyxat Powwow Grounds. Tribal ownership ushered in a new era of Grand Ronde presence and cultural innovation. Achaf-Hammi, the first traditional structure built at Grand Ronde in more than 150 years, opened at the grounds in 2010. Reflecting the diversity of the Tribe, Achaf-Hammi incorporates architectural elements from the plank houses of the Columbia River and the northern Willamette Valley and the semi-subterranean homes of southwestern Oregon. In 2015, the Tribe added a dance arbor to the grounds. It hosts powwows and other events throughout the year.

At community gatherings, the history of the landscape remains ever present. During opening remarks, speakers emphasize that the history of the powwow grounds is also the history of Grand Ronde. The land has borne witness to the hardships after removal, surveillance via Fort Yamhill, allotment and dispossession, and a resurgence of cultural identity and practice in the three decades after restoration. The legacies (and new manifestations) of settler colonialism continue to impact the Tribe in myriad ways. But on the

Uyxat Powwow Grounds, Grand Ronde presence is unmistakable. The Chinuk Wawa word "*uyxat*" translates as "trail," and like any trail, the powwow grounds bring the Tribe and its guests, both settler and Native, into closer connection. A quarter mile up the road, the fort site still provides sweeping views of the surrounding landscape. During powwows and other celebrations, the land below is filled with the sounds, smells, and colors of cultural innovation, teaching and learning, and looking to the future.

An Archaeology of Grand Ronde Survivance

Conducting archaeological investigation on this deeply meaningful landscape began by confronting archaeological expectations of Native disappearance. Historically, archaeologists, like reservation agents, have assumed that when it comes to Native histories, they can "tell it always." As with the GRLTP, a process of learning and unlearning with and from HPO staff proved vital for developing a distinctly Grand Ronde archaeology of survivance.

Collaboration took place as part of Field Methods in Indigenous Archaeology (FMIA), a community-based field school co-directed by the University of Washington and the Grand Ronde HPO (Gonzalez and Edwards 2020; Gonzalez et al. 2018). Established in 2015, FMIA seeks to enhance the capacity of the HPO to protect and care for Grand Ronde land and heritage for the benefit of current and future generations. As part of this goal, project staff work with Tribal members to generate ideas about what archaeology at Grand Ronde can and should be. Some Tribal members associate archaeology (not incorrectly) with the extraction of Native knowledge, bodies, and objects. FMIA staff have addressed this concern by discussing archaeology's potential contributions to the Tribe, especially when it is practiced with the full participation and oversight of the HPO. These conversations have taken place at the annual Grand Ronde History & Culture Summit and during Tribal members' participation in field and laboratory work. HPO staff also regularly conduct formal and informal meetings with Tribal elders and the Grand Ronde Culture Committee. FMIA staff continually reassess whether field and laboratory procedures meet project goals and reflect Grand Ronde knowledge and cultural protocols. All are subject to change, and HPO staff have final say in the implementation of any destructive or nondestructive analytical technique.

In addition to reflecting community goals and interests, FMIA's research at the powwow grounds between 2016 and 2018 incorporated Grand Ronde presence in four ways. First, the project altered basic disciplinary terminology. We described all objects identified at the Uyxat Powwow Grounds as "belongings" rather than as "artifacts." While "artifacts" connotes absence—an "artifact" of past lifeways, for example—"belongings" centers objects' historical and contemporary connections. Regardless of material, place of manufacture, function, or manner of discard, all objects are part of webs of relationship that link people, place, and practice. Belongings are proof of presence, not absence.

Second, FMIA's field and laboratory procedures emphasized description over categorization. Staff and students recorded the size, mass, color, material, possible function(s), and period of manufacture, if known, of identified belongings. Participants did not distinguish between "prehistoric" and "historic" belongings, assume that members of the Grand Ronde community did not use items manufactured in settler factories, or treat belongings as indicators of cultural change or continuity. Dispensing with these dichotomies created an interpretive vacuum that was both freeing and challenging. Being unable to lean on conventional classifications encouraged project participants to imagine diverse histories of use, movement, and meaning for each belonging. Through collaboration with HPO staff and reference to community and archival knowledge, these imagined possibilities were winnowed to likely—and often unexpected—interpretations.

Third, FMIA staff designed the project's field schedule around the community calendar. The field season ran from late June to early August, overlapping with Veteran's Powwow, Youth Culture Camp, and Canoe Journey. When these events took place at the powwow grounds, FMIA backfilled all units and covered or removed field equipment to ensure that fieldwork did not interfere with planned activities. At the community's invitation, FMIA students and staff attended and helped stage events that took place away from the powwow grounds. They packed vans, served lunches, met with the Tribe's guests from other Indigenous nations, and taught Tribal youth about Indigenous archaeologies. These actions inevitably delayed field investigation, but they provided project participants with valuable lessons about Tribal history and culture that enhanced their ability to identify and interpret belongings when fieldwork resumed.

Fourth, FMIA employed a field methodology that was both holistic and low impact (Gonzalez 2016; Gonzalez et al. 2018). Reliance on multiple field strategies, including drone photography, ground-penetrating radar, and 1/8- and 1/16-inch screen sizes provided multiple lines of evidence for identifying Grand Ronde survivance. In addition, the use of minimally invasive and nondestructive approaches addressed Tribal members' concerns about fieldwork. For Grand Ronde and many other Native communities, archaeological investigation, particularly excavation, comes with serious risks to the physical and spiritual well-being of those involved in archaeological research, the community, and/or the world. Guided by the recommendations of HPO staff, FMIA devised an approach to field investigation that proceeded from least to most impactful. Between each step, project staff reviewed preliminary results and discussed whether more invasive testing was justified and appropriate. It was never assumed that fieldwork would eventually proceed to excavation or any other field strategy. If HPO staff believed that current findings were sufficient to answer the project's research questions, no additional work was conducted.

Implementation of this distinctly Grand Ronde archaeology led to new historical insight characterized not by disappearance but by enduring connection to ancestral landscapes and creative adaptation of cultural practices. Fieldwork at the powwow grounds identified deposits of household belongings. The most common finds were mass-produced furnishings such as ironstone flatware, machine-made vessel glass, and wire nails. The manufacture dates for these belongings span the late nineteenth and twentieth centuries, preventing precise assessments about which belongings Grand Ronde families used and which ones post-1923 settler owners used. More direct evidence of Grand Ronde presence was indicated by pre-1900 glass beads, obsidian and cryptocrystalline silicate chipped stone, flaked-vessel glass, and charred seeds of important food and medicinal plants such as tarweed, oak acorns, blue elderberry, and other berries (Figure 2.2). Chipped-stone and macrobotanical remains appeared in all excavation levels, including those dominated by mass-produced objects, suggesting that they were part of reservation lifeways for decades. One unexpected find, a fragment of solarized amethyst vessel glass with a retouched edge, provides a *terminus post quem* of approximately 1870 for knapping activities at the site (Lockhart 2006).

These belongings lend additional nuance to reservation histories. Begin-

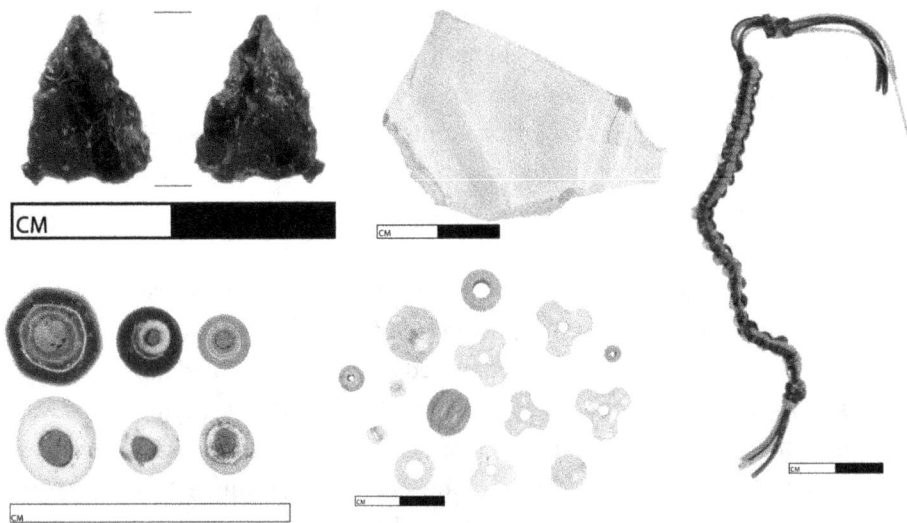

Figure 2.2. Grand Ronde belongings from the Uyxat Powwow Grounds. *Clockwise from upper left*: obsidian projectile point, flaked glass fragment from a solarized amethyst vessel, plastic friendship bracelet, contemporary glass and plastic beads, pre-1900 glass beads. Photograph by the author.

ning as early as 1861, Grand Ronde families pursued off-reservation economic opportunities, particularly during the summer months. Men worked in the timber industry, on farms, and at canneries. Women sold baskets and worked in settler homes. Entire families traveled from farm to farm picking hops, beans, and berries (e.g., Schrock and Zenk 2017, 86–98, 136–140). Off-reservation employment alleviated Grand Ronde's lack of economic opportunity and persistent agricultural deficits. Travel also afforded opportunities for reconnecting with storied landscapes, gathering traditional foods, and affirming bonds with nearby communities and nonhuman relations. Summer travel and employment were the latest expressions of a millennia-old seasonal round (Lewis 2009, 124; see also Raibmon 2005).

FMIA's research showed that families imported many of the items they gathered or purchased during their time off reservation, whether they were plant foods or wire nails, to their homes along Cosper Creek. The assemblage of imported items also includes obsidian. Geochemical sourcing revealed that obsidian from the powwow grounds originated from Inman Creek A, a raw material that is distributed throughout the Willamette Valley (Baxter and

Connolly 2015). The source area closest to Grand Ronde is located 35 miles to the east near present-day Newberg. It would have been en route to many of the employment opportunities reservation families pursued.

Gathering plants, crafting stone tools, and other practices with clear pre-reservation antecedents likely acquired new significance during this period. These activities almost certainly were valuable in a purely functional sense in that they allowed the community to address the challenges of reservation life. Plant foods and medicines would have been vital if crop yields and government-supplied rations proved insufficient, as was so often the case. If metal tools could not be obtained, flaked stone or glass would have been suitable substitutes. Even so, reservation families would have been keenly aware that the continuation of pre-reservation lifeways conflicted with agents' expectations. These practices had become politicized (Silliman 2014). Thus, importing and using culturally significant belongings may have been another way that the Grand Ronde community reshaped the reservation as a Native space. Much like the distribution of allotments, declarations of presence at the household scale may have helped families create spaces of familiarity and a self-determined present.

The archaeological history of the powwow grounds does not end in the early twentieth century. In recent years, the area around Cosper Creek has served as a camping ground for powwows and other community events. These gatherings have produced their own material signature. Pedestrian survey and surface collection documented everyday refuse such as soda cans and tent stakes and more evocative evidence of presence such as plastic friendship bracelets and plastic and glass beads possibly associated with powwow regalia (Figure 2.2). These belongings reminded project staff and students that Grand Ronde presence is not confined to the recent or deep past but is an indelible feature of the contemporary landscape (see Scheiber, this volume).

Conclusion

Archaeology in the United States was not designed to study postcontact Native histories. The US settler colonial project pursued (and continues to pursue) the physical or cultural erasure of Native peoples. The federal government's views and actions have influenced archaeology from the inception of the discipline. Native disappearance infuses standard terminology and categorization strategies and contributes to an emphasis on "contact" and "prehistoric" periods over more recent Native histories. The challenge in developing postcontact Native histories involves not simply filling a gap in existing scholarship but also addressing the practices responsible for this gap in the first place.

Deloria's (2004) discussion of the unexpected offers one path forward. Unlike anomalies, which draw significance by deviating from expectation, the unexpected undermines expectation itself. Centering the unexpected in postcontact Native histories depends on collaborative research partnerships with Native communities. These relationships may take many forms, but all must begin from a place of openness. When archaeologists relinquish their position as self-proclaimed experts of Native histories—acknowledging that they in fact cannot "tell it always"—diverse ways of knowing and relating to the past may be brought to bear on research goals, methodologies, and results. Collaboration provides a setting for identifying latent expressions of Native disappearance and replacing them with methodological and interpretive strategies rooted in Native presence.

Collaborative research conducted in partnership with the Grand Ronde HPO is but one example of how the unexpected may be brought to the fore during archival and archaeological research. At the start of the GRLTP, HPO staff and I focused on tracking changes in reservation land ownership, particularly dispossession introduced by the Dawes Act. The project began as an effort to remember difficult events in Grand Ronde history. During analysis months later, we were surprised to find that the reservation community used allotment location to strengthen relationships among extended families and between historical neighbors. It is worth reiterating that these findings emerged precisely because HPO staff and I critically examined the "tribal" affiliations government agents assigned to allottees. We expected the unexpected and we found it.

Similarly, FMIA's research at the Uyxat Powwow Grounds identified material evidence of Grand Ronde presence from the reservation's founding into the present. The project's holistic, low-impact approach to fieldwork, its use of the term "belongings," and its descriptive recording strategy encouraged project staff and students to see the archaeological record as full of possibility. What emerged was a story of survivance. Grand Ronde families imported mass-produced items, plant foods and medicines, and lithic raw material to households along Cosper Creek. Many of these belongings were likely acquired during summer journeys off reservation to job sites and historically significant landscapes. Today, the powwow grounds continue to be a place of creativity and connection, as demonstrated by the design of Achaf-Hammi, the construction of the dance arbor, and even the presence of plastic beads and friendship bracelets.

The study of postcontact Native histories is an opportunity. This research has the potential to sever archaeology's relationship with settler colonialism more completely and, in the process, generate histories that resonate with Native communities' knowledge and experiences. Expecting the unexpected will foster more precise interpretive and methodological approaches and more fruitful research partnerships. It will, in Rifkin's (2017, 192) words, "make visible the presence of other potential trajectories of Indigenous flourishing." This is a goal to which we can all aspire.

Acknowledgments

Hayu masi (thank you) to the Confederated Tribes of Grand Ronde and the current and former staff of the Historic Preservation Office, especially Briece Edwards, Jessica Curteman, Chris Bailey, and David Harrelson, for the opportunity to learn and study Tribal history. Many thanks to Lee Panich and Tsim Schneider for including me in this volume and to Sara Gonzalez, Allison Acosta, and the reviewers for their insightful comments on previous drafts of this chapter.

References Cited

Applegate, Oliver C. 1905. Report on the Indians of the Grand Ronde Reservation. Letter to the Commissioner of Indian Affairs, January 25. On file at the Confederated Tribes of Grand Ronde Historic Preservation Office.

Atalay, Sonya. 2006. Indigenous Archaeology as Decolonizing Practice. *American Indian Quarterly* 30(3 & 4): 280–310.

Atalay, Sonya, Lee Rains Clauss, Randall H. McGuire, and John R. Welch. 2014. Transforming Archaeology. In *Transforming Archaeology: Activist Practices and Prospects*, edited by Sonya Atalay, Lee Rains Clauss, Randall H. McGuire, and John R. Welch, 7–28. Walnut Creek, CA: Left Coast Press.

Baxter, Paul W., and Thomas Connolly. 2015. Obsidian Use in the Willamette Valley and Adjacent Western Cascades of Oregon. In *Toolstone Geography of the Pacific Northwest*, edited by Terry L. Ozbun and Ron L. Adams, 218–233. Burnaby, British Columbia: Archaeology Press.

Beaudoin, Matthew A. 2016. Archaeologies of Colonizing Canada: The Effects of Unquestioned Categories. *Archaeologies: Journal of the World Archaeological Congress* 12(1): 7–37.

Black, Jason Edward. 2015. *American Indians and the Rhetoric of Removal and Allotment.* Jackson: University Press of Mississippi.

Cavanagh, Edward, and Lorenzo Veracini, eds. 2017. *The Routledge Handbook of the History of Settler Colonialism.* New York: Routledge.

Deloria, Phillip J. 2004. *Indians in Unexpected Places.* Lawrence: University Press of Kansas.

Estes, Nick. 2019. *Our History Is the Future: Standing Rock versus the Dakota Access Pipeline, and the Long Tradition of Indigenous Resistance.* New York: Verso.

Geary, Edward. 1859. Office Superintendent of Indian Affairs, Portland, Oregon, September 1, 1859. In *Annual Report of the Commission of Indian Affairs Accompanying the Report of the Secretary of the Interior, For the Year 1859*, 382–392. Washington, DC: George W. Bowman.

Gonzalez, Sara L. 2016. Indigenous Values and Methods in Archaeological Practice: Low-Impact Archaeology through the Kashaya Pomo Interpretive Trail Project. *American Antiquity* 81(3): 533–549.

Gonzalez, Sara L., and Briece Edwards. 2020. The Intersection of Indigenous Thought and Archaeological Practice: The Field Methods in Indigenous Archaeology Field School. *Journal of Community Archaeology & Heritage* 7(3): 1–16.

Gonzalez, Sara L., Ian Kretzler, and Briece Edwards. 2018. Imagining Indigenous and Archaeological Futures: Building Capacity with the Confederated Tribes of Grand Ronde. *Archaeologies: Journal of the World Archaeological Congress* 14(1): 85–114.

Gould, D. Rae, Holly Herbster, Heather Law Pezzarossi, and Stephen A. Mrozowski, eds. 2020. *Historical Archaeology and Indigenous Collaboration: Discovering Histories That Have Futures.* Gainesville: University Press of Florida.

Kretzler, Ian. 2017. Archives of Native Presence: Land Tenure Research on the Grand Ronde Reservation. *American Indian Culture and Research Journal* 41(4): 45–70.

Lewis, David G. 2009. Termination of the Confederated Tribes of the Grand Ronde Community of Oregon: Politics, Community, Identity. PhD diss., Department of Anthropology, University of Oregon, Eugene.

———. 2014. Four Deaths: The Near Destruction of Western Oregon Tribes and Native Lifeways, Removal to the Reservation, and Erasure from History. *Oregon Historical Quarterly* 115(3): 414–437.

Liebmann, Matthew J. 2012. The Rest Is History: Devaluing the Recent Past in the Archaeology of the Pueblo Southwest. In *Decolonizing Indigenous Histories: Exploring Prehistoric/Colonial Transitions in Archaeology*, edited by Maxine Oland, Siobhan M. Hart, and Liam Frink, 19–44. Tucson: University of Arizona Press.

Lightfoot, Kent G., and Sara L. Gonzalez. 2018. The Study of Sustained Colonialism: An Example from the Kashaya Pomo Homeland in Northern California. *American Antiquity* 83(3): 427–443.

Lockhart, Bill. 2006. The Color Purple: Dating Solarized Amethyst Container Glass. *Historical Archaeology* 40(2): 45–56.

Lopenzina, Drew. 2010. Shadow Casting: William Apess, Survivance, and the Problem of Historical Recovery. In *Gerald Vizenor: Texts and Contexts*, edited by Deborah L. Madsen and A. Robert Lee, 208–230. Albuquerque: University of New Mexico Press.

Lyons, Natasha. 2013. *Where the Wind Blows Us: Practicing Critical Community Archaeology in the Canadian North.* Tucson: University of Arizona Press.

Martindale, Andrew, and George P. Nicholas. 2014. Archaeology as Federated Knowledge. *Canadian Journal of Archaeology* 38(2): 434–465.

McGuire, Randall H. 1992. Archeology and the First Americans. *American Anthropologist* 94(4): 816–836.

McNiven, Ian J., and Lynette Russell. 2005. *Appropriated Pasts: Indigenous Peoples and the Colonial Culture of Archaeology*. Lanham, MD: AltaMira Press.

Olson, Kristine. 2005. *Standing Tall: The Lifeway of Kathryn Jones Harrison*. Seattle: University of Washington Press.

Panich, Lee M., and Tsim D. Schneider. 2019. Categorical Denial: Evaluating Post-1492 Indigenous Erasure in the Paper Trail of American Archaeology. *American Antiquity* 84(4): 651–668.

Pryse, E. Morgan. 1954. *Termination of Federal Supervision over Certain Tribes of Indians*. Subcommittees on Interior and Insular Affairs, Feb. 17. S. Doc. No. 2670, H. Doc. No. 7674, 83rd Congress, 2nd Session.

Raibmon, Paige. 2005. *Authentic Indians: Episodes of Encounter from the Late-Nineteenth Century Northwest Coast*. Durham, NC: Duke University Press.

Rifkin, Mark. 2017. *Beyond Settler Time: Temporal Sovereignty and Indigenous Self-Determination*. Durham, NC: Duke University Press.

Rubertone, Patricia E. 2000. The Historical Archaeology of Native Americans. *Annual Review of Anthropology* 29: 425–446.

———. 2012. Archaeologies of Colonialism in Unexpected Times and Unexpected Places. In *Decolonizing Indigenous Histories: Exploring Prehistoric/Colonial Transitions in Archaeology*, edited by Maxine Oland, Siobhan M. Hart, and Liam Frink, 267–281. Tucson: University of Arizona Press.

Schrock, Jedd, and Henry Zenk, eds. 2017. *My Life, by Louis Kenoyer*. Corvallis: Oregon State University Press.

Silliman, Stephen. 2014. Archaeologies of Indigenous Survivance and Residence: Navigating Colonial and Scholarly Dualities. In *Rethinking Colonial Pasts through Archaeology*, edited by Neal Ferris, Rodney Harrison, and Michael V. Wilcox, 57–75. Oxford: Oxford University Press.

Sinnott, T. R. 1873. Office Grand Ronde Indian Agency, Oregon, September 10, 1873. In *Annual Report of the Commissioner of Indian Affairs to the Secretary of the Interior for the Year 1873*, 320–322. Washington, DC: Government Printing Office.

Stoler, Ann L. 2002. Colonial Archives and the Arts of Governance. *Archival Science* 2(1): 87–109.

Trigger, Bruce G. 1980. Archaeology and the Image of the American Indian. *American Antiquity* 45(4): 662–676.

Two Bears, Davina R. 2008. 'Íhoosh'aah, Learning by Doing: The Navajo Nation Archaeology Department Student Training Program. In *Collaborating at the Trowel's Edge: Teaching and Learning in Indigenous Archaeology*, edited by Stephen W. Silliman, 188–207. Tucson: University of Arizona Press.

Veracini, Lorenzo. 2011. Introducing Settler Colonial Studies. *Settler Colonial Studies* 1(1): 1–12.

Vizenor, Gerald. 1999. *Manifest Manners: Narratives on Postindian Survivance*. University of Nebraska Press, Lincoln.

———. 2009. *Native Liberty: Natural Reason and Cultural Survivance*. Lincoln: University of Nebraska Press.

Wadsworth, F. M. 1885. Siletz Indian Agency, August 10, 1885. In *Annual Report of the Commissioner of Indian Affairs to the Secretary of the Interior for the Year 1885*, 166–168. Washington, DC: Government Printing Office.

Whaley, Gray H. 2016. American Folk Imperialism and Native Genocide in Southwest Oregon, 1851–1859. In *Colonial Genocide in Indigenous North America*, edited by Andrew Wollford, Jeff Benvenuto, and Alexander Laban Hinton, 131–148. Durham, NC: Duke University Press.

Wilcox, Michael V. 2009. *The Pueblo Revolt and the Mythology of Conquest: An Indigenous Archaeology of Contact*. Berkeley: University of California Press.

Wilkinson, Charles. 2010. *The People Are Dancing Again: The History of the Siletz Tribe of Western Oregon*. Seattle: University of Washington Press.

Wilson, Doug. 2018. The Fort and the Village: Landscape and Identity in the Colonial Period of Fort Vancouver. In *British Forts and their Communities*, edited by Christopher R. DeCorse and Zachary J. M. Beier, 91–125. Gainesville: University Press of Florida.

Wolfe, Patrick. 2006. Settler Colonialism and the Elimination of the Native. *Journal of Genocide Research* 8(4): 387–409.

Wylie, Alison. 1995. Alternative Histories: Epistemic Disunity and Political Integrity. In *Making Alternative Histories: The Practice of Archaeology and History in Non-Western Settings*, edited by Peter R. Schmidt and Thomas C. Patterson, 255–272. Santa Fe, NM: School of American Research Press.

Zeitlyn, David. 2012. Anthropology in and of the Archives: Possible Futures and Contingent Pasts. Archives as Anthropological Surrogates. *Annual Review of Anthropology* 41: 461–480.

Zenk, Henry. 1984. Chinook Jargon and Native Cultural Persistence in the Grand Ronde Indian Community, 1856–1907: A Special Case of Creolization. PhD diss., University of Oregon, Eugene.

3

On the Rez, It's All Our History

CATHERINE E. DICKSON AND SHAWN STEINMETZ

Tribal people in the United States often feel the need to remind the world that they continue to exist. This is reflected in a variety of media, usually with the theme "We're Still Here." Examples include museum exhibits ("We're Still Here: Art of Indian New England" at The Children's Museum Collection in 1987; "We're Still Here: The Survival of Washington Indians" at the Columbia Pacific Heritage Museum in 2014), television shows ("We're Still Here," an episode of PBS's *Matters of Race* series), books (Waugaman and Moretti-Langholtz's *We're Still Here: Contemporary Virginia Indians Tell Their Stories* [2000]), and papers (Peck's "We Didn't Go Anywhere: Restoring Jamestown S'Klallam Presence, Combatting Settler Colonial Amnesia, and Engaging with Non-Natives in Western Washington" [2020]), to name just a few.

Why are Indian Tribes usually thought of and referred to in the past tense? Because that is what we learned in school. Shear et al.'s (2015, 68) research shows that US curriculum standards "overwhelmingly present Indigenous Peoples in a pre-1900 context and relegate the importance and presence of Indigenous Peoples to the distant past." Tony Castro, of the University of Missouri, summarizes why this is a problem: "This kind of curriculum, these misconceptions, all that has led to the invisibilization of indigenous people. What we teach acts as a mirror to what we value and what we recognize as legitimate. These standards are perpetuating a misconception and are continuing to marginalize groups of people" (Landry 2014).

Archaeologists tell the stories of people who did not write the histories we are taught, so in theory, we have corrected what we learned in our early years. We are fully versed in the legacy of colonialism. We reject essentialist discourses that project superiority by reducing Native people to "simple, primitive, technologically immature, and (maybe most damaging of all) static in contrast to the complex, modern, technologically advanced and dynamic West" (Liebmann 2008, 76). We archaeologists are different. Or so we tell ourselves. Our language and behavior suggest otherwise.

This chapter describes the experience of two Confederated Tribes of the Umatilla Indian Reservation (CTUIR) Cultural Resources Protection Program (CRPP) archaeologists based in Pendleton, Oregon, each with over twenty years' experience working with federal and state agencies and contract archaeologists to protect, preserve, and perpetuate the CTUIR's culturally significant places and resources for the benefit of current and future generations.

Context

The CTUIR before European/Euro-American Contact

The CTUIR is made up of three Tribes, the Weyíiletpu (Cayuse), Imatalamłáma (Umatilla), and Walúulapam (Walla Walla). These three Tribes have lived in what is now northeastern Oregon and southeastern Washington (Figure 3.1) since time immemorial.

Before there were human beings on the Columbia Plateau, the Creator discussed their impending arrival with the animals. People would be like infants who would need to be taught how to live here. An animal council was held to determine how to proceed. Salmon was first to offer his body and knowledge to the people, and the other plants and animals followed suit (Conner and Lang 2006, 23). The animal council's decisions reflect "tamánwit, the traditional philosophy and law of the people—the foundation of a physical and spiritual way of life that would sustain Plateau peoples for thousands of years" (Conner and Lang 2006, 23).

The Creator decreed that people have a reciprocal responsibility to respectfully care for, harvest, share, and consume traditional foods; if they do not, the foods might be lost. Neither can survive without the other. Since the beginning of time, tamánwit has taken care of the traditional foods and guided the CTUIR in preserving them (Sampson 2006, 248). Tamánwit dictates a deliberate seasonal round migration. With an economy based on seasonally determined fishing, gathering roots and berries, and hunting in geographically localized environments, people moved over large expanses of landscape.

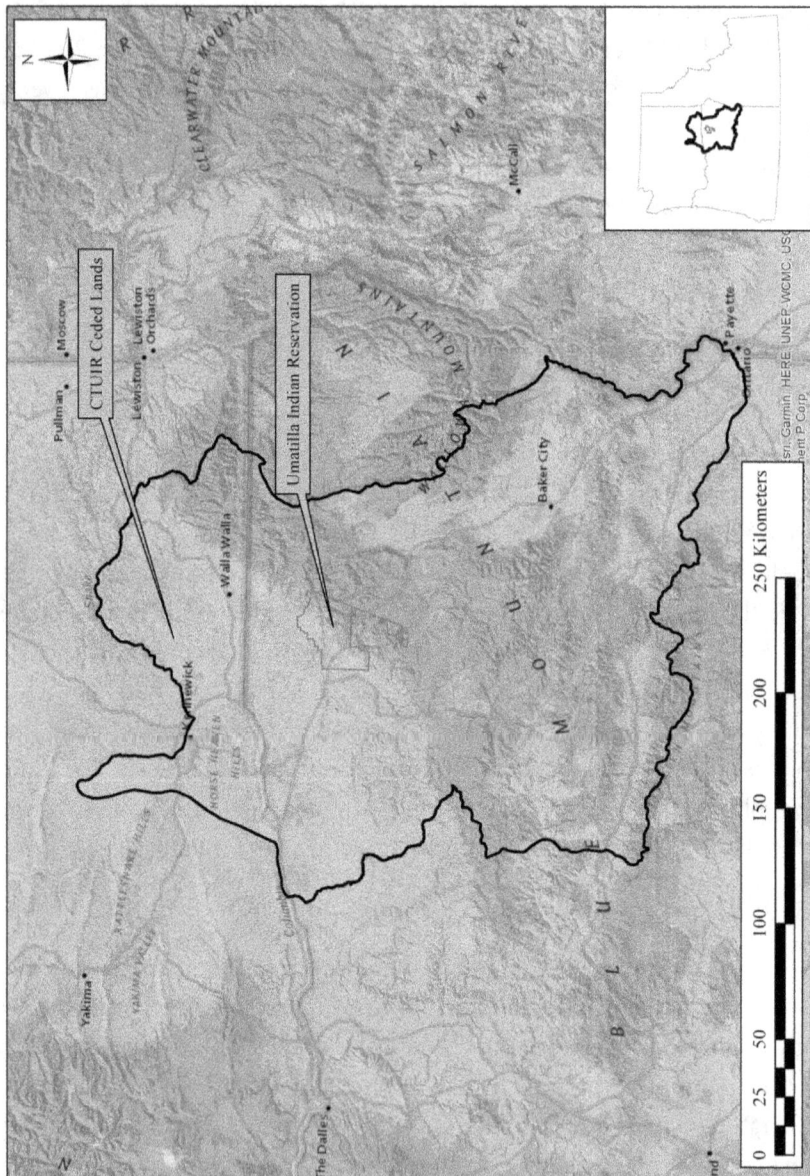

Figure 3.1. Location of CTUIR-ceded lands and the Umatilla Indian Reservation.

The Plateau people were basically riverine in their settlement patterns, and the principal food items in their diet were fish, wild game, and roots. Diets varied from group to group and from family to family depending on personal preference and geographical and seasonal availability or abundance (Anastasio 1972, 119; Marshall 1977, 37; Walker 1971, 10).

Families and bands began a yearly cycle of intensive food procurement in the spring. The harvesting of root crops could begin as early as mid-March and continue until mid-July (Ames and Marshall 1980, 32). Large quantities were prepared for storage (Horr 1974, 332; Spinden 1908, 201). By summer, Plateau bands were fishing, hunting, gathering, and living in camps in the mountains (Chalfant 1974, 106; Horr 1974, 333). Late summer was a time for harvesting berries, trapping, hunting, fishing, and gathering other foods. In the autumn, bands were involved with making final preparations for the winter (Chalfant 1974, 108), including storing harvested food.

Life during the winter was sedentary compared to the rest of the year. Bands of Plateau Tribes wintered in numerous villages situated along several hundred miles of successive rivers (Anastasio 1972, 169; Chalfant 1974, 105–106; Horr 1974, 297, 373; Ray 1974, 255–256; Walker 1978, 128). Bands occupied permanent winter villages with reusable dwellings when they were not engaged in seasonal hunting, fishing, and gathering activities. These villages were the centers of social, economic, and political activities (Chalfant 1974, 129).

With the introduction of the horse, the Weyíiletpu joined with other Tribes "'going to buffalo' on the Plains" (Stern 1998, 396). Raising horses and later cattle became an important part of the economy; the bunchgrass-covered hills in the Tribes' traditional territories provided excellent grazing throughout the year (Burney 1985, 17).

Later Events in CTUIR's History

The members of the CTUIR encountered artifacts from seafaring Europeans before they met any people from those far-off lands or their descendants. The Lewis and Clark journey in 1805 and 1806 through the middle of the Walúulapam and Imatalamłáma homeland was the first direct encounter with non-Native people. Those travelers were followed by numerous other explorers, fur trappers, and then missionaries, including Marcus and Narcissa Whitman in 1836, who built their mission called Waiilatpu near Walla Walla, Washington.

Partly with the Whitmans' encouragement, settlers came in droves beginning in 1843, over what became known as the Oregon Trail through the territory of all three Tribes. The Whitmans sought to supply all of the emigrants' needs (Meinig 1968, 140). By the mid-1840s, it became clear that the mission was failing to convert members of the Weyíiletpu Tribe to Christianity and agriculture. After devastating bouts of scarlet fever and measles that killed perhaps half of the Weyíiletpu, some Tribal members expressed their frustration by killing Marcus and Narcissa Whitman and eleven others beginning on November 29, 1847.

Oregon settlers were horrified and demanded revenge. Lacking federal troops, a volunteer militia formed in the Willamette Valley and headed for Walla Walla to capture the guilty parties. To persuade the volunteers to stay, the territorial superintendent of Indian affairs offered them land in the Walla Walla Valley (Meinig 1968, 153). The death of the Whitmans prompted the US Congress to end debate over slavery in Oregon Territory and pass a bill on August 13, 1848, to establish a territorial government for Oregon (Lyman 1918, 88).

Gold prospecting in Idaho, northeastern Washington, and the Blue Mountains of Oregon encouraged further emigration. It is estimated that over 80,000 emigrants (some calculate as many as a half million) traveled the Oregon Trail by wagon to settle the present-day states of Oregon, Washington, and Idaho (National Historic Oregon Trail Interpretive Center n.d.). At least one Tribal member, a Weyíiletpu, tried to take advantage of the situation by establishing his own toll road in the Grande Ronde Valley (Crawford 1898, 54).

Treaty of 1855

One of the most important events to occur in the region was the negotiation and signing of the Treaty of 1855 between the Imatalamłáma, the Weyíiletpu, and the Walúulapam and the United States government. Treaties became necessary in part because the US government was encouraging its citizens to move to Tribal lands in Oregon Territory without first addressing the Indians' claims to the land and its resources.

The primary purpose of the treaty process from the perspective of the US government was to establish peace by removing the Indians from large portions of the land and make way for industry and settlers. By 1854, Joel Palmer, superintendent of Indian affairs for Oregon Territory, had convinced the Indian Department that no further settlements were to be established east of the Cascade Mountains until the Indians in that area could be moved to reservations by treaty. By the end of July, Congress had authorized the secretary of the interior to negotiate treaties in order to purchase Tribal lands and establish a reservation.

On May 29, 1855, a council was convened on Mill Creek, six miles above Waiilatpu in the Walla Walla Valley. Palmer and Isaac Stevens, governor of Washington Territory, officiated. They met with chiefs, delegates, and headmen from many Tribes. Three treaties were signed that created the Umatilla Indian Reservation, the Yakama Indian Reservation, and the Nez Perce Indian Reservation. Payóopayo Maqšmáqš, chief of the Walúulapam, was open to the idea of a reservation but was cautious: "Let it be as you propose so the Indians have a place to live, a line as though it was fenced in, where no white man can go" (Stevens and Palmer 1855).

Palmer and Stevens originally planned only two reservations, but this was not acceptable to the Tribes who became the CTUIR. Realizing that they had no choice, Palmer outlined the boundaries of the 510,000-acre Umatilla Indian Reservation in the Weyíiletpu homeland and the government services that would come with it. The Tribes ceded 6.4 million acres to the United States but retained the rights to fish, hunt, gather foods and medicines, and pasture livestock in their usual and accustomed areas. The treaty was signed on June 9, 1855, and Congress ratified it on March 8, 1859.

Words Matter

The basic dichotomy in Columbia Plateau archaeology is prehistoric versus historic. The historic era here starts in 1805 with the arrival of Lewis and Clark's expedition. The prehistoric era is everything before that event (at least 16,000 years; Davis et al. 2019), approximately 99 percent of the time people have been living on the Plateau. Since the 1800s, the dominant culture has generally sought to marginalize or outright erase both the people who lived here before and the evidence of their lives (see Trabert, this volume).

Dictionary definitions support an understanding of "historic" and "prehistoric" in keeping with how archaeologists use the terms. However, the definitions of "historic" in *Merriam-Webster.com* include "dating from or preserved from a past time or culture" and those for prehistoric include "regarded as being outdated or outmoded." How does the general public understand those words? We conducted a Google image search for the terms. "Historic" yielded dozens of pictures of buildings. The result for "prehistoric" was mostly dinosaurs. The fourteenth image for "prehistoric" on February 17, 2020, was one labeled "Prehistoric Times: A Stone Age Family," a drawing of a Neanderthal family from 50,000 years ago. Then the images returned to more dinosaurs.

Realizing how the general public uses the terms, we began to wonder how members of the CTUIR understand the terms. Over the years, the CRPP has gathered hundreds of oral histories from Tribal elders. Most have been transcribed, resulting in over 7,500 pages of oral histories. We searched those oral histories for the terms "history," "historic," "prehistory," and "prehistoric" to see how they were used. It became clear that Tribal members understand the terms as the general public and as the deeper dictionary definitions do, not as archaeologists and anthropologists do.

In these oral histories, members of the CTUIR speak of prehistory as the time before there were people. For example, "There's a prehistoric monster with a real long neck, big body, short legs," and "These are old legendary stories . . . Prehistoric animals, I heard our grandmas, how they heard about prehistoric animals, giant animals, that were thousands of years before."

History, on the other hand, is the whole time there were people. The ability to write is not relevant. For instance, "I'm going to all historic sites that mean so much to our people and I'm documenting [them]," and "It seems like, historically, our people, Umatilla, Walla Walla, Cayuse, always had this connection down to the Willamette Valley." For these elders, a historic fishing site is not a place where people fished in the historic era (after Lewis and Clark brought written language), rather it's a place where people fished any time in the past, since time immemorial.

This review is important because it shows that many of the questions that we within the profession ask informants use the terms historic and prehistoric in the archaeological sense; miscommunication between the questioner and the informant may impact the answers. We as archaeologists (and anthropologists) need to be aware of how the people we're talking to understand the words we use and how our interpretation of what they're telling us may hinge on that understanding.

Building Context in Cultural Resource Management

One of the main parts of our jobs as archaeologists for the CTUIR is to write reports prepared as part of the National Historic Preservation Act (NHPA) section 106 process. In these reports, we provide context to help readers understand what we find during an archaeological survey or excavation. We include a fairly detailed history section tailored to the project area. This section generally includes events discussed above, but also information on agriculture, transportation, government development, landownership, and so forth. These are not "Tribal" or "Euro-American" historical themes; they are simply historical themes that impacted all the people in the area.

In 2014, the CTUIR Department of Natural Resources created a timeline of its history. The timeline includes railroads, dams, and changes in the CTUIR's governing structure and body. A more inclusive, longer timeline would include the Missoula floods, volcanic eruptions, the time when the swallow sisters blocked the salmon and coyote broke the dam, strangers, diseases, farming, allotments, and so forth. All along, life was (and is) dominated by adhering to *tamánwit*.

The Impact of the Terms Historic and Prehistoric
on Cultural Resource Management

The CTUIR wears multiple hats in the realm of cultural resource management (CRM). At times, we serve as a contracting company hired to help someone comply with section 106 of the NHPA. We must always be consulted about projects that might affect properties the CTUIR ascribes religious and cultural significance to. That consultation takes place pursuant to section 36CFR800.2(c)(ii) of the Code of Federal Regulations, which says, "Consultation on historic properties of significance to Indian Tribes and Native Hawaiian organizations. Section 101(d)(6)(B) of the act requires the agency official to consult with any Indian Tribe or Native Hawaiian organization that attaches religious and cultural significance to historic properties that may be affected by an undertaking." Nothing in the NHPA or its implementing regulations requires that a historic property be from the prehistoric era. They just require that the Tribe or Native Hawaiian organization ascribe religious and cultural significance to the place. It is really not possible for anyone other than the Tribe to determine whether the property is significant to the Tribe.

And yet, we, representing the CTUIR, are often informed by an agency as we go through the 106 process that the Tribe has no interest in historic-era resources. Examples from a period of approximately six months in late 2018/early 2019 include the following.

The United States Army informed us we were not interested in the Oregon Trail, which was originally a Tribal trail that passes through the reservation, facilitated massive emigration, and certainly impacted the lives of Tribal people. The Base Realignment and Closure process was planning to close the Umatilla Chemical Depot near Hermiston, Oregon. Two segments of the Oregon Trail pass through land that would leave federal ownership. The army did not understand why the CTUIR would want to ensure that the adverse effect of this land transfer on the trail was appropriately mitigated. As Trabert (this volume) notes, thinking of the Oregon Trail as a purely Euro-American site builds Euro-American claim to the area and allows a history that omits Tribal presence.

The U.S. Army Corps of Engineers informed the CRPP we were not interested in Mill Creek Dam, a historic property that adversely impacts fish runs and therefore traditional fishing sites. Corps Regulatory said that we weren't interested in "non-Tribal sites," sites that contain glass and metal. The Oregon State Historic Preservation Office (SHPO) questioned our interest in a road the Works Progress Administration constructed through a traditional gathering area. At the Oregon SHPO, it is architectural historians, not anthropologists, who review elements of the built environment. The Oregon Department of Transportation prepares two separate reports for the 106 process—one covers archaeology and one covers the built environment. They are so confident that Tribes are not interested in the built environment that they do not even provide those reports for review.

We are sure that these agencies mean no harm when they assume or assert lack of Tribal interest in sites from the historic era, but that does not mean they do not cause it. Liebmann (2008, 76) indicates the essentialist perspective sees Native American authenticity as "rooted in an un-changing pre-Columbian essence." Agency staff see the Native American past as so deeply rooted that they act as though it actually stopped in that pre-Columbian essence and never made it into what they think of as the historic era. These perspectives are just another way to place Tribal People "outside their own identity" (Laluk, this volume). Trabert (this volume) highlights problems that arise when Euromericans and Native Americans claim the same *space*. The examples above show that similar problems arise when the two occupy the same *time*. Which brings us to Cowie and Teeman's (this volume) discussion of quantum entanglements and "considerations of place-time in Tribal consultation" and Laluk's perspective that "knowledge, land, and Ndee identity are truly linked and persist across time and space without the need of archaeological categorization or speculation."

Since we operate outside an academic setting, in settings where discussions of essentialism and even colonialism (much less the space-time continuum) would be met with glazed eyes, what we at the CRPP hear in these discussions is an assumption that Tribal members' history, culture, and religion came to an end about 200 years ago. Thus, we feel the need to remind everyone that Tribal people still live. They lived on the land before the new settlers showed up and they still live on and use resources of that same land today. "Our" history is "their" history too, whoever "our" and "their" are. One can easily find photographs of Tribal members from the historic era just living their lives. These snapshots are similar to snapshots any family has. There are photographs of hunting and fishing trips, dogs, horses, cars, kids, and sporting events. Tamástslikt Cultural Institute, the CTUIR's museum, is divided into three sections: "We Were," "We Are," and "We Will Be." The museum describes "We Are" as follows:

> Our Tribes are alive and prospering today. Tribal people have survived and thrive in the contemporary world. WE ARE features our resilient people as soldiers and warriors, players in government and the regional economy, leaders in salmon recovery success, balancing the modern with traditions, and still abiding by the Law of the Salmon.

As much as it seems like one doesn't need to say it, Tribal members are just as much a part of the historic era as any other ethnic group.

Historic Era Sites

Having established that no matter what archaeologists think (or at least how they behave), Tribal people have a history, we consider sites that generally are interpreted as "not Tribal," but certainly involved Tribal members.

More often than not, archaeological reports for the Plateau indicate that in 1855, all members of the CTUIR were rounded up and forcibly moved to the reservation. The implication is they were not allowed to leave. There was indeed a forced geography of the reservation, but as with most things, it's complicated. Tribal members continued to hunt, gather, and fish in their usual and accustomed areas, as they do today.

The reservation era essentially began in 1860, after the US Congress ratified the treaty. During this time, more pressure was applied to Indians who followed the traditional way of living along the rivers for a major part of the year. Despite provisions in the treaty that reserved for Tribal members the right to hunt and fish in usual and accustomed places, people were now systematically removed, sometimes by military force, to the reservations (CTUIR n.d.). On the reservation, Indian agents and missionaries worked to assimilate the Indians. The reservation was not the sanctuary away from non-Indians where Indians could live in peace, as the treaty negotiators and signers had envisioned.

Numerous people continued to leave the reservation to participate in traditional activities (Stern 1998, 415). Among these were large segments of the Walúulapam under the leadership of Homlai and a large portion of the Imatalamłáma who moved seasonally between the Columbia River, the Grande Ronde River, and the reservation. They lived independently and largely rejected the offerings of aid from Indian agents in the form of annuities from the government (Stern 1998, 415).

The religious pressure that the Catholic Church exerted pushed Tribal members away from the reservation. Homlai explained to Indian agent Narcisse A. Cornoyer that his followers were being persecuted by the church; they "cannot stay on the reservation if they are not left alone, allowed to worship God in their own way" (Fisher 2001, 490).

In a report to the secretary of the interior, Agent Cornoyer (1874), described a situation where many Walúulapam, Imatalamłáma, and Weyíiletpu resisted the notion of limited freedom to move about on the land. Many members of these Tribes rejected the geographic limitations of the reservation; they continued to occupy traditional villages and resource procurement sites. Cornoyer (1874) noted that about half of the Indians that participated in the 1855 Walla Walla treaty negotiations, about 2,000 people, were still living along the Columbia River. These river Indians, the agent claimed, were "a great drawback to the improvement of the reservation Indians." He urged that they be placed under "proper control" (Cornoyer 1874).

Cornoyer's report noted that river Indians considered many of the reservation Indians to be culturally assimilated. The reality of the time was that river Indians would come and live on the reservation when they wanted to and reservation Indians would go to the river and live with relatives as desired (Fisher 2001, 475). While there were differences between the two groups, social, cultural, and economic relations remained extensive. Depending on the circumstances, river Indians could become reservation Indians and vice versa (Fisher 2001).

Homlai and the Walúulapam's need for geographic and religious freedom persisted. They continued to hold on to a traditional set of values and beliefs. Chief Johnny Jackson, a contemporary Columbia River Indian, explains why Indians continued to go to their old villages and traditional fishing locations after the reservations were established. He said that they never moved from the villages after the treaties were signed at Walla Walla, because "we reserved the right to live at our usual and accustomed sites along the river. These sites were reserved because they hold all of our religious sacred sites, cemeteries, gathering sites, fishing sites and [they are] where we have always maintained our livelihood" (Fisher 2001, 473).

As you can see, from the beginning of the treaty era, Tribal members have been engaged in off-reservation pursuits. Fisher (2001) points out that many Indians preferred to stay on the Columbia River near the fisheries and the graves of their ancestors. Indian agents tried several tactics to prevent Indians from leaving the reservation, but this hardened the resolve of many and they continued the practice of going to the river. Many Indians believed that not doing so would compromise their very identity as an Indian (Fisher 2001, 486).

Agricultural Work

Tribal members, who were accustomed to a seasonal round lifestyle, were a good fit for short-term agricultural work. It allowed them to bring a little cash into what remained a fairly cashless economy well into the 1900s. When the fish were running or the huckleberries were ripe, it was easy to leave the fields and orchards and access traditional First Foods.

Átway Cecelia Bearchum described the new round: "From here we used to go berry picking up to Mt. Adams. And then from there ... see, that would be in July, August. And then they used to have a big hop farm over to Toppenish, and a lot of people used to pick hops over there. People just kinda moved with the seasons."[1] This new seasonal round demonstrates the blending of a new economy with the traditional Tribal economy.

In oral histories, community members mention harvesting other crops within the ceded lands, including potatoes, peas, apples, cherries, peaches, and strawberries. Labor camps were established in some of these locations. Most of those camps are now gone; what's left are archaeological sites. If archaeologists don't know that history, will Tribal members be recognized in the archaeological record? When documenting such sites, will archaeologists include Tribal people in their hypotheses about who worked there? We fear that we will be subject to what archaeologists think they know, that Tribal people were on the reservations and that temporary farm workers in the area were non-Indians like braceros. However, Drake (2019) demonstrates what can be learned when archaeologist do research and overcome their assumptions.

Civilian Conservation Corps

The Depression took longer to hit Indian Country than urban areas, given that people were used to providing for themselves. One oral history notes, "We still had fish in the river then."[2] But the federal government had significantly cut funding for the Bureau of Indian Affairs (BIA), and the types of resources the Civilian Conservation Corps (CCC) worked to protect were in especially poor condition on reservations.

The CTUIR Tribal Historic Preservation Officer has researched the CCC Indian Division (CCC-ID), especially as it pertains to the Umatilla Indian Reservation (Miller 2017). The CCC-ID was originally funded in 1933 with a goal of establishing "72 camps on 33 reservations which would construct forest roads, trails, and paths, implement fire protection measures, erosion control, and develop water sources" (Miller 2017, 46). Work could be "on tribal, allotted or other lands within Indian reservations and on lands adjacent to reservations when such work is necessary to protect reservation lands" (Office of Indian Affairs 1941, V–1).

The Umatilla Agency CCC-ID opened in 1937. It worked on and off the

Figure 3.2. CCC-ID crew at Old Chief Joseph Gravesite and Cemetery on May 26, 1940. Sitting on the ground (*left to right*) are Leo Sampson, Arthur Motanic, and Andrew Allen. Sitting on the monument are Jack Abraham and John Sampson. Standing are Dave Cowapoo, Joseph Sheoships, Oscar Lawyer, and Cy Wilkinson. Reproduced at the National Archives in Seattle (UM 57, Box 1, District Office Reports.) Source: Miller 2017, Figure 32.

Umatilla Indian Reservation on fifty-eight projects in the period 1937 to 1942. Projects included roads, fences, a fire lookout, check dams, community buildings on the reservation, and work at the Old Chief Joseph Gravesite and Cemetery off the reservation in Joseph, Oregon. Practically every Tribal family worked in the CCC-ID. Not surprisingly, their finished work looked much like work the traditional CCC did (Figure 3.2).

Miller (2017) documented what was left of many features associated with the Umatilla Agency CCC-ID. The fire lookout tower has been removed, but the footings, the collapsed associated cabin, and the fence remain. The artifacts are typical of the time, mainly food and beverage cans. This fence, this cabin, these artifacts look like hundreds of sites found in the forests of Oregon's Blue Mountains. It is only the research that shows this site is associated with Tribal members.

Archaeological Examples Are Paltry

Some sites can be confusing. Have you ever found a cabin with a scatter of historic-era artifacts *and* a lithic scatter? Have you said to yourself, well, a good place to live is a good place to live? Explained it in your mind, first Tribal people lived here and then non-Tribal people lived here. But what if Tribal people lived there on into the historic era? What would that look like? How would an archaeologist recognize such a site? In our many years of reviewing archaeological reports within the CTUIR's area of interest, we are aware of few sites off the reservation that have been clearly documented as Tribal people living on a site in the historic era; both date to the mid- to late 1800s.

Wilke and Dalan (1983) documented Site 45BN281 in Benton County, Washington. Feature 3 contained a pit with many artifacts that included machine-cut nails, cans, two iron skillets, a copper kettle with an iron bail and chain, a metal digging stick, a sheep shear, bullet molds, axe heads, hoe blades, buttons, glass beads, leather, textiles, a belt buckle, basket fragments, a pestle, a few flakes, and faunal remains (shell, modified elk antler, and deer, hare, rabbit, salmonid, and amphibian bones). One of the bones was a cut and polished fragment of a mule deer skull (Wilke and Dalan 1983, 82–86). The artifacts date from the early 1800s to 1863. Wilke and Dalan (1983, 86) note the cache occurred after 1863 (when the belt buckle was patented) but that since some artifacts date to the early 1800s, "some heirlooming of objects may have occurred." Wilke and Dalan (1983, 86) conclude:

> The cultural affiliation of this feature is not known, although some Native American influence is evidenced by the presence of the flakes, beads, pestle, worked antler and shaped deer skull fragment. Owing to the worn condition of the axe heads and pestle and the obviously used copper kettle, it is not believed the cache belonged to a trader or purveyor of new implements. The combination of domestic and land clearing and working tools suggests the possibility of the items belonging to a squatter or early homesteader who either lost track of the cache or did not return to an unsuccessful attempt at homesteading or small-scale farming.

Another feature in this area was a historic dump dating to 1870 to 1900 with (among other things) machine-cut nails, tacks, one spike, one staple, one ceramic fragment, four glass fragments likely from a medicine bottle, glass and iron beads, and many faunal remains, including shell and salmonid, hare, rabbit, mule deer, small and large artiodactyl bones and the bones of a domestic cow with evidence of butchering (Wilke and Dalan 1983, 94). Notably, "Unlike the historic level, prehistoric artifacts were not found at a particular elevation or elevations but rather were dispersed throughout the remaining depths of the units" (94).

Wilke and Dalan (1983, 100) seem to struggle to see just Native Americans in the historic era at this site. They conclude:

> The cultural affiliation of all or any of these deposits is not known although some Native American influence is suspected due to the presence of the digging stick, antler tool, ochre, flakes, and the beads that were recovered from both the cache and the other historic deposits. It is known that Native Americans camped in the area well into historic times, although not in large groups after 1915 or so (Lothson and Lindeman 1980, 23). The historic materials could well be a result of a combination of Euro-American and Native American activities.

This area is known to members of the CTUIR as Tamalám. The village remains important to Tribal members, some of whose grandparents were born there. Hunn et al. (2015, 91–92) indicate:

> According to Átway *Likslaway* (Rose John), "from where the Umatilla River flows into the Columbia, there again my people used to catch the salmon and the eel . . . there was our land for living. All my people from my maternal grandmother's family lived there, and her father and grandfather. And everywhere he had fishing places, *wápyaš*. He had drying sheds—he had them here and there. There were more Indians living there than just my great grandfather. That one had a five fire tule house."

A reasonable interpretation of the site seems to be continued use by Tribal people as their material culture and subsistence practices adjusted to the changed world they found themselves in.

At another archaeological site, Endzweig (1985, 2020) analyzed the results of a River Basin Survey excavation at Site 35GM22 along the reservoir behind the John Day Dam in Gilliam County, Oregon, in 1960 (Cole and Cressman

1961). The excavation involved two house pits, both of which had multiple floors. Endzweig (1985) presented information on various classes of historic artifacts. There were twenty buttons, most of which could have been purchased from the Hudson's Bay Company. One simple buckle was stocked by the Hudson's Bay Company in the period 1829 to 1860 and a fancier one was made during the Civil War. A shoe dating to after 1860 was found. A total of ninety-three glass beads was found, some of which were of the type made in the period 1830 to 1870, others were made in the period 1830 to 1855, and still others were undatable. All of the glass fragments were undatable. All of the nails were machine cut, suggesting manufacture before the 1890s. Twelve straight pins were of a type "manufactured in large quantities by 1840" (Endzweig 1985, 18). A single piece of linoleum dated to after 1860. One metal artifact was probably an iron digging stick.

What might be called precontact artifacts include projectile point fragments, biface fragments, scrapers, cores, gravers, drills, modified flakes, unmodified flakes, anvils, hammers, choppers, milling stones, and multipurpose tools. Other artifacts include a ground bird bone and a rattle made of sawed bovid bone rings on a leather thong. There were four clamshell disk beads and one abalone pendant. A single leather legging was also found. Miscellaneous artifacts included "wood, seeds, stone manuports that are not modified, charcoal, cloth, corroded metal, and feces" (Endzweig 1985, 35).

Endzweig (1985) believed that the site was occupied toward the end of the 1800s, definitely after 1860. She noted the similarity between the assemblage from this site and that from the cache Wilke and Dalan (1983) found. Therefore, Endzweig supported Cole and Cressman's hypothesis that the site was occupied by Native Americans who had left their reservation. She noted that "virtually all of the historic material present is compact and could easily have been carried by one family unit" (Endzweig 1985, 54). She also noted that the house pits were both relatively small and may have had a portable superstructure. Endzweig was interested by the facts that there were no Euro-American weaponry artifacts and that even the number of projectile points was low. She believed that the site may have primarily been used for fishing. Endzweig (1985, 56) believed that the cultural material at sites such as this one "reflects the social changes that its occupants were doubtless undergoing" and argued that archaeologists had consistently undervalued these types of sites and had not researched them.

A third example is located further north. The Pelúucpu (Palouse) are a Columbia Plateau Tribe that did not sign a treaty. They stayed at their home villages (which have substantial archaeological components) on the Snake River as long as they could, as late as into the 1940s. Like their non-Tribal neighbors, they built wooden houses, constructed fences, and developed the property in and around their primary village agriculturally. Individual Tribal members even claimed ownership through a homestead act. When Palúus Village (45FR36) was excavated in 1964, the site was felt to be disturbed, so the focus became the historic-era cemetery where Tribal members had been buried. Historic-era funerary objects include eyeglasses and a Jefferson Peace Medal. Marmes Rockshelter (45FR50), which is adjacent to Palúus Village, became a National Historic Landmark and the subject of years of excavation due to evidence of very early human use. Fielder (1979, 67), who tried to understand "acculturation" based on funerary objects from the historic cemetery, concluded that "the material technology of the Palus changed very little with the introduction of trade goods." Perhaps recognizing the limitations of using burials to understand culture change in this context, Fielder (1979, 39) wrote that "the general pattern of acculturation for the Palus appears to be greater acceptance of Euro-American culture in the realm of material goods than in the ideational realm" (Fielder 1979, 39).

Buckhorn Cabin has been recorded as a multicomponent site within the exterior boundaries of the Umatilla Indian Reservation on land that was lost during the allotment era and restored to the Tribe in 1940. Oral history tells us the location has been used since time immemorial as a base for hunting and gathering. In the late 1800s or early 1900s, a non-Indian squatter appeared and built a cabin. Despite his presence, the area was still important to Tribal members, and once the settler gave up and moved on, Tribal members continued to use the area and its new infrastructure, again for hunting and gathering. From 1937 to 1940, the CCC-ID, recognizing the importance of the area to the Tribe, constructed a picnic shelter, outhouses, camp stoves, picnic tables, incinerators, a spring development, and a well for potable water (Miller 2017, 118). The CCC-ID also cleared brush from the camp area. The artifact assemblage at this site resembles that found at other historic-era homesteads and campsites located on precontact sites.

The lack of documented historic-era sites associated with CTUIR members is not unusual. Panich and Schneider (2019) outline problems not just with recognition but with the requirement to assign sites at the time of recording as historic or prehistoric. They prefer to focus on chronometric dating, noting that "widespread disregard for archaeology of the more recent past supports the mistaken notion that Native Americans vanished early in the colonial period" (Panich and Schneider 2019, 654). Rubertone (2000, 425) notes that the very roots of historic archaeology predispose practitioners to pay "scant attention" to Native Americans. She encourages archaeologists "to take on the daunting challenge posed by acknowledging that persistence sometimes (and perhaps often) means change (rather than a holding onto)" and "recognize that locating community means looking beyond artifacts and sites to the places and, thus, the landscapes that sustained it."

Conclusion

Tribal people are associated with historic-era sites: this basic concept seems so intuitive that it's hardly worth writing about. However, experience has shown that what we learn as children—that Indians exist in the past tense only—is more powerful than common sense. Some archaeologists who talk to Indian people or representatives of a Tribe boldly assert that Tribal members have *no interest* in historic-era archaeological sites. Even when we, as Tribal representatives, walk them through it—we agree there were Tribal people here thousands of years ago; we agree that there are Tribal people here today—it is difficult to get to the third part, that Tribal people were here in the period 1850 to 1970. Whereas Trabert (this volume) highlights the importance of Tribes reclaiming space, especially through place-names, the CRPP has recognized the need to also fight colonialism by reclaiming time.

What we would like archaeologists—academic, CRM, and agency—to take away from this chapter is a reminder from the first archaeology class you ever took. To understand a site, you must know its context and association. Understanding the geomorphology and artifact typology is not the same as understanding the context. At historic-era sites, to understand the context you have to learn the history. You have to abandon your preconceived notions of what is and is not associated with Tribal people. Never assert that a site is not of interest to a group; the group will determine what is of interest to them. Especially if you have not spent enough time in the area, you are unlikely to have a deep understanding of who did what, where, and when. Please, stop telling people they don't have a history. It is not what you mean to say, but it is what they hear.

Notes

1. OHP-285, oral history on file with the CRPP, collected in 2010.
2. OHP-360, oral history on file with the CRPP, collected in 1999.

References Cited

Ames, K. M., and A. G. Marshall. 1980. Villages, Demography and Subsistence Intensification on the Southern Columbia Plateau. *North American Archaeologist* 2(1): 25–52.

Anastasio, Angelo. 1972. The Southern Plateau: An Ecological Analysis of Intergroup Relations. *Northwest Anthropological Research Notes* 6(2): 109–229.

Burney, Michael S. 1985. The Results of Test Excavations Conducted at Sites 45GA119, 45GA120, 45GA122, and 45GA124, in the Blue Mountains South of Pomeroy, Garfield County, Washington. Report submitted to the Umatilla National Forest, Pendleton Oregon. Western Archaeological Consultants, Boulder, Colorado.

Chalfant, S. F. 1974. *Nez Perce Indians, Aboriginal Territory of the Nez Perce Indians.* New York: Garland.

Cole, David L., and Luther S. Cressman. 1961. Interim Report 1960–1961, John Day Reservoir Project, Columbia River. Submitted to the National Park Service. Eugene: University of Oregon Museum of Natural History.

Confederated Tribes of the Umatilla Indian Reservation. n.d. Our History & Culture, Part 2. http://ctuir.org/history-culture/history-ctuir, accessed April 26, 2020.

Conner, Roberta, and William L. Lang. 2006. Early Contact and Incursion, 1700–1850. In *Wiyáay̓t, As Days Go By, Wiyáakaa'awn: Our History, Our Land, and Our People, The Cayuse, Umatilla, and Walla Walla,* edited by Jennifer Karson, 23–57. Portland: Tamástslikt Cultural Institute and Oregon Historical Society Press.

Cornoyer, Narcisse A. 1874. *Annual Report of the Commissioner of Indian Affairs to the Secretary of the Interior for the Year 1874.* Washington, DC: Office of the Commissioner of Indian Affairs.

Crawford, C. H. 1898. *Scenes of Earlier Days in Crossing the Plains to Oregon and Experiences in Western Life.* Petaluma, CA: J. T. Studdert.

Davis, Loren G., David B. Madsen, Lorena Becerra-Valdivia, Thomas Higham, David A. Sisson, Sarah M. Skimer, Daniel Stueber, Alexander J. Nyers, Amanda Keen-Zebert, Christina Neudorf, Melissa Cheyney, Masami Izuho, Fumie Isuka, Samuel R. Burns, Clinton W. Epps, Samuel C. Willis, and Ian Buvit. 2019. Late Upper Paleolithic Occupation at Cooper's Ferry, Idaho, USA, ~16,000 Years Ago. *Science* 365(6456): 891–897.

Drake, Eric C. 2019. Working to Stay Together in "Forsaken out of the Way Places": Investigating Anishinaabeg Family Logging Camps as Sites of Social Refuge and Resilience during the Era of Assimilation in Michigan's Upper Peninsula, 1880–1940. PhD diss., Binghamton University.

Endzweig, Pamela. 1985. 35GM22: Culture Contact on the Lower John Day River. Master's thesis, University of Oregon, Eugene.

———. 2020. Against All Odds: Residential Continuity at Site 35GM22, Lower John Day River. *Journal of Northwest Anthropology Memoir* 19.

Fielder, George F. 1979. Palus Material Technology: Technical Analysis of the Palus Burial Assemblage from 45FR36B. Master's thesis, University of Idaho, Moscow.

Fisher, Andrew H. 2001. They Mean to Be Indian Always: The Origin of Columbia River Indian Identity, 1860–1885. *Western Historical Quarterly* 32: 469–492.

Horr, D. A., ed. 1974. *Nez Perce Indians*. Garland American Indian Ethnohistory Series. Newark, NJ: Garland.

Hunn, Eugene S., E. Thomas Morning Owl, Philip E. Cash Cash, and Jennifer Karson Engum. 2015. *Čáw Pawá Láakni = They Are Not Forgotten: Sahaptian Place Names Atlas of the Cayuse, Umatilla, and Walla Walla*. Pendleton, OR: Tamástslikt Cultural Institute; and Portland OR: Ecotrust.

Landry, Alysa. 2014. "All Indians Are Dead?" At Least That's What Most Schools Teach Children. *Indian Country Today*, Sept. 13. https://newsmaven.io/indiancountrytoday/archive/all-indians-are-dead-at-least-that-s-what-most-schools-teach-children-6Hk8Ahn-r0EG0dsV4MssWcg. Accessed February 8, 2020.

Liebmann, Matthew. 2008. Postcolonial Cultural Affiliation: Essentialism, Hybridity, and NAGRPA. In *Archaeology and the Postcolonial Critique*, edited by Matthew Liebmann and Uzma Z. Rizvi, 73–90. New York: AltaMira Press.

Lothson, Gordon A., and Glen W. Lindeman. 1980. Cultural Resource Reconnaissance and Phase II Testing for the Port of Benton, Near Plymouth, Washington. Unpublished report. Pullman, WA: National Heritage.

Lyman, W. D. 1918. *Lyman's History of Old Walla Walla County Embracing Walla Walla, Columbia, Garfield, and Asotin Counties*. Chicago: S. J. Clarke.

Marshall, Alan G. 1977. Nez Perce Social Groups: An Ecological Interpretation. PhD diss., Washington State University, Pullman.

Meinig, Donald W. 1968. *The Great Columbia Plain: A Historical Geography 1805–1910*. Seattle: University of Washington Press.

Miller, Carey L. 2017. An Analysis of the Work Conducted by the Civilian Conservation Corps-Indian Division for the Benefit of the *Weyíiletpu* (Cayuse), *Imatalamłáma* (Umatilla) and *Walúulapam* (Walla Walla). Master's thesis, St. Cloud State University, Minnesota.

National Historic Oregon Trail Interpretive Center. n.d. Frequently Asked Questions. www.blm.gov/sites/blm.gov/files/learn_interp_nhotic_faq.pdf. Accessed April 25, 2020.

Office of Indian Affairs. 1941. *Civilian Conservation Corps-Indian Division Handbook*. Revised March. Washington, DC: Government Publishing Office.

Panich, Lee M., and Tsim D. Schneider. 2019. Categorical Denial: Evaluating Post-1492 Indigenous Erasure in the Paper Trail of American Archaeology. *American Antiquity* 84(4): 651–668.

Peck, Alexandra M. 2020. "We Didn't Go Anywhere": Restoring Jamestown S'Klallam Presence & Combating Settler Colonial Amnesia in Western Washington. Paper presented at the 73rd Northwest Anthropological Conference, Ellensburg, Washington.

Ray, Verne F. 1974. *Nez Perce Indians, Ethnohistory of the Joseph Band of Nez Perce Indians*. New York: Garland.

Rubertone, Patricia E. 2000. The Historical Archaeology of Native Americans. *Annual Review of Anthropology* 29: 425–446.

Sampson, Donald. 2006. Asserting Sovereignty into the Future. In *Wiyáayҳt / As Days Go By / Wiyáakaaʼawn: Our History, Our Land, and Our People, The Cayuse, Umatilla, and Walla Walla*, edited by Jennifer Karson, 3. Pendleton, OR: Tamástslikt Cultural Institute; and Portland: Oregon Historical Society Press.

Shear, Sarah B., Ryan T. Knowles, Gregory J. Soden, and Antonio J. Castro. 2015. Manifesting Destiny: Re/presentations of Indigenous Peoples in K–12 U.S. History Standards. *Theory and Research in Social Education* 43: 68–101.

Spinden, H. J. 1908. The Nez Perce Indians. *Memoirs of the American Anthropological Association,* Vol. II, Part 3. New York: Lancaster.

Stern, Theodore. 1998. Cayuse, Walla Walla, and Umatilla. In *Handbook of North American Indians*. Vol. 12, *Plateau*, edited by D. E. Walker, 395–419. Washington, DC: Smithsonian Institution.

Stevens, Isaac I., and Joel Palmer. 1855. A True Copy of the Record of the Official Proceedings at the Council in the Walla Walla Valley, held jointly by Isaac I. Stevens, Gov. and Supt. W. T. and Joel Palmer, Supt. Indian Affairs O. T. on the Part of the United States with the Tribes of Indians Named in the Treaties Made at that Council, June 9th and 11th, 1855. On file at the Confederated Tribes of the Umatilla Indian Reservation Cultural Resources Protection Program, Mission, Oregon.

Walker, Deward E., Jr. 1971. *American Indians of Idaho*. Vol. 1. Moscow, ID: University of Idaho.

———. 1978. *Indians of Idaho*. University Press of Idaho, Moscow.

Waugaman, Sandra F., and Danielle Moretti-Langholtz. 2000. *We're Still Here: Contemporary Virginia Indians Tell Their Stories*. Richmond, VA: Palari.

Wilke, Steve, and Rinita Dalan. 1983. Cultural Resource Evaluation of Two Parcels of Land within the Proposed Port of Benton Corridor, Plymouth, WA. Submitted to the U.S. Army Corps of Engineers, Portland District under contract number DACW57–82-C-0110. Geo-Recon International, Seattle, Washington.

4

Why Am I Ephemeral?

Foregrounding Ndee Perceptions of Our Past as Persistence

NICHOLAS C. LALUK

Various terms and descriptions have been used to explain the lack of visibility of Ndee landscape occupations and material traces over time. Such terms as low visibility, highly mobile, and ephemeral are abundant in the archaeological and anthropological literature about historical-period Ndee groups throughout the US Southwest. Such terms imply a lack of material or environmental modification that is equivalent to nonexistence. Archaeologists have spent much time attempting to construct diagnostic material checklists suggesting Ndee landscape presence but often miss the ongoing associations Ndee communities have to the land. Such associations form understandings of the past, present, and future that inform Ndee culture, identity, sovereignty, and overall well-being.

What is needed is not only continued collaborative research with Ndee communities but interactions that move beyond such collaborations as they are defined by western research goals and assumptions. Moreover, restrictive archaeological recording categories and terminologies often perpetuate one-sided and stereotypical understandings of Ndee culture and history.

This chapter attempts to highlight examples of contemporary Ndee lived experiences and cultural resource management strategies with regard to ongoing visibility over time despite the restrictions archaeological and anthropological methods and theories impose. In this chapter, I argue that naming and terminology are powerful vehicles of sovereignty that can lead to better overall understandings of the Ndee past and present. Drawing on Lee Panich's

(2013) notion of persistence, archaeologists can use the Ndee cultural heritage resource strategy of simple avoidance as a tool to guide research about and understandings of Ndee culture and heritage that embrace the persistence of tradition while maintaining senses of community well-being. Standard archaeological methods can limit our understandings of Ndee lifeways; archaeologists can modify these methods to more fully consider the importance of nonmaterial Ndee associations with the landscape. Specifically, archaeologists can explore critical components of Ndee culture that support Ndee-focused research methodologies that persist within Ndee world views. This approach requires researchers to move beyond inferring Ndee presence through analysis of materials such as white chert.

Ndee Communities

Various communities in the US Southwest make up the Ndee, which include the Chiricahua, the Jicarilla, the Kiowa-Apache Lipan, the Mescalero, and the Western Apache (Cibecue, Northern and Southern Tonto, San Carlos, and White Mountain Apache) (Buskirk 1986; Opler 1983a). Although Ndee nations are connected through various cultural, linguistic, and social similarities, each nation is different and exerts its sovereignty and self-determination in its own unique ways. In this chapter, I discuss the Mescalero and the White Mountain in greater detail in terms of Ndee lived experience and cultural heritage resource management perspectives such as persistence (Figure 4.1).

Ndee Archaeology

Ndee sites are notoriously difficult to identify on the ground surface due the high degree of mobility of historical-period Ndee groups, the perishable nature of Apache material items, and difficulties in identifying diagnostic Ndee artifacts (Laluk 2015). As Sechrist (2008, 17–18) states, "in spite of dominating the landscape for at least 300 years[,] Apache sites are rare, material assemblages are sparse, and habitation features are ephemeral." Due to this relatively high degree of invisibility, identifying Apache landscape occupations through material remains is a tenuous and speculative process and a comprehensive Ndee archaeology is elusive (Donaldson and Welch 1991; Ferg 1992; Gregory

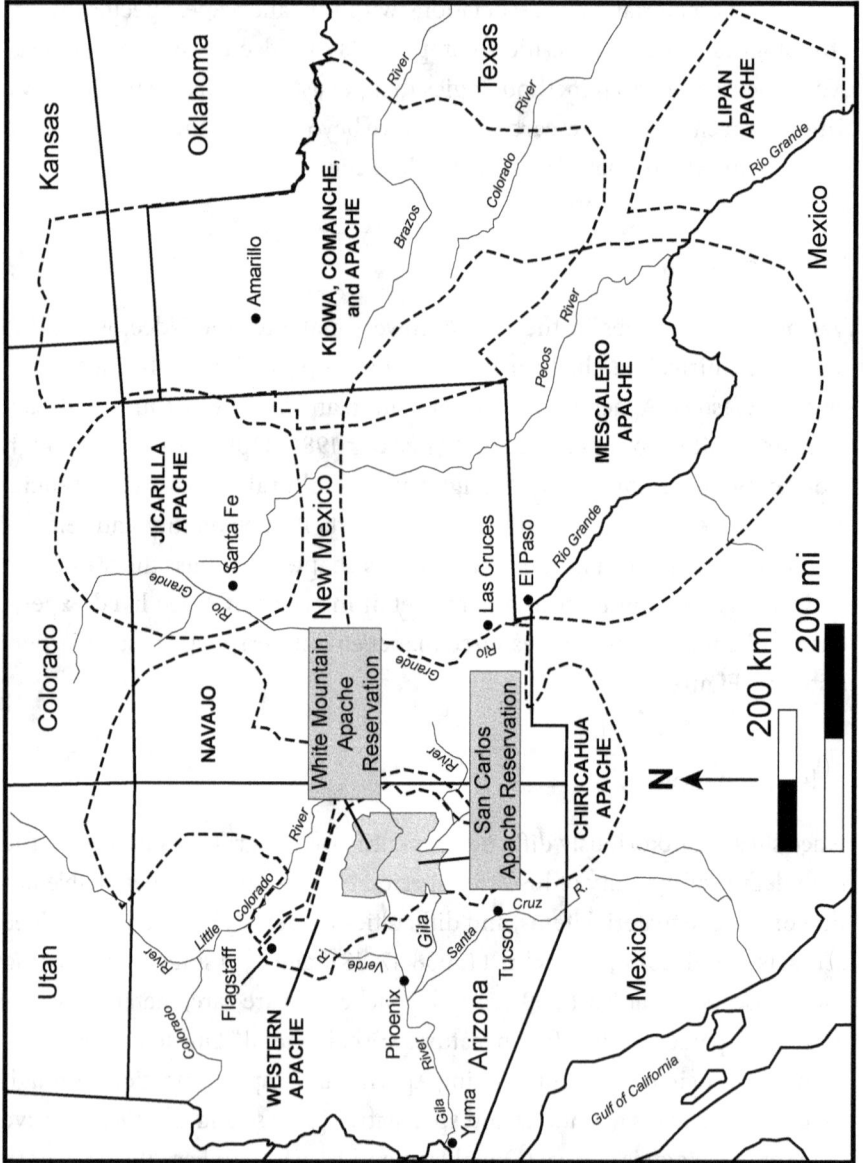

Figure 4.1. Ndee territory. Map adapted from Welch et al. (2017).

1981; Herr et al. 2011, 111). The lack of distinction in Ndee archaeological re-search means that archaeologists must rely on ethnographers, historians, and other non-Ndee researchers regarding understandings of Ndee lifeways and social processes (e.g., Goodwin 1939, 1942; Opler 1965, 1969, 1983a, 1983b, 1983c).[1]

Spanish chronicles (Naylor and Polzer 1986; Spicer 1962; Thrapp 1967) suggest that Ndee were present in the mid-1500s, but there has been much difficulty in locating Ndee sites dating to that time. The perishable organic material Ndee used to construct wickiups disappears rather quickly from the archaeological record. This perishability is attributable to the "leave no trace" practices of Ndee groups (Goodwin n.d.a; Gregory 1981; Herr and Wood 2004; Welch 1997) However, archaeologists' (mostly non-Ndee individuals) speculation about the Ndee past and present is very much alive and has im-plications for contemporary Ndee communities. For this reason, it is neces-sary to refocus attention on the past and persistent presence of Ndee through Ndee cultural resource management strategies and Ndee lived experience.

Ndee versus Apache: Language as an Expression of Sovereignty and Power

Before discussing the past as persistence and how various forms of archaeo-logical knowledge are perpetuated through methodology and terminology that may adversely affect Ndee communities, I want to explain why referring to Apache groups in the Southwest as "Ndee" instead of as "Apache" helps foreground my reasoning throughout this chapter.

In 2013, various Apache nations, including Fort Apache Indian Reserva-tion, leaders of the Jicarilla Apache Nation, Mescalero Apache Tribe, Fort Sill Apache Tribe, San Carlos Apache Tribe, Tonto Apache Tribe, Apache Tribe of Oklahoma, White Mountain Apache Tribe, and Yavapai-Apache Nation, signed the Ndee Iłahík'ai/Nnee Iłahík'ai (Apache People Joining Together, also known as the "Inter-Apache Policy on Repatriation and the Protec-tion of Apache Culture") (Welch et al. 2017). Part of this agreement stated that the Apache term "Ndee" be used to refer to the six Ndee cultural tradi-tions known as Kiowa, Lipan, Jicarilla, Mescalero, Chiricahua, and Western Apaches (Welch 2000).

For the most part, naming and terminology in archaeological discourse have not contributed to the unique ways Ndee communities defined and identified themselves in the past or how they do so in the present. Not only do Ndee orientations help us situate ourselves within our own cultural milieus, but the exertion of naming power and sovereignty through group cohesiveness and identity redirects and reorients an Ndee research stance through the proclamation of the Ndee language as tool of empowerment. Because archaeology within the United States is in many ways a colonial enterprise that has caused unprecedented changes for Ndee people, including "loss of control over the independent shaping of their own names and identities" (Bruchac 2018, 3), exercising self-determination and sovereignty through language grounds the directionality of research from the start. Basic shifts from English to Indigenous language systems can invigorate and enlighten concepts in ways that reach beyond western agendas. For example, I have pointed out (Laluk 2017) in my own collaborative work with Ndee cultural experts that certain components of Ndee culture might not understand English. This reasoning underscores how Ndee thought processes are directly and intimately tied to language and how breaking from this can modify or even fracture reciprocal associations between Ndee communities and the everyday world.

Recently, I have argued (Laluk 2021) that archaeologists need to consider Ndee terminology, language, and thought as ethical and moral tools to guide reflections on past archaeological practices and on their own research methods. Drawing on such understandings, including the inability of English to fully convey Ndee knowledge, researchers can think through why what a seemingly basic name change might mean with regard to the legacies of archaeological research, settler-colonialism, persistence, and Indigenous empowerment. When archaeologists are willing to do this, better paths to collaborative research can be realized. As Bruchac and other colleagues in this volume (Dickson and Steinmetz, this volume) point out, "Names matter. They signify and communicate conceptions of identity, kinship and power" (Bruchac 2018, 3). This quote is a useful guiding tool for the rest of this chapter. Given that western archaeological power structures are very much alive, how can we navigate the use of terminology and methodology to explain that Ndee pasts and present persist beyond archaeological reasoning? A useful path forward is recognizing that Ndee terminological and linguistic sovereignty are powerful ways to foreground Ndee communities as true controllers of their culture, heritage, and identity.

Why "Leave No Trace"?

A discussion of the "leave-no-trace" lifestyle that historical-period Apache groups practiced is warranted. Various researchers (Goodwin n.d.; Gregory 1981; Herr and Wood 2004; Welch 1997) suggest that many Ndee groups intentionally "cleaned up" occupied areas to prevent encroaching Euro-American populations and other American Indian groups from detecting their presence. Herr and her colleagues suggest (Herr et al. 2011, 12) that Ndee artifacts and features on the landscape are "camouflaged from the view of the archaeologist by the Apache practice of residing on earlier prehistoric sites and reusing earlier artifacts." The invisibility resulting from intentional cleanup, high mobility, location of Apache camps on older ancestral sites, and reuse of earlier artifacts continues to present challenges to archaeological researchers.

Ndee representatives have told me that this invisibility could also be attributed to increased interactions with other non-Ndee groups (Laluk 2015). Ramon Riley, a representative of the White Mountain Apache Tribe, states that because Apache people were hunted for their scalps, it was necessary to leave nothing behind to indicate that they had been there (personal communication 2009; see also Laluk 2015). Arden Comanche of the Mescalero Apache Tribe also states that Apache people moved with the seasons and never left anything behind because they did not want anybody to know they were there (personal communication 2010; Laluk 2015).

Another factor that likely contributed to Apache material culture invisibility on the landscape is the erasure of Ndee places. The US military, seeking to subjugate and "pacify" Ndee inhabiting strongholds in the Dragoon and Chiricahua Mountains, spearheaded large-scale burning and destruction of historical-period camps and *rancherías*. Various accounts indicate that when the military came across these areas, they would destroy everything, usually by setting the camps on fire (Bourke 1883; Sechrist 2008).[2] Apache representatives who were interviewed during archaeological work on State Highway Route 260 indicated that when a sickness came to camp or a holy man died, the entire camp was burned (Herr et al. 2011, 106). This is similar to Opler's findings (1965, 473–475) among the Chiricahua Apache that when an individual died, their body was usually interred at another location, their belongings were destroyed, and their campsite was avoided or abandoned altogether. These social and cultural obligations to respect the deceased may also contribute to the great difficulty in identifying Ndee camps in the southwest United States.

Regardless of the factors that contribute to the difficulties of identifying Ndee landscape occupations, the problem is how to move beyond identifying Ndee sites as ephemeral based on leave-no-trace lifestyles. This is connected to a larger and much more important issue: Situating the Ndee past as ephemeral provides a perpetual context of absence that significantly impacts Ndee sovereignty and self-determination with regard to cultural affiliation, identity, heritage, and place. More thorough and well-thought-out discussion about research methods and terminologies with Ndee communities is critical. However, Schneider's warning to archaeologists to "*not* situate something as evidence without regard to audience and context, because to do so would be destructive to Native sovereignty" (Schneider and Hayes 2020, 133) is well taken. This is a crucial point that non-Ndee archaeological researchers in the US Southwest often miss. The focus of researchers on materials and, more importantly, on the lack of materials pushes them to jump to speculations about behavior, material choice, spatial analysis of materials, and sourcing of materials. They fail to widen their analytical and interpretive lenses to consider why "ephemeral" might be a poor descriptive term and how it downplays powerful landscape associations that can drive Ndee sovereignty. What is needed is a more thorough Ndee-driven methodology that contributes to questions that can be used the navigate the social and political nature of Ndee cultural and historical realities. Embracing Ndee cultural heritage resource tenets and diverse Ndee knowledge systems can provide more useful understandings of the past.

Ndee Cultural Knowledge and Tenets as Persistence

Ndee cultural tenets are often used to guide research practice and methodology. On White Mountain Apache lands, they range from simple respect to recognizing that disturbing the past might have detrimental sociocultural effects on individuals and communities. Ndee communities use these tenets to help them maintain cultural balance and ensure the well-being of the overall community. Persistence is one concept that is useful for understanding the "long-term cultural trajectories of indigenous groups, as well as the small-scale negotiations of colonialism that take place through daily practice" (Panich 2013, 118). Panich's statement applies to two unique forms of persistence within Ndee world views: the Ndee negotiation of the tenet of avoidance and the long-term persistence of learned knowledge, or Ndee presence, as demonstrated by the diversity of Ndee knowledge at the Tribal level.

Panich defines (2013, 107) persistence as "a continuation of existence in the face of opposition." This definition works well for Indigenous communities that have maintained their identities distinct from Euro-American colonists. Panich (2013, 107) also notes that "persistence can accommodate change" and at times might require it. In this chapter, I embrace both notions of persistence: as the maintaining of a perpetual static identity in the form of adherence to Ndee cultural heritage preservation tenets such as avoidance and as the recognition on the part of Ndee communities that certain changes need to be made in order to perpetuate notions of avoidance in their own practice of archaeology. Moreover, Panich (2013, 108) argues that "for developing archaeologies of persistence, one of the most the most useful findings of earlier acculturation studies may be that significant variation existed within Native societies in regards to the negotiation of colonialism." Tribal nations throughout the United States negotiated and dealt with colonial activities in unique and diverse ways. This diversity can be found within contemporary intratribal arenas that challenge the notion that full-scale community-based archaeologies can be achieved. Archaeologists do not always recognize the diversity of Tribal knowledge at these levels and as a result fail to appropriately modify their research goals and interests in ways that will enable them to understand issues that go beyond material-based understandings of the Ndee past and present.

Ndee Avoidance

Many Ndee communities strictly follow the cultural tenet of avoidance in reference to dealing with the past and to visiting areas marked by material evidence of ancestors. As Welch et al. (2009, 151) note, "Ndee teachings mandate respect for all ancient places, objects, and intangibles, affirming avoidance as the highest form of respect." The concept of avoidance may be difficult for the archaeologist to comprehend or put into practice, but it can be practiced in ways that are beneficial for both Tribal and Indigenous communities and researchers worldwide. For example, in her work in the Moquegua Valley, Peru, Sharatt (2017) demonstrates how certain communities actively and purposefully avoided burial cemetery components of earlier occupations at the site of Tumilaca la Chimba. Sharatt (656) argues that because her team avoided instead of engaged with the Tumilaca dead, "the Estuquina [people] drew on their program of community building and identity constructions." Although Sharatt states that "we should also make analytical space for interpreting archaeological examples of avoiding the dead," the contemporary meanings of avoidance should also be a part of the analytical space.

The Diné (Navajo Nation) have a similar cultural tenet of avoidance in the American Southwest. As Thompson (2011, 508) points out, the Diné generally practice death avoidance: "Traditionally, once a person passed on their names would no longer be spoken, their possessions would be burned, and their horses would be destroyed." Such conceptions of avoidance extend to the hogan (home) where death has happened and to other Diné archaeological contexts. As Thompson notes, "Like death-hogans, archaeological sites generally are considered to be places that are to be avoided, particularly by people who are not versed in the complexities of Diné philosophy and ceremonialism" (Thompson 2011, 508). When they are asked about the Ndee concept of avoidance in reference to the past and to archaeological site areas, many Ndee representatives adamantly insist that avoidance should be practiced and that it is crucial to Ndee community well-being at the same time that they state that it is a difficult tenet for them to practice.

For example, Arden Comanche (personal communication 2009) has stated that "we (Ndee) avoid the past because it is taboo, but it is not our fault that entities (e.g., museums) have acquired our things without permission. These are still a part of our history and it is hard to stay away." In referring to the difficulties of staying away at times but understanding the overall need to protect and preserve Ndee culture and history including the remains of ancestors, Mr. Comanche goes on to say that he has to be involved because he wants "their souls to go to rest with them." Similarly, Mark Altaha (personal communication 2009) says that "the past is taboo for all Apache Tribes, but we have no choice; now more than ever we have to get involved." To contemporary scholars of Ndee archaeology and to Ndee community experts working within reservations it seems that while the tenet of avoidance needs to be continually practiced, at the same time in certain contexts or situations (i.e., repatriation) avoidance is challenging. Here, we can see a unique sense of persistence at work though a practical embrace of avoidance that can help guide Ndee repatriation practices. The recognition of the absolute need for Ndee community members to be involved in archaeological projects or reburial practices demonstrates a subtler "shift in political organization and group identity that draw[s] on and [is] structured by dynamic cultural values and practices" (Panich 2013, 107). The subtle shift of acknowledging the need to practice avoidance in nontraditional ways by becoming more involved in archaeological projects contributes to a cultural persistence that strengthens overall identity, sovereignty, and well-being for Ndee communities.

For example, Ndee communities strive to achieve various levels of *gózhó*, an Ndee concept of beauty, balance, and harmony. Because Ndee Tribes recognize that repatriating our cultural items and safeguarding our cultures are a part of attaining a state of *gózhó*, varying levels of "necessary permitting" within a practice of avoidance can be made on a case-by-case basis.[3] For example, if Mr. Comanche feels that self-reflection and inherent responsibility are duties to the ancestors, then it is up to Mr. Comanche and appointed and appropriate Mescalero Tribal cultural experts to determine the applicable levels of avoidance while balancing and achieving a continued sense of *gózhó* for the overall Mescalero Tribal community (Laluk 2015). The subtle changes in the Ndee practice of avoidance that embrace protecting the past through recognizing that Ndee individuals are the best equipped to do so not only provides a powerful shift in archaeological practice—by allowing Mr. Comanche to exert sovereignty by choosing the levels of "necessary permitting"—but also demonstrates the persistence of involvement as avoidance in order to achieve individual and community senses of *gózhó*. Since Ndee tribal members are best equipped to preserve and protect Ndee culture and history, the very fact that Ndee cultural resource experts who have the power to guide research methods and practice foregrounds senses of avoidance, especially because Tribal members can stress the need to adhere to cultural tenets/practices during all project-related activities.

However, non-Ndee researchers have to approach working on archaeological projects with Ndee communities on case-by-case basis, respecting the Ndee tenet of avoidance wholeheartedly. Non-Ndee researchers also need to commit to applying Ndee cultural experts' thoughts, words, beliefs, and actions in order to protect the legacies of Ndee culture. That commitment needs to be underpinned by Ndee tenets of respect and avoidance that act as tools of persistence for Ndee communities. The Ndee tenet of respect can also contribute to archaeologists' collaborative research with Native American communities in various ways if the non-Native researchers can critically self-reflect. If researchers can view the tenet of avoidance as a positive opportunity to do research in a constructive way that addresses contemporary and future Ndee concerns regarding cultural heritage resources rather than a hindrance to research, then collaborative research can be much fuller and richer for all parties involved. This would involve respecting Tribal standards of care and management. Kovach (2010, 32) defines reflexivity as "the researcher's own self-reflection in the meaning making process." Ndee individuals who are willing to collaborate with non-Ndee researchers have done this process of self-reflection and concluded that it is necessary for them to be involved "more than ever."

Such an involvement underpins my point that definitions of Ndee culture rely on how non-Ndee archaeologists continue to define Ndee culture as something that is hard to see, something that is composed of minimal traces or is ephemeral. Avoidance, which has persisted in varying ways as needed as an experiential way of knowing, "challenges dominant views of what constitutes intelligence" (Magnat 2012, 34). Avoidance highlights the persistence of the Ndee past through a methodology that recognizes that a) disturbance of the past might result in negative consequences; and b) avoidance persists as direct experience and as the best practice for managing Tribal cultural heritage.

However, this involvement cannot be misconstrued as fully integrated archaeological research, as is often the case with proposals for archaeological research projects that suggest fully collaborative research with Native American communities. Moreover, collaboration cannot be limited to interpretation. Participation as equal players also has to occur at the practical and methodological levels when important choices can still be made, not only regarding cultural heritage resources but also regarding the association of Ndee resources with the contemporary Indigenous livelihoods of Ndee people. Just because Ndee people have a cultural tenet of avoidance does not mean that we should be avoided during decision-making processes (Laluk 2015).

In my experience, the quest of archaeologists to collect, record, analyze, and interpret contributes to non-Ndee researchers viewing avoidance as a hindrance. This view of avoidance needs to be critically and creatively thought out and integrated into research plans so that researchers can identify and embrace their own social and moral responsibilities beyond paternalistic notions of saving "the Indian" or internalized romanticized notions of what archaeology should be (e.g., excavation, invasive and destructive research). Determining what avoidance means should not be predetermined. In the Ndee sense, avoidance refers to a whole lifeway of traditional community practice grounded in respect and reciprocity.

Finally, non-Ndee archaeological perspectives on the limitations of the tenet of avoidance might perpetuate stereotypes about Ndee people. For example, because disturbing the past was and still is considered a taboo, stereotypes surrounding the term avoidance perpetuate the idea of lack of material remains and lead to the idea that "leave no trace" is equivalent to nonexistent. In other words, the fact that Ndee individuals might have in the past and still do avoid certain elements of their history does mean that their connections to the past have been minimized and thus are invisible or disconnected. Rather, because we continue to practice the cultural tenets of avoidance and respect that our ancestors have passed down over time, our ongoing connections of the present with the past persist beyond objective material-based affiliations. Academic literature perpetuates the concept of nonexistence based on a "lack" of archaeological evidence. This places Ndee individuals outside their own identity and their own heritage as ephemeral. If Ndee community members state they were present on the past landscape, *then they were!*

White Chert: Ndee Persistence beyond Material Presence

Various archaeologists and ethnographers have suggested that the presence of white chert chipped-stone artifacts might be used as a possible diagnostic trait of Western Apache affiliation (Bourke 1890; Buskirk 1949; Goodwin n.d.; Gregory 1981). However, archaeologists fail to address other potential questions associated with the presence of white chert that might signal more in-depth understandings of reservation lifeways and Ndee identities beyond simple presence. The persistence of Ndee presence on the landscape is held together not only through material components of the Ndee past but also through the direct intergenerational experience of Ndee individuals. Such persistence allows for more Ndee community-based and lived experiential realities to be highlighted that not only enhance archaeological understandings but guide research methodologies and practice with Ndee communities.

For example, after consulting with Western Apache communities during the Highway 260 Project near Little Green Valley, Arizona, Cibecue Apache cultural expert Levi Dehose wrote that "Apaches coveted white flint or chert for points because white symbolically represents the female" (Krall et al. 2011, 110). However, Victor Smith, who lived near Middle Verde (Verde Valley) when he was younger (Krall et al. 2011, 107) states that "obsidian was often the material of choice to make projectile points" (Krall et al. 2011, 110). Intrigued by Mr. Dehose's recognition of the significance of white chert to the Cibecue Apache and Mr. Smith's recognition of the importance of obsidian to Ndee individuals in the Verde Valley area of Arizona, I researched the issue.

I first interviewed White Mountain Apache NAGPRA coordinator Ramon Riley (personal communication 2014; see also Laluk 2015) and asked if he had ever heard of an Ndee preference for white chert. Riley responded that "the only very significant arrowhead I know about is the black ones, all hold some kind of power but the black one I know for sure. Black arrowheads is used for healing and warding off evil, people today wear it around their neck and others have it in their pouch." Riley's statement is interesting because he and Mr. Dehose are both members of the White Mountain Apache Tribe but they are from different communities within the Tribe. Cibecue, where Mr. Dehose lives, is somewhat isolated from other White Mountain communities. Mr. Riley lives in the Seven Mile community located near Fort Apache and the Tribal headquarters in Whiteriver, Arizona. Riley and Dehose's statements both draw an association between power and the ongoing importance of certain materials in Ndee belief systems. This is important because it demonstrates how diverse Ndee and Native American knowledge systems can be. These relationships are important to the identification and management of potential Ndee sites that exhibit black and white chipped-stone materials (Laluk 2015).

In addition to reflecting past social processes such as resource preference and social ties to resources that embody important colors of power (i.e., white and black) the statements of Riley and Dehose also demonstrate the uniqueness of interpretations at the intratribal and intertribal social level. Although both are cultural experts who are enrolled in the same Tribe, they provided their own unique explanations about white chert material. This touches on the absolute necessity for researchers to question their research methodologies and to modify them so they reflect the reality of multiple layers and dimensions of diverse but equal knowledge from within the same Tribal nation.

The knowledge Mr. Dehose and Smith shared demonstrate equally important yet unique statements that result from living and learning in different communities within the same reservation. The observations and lived experiences of Mr. Dehose and Riley show how knowledge, land, and Ndee identity are linked and how those links persist across time and space without the need for archaeologists to categorize them or speculate about them. The presence of white chert brought to life questions and responses that are integral for understanding how Ndee folks connect to the landscape. The learned knowledge systems of two highly respected Tribal cultural experts who were raised in two distinct communities of the same reservation demonstrate lived and ongoing connections to the landscape. These connections may be manifested regionally though the presence and power of important colors of material remains that may be present across possible Ndee sites throughout the southwest United States (Laluk 2015). The persistence of Ndee reasoning and reality is grounded in the land base that might have material traces of white chert, but the inner Tribal dynamics underscore social, spiritual, and political realities of Ndee presence that have been maintained since time immemorial. Material remains are only one part of the interrelated story.

Field Methodology: A Note

So far, I have argued that certain terms archaeologists use to refer to past Ndee presence on the landscape need to be rethought in terms of how Ndee communities actually were present on the landscape and how they have persisted in the present. I have also demonstrated the limitations of archaeological methodology with regard to consultation and collaborative work through a local example in my own community. Here, I would like to discuss how archaeological field methodologies might be contributing to the lack of identification of Ndee sites due to the often one-dimensional thinking that informs archaeological methods and practice.

I use the term "one-dimensional" to mean a focus on western methods, including those that stress the importance of material over other components of agency and reasoning. Because archaeologists are trained to "seek out, collect, and study human-modified things" (Cipolla et al. 2019, 132), there is a huge potential that they will miss evidence that does not fit the category of human-modified material remains. Archaeologists need to modify their survey techniques so they can better identify evidence of past Ndee presence that goes beyond material remains. During my dissertation research, I spent time contemplating various ways to identify Ndee sites in southern Arizona more effectively.

I initially thought that modifying pedestrian survey intervals and even focusing on higher-altitude, steeper terrain might help identify sites that might be associated with past Ndee presence. However, although this modified survey methodology covered more ground, it did not contribute to better understandings of historical-period Ndee lifeways within the mountainscape. Instead, listening to and watching venerated Ndee elders and cultural experts associate with the land base during collaborative site visits and discussions helped me see powerful Ndee ties to the past and present land base (Laluk 2017). For example, during a site visit, I listened to cultural experts describe how century plants were often present at campsites (Laluk 2015). I realized that insights gleaned from such experts could be deepened with modifications of archaeological methods.

Although large-above ground agave roasting pits and processing tools have long been considered a hallmark of past Ndee presence, agave plants themselves do not necessarily need to be associated with material components of the Ndee past to make places important to Ndee communities. Here, if we adapt a pedestrian survey strategy similar to Cipolla et al.'s (2019, 134) method, which focused on identifying local plant species Ndee communities used in the past and still use in the present for subsistence and for medicine at different seasonal intervals, we might better understand how Ndee communities related in the past (and still relate today) to the mountainscape and the natural world. It is equally important to understand that such Ndee expertise comes from a lifetime of experiences, careful observations and trial and error (Grenier 1998). These ways of gaining knowledge can contribute to multiple ontologies within Indigenous communities.

Cipolla et al. (2019) note that that their recognition that as archaeologists they needed make room for multiple ontologies was useful in their work. The example of materials used in the past for arrowheads illustrates how intratribal ontologies guide interpretation and reasoning. This does not mean that one Tribal ontology might be more important than another; what is important is the persistence of reality-based relationships Ndee cultural experts voice. These powerful forms of knowledge can guide us as we learn to replace or modify archaeological methods. Methodology guided by Tribal ontological reasoning (Cowie and Teeman, this volume) not only creates space for Indigenous knowledge systems but maintains and reinvigorates the associations Tribal communities have to the land base in ways that go beyond how archaeologists discern the past. Archaeologists who want to better understand post-1492 Indigenous lifeways need to identify the needs and wants of Tribal entities. Modifying standard archaeological methods to be more inclusive of Tribal interests and thought processes is absolutely critical, but forming better understandings of the diverse reasoning that goes beyond human-based agency leads to more inclusive and holistic interpretation and methodology.

Conclusion

In essence, I agree with Bruchac's (2018, xi) call to reevaluate ethics of engagement with Indigenous communities. If we are to recover as Indigenous peoples from various issues anthropologists and archaeologists have created—including harmful assumptions and practices that violate Tribal research protocols—those researchers need to reassess the ethics of engagement with Indigenous communities. I have outlined a potential ethics of engagement from my own Ndee view and as an Indigenous archaeologist. I discussed the tenet of avoidance and highlighted an example of material culture (white chert) that some researchers see as a sign of past Ndee presence on the landscape. However, if archaeology is to truly embrace Panich's (2013) call for more "archaeologies of persistence," more archaeologists will need to question their own training and thought processes to look for meaning and persistence in evidence other than material remains.

The Ndee philosophy of avoidance has contributed to reasoning that suggests that Ndee archaeology has to be determined by the "ephemerality" of sites. In the past, archaeologists have not thought beyond material evidence of Ndee culture that fits categories they have created and rely upon (Donaldson and Welch 1991; Gregory 1981; Welch et al. 2017). However, foregrounding avoidance as a way of approaching the Ndee past brings Ndee culture to life. The Ndee practice of avoidance highlights a management practice driven by sovereignty and cultural tenets that respectfully shifts the focus away from material categories and toward the principle that "absence = presence through Ndee perspectives and knowledge systems concerning their own past."

As an Ndee Tribal member, I know that my ancestors moved swiftly on the landscape and exploited resources over their vast traditional homelands in present-day Arizona, New Mexico, Mexico, and Texas. Referring to my past as ephemeral, or nearly invisible, takes away the ongoing persistence of my culture, which is held together powerfully by tenets such as avoidance or through knowledge that is passed from generation to generation within distinct Tribal communities on my reservation. For most western, Euro-American archaeologists, the words "absence" and "ephemeral" fail to capture the beautiful presence of Ndee culture, history, and world views that are very much alive within the context of what Ndee folks know all too well about themselves: *That we have always been here and that we persist in ways that exist outside of current archaeological thinking.*

Notes

1. See also "Dwellings of the White Mountain Apache, Artifacts, Fire and Tobacco," unpublished field notes on file in the Arizona State Museum Library, A-71, 1932, Folder 31, Grenville Goodwin Collection, M 517, Arizona State Museum, Tucson; and Grenville Goodwin, "Dwellings of the White Mountain Apache, Artifacts, Fire and Tobacco," n.d., unpublished field notes on file in the Arizona State Museum Library, A-71, Tucson.

2. See also E. J. Harrington to Major W. Harvey Brown, Commanding Camp Wallen, Arizona Territory, June 24, 1867, House Executive Documents 1324, Report of the Secretary of War, D-XV; Reuben F. Bernard to Brevet Lieutenant Colonel Thomas S. Dunn, February 1, 1870, transcript on file at Fort Bowie National Historic Site; J. Gorman to Captain John A. A., November 9, 1865, manuscript on file at Fort Bowie National Historic Site.

3. "Yavapai-Apache Nation Signs Historic Apache Alliance Document," *Gah'nahvah/ YaTi'* (newspaper of the Yavapai-Apache Nation), June, 1–2, 2013.

References Cited

Bourke, John G. 1883. *An Apache Campaign in the Sierra Madre: An Account of the Expedition in Pursuit of the Hostile Chiricahua Apaches in the Spring of 1883.* New York: Charles Scribner's Sons.

Bruchac, Margaret M. 2018. *Savage Kin: Indigenous Informants and American Anthropologists.* Tucson: University of Arizona Press.

Buskirk, Winfred. 1986. *The Western Apache: Living with the Land before 1950.* Norman: University of Oklahoma Press.

Cipolla, Craig N., James Quinn, and Jay Levy. 2019. "Theory in Collaborative Indigenous Archaeology: Insights from Mohegan." *American Antiquity* 84(1): 127–142.

Donaldson, Bruce R., and John R. Welch. 1991. Western Apache Dwellings and Their Archaeological Correlates. In *Mogollon V*, edited by Patrick Beckett, 93–105. Las Cruces: COAS.

Ferg, Alan. 1992. Western Apache and Yavapai Pottery and Features from the Rye Creek Project. In *The Rye Creek Project: Archaeology in the Upper Tonto Basin*. Vol. 3, *Synthesis and Conclusions*, edited by Mark D. Elson and Douglas B. Craig, 3–27. Anthropological Papers 11. Tucson, AZ: Center for Desert Archaeology.

Goodwin, Grenville. 1939. *Myths, and Tales of the White Mountain Apache*. Memoirs of the American Folklore Society Volume 33. New York: American Folklore Society.

———. 1942. *Social Organization of the Western Apache*. University of Chicago Press, Chicago.

———. N.d. Dwellings of the White Mountain Apache, Artifacts, Fire and Tobacco. Unpublished field notes on file in the Arizona State Museum Library, A-71.

Gregory, David A. 1981. Western Apache Archaeology: Problems and Approaches. In *The Protohistoric Period in the North American Southwest, AD 1450–1700*, edited by David R. Wilcox and W. Bruce Masse, 257–274. Anthropological Research Papers No. 24. Tempe: Arizona State University.

Grenier, Louise. 1998. *Working with Indigenous Knowledge: A Guide for Researchers*. Ottawa: International Development Research Centre.

Herr, Sarah A., ed. 2011. *Dilzhe' 'e bii tian*: Archaeological Investigations of Apache Sites Near Little Green Valley, Arizona, State Route 260 Payson to Heber Archaeological Project, Gila County, Arizona. Technical Report no. 2006-05, Desert Archaeology, Inc., Tucson, AZ.

Herr, Sarah, and Scott Wood. 2004. Apache Archaeology in Central Arizona: The Origins of the 'Leave No Trace' Camping Movement? Paper presented at the conference Faint Traces of Past Places: The Archaeology of High-Mobility Groups in Arizona, A.D. 1330–1750, October 22–23, Tucson, AZ.

Kelly, W. 1871. Letter to Post Adjutant, Fort Bayard, N.M., February 19.

Kovach, Margaret. 2010. *Indigenous Methodologies: Characteristics, Conversations and Contexts*. Toronto: University of Toronto Press.

Krall, Angie, Chip Colwell-Chanthaphonh, and T. J. Ferguson. 2011. Apache Interpretations of the Plymouth Landing Site. In *Dilzhe' 'e bii tian: Archaeological Investigations of Apache Sites near Little Green Valley, Arizona, State Route 260 Payson to Heber Archaeological Project, Gila County, Arizona*, edited by Sarah Herr, 105–111. Technical Report no. 2006-05. Desert Archaeology, Inc., Tucson, AZ.

Laluk, Nicholas C. 2015. Historical-Period Apache Occupation of the Chiricahua Mountains in Southeastern Arizona: An Exercise in Collaboration. PhD diss., University of Arizona.

———. 2017. The Indivisibility of Land and Mind: Indigenous Knowledge and Collaborative Archaeology within Apache Contexts. *Journal of Social Archaeology* 17(1): 92–112.

———. 2021. Changing How Archaeology Is Done in Native American Contexts: An *Ndee* (Apache) Case Study. *Journal of Social Archaeology* 21(1): 53–73.

Magnat, Virginie. 2012. Can Research Become Ceremony? Performance Ethnography and Indigenous Epistemologies. *Canadian Theatre Review* 151: 30–36.

Naylor, Thomas H., and Charles W. Polzer, eds. 1986. *The Presidio and the Militia on the Northern Frontier of Spain*. Vol. 1. Tucson: University of Arizona Press.

Opler, Morris E. 1965. *An Apache Life-Way: The Economic, Social, and Religious Institutions of the Chiricahua Indians*. New York: Cooper Square Publishers.

———. 1969. *Apache Odyssey: A Journey between Two Worlds.* New York: Holt, Rinehart and Winston.

———. 1983a. The Apachean Culture Pattern and its Origins. In *Handbook of North American Indians.* Vol. 10, *Southwest,* edited by Alfonso Ortiz, 368–392. Washington, DC: Smithsonian Institution.

———. 1983b. Chiricahua Apache. In *Handbook of North American Indians.* Vol. 10, *Southwest,* edited by Alfonso Ortiz, 401–418. Washington, DC: Smithsonian Institution.

———. 1983c. Mescalero Apache. In *Handbook of North American Indians.* Vol. 10, *Southwest,* edited by Alfonso Ortiz, 419–439. Washington, DC: Smithsonian Institution.

Panich, Lee M. 2013. Archaeologies of Persistence: Reconsidering the Legacies of Colonialism in Native North America. *American Antiquity* 78(1): 105–122.

Schneider, Tsim D., and Katherine Hayes. 2020. Epistemic Colonialism: Is it Possible to Decolonize Archaeology? *American Indian Quarterly* 44(2): 127–148.

Sechrist, Mark. 2008. Archaeological Reconnaissance Survey in the Sulphur Canyon Area of the Chiricahua Mountains, Arizona: An Apache Landscape. Masters report, Department of Sociology and Anthropology, New Mexico State University.

Sharratt, Nicola. 2017. Steering Clear of the Dead: Avoiding Ancestors in the Moquegua Valley, Peru. *American Anthropologist* 119(4): 645–661.

Spicer, Edward H. 1962. *Cycles of Conquest: The Impact of Spain, Mexico, and the United States on the Indians of the Southwest, 1533–1960.* Tucson: University of Arizona Press.

Thompson, Kerry F. 2011. The Navajo Nation, Diné Archaeologists, Diné Archaeology, and Diné Communities. *Archaeologies* 7(3): 502–517.

Thrapp, Dan L. 1967. *The Conquest of Apacheria.* Norman: University of Oklahoma Press.

Welch, John R. 1997. White Eyes' Lies and the Battle for *Dził Nchaa Si'An. American Indian Quarterly* 21: 75–109.

Welch, John R., and Todd W. Bostwick, eds. 1998. *The Archaeology of Ancient Tactical Sites.* Tucson: Arizona Historical Society.

Welch, John R., Mark T. Altaha, Karl A. Hoerig, and Ramon Riley. 2009. Best Cultural Heritage Stewardship Practices by and for the White Mountain Apache Tribe. *Conservation and Management of Archaeology Sites* 11(2): 148–160.

Welch, John R., Sarah A. Herr, and Nicholas C. Laluk. 2017. Ndee (Apache) Archaeology. In *The Oxford Handbook of Southwest Archaeology,* edited by Barbara Mills and Severin Fowles. Oxford: Oxford University Press.

5

Considering the Long-Term Consequences of Designating Native American Sites as European Creations

SARAH TRABERT

The Europeans who colonized North America sought to remake the continent into something familiar to them while also erasing the long-held claims Native Americans had to these landscapes. Europeans used cartography to support imperial agendas as they assigned altered or entirely new names to prominent landforms, rivers, and landscapes that had been known to Native peoples for countless generations. This was and is a global process, and scholars around the world have recently highlighted the counterhistories of many descendant communities who are reclaiming landscapes and returning traditional names to places (e.g., Basso 1996; Blu Barnd 2017; Cogos et al. 2017; Fitznore 2006; Kapä'anaokaläokeola Näkoa Oliveira 2009; Guyot and Seethal 2007; Rose-Redwood 2016; Steinman 2016; Uluochoa 2015). However, before place-names can be reclaimed for some archaeological sites, descendant communities have to navigate the fact that some of their sites have been claimed by Euro-American communities as their own.

In North America, Euro-Americans not only renamed landscapes but also rewrote histories and attributed the origins of some Native American archaeological sites to Europeans. Remnants of villages and fortifications on the Great Plains that Native peoples were forced to abandon because of population loss, conflict, and forced resettlement were left out of written histories. In many cases, Euro-Americans in the nineteenth and twentieth centuries chose to believe that the ruins of Indigenous villages and fortifications were the products of Spanish and/or French settlement centuries before. Although many local historians and later archaeologists found these sites to be of Native American rather than European origin, they published their findings after those initial European designations were given. The damage was already done to local community memories and long-term Indigenous histories were severely undermined. As part of broader colonial legacies, archaeologists today continue to give shorthand names to Indigenous sites that refer to nearby landforms or rivers with European names, the last names of American landowners, or events (for example, "the car crash site"). While these naming practices can be problematic, the examples I provide here go beyond assigning Euro-American names to sites; they assign Euro-American origins, thus rebranding Indigenous sites as European creations.

In this chapter, I briefly discuss the broader literature surrounding place making and the importance of reclaiming named places, contextualizing these ideas within colonial processes. Newly developing pericolonial frameworks can be used to model the consequences of these designations, especially given that many of these spaces were part of—yet viewed as apart from—the main vanguard of settler colonialism. I provide examples of four Native American sites from the Central and Southern Plains (El Cuartelejo, Deer Creek, Neodesha Fort, and Spanish Fort; see Figure 5.1) that were all incorrectly assigned European rather than Native American origins. In most cases, local American communities persist in privileging these inaccurate origins, a practice that undermines long-term Indigenous histories of occupying these places. Names have power, and Indigenous and non-Indigenous researchers can help rewrite these narratives by recognizing Indigenous perspectives, Indigenous claims, and the importance of Indigenous-centered histories.

Place Making, Naming, and Colonial Processes

Power in Names

Place-names hold layers of significant meaning. Even though some scholars in other disciplines argue that names themselves are simply labels without intrinsic importance (see Nyström 2016, 39, for a review), this sentiment does not recognize that the places and their names encode a great deal of meaning and history (Panich and Schneider, this volume). Place-names connect people with their pasts, they act as literal and figurative guideposts, and they can

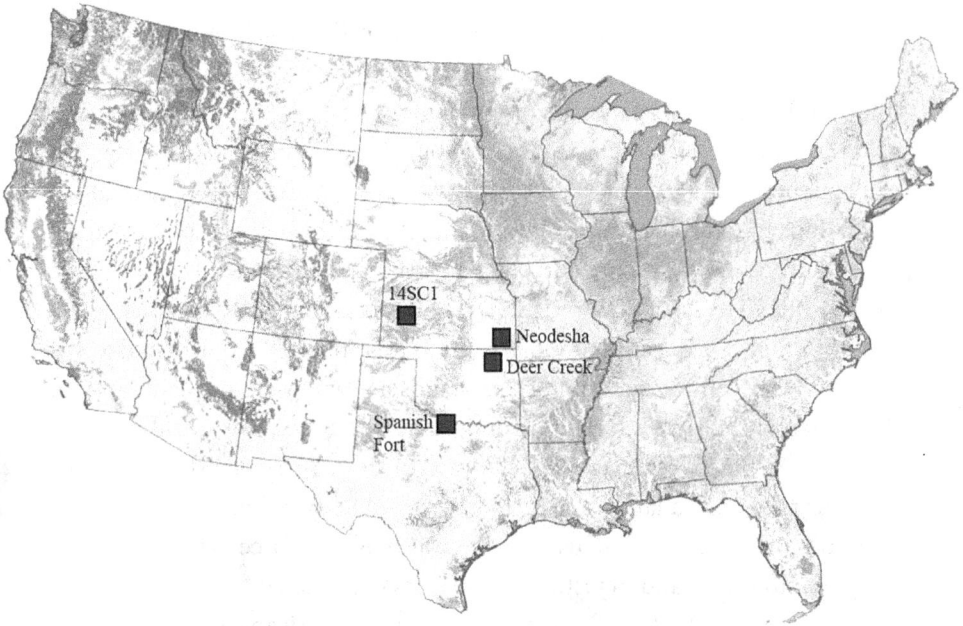

Figure 5.1. Locations of Site 14SC1, Neodesha, Deer Creek, and Spanish Fort. Map produced by Sarah Trabert.

hold a great deal of power in themselves (Cowie and Teeman, this volume; Kostanski 2016). Western cartographic methods do not preserve larger histories and knowledge sets. But that does not mean that nonwestern toponyms have disappeared (Cogos et al. 2017, 49). As Basso states, "place-names anchor historical narratives. . . . A single place-name may accomplish the communicative work of an entire saga or historical tale" (1996, 89). Many Indigenous communities argue that naming a place gives life to it and that removing that name harms the landscapes and peoples who live there (Kapä'anaokaläokeola Näkoa Oliveira 2009, 105). Scholars across many disciplines, particularly in geography and ethnohistory, are increasingly aware of the political struggles of Indigenous peoples over the issue of naming places and how taking back place-names is part of a growing political struggle over space and place (e.g., Barr 2011, 2017; Rose-Redwood 2016, 192).

Many Indigenous landscapes were renamed during colonization as European settlers assigned labels to landforms, rivers, and other spaces using names that were similar to those used in their homelands (Blu Barnd 2017;

Calloway 2013; Cogos et al. 2017; Guyot and Seethal 2007; Uluochoa 2015). In North America, Europeans established settlements that mirrored those they left behind, sometimes assigning names like New France or Nova Scotia. Europeans often established their colonies in or around Native American settlements, keeping some Native American place-names while excluding or changing others arbitrarily (Calloway 2013, 11–12). This settlement pattern enabled Europeans to obscure and often erase Native American connections to these lands (Barr 2011; Blu Barnd 2017; Calloway 2013; Panich and Schneider, this volume). European and American cartographers further dispossessed Native Americans by describing their lands as "wilderness, vacant land, or terra incognita . . . effectively excluding [them] from the new world they created on parchment and paper" (Calloway 2013, 13). These pen strokes helped colonizers remake a landscape that was neither new nor uninhabited. These methods of remaking local histories were also used to force nationalistic ideologies into reality and to justify mythologies of so-called frontiers and "new lands" (Grounds 2001, 288). This enabled Euro-Americans to forget the Native American nations that originally claimed these lands, and this collective forgetting removed conflicts in thinking about America as a land of liberty (Barr 2011; Grounds 2001; Shackel 2001; Zappia 2012).

Archaeologists are regularly confronted with many different types of purposeful forgetting and with changing social, cultural, and public memory (Kryder-Reid 2016; McAnany 2016; Panich and Schneider, this volume; Van Dyke 2019). Public memory can form as a kind of counterhistory that serves one community, sometimes at the expense of another (Shackel 2001; Van Dyke 2019). It can be built around touchstones—symbolic places, artifacts, events, or documents that work to ground memory even as public discourse shifts and change (Watts 2020). In some places, these touchstones are ruins that Americans claimed as they created their alternative histories that emphasized European rather than Native American claims to North American landscapes. Americans then publicly claimed many Native sites and places by erecting monuments, and local histories became part of "American" history as colonizers shared physical space with previous events and peoples (e.g., Shackel 2001).

American communities can form a strong sense of nostalgia for this manufactured history that links present-day peoples with distant and often non-European pasts. An example of these connections is seen in Cameron Wesson's (2012) work about the tensions between archaeologists and the public in Childersburg, Alabama, over Hernando de Soto's supposed expedition route in the sixteenth century. When archaeologists presented local communities with an alternative trail for de Soto's route that contradicted local historical narratives, they encountered harsh backlash as they hit the wall of public memory. The people of Childersburg strongly believed that their community was connected with de Soto's expedition, and when archaeologists suggested otherwise, members of the public created a narrative that outsiders were attempting to take their history away, calling into question the basis of their social identity and pride (Wesson 2012, 430). Scheiber (this volume) describes examples of communities in Wyoming that have claimed and attempted to remake Crow tipi ring sites, viewing these Native American sites as a common resource for recreation that the larger community "owns." Americans commonly use links with historic Native American settlement sites, European expedition routes, battle sites, or forts to foster a stronger claim to the places they occupy and to create a history that begins with colonization instead of with the longer-held Native connections to those same places.

Remodeling Colonial Processes with Links to Renaming

European and later American efforts to reimagine and rename Native American spaces as part of the colonial process are in part a reaction against centuries of Native hegemony in much of North America. Native Americans, especially in the West, retained a great deal of power and influence during early colonial encounters and were able to manipulate European individuals and interests (DuVal 2016; Hämäläinen 2014; Radding 2014). For much of the early "colonial" period, Native Americans outnumbered and outmaneuvered Europeans, forcing them to follow Indigenous rules for economic, social, and political engagement, all the while manipulating terms to best fit Indigenous rather than European interests (see Barr 2011, 2017; DeCoster 2013; DuVal 2007; Schwartz and Green 2013; and Zappia 2012 for examples). By removing Indigenous peoples and their territories from maps, colonizers were able to erase this earlier history of Native American hegemony and declare even the most powerful of Tribes as dispossessed (Barr 2011; Scheiber, this volume).

Another product of European- and American-centered narratives is the notion that colonization was a largely homogenous process that began with the establishment of forts and colonies in Native American territories. I contend here and elsewhere (Trabert 2017, 2018, 2019), however, that contact, social interaction between Indigenous and European peoples, and colonial policies were processes that unfolded in many ways across North America. For example, throughout the Great Plains, few Native peoples made direct contact with Europeans until the eighteenth or nineteenth centuries, despite earlier Spanish and French expeditions to the region (Mitchell and Scheiber 2010; Rogers 1990; Vehik 2006). Colonialism did not begin with sustained contacts between Native Americans and Europeans in the nineteenth century. Instead, Plains peoples experienced the indirect effects of European and Euro-American expansion as social, economic, demographic, and political changes that stemmed from colonial interference in neighboring regions and spilled over to their homelands (Trabert 2017, 2019). European manufactured goods, domestic animals, and disease preceded Europeans in all areas of the Plains, and the timing and intensity of Euro-American contact, interaction, and colonization varied considerably (DuVal 2006; Rogers 1990; Mitchell and Scheiber 2010; Trabert 2017; Vehik 2006).

This means that for hundreds of years, a number of Native American groups living on the Plains were neither colonized nor completely apart from the colonization process. They built and maintained fortifications, used their villages as trading centers, and maintained critical connections with other Native groups and with Europeans for decades, if not centuries, after initial contacts and after Europeans established colonies elsewhere (Trabert 2018; Trabert and Bethke forthcoming). Rather than considering these processes as "incomplete colonization," I draw on the concept of pericolonialism as a process and a model because it recognizes that groups might be economically and politically independent and yet still be affected by colonial activities in adjacent regions (Acabado 2017; Trabert 2019; Weaver et al. 2006). The concept of pericolonialism forces us to focus our research specifically on spaces where Native peoples were living beyond sight of most European and American colonizers, spaces where few written documents exist for autonomous Native American communities that thrived. Euro-American histories of the Great Plains often downplay the incomplete nature of colonialism in these spaces. Later Americans assigned European origins to some Native American sites, assuming that Spanish and/or French colonization was total (i.e., the remnants of fortifications must be a European fort). American settlers did not realize that many Native American nations lived independently and well beyond European settlements well into the nineteenth century, hundreds of years after contact and "colonization." In regions where pericolonial processes were at work, later Euro-American colonizers misattributed Native American sites to European origins, thus perpetuating the colonial process of claiming others' histories and spaces as their own.

Colonizing and Renaming the Plains

Archaeologists often use colonial processes such as the Spanish colonization of New Mexico or the movement of French agents through the Southern Plains as a temporal boundary to separate Native American history and experiences into "prehistoric" and "historic" periods (see Panich and Schneider, this volume). Yet few Native peoples on the Great Plains had sustained contact with European colonizers. This means that very little of their early experiences and communities are described in historic documents. The Native American communities described below existed in regions that were part of yet were often viewed as apart from early settler colonialism. Because of that, later American settlers to these regions had little understanding of the long-term Indigenous connections to these places and viewed their history of occupation as related to only Spanish and French colonial expansion. Euro-Americans attempted to remake the Central and Southern Plains in their own image using toponyms and cartography as tools for privileging Eurocentric histories.

El Cuartelejo: Contested Histories in the Central Plains

Although Spain controlled only a small portion of the Great Plains, the Spanish presence in the American Southwest had far-reaching implications for Native peoples living in the Central and Southern Plains. Spanish colonization introduced new diseases, conflict, and religion to northern Rio Grande Puebloan communities, disrupting their subsistence, economic, and religious practices (Kulisheck 2010; Spielmann et al. 2006). Many Puebloan groups enacted mobility practices to avoid Spanish rule and to maintain their autonomy and cultural practices (Kulisheck 2003, 2010). The Puebloan diaspora led refuge communities to develop in parts of present-day Arizona, Texas, and Kansas (Anderson 1999; Barr 2005; Beck and Trabert 2014; Herr and Clark 1997; Liebmann and Preucel 2007). Some refugees from northern Rio Grande pueblos relied on their relationships with ancestral Dene groups (known to archaeologists as the Dismal River complex) living in western Kansas for shelter after 1600 (Beck and Trabert 2014; Hill et al. 2018). They traveled several hundred kilometers to the Ladder Creek valley in Scott County, Kansas, where they built a seven-room masonry pueblo (known as El Cuartelejo or the Scott County Pueblo, 14SC1). They lived in the area for several generations alongside Dene residents (Beck and Trabert 2014; Hill et al. 2018; Trabert 2017, 2019) (Figure 5.1).

El Cuartelejo (14SC1) is a key example of an Indigenous site that early American settlers and researchers originally assigned a European origin. In 1899, Americans living in Scott County notified paleontologists about ruins of a structure in the area. S. W. Williston, who visited the site, noted the presence of a large, low mound that locals thought was a sod house or perhaps a Jesuit mission (Williston 1899). Despite the fact that the local residents had recovered large quantities of burned corn, southwestern-style pottery, and stone tools from the site, Williston initially theorized that white men built the structure, possibly when Coronado was in the area, because he believed that Puebloan peoples would not have ventured so far north (Williston 1899, 113). After Williston received several letters contesting his suggestion that El Cuartelejo was the work of members of Coronado's expedition, he returned to the site and excavated it, uncovering the remains of a seven-room structure and a great deal of Puebloan and Dene material culture. Williston and his research partner H. T. Martin concluded that the El Cuartelejo site was undoubtedly built by Puebloan peoples, although they argued that "it is very probable that both the Spaniards and French may have occupied this and other structures at this locality at later times, or even contemporaneously with the Pueblo" (Williston and Martin 1900, 126). They also claimed that "the finding of an iron ax of rude and primitive workmanship . . . indicates white men's skill" (Williston and Martin 1900, 126). After conducting further excavations at the site in the 1970s, Thomas Witty wrote that although the site had been built by Puebloan people, it was important to the Spanish because it served as a key northern outpost during their conflicts with the French over lands located farther north (Witty 1971). In 1720, the Pawnee and their French allies attacked a Spanish party led by Villasur somewhere in Nebraska, and Spanish officials later suggested El Cuartelejo as the location of a military outpost, although it was never built (Witty 1971, 2).

Despite Williston and Martin's statements that Puebloan peoples built El Cuartelejo, the Kansas Society Daughters of the American Revolution erected a monument at the site in 1925 that reads: "This marks the site of the Picurie Indian Pueblo 1604 which became an outpost of Spanish civilization and a rendezvous for French traders prior to 1720." Local residents continued to stress the European connections to the site instead of its Native American history. The Kansas Historical Society erected a second marker on the site in 1971 that gave a narrative centered on historical European documents and Spanish connections rather than the archaeological work at the site that confirmed its Indigenous origin. The state of Kansas erected a third marker in 2012 that does not state or imply that the site was a fort or had been used by Europeans. It says only that it was the site of a Native American community that the Spanish visited. In the nearby town of Scott City, the El Quartelejo Museum assigns a Native American origin to the pueblo but also stresses the importance of Spanish connections to site.

The Deer Creek Site: Wichita Village or French Trading Post?

In contrast to Spanish officials, French officials chose to build alliances with Native American nations rather than assert military and religious control (DuVal 2006; Hämäläinen 1998). France wanted to connect its Louisiana colony with the economic exchange centers in Santa Fe and needed economic partners on the Southern Plains and safe passage through Native territories (Morris 1970; Trabert and Bethke forthcoming). In exchange for furs, hides, and often horses, French traders gave their hosts firearms, ammunition, cloth, glass beads, copper and brass kettles, iron axes and hoes, and metal knives (Schilz and Worcester 1987). Ancestral Wichita communities were especially important for the French. The Wichita were organized into a loose confederation of bands whose combined territories covered more than 120,000 square kilometers that included dozens of large villages (Perkins and Baugh 2008; Smith 2008; Trabert and Bethke forthcoming). The Wichita controlled local resources and exchange networks and had social relations with neighboring Native groups. As a result, their villages were prime centers for Native American and French trade (Trabert and Bethke forthcoming).

French traders traveled to several settlements in southern Kansas and Oklahoma, including villages known to archaeologists as Deer Creek (Trabert 2019), Fort Neodesha (Weston and Lees 1994), and Spanish Fort (Friend

1940; Perttula 2012) (see Figure 5.1). While archaeological investigations at each of these villages have uncovered a wide variety of European manufactured goods, researchers have also demonstrated the continuation of traditional Wichita technologies and practices (Drass et al. 2018; Trabert 2018; Vehik 2006). Evidence for fortifications is found at all of these ancestral Wichita sites; they were either protecting themselves from raids or signaling to others that they had valued objects to protect (Vehik 2018).

Today, the Deer Creek site in northeastern Oklahoma is largely recognized as a significant ancestral Wichita fortified village and trade center that dates to the mid-seventeenth and early eighteenth centuries (Trabert 2018). In 1914, local residents notified historian Joseph Thoburn that they had collected Native American and European artifacts from plowed portions of the site (Wedel 1981). Although Thoburn and his colleague Otto Spring were not able to secure permission to excavate the site, they theorized that the site was a lost French trading post called Ferdinandina. They based this theory on an 1868 map of the western United States that circulated in England and Scotland. The map marked a trading post that shared a location with the Deer Creek site as Ferdinandina (McRill 1963; Wedel 1981). Later publications also referred to the site as Ferdinandina without critically evaluating the origin of the name or the potential issues with labeling it a French trading post (e.g., Bell et al. 1974). Deer Creek/Ferdinandina was soon viewed beyond archaeological circles as the "first white settlement in Oklahoma." In 1956, the *Daily Oklahoman* published an article titled "Oklahoma Reclaims Its Past: Relics of Fernandina [sic], First White Settlement in State" that discussed French settlement in Oklahoma and provided an artist's reconstruction of the site that depicted a typical French trading post surrounded by a wooden palisade (Perkins and Baugh 2008).

Later visits to the site and geophysical surveys in the 1970s identified the presence of two circular fortification ditches and a number of mounds (Corbyn 1976). Archaeological work at a second fortified village nearby and analyses of artifacts from the Deer Creek site confirmed that ancestral Wichita groups built and occupied these villages and that they were not French trading posts (Hartley and Miller 1977; Sudbury 1976). Ethnohistorian Mildred Wedel (1981), who disagreed with labeling a Native American site as a "white settlement," tracked down a copy of the map that Thoburn and Spring likely used and several other pre-1868 maps to determine if other cartographers had recorded a French trading post in the vicinity of the Deer Creek site. Wedel could not find other maps to support this designation and found at least one other map that placed Ferdinandina on an entirely different river. She also found that this name/label was not in any historic French-language documents regarding French trade in the Southern Plains. She concluded that the name Ferdinandina was likely an error that mapmakers replicated as they copied from each other without verifying the accuracy of place-names and locations (Wedel 1981).

Despite almost a century of archaeological work at Deer Creek and other Wichita sites in the area, the notion that Wichita fortified sites were European trading posts persists in public memory. In 2008, an Oklahoma newspaper ran an article that stated that while archaeological work hadn't uncovered Ferdinandina yet, it could very well still be out there in the area.[1] When I led the first formal excavations of Deer Creek in 2016 and 2017, I was surprised that the proportion of local residents who believed the site was a Wichita village and those who believed it was the first white settlement in the state was equal. Our excavations yielded evidence of a significant ancestral Wichita occupation of the site, including midden mounds, storage/trash pits, an exterior fortification ditch, and an interior shelter ditch that likely was covered to protect noncombatants (Trabert 2018). While French trade goods were present, there was no other evidence to suggest this was a French trading post.

Wichita Sites as European Forts: Neodesha Fort and Spanish Fort

The Deer Creek village was one of several important trading centers for economic exchange between Wichita groups and Europeans. Neodesha Fort in southeastern Kansas is likely the location of the earliest Wichita-French contact, as it was here that Wichita peoples met French trader Claude-Charles Dutisné in 1719. Although Dutisné traded axes, knives, firearms, and powder for horses and a mule that year, historical records indicate that neither he nor other French traders recorded other visits to this village (Bell et al. 1974; Wedel 1981). In 1901, a Kansas newspaper reported the site of Neodesha Fort and local American residents wrote to the Kansas Historical Society describing significant features at the site, including a prominent horseshoe-shaped earthwork. The earthwork was later identified as part of a system of fortifications (Weston and Lees 1994).

Despite the fact that local residents found large quantities of Native American pottery, chipped-stone debris, and stone tools on the surface of the site (Wedel 1959; Weston and Lees 1994), there was disagreement in the early twentieth century about whether the site was built by white settlers or by Native Americans. The presence of some European goods (lead bullets, a sword hilt, and other fragmented metal objects) and the evidence of fortification works encouraged some to believe that white settlers built the earthworks next to a Native American village (Wedel 1959, 526). Local residents named the site "Neodesha Fort," using European military terminology to classify the earthworks as fortifications. This name contributed to a European-centered history of the region. Weston and Lees (1994) provide archaeological evidence to that refuted this identification. Their testing of the site yielded evidence of Wichita, rather than European, fortifications and occupation.

Neodesha Fort is not the only fortified Wichita site that was labeled as a European creation. Americans also assigned Spanish Fort, located to the south on the Red River, a European origin, albeit with a more complicated history. In the mid-eighteenth century, one ancestral Wichita village (known today as the Longest site) was located on the north side of the Red River. On October 7, 1749, Spanish forces attacked it in reprisal for the destruction of San Saba Mission to the south by Wichita bands and other Native Americans (Drass et al. 2018; John 1975; Weddle 2007). The attack was a failure because Wichita forces outnumbered the Spanish and their villages were fortified. A Spanish officer described the village as having a stockade and a moat with an enclosed entrance (Weddle 2007, 124). In 1772, the Taovayas band of the Wichitas built a second village (known today as Spanish Fort) on the south side of the Red River (Perttula 2012, 64; Smith 2008, 409). Athanase de Mezieres visited both villages in 1778 and named the village on the north side of the river San Bernardo (Longest) and the village to the south San Teodoro (Spanish Fort) after prominent Spanish officials (Drass et al. 2018; Witte 1938). It is possible that the fortifications at San Teodoro were rebuilt several times over the life history of the village (Perttula 2012). Even though the villages were most likely abandoned by the 1840s, remnants of the houses and fortification works were still visible as late as 1939 (Donnell 1940; Friend 1940).

In the late nineteenth century, Americans concluded that the Spanish built the substantial fortifications at San Teodoro rather than the Wichita or other Native American groups (Perttula 2012). The first American settlers to the area named the ruins Spanish Fort (likely unaware of the San Teodoro name from the eighteenth century) because they believed that a large battle had taken place there and knew the area was formerly Spanish territory (Donnell 1940; Wilson 1958). After additional exploration of the ruins, local American residents suggested several possible explanations for its origins. One theory was that the site was the remnants of an outpost from Coronado's 1541 expedition, the location where he divided his forces, one part of which returned to New Mexico and the second part continued north. A second theory argued it was somehow related to the de Soto expedition. A third theory was that it was a French trading post (Donnell 1940, 101). A fourth theory suggested Spanish Fort might be the location of the first decisive battle against Spanish encroachment in Texas; those who believed this called it the "North Texas Alamo" (Donnell 1940; Friend 1940).

American settlement of the immediate area began after 1850 and the town of Burlington was platted in 1854 near the fortification ruins. The residents changed the name of their town to Spanish Fort in 1878 to recognize the battle between the Spanish and the French that supposedly took place there over the territory (Wilson 1958). By the early 1900s, local residents and researchers who had explored the site in more detail and studied historical documents concluded that the name of the site and their town was the result of a misunderstanding and that the Taovayas band had built the fortifications and occupied the area (Donnell 1940; Friend 1940; Wilson 1958). In 1937, the town of Spanish Fort erected a monument commemorating the defeat of Spanish forces in 1759 by Native American forces: "The town of Spanish Fort occupies the site of an Ancient Taovayas Indian Village. Scene of first severe defeat in Texas of Spanish Troops by Indians in 1859. Named Fort Teodoro in 1778 by De Mezieres in honor of Teodoro De Croix, Commander of the Interior Provinces of Mexico. Permanent white settlements began in this vicinity after 1850" (King and Harris 1961, 2).

The Long-Term Consequences for Descendant Communities

This sample of Native American settlements presents a pattern whereby remnants of Native fortifications and structures were attributed to European construction. These are not isolated examples—the dismantling of Indigenous landscapes and creation of alternative histories happened around the world, particularly in places where pericolonialism was the dominant process for decades or centuries before settler colonization. A lasting legacy of colonization is the unmaking of Indigenous geographies. This process still happens today and continues to impact Indigenous communities (Blu Barnd 2017, 79). Our continued use of colonizers' place-names and manufactured histories of space and place sends a political message that Indigenous peoples are separate from these conquered lands (Uluochoa 2015). This directly counters widely shared beliefs among Indigenous and First Nations peoples that their connection to these spaces remains intact and dynamic (Schneider et al., this volume).

The examples provided here from the Great Plains move beyond reassigning names to Indigenous landscapes to reassigning the identity of Native American sites themselves. When Euro-American communities formed on the Plains in the nineteenth and twentieth centuries, they constructed their own histories of the lands they inhabited, creating memories of place that were immortalized in monuments and written histories. These histories persist and are very difficult for outsiders to challenge or change. There are long-term consequences to assigning European origins to Native American sites, even if those assignments happened over a century ago and have since been corrected. While the residents of Scott City, Kansas, originally believed that the El Cuartelejo pueblo was related to Jesuit or Spanish occupations of the region, they now recognize Puebloan origins for the site. Although the community recently invited Puebloan peoples from Taos and Picuris Pueblos to visit and hold ceremonies at El Cuartelejo, the site's significance in public discourse is nevertheless centered on the Spanish interests in the area rather than the more complex Indigenous histories. The identification of Deer Creek site, or "Ferdinandina," as the first white settlement in Oklahoma still persists today despite decades of archaeological work that disproves this manufactured history. Neodesha Fort was also initially determined to be a European creation because fortification works and a handful of European manufactured goods were recovered from the site even though the quantity of ancestral Wichita material culture also recovered at the same time was much larger. Spanish Fort on the Red River was also initially believed to be a European fort. The present-day community of Spanish Fort recognizes that the naming of the fortification ruins was a misunderstanding of local history and that it was a Wichita village. However, they also claim that the documented battle between Wichita and Spanish forces that took place there is part of *their* town's history, referring to it as the North Texas Alamo.

While strong local connections to these Indigenous sites can have positive outcomes—such as a sense of stewardship as local communities work to preserve archaeological sites—there is a greater cost to this. When Euro-American communities claim Indigenous sites as part of their own heritage, they essentially reinforce barriers between Euro-American and Native American communities as each group lays claim to the same spaces. Archaeologists and members of the local public are also likely to clash over conflicting narratives as community memory is challenged. Public memory, both written and monumentalized, has attempted to erase entirely or at least downplay Indigenous connections to these spaces. If the long-term practice of misattributing Indigenous sites as European creations can be corrected and if the histories of places can be rewritten to include Indigenous connections, then descendant communities can work to retake their ancestral landscapes and place-names.

Many Indigenous peoples around the world view place-names as an opportunity to reclaim space as part of larger decolonizing efforts to reconnect their people, culture, and history to traditional lands (Kapä'anaokaläokeola Näkoa Oliveira 2009). As Uluochoa (2015, 186) explains, "place-name decolonization is an attempt to eliminate garbled, derogatory or erroneous names and, by so doing, restore the indigenous cartography of the natives." This counter-mapping or toponymic resistance disrupts colonial images and claims to landscapes, works to restore the heritage of Indigenous peoples, and reminds everyone that settler colonialism and European authority were never comprehensive (Brattland and Nilsen 2011, 275; Cogos et al. 2017, 50; Steinman 2016, 225; Uluochoa 2015, 188). Local histories can be corrected, spaces can be renamed, and places can be reclaimed by descendant groups as links are strengthened between ancestral and contemporary communities.

Moving forward, it is especially important for archaeologists to understand the history of place-names, especially in pericolonial contexts, if we are to have any hope of identifying Native American sites from these periods and establishing and maintaining meaningful collaborations with descendant communities. As Beaudoin (this volume) argues, archaeologists must be cautious in assuming that sites are European in origin by default when European objects are found there. Instead, archaeologists must continue working toward developing methods and models that do not privilege Europeans or Euro-American histories. Archaeologists can change their practices, for example by using Native American terms rather than European labels (i.e., forts, etc.) to describe Native American sites (Panich and Schneider, this volume; Schneider et al., this volume). When possible, archaeologists should research and use Indigenous place-names for landforms, rivers, and villages or sites. This can be particularly challenging with some communities. For example, the Wichita and Affiliated Tribes have names in their own language for only a few historic villages. Nevertheless, if those names are shared with and are known to archaeologists, they should become part of the site's official records. We also still have a commitment to work with local communities, be they Native American and/or Euro-American, whenever possible to openly discuss different narratives instead of attempting to present just one view of historical events. Explaining these different narratives to local communities and showing them how archaeology can link the past with the present may also help change people's perceptions of their local histories. Public memory is not easy to challenge or change, but we may be able to encourage communities to recognize the connections that Native peoples had to these lands and that there is never only one version of history.

Note

1. "Was Fernandina [*sic*] the 1st White Settlement?" *Enid News and Eagle*, August 10, 2008.

References Cited

Acabado, Stephen. 2017. The Archaeology of Pericolonialism: Responses of the "Unconquered" to Spanish Conquest and Colonialism in Ifugao, Philippines. *International Journal of Historical Archaeology* 21: 1–26.

Anderson, Gary Clayton. 1999. *The Indian Southwest 1580–1830*. Norman: University of Oklahoma Press.

Barr, Juliana. 2005. Beyond Their Control: Spaniards in Native Texas. In *Choice, Persuasion, and Coercion: Social Control on Spain's North American Frontiers*, edited by Jesus F. de la Teja and Ross Frank, 149–177. Albuquerque: University of New Mexico Press.

———. 2011. Geographies of Power: Mapping Indian Borders in the "Borderlands" of the Early Southwest. *The William and Mary Quarterly* 68(1):5–46.

———. 2017. There's No Such Thing as "Prehistory": What the Longue Duree of Caddo and Pueblo History Tells Us about Colonial America. *William and Mary Quarterly* 74(2): 203–240.

Basso, Keith H. 1996. *Wisdom Sits in Places: Landscape and Language among the Western Apache*. Albuquerque: University of New Mexico Press.

Beck, Margaret E., and Sarah Trabert. 2014. Puebloan Occupation of the Scott County Pueblo, Western Kansas. *American Antiquity* 79(2): 314–336.

Bell, R. E., E. B. Jelks, and W.W. Newcomb. 1974. *Wichita Indian Archaeology and Ethnology: A Pilot Study*. New York: Garland.

Blu Barnd, Natchee. 2017. *Native Space: Geographic Strategies to Unsettle Settler Colonialism*. First Peoples: New Directions in Indigenous Studies. Corvallis: Oregon State University Press.

Brattland, Camilla, and Steinar Nilsen. 2011. Reclaiming Indigenous Seascapes: Sami Place Names in Norwegian Sea Charts. *Polar Geography* 34(4): 275–297.

Calloway, Colin G. 2013. *New Worlds for All: Indians, Europeans, and the Remaking of Early America*. 2nd ed. Baltimore, MD: John Hopkins University Press.

Cogos, Sarah, Marie Roue, and Samuel Roturier. 2017. Sami Place Names and Maps: Transmitting Knowledge of a Cultural Landscape in Contemporary Contexts. *Arctic, Antarctic, and Alpine Research* 49(1): 43–51.

Corbyn, R. C. 1976. Archaeological Photointerpretation of the Deer Creek Site, Kay County, Oklahoma. Manuscript on file, Department of Anthropology, Pennsylvania State University, University Park.

DeCoster, Jonathan. 2013. Entangled Borderlands: Europeans and Timucuans in Sixteenth-Century Florida. *Florida Historical Quarterly* 91(3): 375–400.

Donnell, Guy Renfro. 1940. The History of Montague County, Texas. Master's thesis, University of Texas Graduate School, Austin.

Drass, Richard R., Stephen M. Perkins, and Susan C. Vehik. 2018. Digging Ditches: Archaeological Investigations of Historically Reported Fortifications at Bryson-Paddock (34KA5) and Other Southern Plains Village Sites. In *Archaeological Perspectives on Warfare on the Great Plains*, edited by Andrew J. Clark and Douglas B. Bamforth, 211–236. Louisville: University Press of Colorado.

Duval, Kathleen. 2006. *The Native Ground*. Philadelphia: University of Pennsylvania Press.

———. 2007. Cross-Cultural Crime and Osage Justice in the Western Mississippi Valley, 1700–1826. *Ethnohistory* 54(4): 697–722.

———. 2016. Living in a Reordered World, 1680–1763. In *The Oxford Handbook of American Indian History*, edited by Frederick E. Hoxie, 56–75. Oxford: Oxford University Press.

Fitznore, Laara. 2006. The Power of Indigenous Knowledge: Naming and Identity and Colonization in Canada. In *Indigenous Peoples' Wisdom and Power: Affirming Our Knowledge through Narratives*, edited by Julian E. Hunnie and Nomalungelo I. Goduka, 51–77. Burlington, VT: Ashgate.

Friend, Llerena. 1940. Old Spanish Fort. *West Texas Historical Association Year Book* 16: 3–27.

Grounds, Richard A. 2001. Tallahassee, Osceola, and the Hermeneutics of American Place-Names. *Journal of the American Academy of Religion* 69(2): 287–322.

Guyot, S., and C. Seethal. 2007. Identity of Place, Places of Identities: Change of Place Names in Post-Apartheid South Africa. *South African Geographical Journal* 89(1): 55–63.

Hämäläinen, Pekka. 1998. The Western Comanche Trade Center: Rethinking the Plains Indian Trade System. *Western Historical Quarterly* 29: 485–313.

———. 2014. The Shapes of Power: Indians, Europeans, and North American Words from the Seventeenth to the Nineteenth Century. In *Contested Spaces of Early America*, edited by

Juliana Barr and Edward Countryman, 32–68. Philadelphia: University of Pennsylvania Press.

Harris, R. King, and Inus Marie Harris. 1961. Spanish Fort, A Historic Trade Site. *Dallas Archeological Society* 16(1): 2–5.

Hartley, J. D., and A. F. Miller. 1977. Archeological Investigations at the Bryson-Paddock Site. Oklahoma River Basin Survey Archeological Site Report 32. Norman, OK.

Herr, Sarah, and Jeffery J. Clark. 1997. Patterns in the Pathways: Early Historic Migrations in the Rio Grande Pueblos. *Kiva* 62(4): 365–389.

Hill, Matthew E., Margaret E. Beck, Stacey Lengyel, Sarah Trabert, and Mary Adair. 2018. A Hard Time to Date: The Scott County Pueblo (14SC1) and Puebloan Residents of the High Plains. *American Antiquity* 83(1): 54–74.

John, Elizabeth A. H. 1975. *Storms Brewed in Other Men's Worlds: The Confrontation of Indians, Spanish, and French in the Southwest, 1540–1795*. College Station: Texas A&M University Press.

Kapä'anaokaläokeola Näkoa Oliveira, Katrina-Ann R. 2009. Wahi a kahiko: Place Names as Vehicles of Ancestral Memory. *AlterNative* 5(2): 101–115.

Kostanski, Laura. 2016. Toponymic Attachment. In *The Oxford Handbook of Names and Naming*, edited by Carole Hough, 412–426. Oxford: Oxford University Press.

Kryder-Reid, Elizabeth. 2016. *California Mission Landscapes: Race, Memory, and the Politics of Heritage*. Minneapolis: University of Minnesota Press.

Kulisheck, Jeremy. 2003. Pueblo Population Movements, Abandonment, and Settlement Change in Sixteenth and Seventeenth Century New Mexico. *Kiva* 69(1): 30–54.

———. 2010. "Like Butterflies on a Mounting Board": Pueblo Mobility and Demography before 1825. In *Across a Great Divide: Continuity and Change in Native North American Societies, 1400–1900*, edited by Laura L. Scheiber and Mark D. Mitchell, 174–191. Tucson: University of Arizona Press.

Liebmann, Matthew, and Robert W. Preucel. 2007. The Archaeology of the Pueblo Revolt and the Formations of the Modern Pueblo World. *Kiva* 73(2): 195–217.

McAnany Patricia A. 2016. *Maya Cultural Heritage: How Archaeologists and Indigenous Communities Engage the Past*. Lanham, MD: Rowman & Littlefield.

McKill, L. A. 1963. Ferdinandina: First White Settlement in Oklahoma. *Chronicles of Oklahoma* 41(1): 126–159.

Mitchell, Mark D., and Laura L. Scheiber. 2010. Crossing Divides: Archaeology as Long-Term History. In *Across a Great Divide: Change and Continuity in Native North America, 1400–1900*, edited by Laura L. Scheiber and Mark D. Mitchell, 1–22. Tucson: University of Arizona Press.

Morris, Wayne. 1970. The Wichita Exchange: Trade on Oklahoma's Fur Frontier, 1719–1812. *Great Plains Journal* 9: 80–81.

Perkins, S. M., and T. G. Baugh. 2008. Protohistory and the Wichita. *Plains Anthropologist* 53(208): 381–394.

Perttula, Timothy K. 2012. Long Unreported Artifact Collections from Spanish Fort Bend Wichita Indian Sites in Oklahoma and Texas. *Plains Anthropologist* 57(221): 63–69.

Radding, Cynthia. 2014. Colonial Spaces in the Fragmented Communities of Northern New Spain. In *Contested Spaces of Early America*, edited by Juliana Barr and Edward Countryman, 116–141. Philadelphia: University of Pennsylvania Press.

Rogers, J. Daniel. 1990. *Objects of Change: The Archaeology and History of Arikara Contact with Europeans.* Washington, DC: Smithsonian Institution Press.

Rose-Redwood, Reuben. 2016. "Reclaim, Rename, Reoccupy": Decolonizing Place and the Reclaiming of PKOLS. *ACME: An International E-Journal for Critical Geographies* 15(1): 187–206.

Schilz, Thomas Frank, and Donald E. Worcester. 1987. The Spread of Firearms among the Indian Tribes on the Northern Frontier of New Spain. *American Indian Quarterly* 11(1): 1–10.

Schwartz, Saul, and William Green. 2013. Middle Ground or Native Ground? Material Culture at Iowaville. *Ethnohistory* 60(4): 537–565.

Shackel, Paul A. 2001. Public Memory and the Search for Power in American Historical Archaeology. *American Anthropologist* 103(3): 655–670.

Smith, F. Todd. 2008. Wichita Locations and Population, 1719–1901. *Plains Anthropologist* 53(208): 407–414.

Spielmann, Katherine A., Jeannette L. Mobley-Tanaka, and James M. Potter. 2006. Style and Resistance in the Seventeenth Century Salinas Province. *American Antiquity* 71(4): 621–647.

Steinman, Erich W. 2016. Decolonization Not Inclusion: Indigenous Resistance to American Settler Colonialism. *Indigenous Sociologies* 2(2): 219–236.

Sudbury, Byron. 1976. Ka-3, The Deer Creek Site: An Eighteenth Century French Contact Site in Kay County, Oklahoma. *Bulletin of the Oklahoma Anthropological Society* 24: 1–136.

Trabert, Sarah. 2017. Considering the Indirect Effects of Colonialism: Example from a Great Plains Middle Ground. *Journal of Anthropological Archaeology* 48: 17–27.

———. 2018. Partners and Power: Understanding Ancestral Wichita and French Trade at the Deer Creek Site. *International Journal of Historical Archaeology* 23: 444–461.

———. 2019. Reframing the Protohistoric Period and the (Peri)Colonial Process for the North American Central Plains. *World Archaeology* 50(5): 820–834.

Trabert, Sarah, and Brandi Bethke. 2021. Reconceptualizing the Wichita Middle Ground in the Southern Plains. In *The Routledge Handbook of the Archaeology of Indigenous-Colonial Interaction in the Americas*, edited by Lee M. Panich and Sara L. Gonzalez, 261–275. Routledge, London.

Uluochoa, Nna O. 2015. Decolonizing Place-Names: Strategic Imperative for Preserving Indigenous Cartography in Post-Colonial Africa. *African Journal of History and Culture* 7(9): 180–192.

Van Dyke, Ruth M. 2019. Archaeology and Social Memory. *Annual Review of Anthropology* 48: 207–225.

Vehik, Susan C. 2006. Wichita Ethnohistory. In *Kansas Archaeology*, edited by R. J. Hoard and W. E. Banks, 206–218. Lawrence: University Press of Kansas.

———. 2018. Why Fortify? Force-to-Force Ratios and Fortification on the Southern Plains. In *Archaeological Perspectives on Warfare on the Great Plains*, edited by Andrew J. Clark and Douglas B. Bamforth, 190–210. Denver: University Press of Colorado.

Watts, Amanda C. 2020. Archaeological Interpretation: The Rhetorical Shaping of Public Memory. In *Developing Effective Communication Skills in Archaeology*, edited by Enrico Proietti, 34–52. Hershey, PA: IGI Global.

Weaver, J., C. S. Womack, and R. Warrior. 2006. *American Indian Literary Nationalism.* Albuquerque: University of New Mexico Press.

Wedel, Waldo R. 1959. *An Introduction to Kansas Archaeology*. Washington, DC: Bureau of American Ethnology.

Wedel, Mildred Mott. 1981. *The Deer Creek Site, Oklahoma: A Wichita Village Sometimes Called Ferdinandina, An Ethnohistorian's View*. Oklahoma Historical Society Series in Anthropology, Oklahoma. Oklahoma City: Oklahoma Historical Society.

Weddle, Robert S. 2007. *After the Massacre: The Violent Legacy of the San Sabá Mission*. Lubbock: Texas Tech University Press.

Wesson, Cameron B. 2012. De Soto (Probably) Never Slept Here: Archaeology, Memory, Myth, and Social Identity. *International Journal of Historical Archaeology* 16: 418–435.

Weston, T., and W. B. Lees. 1994. History and Status of an Earthwork Known as "Neodesha Fort," Kansas. *Plains Anthropologist* 39(150): 415–428.

Williston, S. W. 1899. Some Prehistoric Ruins in Scott County, Kansas. *Kansas University Quarterly* 7(4): 109–114.

Williston, S. W., and H. T. Martin. 1900. Some Pueblo Ruins in Scott County, Kansas. *Transactions of the Kansas State Historical Society, 1897–1900* 6: 124–130.

Wilson, Glenn O. 1958. Montague County: The Texas County of Trails. In *100 Years in Montague County, Texas*, edited by Jeff S. Henderson. Saint Jo, TX: IPTA Printers.

Witte, Adolph Henry. 1938. Spanish Fort, An Historic Wichita Site. *Bulletin of the Texas Archeological and Paleontological Society* 10:115–119.

Witty, Thomas A. 1971. Archeology and Early History of the Scott Lake Park Area. *Kansas Anthropological Association Newsletter* 16(5): 1–5.

Zappia, Natale A. 2012. Indigenous Borderlands: Livestock, Captivity, and Power in the Far West. *Pacific Historical Review* 81(2): 193–220.

6

The Struggle to Identify Nineteenth-Century Indigenous Sites in Cultural Resource Management

MATTHEW A. BEAUDOIN

During cultural resource management (CRM) projects in Ontario, members of Indigenous communities often ask archaeologists "How do you know that this nineteenth-century site is not Indigenous?" Practitioners handle these inquiries with a wide variety of responses that range from being dismissive of the question (e.g., "these are nineteenth-century ceramics, so they are obviously Euro-Canadian") to a more thoughtful consideration of what is actually being asked. While this can be understood as a seemingly innocuous question that asks practitioners to discuss the background research they did to justify their interpretation, it may also be about the larger point of how archaeologists connect the "precontact" Indigenous past with the reality that Indigenous peoples are still here today.

This latter understanding questions the common unspoken precontact/Indigenous versus historic/European divide that remains prevalent in archaeological thinking as a conceptual shortcut (Beaudoin 2016, 2019; Lightfoot 1995; McNiven and Russell 2005; Panich and Schneider 2019). Many researchers have been critiquing this divide and searching for ways to directly connect deeper Indigenous pasts and histories to the era of mass-produced modernity through an archaeological lens (Cipolla 2013, 2017; Cipolla and Hayes 2015; Croucher and Weiss 2011; Liebmann 2008, 2012; Silliman 2009, 2010, 2012, 2014; Silliman and Witt 2010; Thomas 2004; Whitridge 2008). However, much of this research is conducted in an academic context and is usually carried out by studying sites or communities that have been predetermined to have an Indigenous association.

To provide an alternative perspective to this research, this chapter reviews the question from a CRM context, where the association of a site is often not understood from the outset. The fact that commonsense and expedient practices often drive the interpretive process acts to eliminate the possibility of Indigenous associations from the outset. Because of this, we must highlight the assumptions and practices applied to archaeological data and question whether they are appropriate tools to determine if a nineteenth-century site is Indigenous.

Seeing Indigenous Peoples though an Archaeological Lens

The core of the problem is the low visibility of nineteenth-century Indigenous sites. The term "low visibility" does not refer to the common adage that Indigenous peoples "lived light on the land" (but see Laluk, this volume, for the Ndee perspective); instead, it refers to that lack of easily visible markers in the archaeological record that would indicate that the past occupants of a site were Indigenous peoples. Archaeologists have used many objects and signifiers to identify nineteenth-century Indigenous sites, including pierced coins, chipped glass, hunting tools, and the presence of "precontact" artifacts, to name a few common ones. These markers are based on an assumption that they were continuously and exclusively used for a practice associated with Indigenous people from earlier periods of time into the nineteenth century, when mass-produced goods dominated the market economy.

A more insidious problem with the current practice is that only the researchers who are aware of and concerned with the presence of nineteenth-century Indigenous sites are actively searching for ways to see them. Most other archaeologists harbor a default assumption that a nineteenth- or twentieth-century site is associated with peoples of European descent. They often assume that the presence of nineteenth-century mass-produced artifacts indicates the presence of person of European descent unless there is some significant documentation that suggests otherwise (see Hull, this volume). This is most commonly represented in the almost unconscious practice of referring to nineteenth- and twentieth-century sites as "Euro-Canadian" or "Euro-American" by default (Beaudoin 2016, 2019). While it could be argued that this assumption is based on the very strong likelihood that in most places this would be correct and is thus is a valid starting point, it risks homogenizing the past into an assumed European world. Given that Indigenous peoples and various Others did not entirely restrict their populations to known reserves, reservations, or other easily defined ghettoized areas so that future archaeologists could easily identify their sites, this is a dangerous assumption that acts to prevent these Others (however defined) from being regarded as legitimate actors in the dominant narrative and further disenfranchise them from their heritage (see Scheiber, this volume). I do not believe that practicing archaeologists actively make these decision; instead, they are a reflection of the insidious impacts of settler colonialism in which we are all embedded (Snelgrove, et al. 2014).

Legal and social restrictions in the past and present pressured Indigenous peoples to stay within defined regions and tracts of lands. The majority of the populations likely stayed within these boundaries for significant periods of the time when these restrictions were in place. However, this does not mean that everyone abided by the restrictions. Many individuals lived outside them (see Kretzler, this volume; Scheiber, this volume). Detailed study of local histories and primary documents often shows that Indigenous peoples lived in various urban and rural areas outside reserve lands. The number who did so is likely underrepresented because of numerous structural inequalities in how people were recorded (Faux 1984, 2002; Hamilton 2007).

This issue varies across regions and times. When working on known nineteenth-century Indigenous communities or settlements, it is easy to assume that the sites found are likely of Indigenous affiliation or that other lines of past or present community-based knowledge exist that can strengthen that assumption. Also, in areas and times where continuous, distinct local object production that was predominantly for personal use by Indigenous peoples is documented, these objects can be used as highly probably indicators of Indigenous association. However, this connection must also be used with caution to ensure that this practice is not simply inverting the assumption that European mass-produced goods reflect European peoples. Making the opposite assumption would inadvertently perpetuate another facet of the same problem.

Ontario CRM as a Testing Ground for Archaeological Interpretation

I primarily work in the private CRM industry in Ontario, Canada. This is a unique context for research because the regulations in this context mandate a more inductive research structure. The regulations that pertain to the Ontario CRM industry require a significant amount of archaeological study on both public and private lands in advance of development (Ferris 1998, 2002, 2003). Because of that, a larger sample of lands are subject to standardized archaeological assessment than is typical in other Canadian locations. In addition, the archaeological process in this context is more inductive than deductive. Evaluation of the importance of a site primarily follows the method of recovering artifacts in the field throughout the research process, then making a broad interpretation instead of developing a research plan or goal that is then tested against the archaeological findings.

Rigid and prescriptive criteria in the current CRM structure in Ontario determine the level of cultural heritage value or interest (CHVI). These are primarily based on the quantity and date range of artifacts. For example, during a Stage 2 field survey, if you encounter a site through pedestrian or test-pit survey and at least twenty artifacts are identified that pre-date 1900, the site will require additional Stage 3 site-specific testing. The Stage 3 testing usually consists of additional background research and the systematic excavation of one-meter test units across the site area to gather a larger collection of artifacts. At this stage of the process, if it is determined that the majority of the occupation of the site pre-dates 1870, then it is determined to have CHVI and requires full mitigation from construction impacts through excavation or protection. This pre-1870 date is predominantly drawn from the date range derived from the recovered diagnostic artifacts that are supplemented by background research.

There are a couple of broad trends to be aware of concerning the how practicing archaeologists in Ontario apply this process. While the number of archaeologists formally trained in the analysis of nineteenth-century artifacts and background research is growing, the majority of this training is still informal (Ferris 2007; Kenyon 1986). Most of the archaeology training at Ontario universities is focused on Indigenous artifacts and histories and is more focused on anthropology. Archaeologists are usually trained in nineteenth-century methods and strategies on the job by people who were also not likely formally trained. This lack of formal training is further problematized by the paucity of published historical archaeology literature that is specific to Ontario or to Canada (Doroszenko 2009). Most of the CRM practitioners who study the nineteenth century are forced to rely on local or company-specific gray literature or published sources from other countries for processes, standards, and interpretations. These critiques are not meant to imply that people are doing poor work; people are working to the best of their ability or knowledge to gather relevant data and make relevant interpretations about the archaeological record. Instead, my comments highlight the methodological or interpretative gaps that emerge from and are perpetuated by the absence of robust and engaged archaeological and historical knowledge bases.

Since revised regulations were implemented in 2011, the rigid CRM process has exponentially increased the documentation and excavation of nineteenth-century sites. As the prescriptive requirements for site excavation are based primarily on the quantity and date of the artifacts rather than the historical documentation or people associated with the site, this means that many sites that are excavated and analyzed are only loosely tied to a family or a background. In some instances, there is good background research and documentation to associate a site or an assemblage to a specific family or occupation, but in most cases the historical context is much more ambiguous or is complicated by the fact that the commonly available historical records provide only a small window of information for a site or by the fact that a site was repeatedly reoccupied by numerous families over a relatively short period of time. This context provides a unique opportunity to highlight the value of archaeology as the primary lens for understanding the past in the absence of other data sources that can be used to initially structure interpretation. However, the absence of any regional, temporal, or ethnic studies that synthesize this growing data set means that the potential of this research has not been realized to date.

The common practice for nineteenth-century sites in Ontario is to label them as "Euro-Canadian." The archaeological community here commonly uses the term "Euro-Canadian" as a synonym for "historical" or "nineteenth century" and there has been limited critical analysis and deconstruction of that practice. There is no accepted standard for determining who specifically would or would not be defined as Euro-Canadian, but it is generally assumed that sometime between the first and second generations of settlement in Ontario, an ethnogenesis occurred. Akenson (1995, 395) notes that it was not until 1961 that the federal government coalesced the varied British Isles identities into a single analytical category as part of the process of defining a distinct Canadian identity. This suggests that the Euro-Canadian identity is a recent political construct rather than a historically experienced one and one that emerged as a category of analysis due to "the confusion of English-language culture with English national origin" (Akenson 1995, 399). I do not think that the Euro-Canadian moniker is solely of recent origin, but this debate highlights the need for further research into what it might have meant to be Euro-Canadian in the past. A common element of this term, albeit an unstated one, is assumption that it does not include Indigenous peoples or African-Canadian people.

The uncritical default use of Euro-Canadian dovetails with the regulation of Indigenous participation in Ontario archaeology in a way that creates additional problems within the discipline. The current regulations (Ontario Ministry of Tourism and Culture 2010, 2011) requires archaeologists to engage with Indigenous communities if a site has an "Aboriginal" ethnic association. This requirement has resulted in a significant increase in Indigenous participation on CRM projects and has shifted the nature of the relationship between practicing archaeologists and Indigenous communities (Ferris and Dent 2020). Whereas from a regulatory perspective, the ultimate authority and decision-making responsibility rests with the licensed professional archaeologist, the reality on the ground is that the voices, opinions, and perspectives of the Indigenous communities are becoming a more prominent part of the process. This shift is having significant impacts on how commercial archaeology is practiced in Ontario, and the perceived threat to the state-sanctioned authority of the archaeologist is creating highly varied responses from provincial regulators and archaeologists (Ferris and Dent 2020).

Despite the growing participation by Indigenous communities in the CRM process, a site must be identified as "Aboriginal" before engagement occurs. Without this trigger, there is no regulatory requirement for archaeologists to engage with Indigenous communities. This removes opportunities for Indigenous communities to share their knowledge, interests, and histories that might have significant impact on the archaeological process and outcomes. In practice, archaeologists uncritically assume that nineteenth-century sites are Euro-Canadian unless the site is located within previously identified or contemporary Indigenous communities. The common assumption that Indigenous peoples were restricted to present-day reserve lands precludes community interest and participation in spaces or buildings located outside reserves.

For example, during archaeological work on a property associated with the Livingston (Caradoc) Academy, a nineteenth-century boarding school in Middlesex County, Ontario, an Indigenous participant on the project indicated that the headmaster had a strong relationship with the nearby Indigenous community and that his daughter was thought to have married an Indigenous person from the community. Even though the headmaster was a recent immigrant from Scotland and the institution was associated with enculturating and socializing the children of elite government and business leaders in the region, this site was also of Indigenous interest because of the wider associations. Even though there is no evidence that an Indigenous person ever lived on this property, it was in some ways still an Indigenous site because of these connections. In this instance, we were fortunate to have an Indigenous participant in the fieldwork because of the wider nature of the project, but in most other instances an Indigenous person would not have been present and the potential Indigenous association and knowledge of the local community interest would have been unrecognized.

Searching for Signifiers

Because of the nature of our discipline, we are searching for the connections between material signifiers and various forms of identity. This is not inherently problematic, but the unquestioned conceptual baggage and "practical" frameworks that are considered integral to archaeological research can greatly skew our interpretations. In the absence of a robust historical or analytical framework to help identify Indigenous presence in the past, CRM archaeologists have been searching for key objects or practices that can be used to support an artifact-based way to identify Indigenous peoples in the archaeological record. While people have postulated many different signifiers as likely indicators of Indigenous peoples, two of the more common ones require unpacking: pierced coins and chipped glass.

Pierced Coins

Pierced coins are commonly used as a marker of Indigenous occupation. Archaeologists, members of the public, and members of descendant communities frequently experience an "aha" moment when they see them. The assumption is that among many Indigenous populations coins had a greater significance as decoration for clothing or as ceremonial objects than as legal currency. For example, Briggs (2012, 48–50) associated the presence of bent and pierced silver coins at the nineteenth-century Haney Site with the Upper Creek occupation. Similarly, Beaudoin et al. (2010) associated two pierced coins with a nineteenth-century NunatuKavut (formerly known as Labrador Métis) site along North River in Labrador.

The practice of piercing coins is not exclusive to Indigenous populations. In many contexts, researchers have suggested that pierced coins may have had a connection to the Underground Railroad (Clemens 2018) or to a continuation of African traditions (Baker and Baker 1996; Lee 2011; Leone and Fry 1999). Davidson (2004) documents the long history of coin perforation as a form of charm or folk magic in the nineteenth-century settler society. Timmins Martelle Heritage Consultants (2014, 2017, 2019) have identified pierced coins at three nineteenth-century sites associated with European populations: AkGw-77, a circa 1859–1880 site in Toronto associated with the Moore family; AhGs-381, a nineteenth- and twentieth-century site in Niagara-on-the-Lake; and AgHf-50, a circa 1853–1863 site in Oxford County associated with the Chrystal family. None of these contexts are associated with people of non-European descent, and the prevalence of these pierced coins in this limited CRM sample suggests that the practice is more common in general settler contexts than is often considered.

Researchers who conduct in-depth research about the significance of pierced coins often acknowledge that pierced coins are not indicative of a particular time period or ethnicity (e.g., Briggs 2012, 50). However, these assertions are often forgotten or ignored in more isolated or superficial studies. While pierced coins might have a vastly differing meaning in an Indigenous, African American, or settler site, their relatively broad tradition makes them of somewhat limited value in identifying the association of a site on their own.

Knapped Glass

Knapped or reworked glass is another commonly discussed marker of Indigenous presence (Russell, this volume). In most publications and conversations, people assume that the use or reworking of broken glass is a continuation of the knapping tradition among Indigenous peoples that has extended into the nineteenth and twentieth centuries. Many people assume that if a piece of glass has edge damage that macroscopically resembles use wear or retouching, it was used by an Indigenous person in the past.

Recently, archaeologists have been paying greater attention to the presence of worked glass at nineteenth-century Indigenous sites across North America (Martindale and Jurakic 2006; Neill 1955; Pilon 1990; Silliman 2009; Warrick 2009) and at Aboriginal sites in Australia (Cooper and Bowdler 1998; Harrison 2003; Tindale 1941). These studies complement contemporary interpretations of residence and survivance (Beaudoin 2017, 2019; Silliman 2014). However, it is important to note that in most of these studies researchers are identifying expedient tools made of retouched glass sherds rather than more formal tools such as scrapers or projectile points. The knapping tradition likely continued in Indigenous communities into more recent periods of time, and these arguments are stronger for sites where formal tools are identified, but the use of reworked glass is not exclusive to one group of people.

Reworked glass tools have also been identified as expedient tools on African American sites in North America and the Caribbean (Ahlman, et al. 2014; Armstrong 1998; Boling 2005; Farnsworth 1999; Klingelhofer 1987; Patten 1992; Wilkie 1996). The majority of researchers who work on such sites relate the use of expedient glass tools to a continuity of tradition and practice. Further complicating the association between knapped glass and Indigenous peoples is a growing number of studies that demonstrate that there was a folk tradition of working glass among settler populations in North America. Nicole Brandon (in press) describes this in her study of a series of case studies from Ontario, and several other studies from the 1980s look at European traditions of worked-glass tools in North America (Clark 1981; Poplin 1986). Based on the data she analyzed and on background research, Brandon connects the use of chipped glass and ceramic expedient tools in nineteenth- and twentieth-century Ontario to a pragmatic folk tradition of taking advantage of the sharp edges created by these breakages. Brandon also explored some recorded traditions that document a preference for chipped-glass tools for woodworking and shaving for some projects. However, at this time, she has been unable to connect this practice to any specific archaeological site or signature.

The presence of chipped glass can provide a dynamic and compelling interpretive lens depending on the context where it is found. Among Indigenous communities, it can be a symbol of survivance and continuity of practice despite colonial impingements. Among African American communities, it can be understood as evidence of the creation of expedient tools in a context where access to formal tools was limited. Among European communities, it represents the pragmatic use of broken objects and/or a preferred material for woodworking tools. Chipped glass can support any or all of these narratives, and many others. However, the starting point of the discussion must be identifying the occupants of the site where it is found.

What Are We Actually Trying to Say?

In the end, a researcher's individual experiences and perceptions of the present and the past contribute to which objects or patterns they deem significant for identifying nineteenth-century Indigenous presence in the archaeological record. The imaginary that each of us superimposes onto present data to create meaningful narratives of the past is informed by our own understandings, readings, and experiences. Unfortunately, this often results in the development of gross generalizations, stereotypes, or homogenized narratives to make sense of inherently complicated and partially understood realities. This is further compounded during the study of the nineteenth and twentieth centuries, periods when the use of mass-produced goods was ubiquitous across the majority of sites. The conceptual shortcut many people make that European objects = European people is inadequate.

In the current state of the discipline, archaeology is very good at drawing out the complex meanings and understandings of the past from objects when we have a known association to use when creating an interpretation of a site. For example, many interesting and detailed interpretations have been made from the analysis of pierced coins or chipped glass on Indigenous sites that tie these artifacts to the continuation of Indigenous traditions or sensibilities in relation to an emergent settler colonialism. Many other valuable research and interpretations have been made from numerous data sets. However, this research almost always starts from a position where historical data or ethnographic information has already determined Indigenous presence at a site. In these studies, the initial step of determining that a site is Indigenous and thus providing an interpretive roadmap for these studies, did not rely on the archaeological record. In this sense, nineteenth-century archaeology remains the "handmaiden to history" (Hume 1964). However, even though "history" now includes ethnographic or community data, it might still be ill suited as a tool for making initial determinations. For example, if a series of nineteenth-century assemblages were provided to researchers without historical documentation, there would be some level of consistency in the identification and dating of those artifacts. However, I am less confident about the interpretations that would be drawn from those artifacts. Similar exercises conducted with lithic assemblages show a high level of variability in the interpretive process (Keron 2003), but I am not aware of similar exercises to assess interpretations for nineteenth-century sites.

Some might argue that the presence of historical and ethnographic records is what allows for the development of a robust and deep interpretation of the archaeological record and that such records are required for historical archaeology. I would not disagree that these additional data sets allow the interpretive process to go quickly in a variety of directions, but relying on these data sets can limit the value of the archaeological record when they are not available or present ambiguous information. Most historical archaeologists have experience with using these data sets to draw out nuanced and hidden patterns and histories (as described by Hull, this volume). However, within a CRM industry that is primarily focused on the presence or absence of artifacts and that is practiced by individuals who do not have a strongly developed education in historical archaeology, these nuances are often lost. In many cases, the capitalistic, expedient, and regimented regulations of the industry do not permit archaeologists to search for these additional data sources or actively prevents them from doing so. The often superficial nature of the background research forces archaeologists into an archaeological-centric process that is driven by the artifacts that have been found.

My suggestion that the archaeology of the nineteenth century is reliant on other data sets to frame site interpretation is not intended to diminish the importance of archaeology's role in knowing the past. Recently, researchers have been critically using other data sets, such as maps (Panich et al. 2018), ethnography (Russell 2016), and collaborative community-based research (Cipolla et al. 2019) to create new and more robust ways of knowing the past through archaeology. Archaeology has a unique role to play in these studies. It can make more abstract histories accessible and can provide novel and imaginative narratives that flesh out core understandings. However, the findings of archaeologists often seem to respond to existing narratives instead of forming the structural core of a new narrative. This is an important role that should not be lost. However, we need to acknowledge the current limitations of the discipline in an effort to identify what an starting point that centers archaeology might be missing.

Despite this critique of the current state of affairs, I believe that there is still the potential to make core identifications of Indigenous sites using archaeological methods and interpretations. To do so, we must think through simple and expedient practices that rely on temporal, regional, or cultural assumptions with a critical eye. These assumptions restrict our understanding of Indigenous existence in the nineteenth and twentieth centuries to known reserve lands or traditions removed from modernity (Cipolla 2013). Indigenous peoples had varied levels of access to the market economy and many had access to mass-produced objects. We cannot continue to search for stone tools as indications of Indigenous presence. Studies have shown patterns in how Indigenous people used mass-produced objects in both creative and conventional ways. These findings can be used to help us identify Indigenous presence. For example, Mrozowski et al. (2015) demonstrated that the presence of a larger-than-usual quantity of utensils at Indigenous sites in New England was indicative of communal feasting. Beaudoin (2019) suggested that a greater quantity of bowls were present on Indigenous sites. There are undoubtedly other material patterns that can be used to identify Indigenous presence. However, all of the patterns are difficult to identify in the early stages of the CRM process, when the determination of Indigenous presence can have a significant impact on whether a site will be excavated, protected, or destroyed.

We must ask ourselves a core question: "What makes a site Indigenous?" Is it Indigenous peoples using the site, the presence of Indigenous-made artifacts, the fact than an area is significant to contemporary Indigenous peoples, or a combination of these factors? A corollary of this line of questioning that must also be asked is, "What makes a site a settler site?" Unless both essentialized categories are deconstructed and defined, we will be forever forced to define Indigenous sites against an amorphous and ever dominant settler site type (Beaudoin 2019).

Until better regional and temporal patterns are developed to identify Indigenous sites through archaeological materials, I advocate that we assume that all sites have the potential to be Indigenous, settler, or any other determined category until it can be proven otherwise. Within this assumption, we should not be assigning seemingly "practical" categories (such as Euro-Canadian or Euro-American) from the outset. Instead, we should frame them using a temporal period (e.g., nineteenth century, ca. 1850–1870, etc.) until better data can be determined. Regulators and members of the archaeological community have strongly resisted this suggestion when it has been made in the past. The common response is that "we need to say something" about the cultural affiliation of a site, even if what we say is based on assumptions. In response to this, I question what is added to the understanding of a site by ascribing it a potentially erroneous cultural affiliation that might not reflect the reality of the lived existence of the time, especially when such assumptions eliminate the participation of various Others. While the choice not to assign a cultural affiliation to a site without additional information might seem like a somewhat pedantic change, it can have significant consequences. For example, in the Ontario CRM context, the seemingly arbitrary association of nineteenth-century sites with a "Euro-Canadian" identity precludes the site from having other affiliation and eliminates the regulatory triggers that might require descendant populations to participate in the archaeological process (Beaudoin 2016). I acknowledge that most nineteenth- and twentieth-century sites in Ontario are likely associated with someone of European descent. However, additional research should be conducted to demonstrate a Euro-Canadian association before it is arbitrarily made, since the decision to make that identification has significant consequences.

References Cited

Ahlman, Todd M., Bobby R. Braly, and Gerald F. Schroedl. 2014. Stone Artifacts and Glass Tools from Enslaved African Contexts on St. Kitts' Southeast Peninsula. *Journal of African Diaspora Archaeology and Heritage* 3(1): 1–25.

Akenson, Donald Harman. 1995. The Historiography of English Speaking Canada and the Concept of Diaspora: A Sceptical Appreciation. *The Canadian Historical Review* 76(3): 377–409.

Armstrong, Douglas. 1998. Cultural Transformation within Enslaved Laborer Communities in the Caribbean. In *Studies in Culture Contact: Interaction, Culture Change, and Archaeology*, edited by James G. Cusick, 378–401. Carbondale: Southern Illinois University.

Baker, T. Lindsay, and Julie Philips Baker. 1996. *The WPA Oklahoma Slave Narratives*. Norman: University of Oklahoma Press.

Beaudoin, Matthew A. 2016. Archaeologists Colonizing Canada: The Effects of Unquestioned Categories. *Archaeologies: Journal of the World Archaeological Congress* 12(1): 7–37.

———. 2017. A Tale of Two Settlements: Consumption and the Historical Archaeology of Natives and Newcomers in the Nineteenth-Century Great Lakes Region. In *Foreign Objects: Rethinking Indigenous Consumption in American Archaeology*, edited by Craig N. Cipolla, 44–58. Tucson: University of Arizona Press.

———. 2019. *Challenging Colonial Narratives: Nineteenth-Century Great Lakes Archaeology.* Tucson: University of Arizona Press.

Beaudoin, Matthew A., Richard L. Josephs, and Lisa K. Rankin. 2010. Attributing Cultural Affiliation to Sod Structures in Labrador: A Labrador Métis Example from North River. *Canadian Journal of Archaeology* 34(2): 148–173.

Boling, Melissa Diana. 2005. A Contextual Study of Expedient Glass Tool Use by Europeans and African Americans at Late 18th-Early 20th Century Historic Sites in the Southeastern US and Caribbean. Master's thesis, University of South Carolina, Columbia.

Brandon, Nicole E. In press. Sharpening the Perception of Euro-Canadian Use of Glass Shard Tools in Ontario. *Ontario Archaeology.*

Briggs, Rachel V. 2012. Landscape Analysis of a Late Eighteenth- to Early Nineteenth-Century Upper Creek Camp. *Journal of Alabama Archaeology* 58(1 and 2): 39–61.

Cipolla, Craig N. 2013. Native American Historical Archaeology and the Trope of Authenticity. *Historical Archaeology* 47(3): 12–22.

———. 2017. Postscript: Postcolonial Archaeology in the Age of Things. In *Foreign Objects: Rethinking Indigenous Consumption in American Archaeology*, edited by Craig N. Cipolla, 222–229. Tucson: University of Arizona Press.

Cipolla, Craig N., and Katherine Howlett Hayes, eds. 2015. *Rethinking Colonialism: Comparative Archaeological Approaches.* Gainesville: University Press of Florida.

Cipolla, Craig N., James Quinn, and Jay Levy. 2019. Theory in Collaborative Indigenous Archaeology: Insights from Mohegan. *American Antiquity* 84(1): 127–142.

Clark, Jeffrey T. 1981. Glass Scrapers from Historic North America. *Lithic Technology* 10(2–3): 31–34.

Clemens, Aaron. 2018. A Tavern on the Puce River. Paper presented at the 45th Annual Ontario Archaeological Symposium, Chatham-Kent.

Cooper, Zarine, and Sandra Bowdler. 1998. Flaked Glass Tools from the Andaman Islands and Australia. *Asian Perspectives* 37(1): 74–83.

Croucher, Sarah K., and Lindsay Weiss. 2011. The Archaeology of Capitalism in Colonial Contexts, an Introduction: Provincializing Historical Archaeology. In *The Archaeology of Capitalism in Colonial Contexts: Postcolonial Historical Archaeologies*, edited by S. K. Croucher and L. Weiss, 1–37. New York: Springer.

Davidson, James M. 2004. Rituals Captured in Context and Time: Charm Use in North Dallas Freedman's Town (1869–1907), Dallas, Texas. *Historical Archaeology* 38(2): 22–54.

Doroszenko, Dena. 2009. Exploration, Exploitation, Expansion, and Settlement: Historical Archaeology in Canada. In *International Handbook of Historical Archaeology*, edited by T. Majewski and D. Gaimster, 507–524. New York: Springer.

Farnsworth, Paul. 1999. From the Past to the Present: An Exploration of the Formation of African-Bahamian Identity during Enslavement. In *African Sites Archaeology in the Caribbean*, edited by J. B. Haviser, 94–130. Princeton, NJ: Marcus Weiner; and Kingston, Jamaica: Ian Randle.

Faux, David. 1984. The Mohawk Village: An Interpretive Approach to Historical, Archaeological, and Genealogical Investigations. Paper presented at the Iroquoian Historical Conference, Woodland Indian Cultural Educational Centre, Brantford, Ontario.

———. 2002. *Understanding Ontario First Nations Genealogical Records: Sources and Case Studies*. Ontario Genealogical Society, Toronto.

Ferris, Neal. 1998. 'I don't think we're in Kansas anymore . . . ': The Rise of the Archaeological Consulting Industry in Ontario. In *Bringing Back the Past: Historical Perspectives on Canadian Archaeology*, edited by Pamela Jane Smith, 225–247. Ottawa: University of Ottawa Press.

———. 2002. When the Air Thins: The Rapid Rise of the Archaeological Consulting Industry in Ontario. *Revista de Arqueología Americana* 21: 53–88.

———. 2003. Between Colonial and Indigenous Archaeologies: Legal and Extra-Legal Ownership of the Archaeological Past in North America. *Canadian Journal of Archaeology* 27(2): 154–190.

———. 2007. "From Crap to Archaeology": The CRM Shaping of Nineteenth Century Domestic Site Archaeology. *Ontario Archaeology* 83–84: 3–28.

Ferris, Neal, and Joshua Dent. 2020. Wringing Hands and Anxious Authority: Archaeological Heritage Management beyond an Archaeologist's Ontology. *Archaeologies* 16:1–28.

Hamilton, Michelle. 2007. "Anyone not on the list might as well be dead": Aboriginal Peoples and the Censuses of Canada, 1851–1916. *Journal of the Canadian Historical Association/ Revue de la Société historique du Canada* 18(1): 57–79.

Harrison, Rodney. 2003. 'The Magical Virtue of These Sharp Things': Colonialism, Mimesis and Knapped Bottle Glass Artefacts in Australia. *Journal of Material Culture* 8(3): 311–336.

Hume, I. Noel. 1964. Archaeology: Handmaiden to History. *North Carolina Historical Review* 41(2): 214–225.

Kenyon, Ian. 1986. "That Historic Crap!" Historic Archaeological Resource Management. In *Archaeological Consulting in Ontario: Papers of the London Conference 1985*, edited by W. Fox, 41–50. London, Ontario: London Chapter of the Ontario Archaeological Society.

Keron, Jim. 2003. Comparability of Published Debitage Analysis: An Experimental Assessment. *KEWA: Newsletter of the London Chapter, Ontario Archaeological Society* 3(1): 1–13.

Klingelhofer, Eric. 1987. Aspects of Early Afro-American Material Culture: Artifacts from the Slave Quarters at Garrison Plantation, Maryland. *Historical Archaeology* 21(2): 112–119.

Lee, Lori. 2011. Beads, Coins, and Charms at a Poplar Forest Slave Cabin (1833–1858). *Northeast Historical Archaeology* 40(1): 104–122.

Leone, Mark P., and Gladys-Marie Fry. 1999. Conjuring in the Big House Kitchen: An Interpretation of African American Belief Systems Based on the Uses of Archaeology and Folklore Sources. *Journal of American Folklore* 112(445): 372–403.

Liebmann, Matthew. 2008. Postcolonial Cultural Affiliation: Essentialism, Hybridity, and NAGPRA. In *Archaeology and the Postcolonial Critique*, edited by Matthew Liebmann and Uzma Z. Rizvi, 73–90. New York: Altamira Press.

———. 2012. The Rest Is History: Devaluing the Recent Past in the Archaeology of the Pueblo Southwest. In *Decolonizing Indigenous Histories: Exploring Prehistoric/Colonial Transitions in Archaeology*, edited by Maxine Oland, Siobahn M. Hart, and Liam Frink, 19–44. Tucson: University of Arizona Press.

Lightfoot, Kent G. 1995. Culture Contact Studies: Redefining the Relationship between Prehistoric and Historical Archaeology. *American Antiquity* 60(2): 199–217.

Martindale, Andrew, and Irena Jurakic. 2006. Identifying Expedient Glass Tools in a Post-Contact Tsimshian Village. *Journal of Archaeological Science* 33: 414–427.

McNiven, Ian J., and Lynette Russell. 2005. *Appropriated Pasts: Indigenous Peoples and the Colonial Culture of Archaeology.* Lanham, MD: Altamira Press.

Mrozowski, Stephan A., D. Rae Gould, and Heather Law Pezzarossi. 2015. Rethinking Colonialism: Indigenous Innovation and Colonial Inevitability. In *Rethinking Colonialism: Comparative Archaeological Approaches,* edited by Craig N. Cipolla and Katherine Howlett Hayes, 121–142. Gainesville: University Press of Florida.

Neill, Wilfred T. 1955. The Site of Osceola's Village in Marion County, Florida. *Florida Historical Quarterly* 33(3/4): 240–246.

Ontario Ministry of Tourism and Culture. 2010. *Engaging Aboriginal Communities in Archaeology: A Draft Technical Bulletin for Consultant Archaeologists in Ontario.* Toronto: Queen's Printer for Ontario.

———. 2011. *Standards and Guidelines for Consultant Archaeologists.* Toronto: Queen's Printer for Ontario.

Panich, Lee M., and Tsim D. Schneider. 2019. Categorical Denial: Evaluating Post-1492 Indigenous Erasure in the Paper Trail of American Archaeology. *American Antiquity* 84(4): 651–668.

Panich, Lee M., Tsim D. Schneider, and R. Scott Byram. 2018. Finding Mid-Nineteenth Century Native Settlements: Cartographic and Archaeological Evidence from Central California. *Journal of Field Archaeology* 43(2): 152–165.

Patten, Drake. 1992. Mankala and Minkisi: Possible Evidence of African American Folk Beliefs and Practices. *African-American Archaeology* 6: 5–7.

Pilon, Jean-Luc. 1990. Historic Native Archaeology along the Lower Severn River, Ontario. *Canadian Journal of Archaeology/Journal Canadien d'Archéologie* 14: 123–141.

Poplin, Eric C. 1986. Expedient Technology in European North America: Implications from an Alternate Use of Glass by Historic Period Populations. PhD thesis, University of Calgary, Alberta.

Russell, Lynette. 2016. Fifty Years On: History's Handmaiden? A Plea for Capital H History. *Historical Archaeology* 50(3): 50–61.

Silliman, Stephen W. 2009. Change and Continuity, Practice and Memory: Native American Persistence in Colonial New England. *American Antiquity* 74(2): 211–230.

———. 2010. Indigenous Traces in Colonial Spaces: Archaeologies of Ambiguity, Origin, and Practice. *Journal of Social Archaeology* 10(1): 28–58.

———. 2012. Between the Longue Durée and the Short Purée: Postcolonial Archaeologies of Indigenous History in Colonial North America. In *Decolonizing Indigenous Histories: Exploring Prehistoric/Colonial Transitions in Archaeology,* edited by Maxine Oland, Siobahn M. Hart, and Liam Frink, 113–131. Tucson: University of Arizona Press.

———. 2014. Archaeologies of Indigenous Survivance and Residence: Navigating Colonial and Scholarly Dualities. In *Rethinking Colonial Pasts through Archaeology,* edited by Neal Ferris, Rodney Harrison, and Michael V. Wilcox, 57–75. Oxford: Oxford University Press.

Silliman, Stephen W., and Thomas A. Witt. 2010. The Complexities of Consumption: Eastern Pequot Cultural Economics in Eighteenth-Century New England. *Historical Archaeology* 44(4): 46–68.

Snelgrove, Corey, Rita Kaur Dhamoon, and Jeff Corntassel. 2014. Unsettling Settler Colonialism: The Discourse and Politics of Settlers, and Solidarity with Indigenous Nations. *Decolonization: Indigeneity, Education & Society* 3(2): 1–32.

Thomas, Julian. 2004. *Archaeology and Modernity*. London: Routledge.

Timmins Martelle Heritage Consultants. 2014. Stage 3 Archaeological Assessment, Enbridge Gas GTA Project—Segment A, AkGw-477, West Half of Lot 13, Concession 4 EHS, Geographic Township of Toronto (North), City of Brampton, Regional Municipality of Peel, Ontario.

———. 2017. Stage 3 Archaeological Assessment, Cassady Site (AhGs-381), Registered Development Plan TP-86, 135 Queen Street, Town of Niagara-on-the-Lake, Part of Lots 42, 43, 54, 55, Geographic Township of Niagara, Regional Municipality of Niagara, Ontario.

———. 2019. Stage 4 Archaeological Assessment, Existing Aggregate Pit, Putnam Pit 8–Blythe Dale Aggregates, AgHf-50–Location 1, Part of Lot 23, Concession 5, Geographic Township of North Oxford, Oxford County, Ontario.

Tindale, Norman B. 1941. A Tasmanian Stone Implement Made from Bottle Glass. *Papers and Proceedings of the Royal Society of Tasmania, 1941*, 1–2.

Warrick, Gary. 2009. Glass Tools at the Eagles Nest Site, Brantford, Ontario. *KEWA: Newsletter of the London Chapter, Ontario Archaeological Society* 9(3): 1–16.

Whitridge, Peter. 2008. Reimagining the Iglu: Modernity and the Challenge of the Eighteenth Century Labrador Inuit Winter House. *Archaeologies: Journal of the World Archaeological Congress* 4(2): 288–309.

Wilkie, Laurie A. 1996. Glass-Knapping at a Louisiana Plantation: African-American Tools? *Historical Archaeology* 30(4): 37–49.

7

Distrust Thy Neighbor

Seminole Florida Camps from the Aftermath of the Seminole War to the Twentieth Century

DAVE W. SCHEIDECKER, MAUREEN MAHONEY,
AND PAUL N. BACKHOUSE

In the early twentieth century, anthropologists and journalists began to bring pictures and video from Florida of "forgotten Indians," the Seminole. These documents and the writings that went with them spoke of survivors keeping to old ways who were living in a ramshackle state, tenacious in the face of poverty, and only starting to be seen once more by Americans as they lost more and more of the land they lived on.[1] Showcasing the inherent biases of the time, the Americans making these recordings failed to pick up on a very important detail: that the Seminole were carefully controlling what outsiders were able to see. The decision to engage with American journalists and academics was made cautiously and carefully, ensuring that the glimpses of Seminole life and land would not inspire a new wave of invasion. Even sixty years after the Seminole War officially ended, the lessons learned through more than four decades of violence were not forgotten.

Much of the study of Native American culture and history has been done, intentionally or not, from a mindset of settler colonialism that has tainted the results (Panich and Schneider, this volume; Schneider et al., this volume). Scholars have prioritized personal theories and biases over information that could be gained from the most seemingly obvious of sources, the people themselves. This combination of paternalistic attitudes and belief in stereotypes colored Native interactions to the point where many decided it was easiest just to tell outsiders what they wanted to hear. Only when one listens to the people of the Seminole Tribe of Florida talk about the early twentieth century, the time when many Tribal members began to cautiously move from hidden hammock camps to designated reservation lands, can the true nature and importance of this change be seen.

In contrast to many other Native groups in the United States, the Seminole Tribe of Florida has members spread over seven separate reservations. Each one was founded with a unique story (Figure 7.1). The Big Cypress Reservation sits where Abiaka led the surviving Seminole to safety near the end of the Seminole War. The Dania Reservation (now the Hollywood Reservation) became a home for those of the Tribe most willing to engage with American settlers and was established on Big City Island, a former home of the Seminole and their ancestors. The people who settled the Brighton Reservation were members of the Cow Creek Seminole, Muscogee speakers led by Chipco. Through the later twentieth century the Tribe added the reservations of Immokalee, Fort Pierce, Tampa; and in the twenty-first century, it added Lakeland. Every reservation is part of one Tribal government, but each has its own individual culture. The separations and the binding ties are best understood by talking to the people who live there (see Backhouse et al. 2017). But to understand their stories, one needs to understand the history behind them.

Seminole History

The first Seminole ancestors set foot in Florida over 12,000 years ago. The origin story of the Tribe says they originally came from across a large river to the west and spread from there (Griffis 2015). Incredible changes followed, each one requiring adaptation to the lives and culture of the Florida people. The people of the peninsula adapted to the reshaping of the land by the rising waters, the loss of the megafauna they had followed, and even the hurricanes that would somewhat regularly tear through the skies. But after the ancestors of the Seminole had lived on the peninsula for millennia and learned it intimately, the most impactful change was the arrival of new people from across the eastern ocean (Worth 2009). The Europeans brought unexpected demands, slavery, violence, and disease down on the people of Florida (Reséndez 2016). Spanish mission colonies sought to destroy Native culture and life

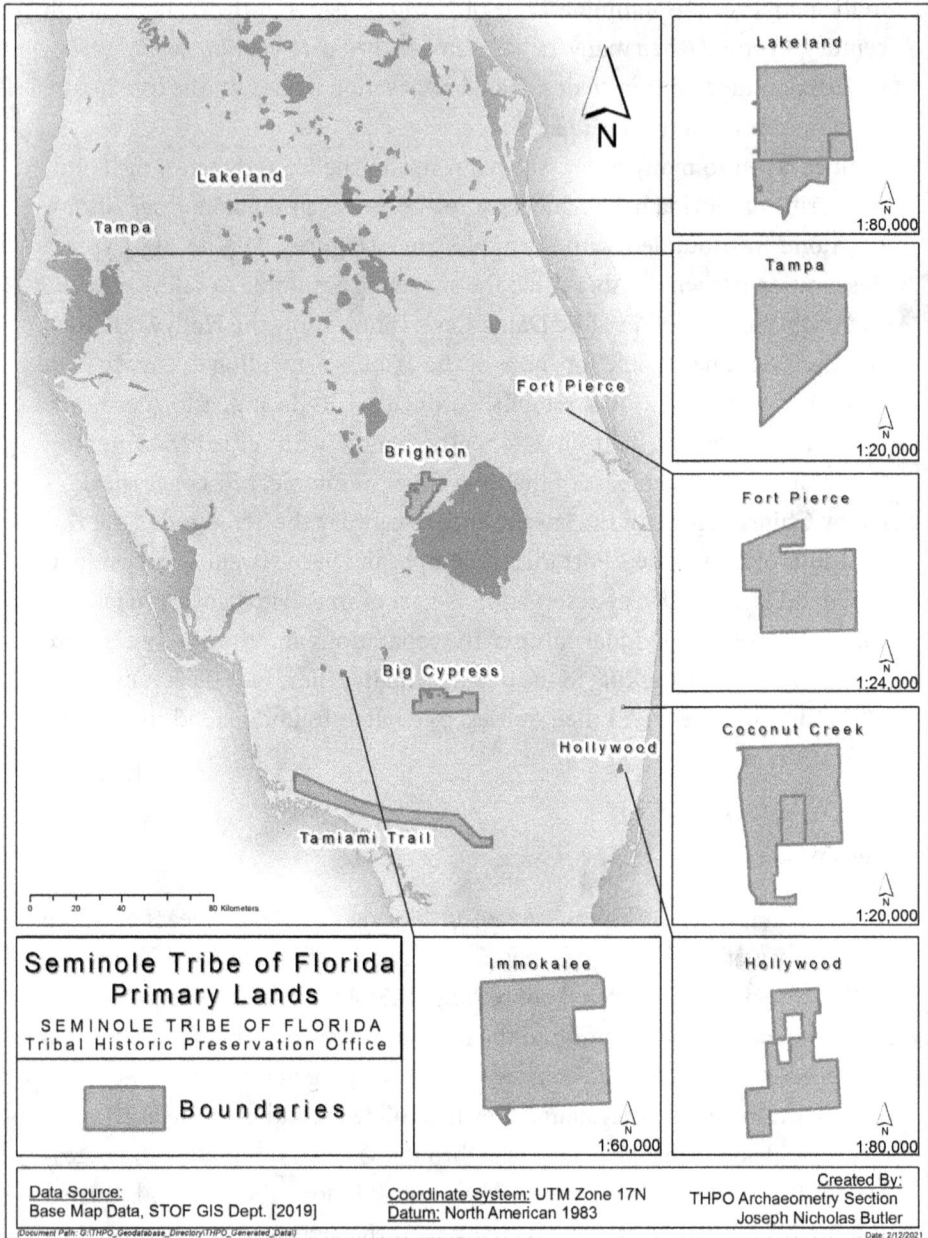

Figure 7.1. Seminole Tribe of Florida primary lands.

through forced assimilation (Milanich 1995). Invading forces from the United States of America sought the farm and pasture land of the Native people. This began in 1812, when American militia groups attacked in the "Patriot War of East Florida," killing the Alachua leader King Payne and destroying Paynes Town. Hostilities continued, inflicting half a century of war during which all but a few hundred of the Indigenous population were killed or "removed" to reservations west of the Mississippi river (Monaco 2018; Sprague 1848). During this time, the United States declared three separate "Seminole Wars" (1817–1823, 1835–1842, and 1855–1858). For the Native people of Florida, it did not matter if the Americans attacking or taking land were military or civilian; they remember the entire period as one long war.

Those who remained, now called "Seminole" by most Americans, were descendants of a number of Native groups. Miccosukee who were originally from North Florida and Muscogee and Yuchi from even farther north were joined by people of the Calusa, Apalachee, and other Native groups that had survived the European powers' greed for new and exotic territories (Scheidecker 2019). Seminole camps and warrior bands often broke down along lines of language and culture. One of the strongest groups within the Seminole coalition were the Miccosukee, one of the southernmost Muscogee groups that had never joined the Creek Confederacy. From the beginning of the wars, a medicine man named Abiaka was one of the most outspoken voices against leaving Florida. American officers, who knew him as "Sam Jones," often noted in reports that he led a group that would never agree to removal (Sprague 1848). Even Billy Bowlegs, whom Elias Rector, the superintendent of Indian Affairs, interviewed in 1858 on board the *Grey Cloud*, the ship used to transport the Seminoles on the Trail of Tears, stated that Sam Jones's party would never leave.[2] He was correct. Sam Jones led his followers deep into the Florida wetlands to an area he knew well, where they were able to survive away from the eyes of American settlers (Griffis 2015).

The History of Big Cypress

When the Seminole settled in the place that would become the Big Cypress Reservation, it consisted of open wetlands interspersed with tree islands rising just enough above the water line to remain dry land during the summer wet season. In between the tree islands, also known as hammocks, there were rivers, shallow wetlands, muddy sloughs, and other wetland environments that were even less hospitable to foreign eyes (Parker 1984).

In the hammocks, the Seminole found both good high ground and natural cover from sight. The borders were naturally dense, with tangles of trees and vines that obscured interior chickees and gardens from anyone passing by (Dilley 2018). This combined perfectly with the open wetlands in between, which enabled the inhabitants of the hammock to easily spot anyone approaching their homes. Within the hammocks the Seminole were able to remain hidden from US troops even when they built blockhouse forts and sent patrols in seemingly every direction. This was put to the test when the military deliberately established Fort Shackleford in the middle of Seminole territory, in an area that is now part of the reservation. The soldiers remained in Fort Shackleford for only three months. They failed to find any Seminole camps and abandoned the fort when the harsh Florida wet season arrived. Shortly after they left, the Seminole burned the fort to the ground (Snapp 2017).

The larger tree island hammocks could support a full camp with multiple chickees. These structures thatched with palmetto leaves formed the core of the camp. Chickees served individual purposes such as cooking, eating, and sleeping units. Trails connecting to a separate section of the hammock would often contain a garden, a cleared area for growing domestic plants that could not be seen from the outside. Each camp belonged to members of one clan, matrilineal family lines that form the core of Seminole culture. Members of the same clan commonly chose hammocks near each other, forming a cohesive area.

After the United States declared an end to the war, the Seminole continued the strategy of covert camp settlement through the end of the nineteenth century. For the Seminole, the war continued, and the encroachment of American settlers into Florida meant that it was necessary to stay hidden and discreet, lessons learned from the historical trauma of war and structural violence that the Seminole passed on for generations (see also Cowie & Teeman, this volume, Laluk, this volume). Big Cypress was continuously occupied by Seminole as the Tribe recovered during this period. Trade continued with carefully chosen Americans and was mostly conducted in frontier settlements that Seminole families would travel to by canoe. The people trusted to do this made efforts to ensure they were not followed back to their camps (Covington 1993). The first trading post within Big Cypress was not established until the early twentieth century, when Bill Brown opened his post. Brown, an English expatriate, was the first outsider allowed to settle on Seminole land; he brought his family with him (Kersey 1971). His post quickly became a community center within Big Cypress.

In 1936, after dealings between the Seminole Tribe and the US government had resumed peacefully, the Big Cypress area was declared an official Indian reservation. It is one of the few reservations that was established where Native people were currently living and thus were not required to relocate. A Bureau of Indian Affairs (BIA) local headquarters was built on the reservation along the main route to serve as a center for goods and services for the Tribe. In the 1930s, the Big Cypress Red Barn was built approximately one-half mile from this headquarters to be the center of the returning Seminole cattle tradition in Big Cypress. The Ahfachkee School was constructed in 1968 directly next to the BIA headquarters (West 2008).

The camps changed steadily as the new century continued. As relationships between the Tribe and the American government changed, the camps began to move from the centers of the hammocks to the sides of roads. Many Seminole established trade chickees along the Florida roadways, places to sell tribally created goods and souvenirs to curious visitors. Thus, the Seminole became pioneers in the Florida tourist trade. The multiple-use chickees were added to and adapted. Then, as developed land and modern housing were embraced, they became outside additions. Despite all these changes within one century, the camp tradition still shows. Many Tribal members claim home sites that are located where their parents and grandparents made camp, or in close proximity to those sites. Traditional chickees sit alongside modern houses, and nearly every Seminole home has one. When sites for new homes are chosen, the clan connection remains a strong priority (Dilley 2018).

The Archaeological Signatures of the Big Cypress Camp Settlements

For archaeologists working for the Tribal Historic Preservation Office (THPO), recognizing the signature of a camp is a necessity, but one that remains incredibly difficult due to the preservation conditions in the Florida wetlands and the Florida climate. The oral histories of the Tribe, which provide the rich context and information that is needed for proper archaeological work to be done, inform all investigations performed by Tribal archaeologists. Signs of habitation in the tree islands are common in and around the Seminole Tribe's reservations. Oftentimes, the signs of habitation may simply look like a jumble of historic objects. However, if these objects are put into context with oral histories and historic aerial photographs, the makeup of Seminole camps emerges (Mahoney 2017; and see Cowie and Teeman, this volume; Dickson and Steinmetz, this volume).

Based on their examination of fourteen camps archaeologically recorded on the Big Cypress Reservation, THPO archaeologists have found that the signature of the pre-reservation period camps, mostly dating to the late nineteenth and early twentieth centuries, include faunal bones, glass beads, and glass bottles. The reservation period camps (dating to after 1936) contained faunal material (mostly deer bones), glass sherds and bottles, and metal objects. The items from both periods are generally not in one specific level of stratigraphy and are often even on the ground surface. Many camps have heavy disturbance since younger generations of the original occupants' family have developed the sites. Added to these difficulties are the impacts of semi-regular tropical storms and a very limited depositional environment. Since archaeological features are not readily apparent at camps from either period, the THPO archaeologists often combine what is found in the field with other sources (see also Laluk, this volume). For example, historic aerials may show signs of clearings in the hammocks or trails leading to camps. Additionally, oral histories provide details about the makeup of the camps and the people living in them (Mahoney 2017).

Big Cypress Reservation Period Camps: Two Examples

Every Seminole camp is unique, crafted by individual people and families who have learned skills, knowledge, and culture handed from previous generations. The camp is made to fit the needs of the people and to fit within the specific environment. During the war years and up through the establishment of the Florida reservations, this uniqueness was curtailed by secrecy and defense needs. As Tribal members adjusted to the changing times, their ability to shape their places of living to their own desires and needs grew.

The camps of Lee Billie and Charlie Cypress and of Morgan Smith were both established in this period. Both belonged to respected Tribal elders in positions of responsibility and leadership and both show adaptations to the changing times of the twentieth century. The two camps also contrast starkly. The camp of Lee Billie and Charlie Cypress shows how the traditional Seminole culture adjusted to modern times, whereas the Morgan Smith camp shows intense changes and the use of concepts and products from outside the traditional Seminole ways that depart from the commonly accepted signs of a Native camp (Dickson and Steinmetz, this volume).

The Lee Billie and Charlie Cypress Camp

The Lee Billie and Charlie Cypress camp was first recorded on the Tribe's Seminole Site File (SSF) in 2014, when a Tribal elder pointed out where its location had been on Big Cypress. It was fully investigated in 2017 for the Tribal Register of Historic Places due to the significant role Charlie Cypress played in Seminole history. The investigation included archival research, the examination of historical aerial photographs, a limited pedestrian survey, and conversations with family members about the camp (Morgan 2017).

One of the first steps in recording a camp is examining historic aerials that date from the 1940s to 1960s and show the clearings for the camp. For the Lee Billie and Charlie Cypress camp, the aerials highlight how the camp continued to be cleared of vegetation over a fourteen-year period from 1940 to 1953. Similarly, archival research often contributes information about where other earlier camps may have been situated. With this information, the THPO was able to learn the location of the Lee Billie and Charlie Cypress camp in 1930 (Densmore 1956).

One of the most important parts of recording any historic camp on the reservations is working with members of the family of the original occupants. The family helps make sure the information is correct and that it is collected appropriately and respectfully. Family members also add important historic context through oral histories. Fieldwork at this camp was limited to a pedestrian survey, since the THPO was asked not to proceed with ground disturbance. While we often do shovel testing for development activities, it was deemed unnecessary in this instance. Similarly, as part of the survey, no artifacts were collected; instead, they were recorded in place and photographed. The pedestrian survey revealed that a modern home (occupied by a descendant of Lee Billie and Charlie Cypress) was located where the camp once stood. As was the case with other camps on Big Cypress, cultural material that may have once been associated with the camp was pushed to the edges of the home site. These items included a concrete pad, a 1967 soda bottle, a wire bed frame, tires, and a motor (Morgan 2017).

If the THPO only used the aerial photographs, the pedestrian survey, and archival research, we would still have known very little of the makeup of the camp and its occupants. The photos point us to a rough size and shape and the archival research shows us the family's movement and one camp layout, and while it is interesting to note the artifacts we recorded, the oral histories add a needed cultural context. While some may argue that further excavations may provide more physical information, we have often found that this is not the case. As Tribal archaeologists, we have to earn the trust of the Tribal members, and for many traditional members this means no unnecessary excavation, especially in an area with such strong family ties (see also Laluk, this volume; Schneider et al., this volume).

It is crucial to work with the family members of the camp throughout the entire process of its recording. Many individuals provided personal stories about family members who lived in these camps and helped us determine the layout of the camp. When all of these types of sources were taken together, the entire history of the camp emerged.

The camp of Lee Billie (Panther Clan) and Charlie Cypress (Otter Clan) is in many ways the classic early twentieth-century Seminole camp (Figure 7.2). Charlie Cypress and his three brothers (named Futch, Wilson, and Whitney) played important roles in settling the area and building relations that led to the land being brought into trust. Charlie and his wife Lee Billie were able to pick a central location for their camp. The area they chose was outside the tree islands but had ground high enough to remain dry throughout the year even before the state's mass drainage and canal projects changed the landscape. The camp also sat along the main road that passed through the reservation, leading north to the community of Clewiston, east to the edge of the Everglades, and south toward where Brown's Trading Post had stood at the start of the century. According to their great-granddaughter, Mary Jene Koenes (Panther Clan), the couple also maintained a separate garden roughly two miles away from their home, but its exact location is not a matter of record. The separation of the garden from the camp was one feature that remained from the years of conflict, as the source of food was hidden away from those who would pass by. The home site, in contrast, was open and welcoming. Lee and Charlie referred to their home in Big Cypress

Figure 7.2. The Lee Billie and Charlie Cypress Camp (*above*) and the family at work in the craft chickee (*below*). Courtesy of the Ah-Tah-Thi-Ki Museum.

as "a happier place" in contrast to the years of distrust and conflict that had shaped their previous lives (Morgan 2017).

Lee Billie and Charlie Cypress were respected leaders in the community who embraced and exemplified traditional practices. Lee was a local leader in the community and in the women's circle. Charlie was a respected medicine man of the Tribe and was particularly well known for preserving the Seminole canoe crafting tradition. In Seminole tradition, a camp is owned and run by the matriarch of the family living on it and belongs to her clan. In this tradition, their home was a Panther clan camp under Lee Billie's leadership. It was the primary home not only for Lee and Charlie but over time for the ten children they brought into the world.

The camp was composed of three chickees, each one built with a specific purpose. The cooking chickee at the center was considered the heart and soul of the camp. It was the center of life at the camp. The tradition is that the first chickee is built on the highest spot, and that is where the cooking chickee was located in this camp. It was there that Charlie Cypress, in his role as medicine man, performed the ceremony that officially made Lee Billie the camp matriarch. The other chickees were sleeping areas for Lee and Charlie and their children. Within the camp, Lee Billie taught cooking, sewing, and basket weaving to Tribal children (Figure 7.2). Charlie Cypress gained renown as a canoe maker, preserving the style and tradition even after the draining of the everglades caused the Tribe to stop needing them. He often made miniature canoes for his grandchildren.[3]

The camp grew through the years as the family changed and expanded, as children were born, left, and married. One daughter, Willie Mae Cypress Billie (Panther Clan), stayed at the camp after marrying. Her husband joined her there in the traditional Seminole pattern, and she raised her children at the camp. After Charlie and Lee's son, Stanley Cypress (Panther Clan), married, the family built an adjacent camp for the new couple. Stanley broke with tradition in his camp by building an American-style wood-framed house in addition to the chickees. This was increasingly common among the newer generations within the Tribe as the reservation brought in more and more technology from the surrounding areas (Morgan 2017).

The central location of the camp led the Bureau of Indian Affairs to build their reservation complex next door to Lee and Charlie's camp in 1937. This was the beginning of sweeping changes to the reservation that took place as the Tribal community adapted to the changing world around them. Soon after that, the nearby road was paved and more families and services moved to the centralized location. In 1968, the Ahfachkee school was built on the western edge of the camp, where the BIA complex had previously stood. When Charlie Cypress passed on in 1960, he was at least 98 years old, although some in the family claimed he was over 100. He had seen and helped shape the incredible changes his Tribe had gone through, from the years of distrust and hiding to the establishment of the reservation to the formal establishment of the Seminole Tribe of Florida two years before he passed. All of these affected him, his family, and the camp they called home (Morgan 2017).

Morgan Smith Camp

The Morgan Smith camp was recorded in the 1990s by a cultural resource management (CRM) firm and was added to the Tribal Register of Historic Places in 2017. THPO archaeologists followed the same investigatory process to document the camp as they had with the Lee Billie and Charlie Cypress camp. Aerials from 1953 show previous camps occupied by Morgan Smith and the 1968 aerial photograph highlights the location of the camp, some cow pens, and a possible grazing area. Artifacts noted in the earlier CRM survey include a large amount of diagnostic pottery that dates to the Glades period (500 BCE to CE 1750) and shows the continual use of hammocks from the prehistoric to historic periods (Freeman 2017).

The THPO survey of the Morgan Smith camp was restricted to a pedestrian survey at the request of a family member. No artifacts were collected, although they were photographed and their locations were digitally recorded. Unlike the Lee Billie and Charlie Cypress camp, no home site exists where the camp once stood. This means that some artifact locations are more intact. Many of the objects found at this camp are tied to Morgan Smith's involvement in the cattle industry. These include a concrete water trough, a low wire fence (possibly from a hog pen and/or horse corral), numerous condiment bottles and jars, soda bottles of various brands dating to the 1950s, and one spirits bottle. Metal artifacts found there include pans and pots, steel wire mesh, large barrels, a cabinet, and a Royal Crown Cola cooler. Several short concrete pillars were also identified as the structures used to support the house located at the camp, the first house erected on the Big Cypress Reservation.

Much of the information about the Morgan Smith camp is from a Tribal elder who was raised by Morgan. By speaking with him, the THPO learned about the camps Morgan lived in and about who he was as a person. If we had used only traditional archaeological practices, this information would be missing (Griffis et al. 2016).

While the Lee Billie and Charlie Cypress Camp exemplifies the changes traditional camps went through in the early twentieth century, the Morgan Smith camp illustrates how other Tribal members chose to make immediate and drastic breaks with tradition. The Morgan Smith camp sits far from the central community, out on the western end of Big Cypress on the edge of the Kissimmee Billie Slough. Morgan Smith (Bird Clan) chose this location so he would be close to his cattle pens. Smith was a proud proponent of the Seminole cattle tradition. The pens, which were located roughly 350 yards northwest of the camp, are considered to be the birthplace of the Big Cypress cattle program (Griffis et al. 2016).

This location was not the primary camp for Morgan Smith and his wife Katie Tommie Huff (Panther Clan). That was located next to the Big Cypress Red Barn, the central building for the growing cattle industry. During this period, the modern Seminole cattle program was forming, rebuilding a tradition the Tribe had practiced until the Seminole War forced its end. Morgan Smith had grown up working in the cattle industry around the Bluefields and Brighton areas. He was also instrumental in organizing for the Tribal constitution that officially founded the Seminole Tribe of Florida in 1957. His abilities and experience made him one of the leaders of the Tribe, and he was elected to the first board of trustees for the cattle program (Figure 7.3). Today the Morgan Smith Cattle & Range headquarters on Big Cypress, the modern center of operations, is named in his honor.

The new camp was placed so that Morgan could keep a close eye on the cattle while he was tending to them (Figure 7.3). One of the major cow pens on the Big Cypress Reservation was located about 350 meters (1,148 feet) northwest of the camp, and a large grazing area lay to the south. Morgan and Katie chose a hammock with higher ground on the edge of the slough when they established this camp in the early 1940s. The camp was relatively small and exhibited many of the changes to Seminole life in the twentieth century. Because the camp was not a primary home, it did not feature the traditional-style chickees. Instead, it consisted of several makeshift tents made out of four posts and canvas tops near the stables and cow pens. Morgan's cow-

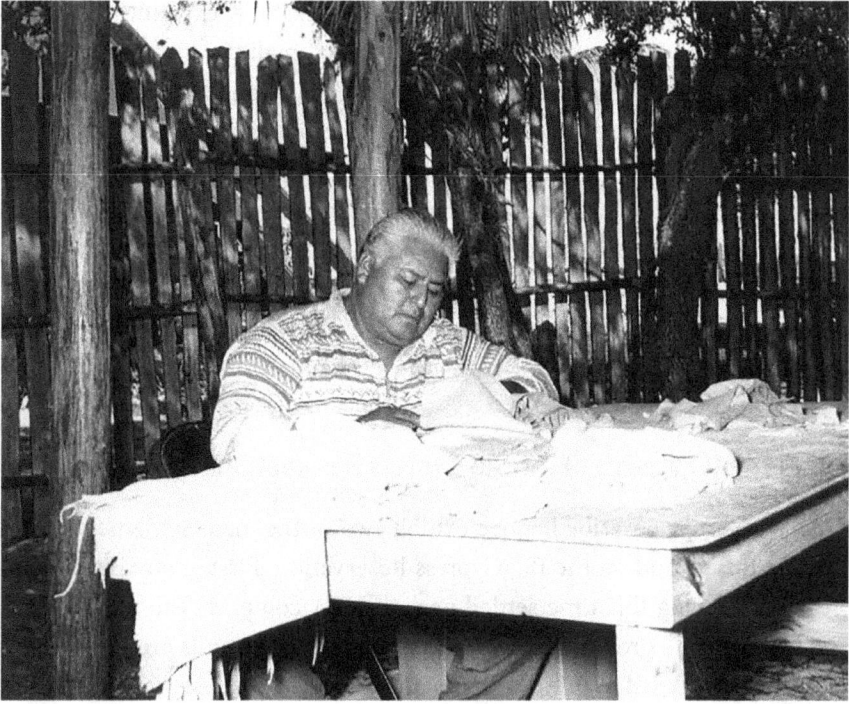

Figure 7.3. Morgan Smith at work (*above*) and cattle being loaded at the Morgan Smith Camp (*below*) (courtesy of the Ah-Tah-Thi-Ki Museum).

hands would also set up temporary camps in the area, expanding the footprint. Sometime before 1949, Morgan bought a small two-room house from Joe Flint, a former tax appraiser from Glades County, and had it moved to this camp from Immokalee, hiring help to cut the way through the wetlands to the intended location of the prebuilt home. The house was placed on several concrete pillars and had steps leading up to the entrance. With this purchase, Morgan Smith became one of the first on the Big Cypress reservation to have an American-style house. Morgan and Katie used the camp for over twenty years, until the late 1960s. After that, the camp was left untended and was reclaimed by the fast-growing native flora (Freeman 2017).

Settlement Patterns of the Big Cypress Reservation

The two camps described above exhibit two of the main settlement trends during this period on the Big Cypress Reservation. First, many Big Cypress residents during this time settled near the BIA complex. The second trend centered on the growing cattle industry. These two trends are quite different from what existed prior to the establishment of the reservation. Historic maps and archaeological discoveries indicate that the Seminole camps of the early 1900s were primarily located near other similar camp types on the east side of what would become the reservation (Mahoney 2017).

Beginning in the 1930s, most likely with the establishment of the reservation, settlement locations changed drastically. Camps were clustered in what would later be called the "community" and generally along the Josie Billie Highway, the major road of the reservation. Camps were clustered around the BIA complex and the Red Barn, highlighting the importance of this infrastructure. Four of the fourteen camps the THPO recorded were located near the BIA Complex and five were located close to the Red Barn. At times, a location near these or other work areas ranked higher in decisions about placement than locations near similar clan camps, which had once been the main consideration for settlements.

Other Twentieth-Century Seminole Reservations

The Big Cypress Reservation is only one of the Seminole Reservations established during the twentieth century, and much like the camps within them, each reservation was formed in a unique way that featured both individual characteristics and elements that were common among the reservations. Big Cypress has a distinct community that varies considerably from other reservations, specifically the Hollywood, Brighton, and Immokalee reservations, which were established in the same early twentieth-century period. The differences in settlement choices between the reservations highlights the social and economic contrasts between the various communities that founded them.

Brighton

Before the Brighton Reservation was established in 1935, the Seminole community that made up this area primarily settled to the east-northeast of Lake Okeechobee in an open wetland area interspersed with hammocks called the Bluefields. Most of the Seminole in this region were Muskogee speakers. Often called the Cow Creek Seminole, they were descendants of the Red Stick Creek who had joined the Seminole after the Creek Civil War. While long years of shared conflict had united the groups into one Tribe, they still had different cultures and languages. Many Muskogee followed Chipco, an elder who had led the Creek contingent that joined the Seminole following the Creek Civil War. Chipco led his followers north and east, settling around the northern edges of Lake Okeechobee (Spoehr 1941).

In the early 1900s, Cow Creek camps were located throughout the Bluefields and included a local trading post. The trading post eventually grew into the city of Indiantown. However, as more American settlers moved into the region and bought up land during the Florida land boom, the Seminole were steadily pushed out of the region. Talks began of establishing a reservation for this northern Seminole community. A region was settled north of the lake and just south of the growing (but soon to vanish) community of Brighton that would give the new reservation its name. With the move to this new land, the trend of settling near roads and work areas that had been growing in the twentieth century became clear (Mahoney 2017). When the Brighton community first formed, camps were primarily settled in the northern part of the reservation so residents could easily access the roads that led to fields where Seminoles were employed to pick crops. This choice served a second purpose that was still in the minds of the Tribe, as the roads also allowed for an easy escape from the reservation if US troops returned to the area. As new programs were established on the Brighton Reservation, camp occupants began to settle their camps near these developments. In the 1940s, people still settled near work areas, but work by that time meant the growing Tribal cattle enterprises, such as the Red Barn and the cow pens. During this time, Seminoles on Brighton also began occupying camps near the BIA complex, which contained a school, a medical office, and a store. Instead of continuing to be hidden away as they once were, Seminole camps on Brighton became more visible to outsiders. In the 1950s, camps were settled near the main road of the reservation so that children could catch the school bus and passersby could buy items from the newly created craft chickees.

Hollywood

Much like Brighton, the BIA established the Hollywood Reservation (originally the Dania Reservation) as a place for the Seminole to relocate to. As many Seminole were being forced out of their homes in the Bluefields region, the agency decided to place a reservation south in Broward County for these and other Seminole who were looking to relocate to an area closer to the developed Fort Lauderdale area. While the area the BIA chose included a portion of Big City Island, an area Seminole had occupied in the 1800s, there were no Native people living there in 1926 when the reservation opened (Steel and Cancel 1995).

The first Tribal members to move to the reservation were able to use structures previous occupants had left behind land. Betty Mae Tiger Jumper (Snake Clan), a future chair of the Tribe, recalled her family arriving from the Bluefields region after her mother, Ada Tiger (Snake Clan), sold off most of her cattle. They undertook the journey south and moved into the abandoned home of a former settler. Many of the earliest arrivals were Christian converts, like the Tiger family, a fact that had created a significant rift within the Bluefields community. Their family moved to the area in order to keep young Betty Mae safe, whose mixed blood put her at risk, because she would be more accepted in the reservation managed by the Bureau of Indian Affairs (Jumper and West 2001).

Settlement in the Dania reservation was largely determined by the more urban infrastructure that surrounded them; families claimed homes or established camps close to the BIA complex or the major roads. Whereas in Big Cypress, the infrastructure brought in was made to adapt to the Seminole, in Dania, the Seminole had to adapt to the developed land they were in.

Immokalee

Like Hollywood, the Immokalee Reservation was established in a region the Seminole people had previously inhabited but had abandoned during the Seminole Wars. In Immokalee, however, the Seminole returned of their own volition to make use of the area and to take advantage of the opportunities for trade and paid work that the growing frontier settlement that formed in the 1870s and 1880s provided (Kersey and Pullease 1973). In 1921, a railway was laid through the area, bringing in new opportunities and new investments. This led to the creation of another seasonal camp near the depot for Seminole working in the lumber industry.

In Immokalee, the Seminole in the main camp were integrated into the local community more thoroughly than in other reservations, presumably because it was closer to the center of a town. The community remained there until the 1960s, when officials from the Collier Company struck a deal with the four women who ran the camp to trade the land for an equal amount southeast of town. The deed for the new land was signed into trust in 1970 and that land became the first segment of the newly formed Immokalee Reservation. The reservation grew through new deeds and purchases in the 1980s and 1990s. In contrast to Hollywood, where the federal government allotted reservation land and asked the Seminole to move there, in Immokalee the Seminole moved to the land and informed the federal government that it would become a reservation.

Twentieth-Century Seminole Camps in Context

These different but linked stories, drawn from four geographically separate reservations, demonstrate the complex cultural, economic, and traditional mechanisms at work when considering the placement of historic, reservation period Seminole camps. One common factor that is clear across all Tribal lands is how quickly these places are given local importance and continue to be of great significance to the community. Different clans and families carefully choose where to move to, and individuals addressed how to meet the needs of their family and the changing economic and cultural environment in well-thought-out ways. Put another way, the infrastructure that exists on reservations today is a response to those founding families' decisions rather than a structure that was imposed upon them, as was the case with westernized planned developments that were spreading through Florida. The traditional process of deciding to place a camp close to other clan camps and to goods and services has enabled the reservations to retain a strong local identity into the early twenty-first century. Still today when home sites are granted, new generations of Tribal members seek to place their camps close to places that their ancestors chose. There are very few exceptions to this rule, but those that do occur are notable (e.g., Morgan Smiths Camp, Big Cypress Reservation) and are best explained by exploring the oral histories of community members.

Archaeologists who want to understand the population dynamics of early reservation period communities and the settlement patterns from earlier time periods should take note of the internal Tribal decision making that informs adaptation (see Dickson and Steinmetz, this volume; Kretzler, this volume). People mapped their lives onto these spaces in very different ways that cannot be adequately explained through a lens that does not consider sociopolitical factors. Camp locations were and are idiosyncratic and were strongly influenced by sociocultural factors. Viewed from broad scales, these combined individual decisions reveal patterns of resistance and distrust of the US government and American settlers. This happened even while community members took advantage of the new economic opportunities created by the rapid social and technological change that came with greater interaction with nontribal communities outside the reservation. The death, betrayal, and loss the Seminole Tribe experienced during the Seminole War left a mark on the Seminole people that led to half a century of stoic and cautious survival. The word "distrust" best reflects the cautious adaptation to the spread of Americans through Florida. The Seminole did their best to interact with these new arrivals and benefit from new opportunities while simultaneously remaining secluded and drawing as little attention to themselves as possible, ready to move swiftly if America decided once again to remove them by force.

Conclusion

The THPO was established to serve the cultural and historical interests of the Seminole people. Our work has found that the exploration of historic period camps on the Seminole Tribe of Florida's trust lands is of great importance to the communities served. Community members are proud of the families who first moved on to reservation land and this is expressed in the number of nominations the THPO has received to place historic period camps on the Tribal Register of Historic Places and also in the consistent reuse of specific areas by clans and families seeking to identify with their immediate ancestors. Archaeologically, the signature for historic camps is of extreme interest as these locations provide opportunities to test correlations between oral histories and physical evidence. It is of particular note that the combination of the South Florida environment and the organic material used to construct early reservation period Seminole camps effectively renders many camp signatures invisible in very short amounts of time. Often this means that the record for the camps' structure and layout is much better retained in the oral history of the descendent family than it is the archaeological record. An important conclusion is that the location of historic camps retains a strong geographic consistency that reflects clan and family units through time. However, placement of camps cannot be easily interpreted or predicted at local scales without access to the oral historical record of the communities.

Acknowledgments

We thank the members of the Seminole Tribe of Florida who took the time to help us and guide our research, James Billie (Bird Clan) and Neal "Marty" Bowers (Wind Clan). We also thank the members of the Big Cypress and Brighton Communities.

Notes

1. *Proudest Americans*, dir. A. B. Carrick, 1938, Veribest; 1951. *Seminole Indians*, dir. H. Webb, 1951, International Film Bureau Inc.
2. Elias Rector, onboard the steamer *Gray Cloud*, Egmont Key, May 6, 1858, letter on file at the Ah-Tah-Thi-Ki Museum, Clewiston, Florida.
3. J. Robinson, "Cypress Charley Fashioned Fine Canoes," *Orlando Sentinel*, May 17, 1998.

References Cited

Backhouse, Paul N., Brent R. Weisman, and Mary Beth Rosebrough, eds. 2017. *We Come for Good: Archaeology and Tribal Historic Preservation at the Seminole Tribe of Florida.* Gainesville: University Press of Florida.
Covington, James W. 1993. *The Seminoles of Florida.* Gainesville: University Press of Florida.

Densmore, Frances. 1956. *Seminole Music*. Washington, DC: United States Government Printing Office.

Dilley, Carrie. 2018. *Thatched Roofs and Open Sides: The Architecture of Chickees and Their Changing Role in Seminole Society*. Gainesville: University Press of Florida.

Freeman, Jessica. 2017. Morgan Smith Camp Nomination Packet, February 3. Report on file at the Seminole Tribe of Florida Tribal Historic Preservation Office, Clewiston, Florida.

Griffis, Eric. 2015. Interview with Bobby Henry. October 23. Oral history interview on file at the Ah-Tah-Thi-Ki Museum, Clewiston, Florida.

Griffis, Eric, Kate Macuen, Quintin Cypress, and Tucomah Robbins. 2016. Interview with James Billie. June 8. Oral history interview on file at the Ah-Tah-Thi-Ki Museum, Clewiston, Florida.

Jumper, Betty Mae Tiger, and Patsy West. 2001. *A Seminole Legend: The Life of Betty Mae Tiger Jumper*. Gainesville: University Press of Florida.

Kersey, Harry. 1971. Interview with Frank Brown. Samuel Proctor Oral History Program, September 24. Oral history interview on file at the Ah-Tah-Thi-Ki Museum, Clewiston, Florida.

Kersey, Harry A., and Donald E. Pullease. 1973. Bishop William Crane Gray's Mission to The Seminole Indians of Florida, 1893–1914. *Historical Magazine of the Protestant Episcopal Church* 42(3): 257–273.

Mahoney, Maureen. 2017. Tarakkvlkv (Land of Palms): Bridging the Gap between Archaeology and Tribal Perspectives. In *We Come for Good: Archaeology and Tribal Historic Preservation at the Seminole Tribe of Florida*, edited by Paul N. Backhouse, Brent R. Weisman, and Mary Beth Rosebrough, 179–205. Gainesville: University Press of Florida.

Milanich, Jerald T. 1995. *Florida Indians and the Invasion from Europe*. Gainesville: University Press of Florida.

Monaco, C. S. 2018. *The Second Seminole War and the Limits of American Aggression*. Baltimore, MD: Johns Hopkins University Press.

Morgan, Rachel. 2017. Lee Billie and Charlie Cypress Nomination Packet, July 17. Report on file at the Seminole Tribe of Florida Tribal Historic Preservation Office, Clewiston, Florida.

Parker, Gerald G. 1984. Hydrology of the Pre-drainage System of the Everglades in Southern Florida. In *Environments of South Florida: Present and Past II*, edited by Patrick J. Gleason, 28–37. Coral Gables, FL: Miami Geological Society.

Reséndez, Andrés. 2016. *The Other Slavery: The Uncovered Story of Indian Enslavement in America*. Boston: Houghton Mifflin Harcourt.

Scheidecker, Dave. 2019. Interview with Willie Johns. Seminole and Florida Origins, May 20. Oral history interview on file at the Ah-Tah-Thi-Ki Museum, Clewiston, Florida.

Snapp, Annette L. 2017. Everything You Know Is Wrong! Community Archaeology at Fort Shackelford. In *We Come For Good: Archaeology and Tribal Historic Preservation at the Seminole Tribe of Florida,* edited by Paul N. Backhouse, Brent R. Weisman, and Mary Beth Rosebrough, 158–178. Gainesville: University Press of Florida.

Spoehr, Alexander. 1941. Camp, Clan, and Kin among the Cow Creek Seminole of Florida. *Publications of Field Museum of Natural History Anthropological Series* 33: 7–27. Chicago, IL: Field Museum of Natural History.

Sprague, John T. 1848. *The Origin, Progress, and Conclusion of the Florida War*. New York: Appleton & Company.

Steel, W., and J. Cancel. 1995. Big City Island and the Snake Creek Community: An Historical Perspective. Document on file at the Big Cypress Reservation, Clewiston, Florida.

West, Patsy. 2008. *The Enduring Seminoles: From Alligator Wrestling to Casino Gaming.* Gainesville: University Press of Florida.

Worth, John E. 2009. Razing Florida: The Indian Slave Trade and the Devastation of Spanish Florida, 1659–1715. In *Mapping the Mississippian Shatter Zone: The Colonial Indian Slave Trade and Regional Instability in the American South*, edited by Robbie Ethridge and Sheri M. Shuck-Hall, 295–311. Lincoln: University of Nebraska Press.

II

CONCEPTUAL AND PRACTICAL ADVANCES

8

Recognizing Post-Columbian Indigenous Sites in California's Colonial Hinterlands

KATHLEEN L. HULL

In recent decades, archaeological investigation of the Indigenous experiences of European colonialism and subsequent American hegemony have provided important insights into how Native communities resisted and persisted from the past to the present in North America (e.g., Hunter et al. 2014; Hull and Douglass 2018; Liebmann 2012; Panich 2013, 2020; Panich and Schneider 2014; Wilcox 2009). As Panich and Schneider (2019, this volume) note, however, the pernicious effects of embedded biases in archaeological practice undermine this effort. This is especially notable in the failure of researchers to identify and properly record archaeological traces of post-1492 Native life outside colonial institutional settings. For example, simplistic assumptions about the use of non-Native goods and introduced materials often rooted in outdated notions such as acculturation or "terminal narratives" (Panich 2013; Wilcox 2009) result in the misattribution of sites or the incorrect identification of relatively late components within multicomponent sites to non-Native people. Instead, such deposits document the flexibility and resilience of Indigenous people who confronted displacement or even genocide. To overcome such methodological problems, Panich and Schneider (2019, 3) call for the development of a wider array of archaeological approaches to identifying post-1492 Indigenous presence, beyond the typical reliance on a few "index artifacts" such as glass beads (Panich and Schneider 2019, 654).

Such efforts to recognize colonial-era Indigenous sites are especially important in "hinterland" areas that were far removed from European colonial institutions. Ethnohistoric information, Native oral history, and archaeological data reveal that Indigenous people living at great distance from areas that were permanently occupied—or even periodically visited—by Euro-American colonists experienced profound effects of colonialism, such as demographic collapse due to introduced, non-native diseases and the unforeseen repercussions of changing economic entanglements. In addition, Native survivors of fatal epidemics were often relegated to peripheral or marginal areas either by mandate or choice in the face of non-Native antipathy after Euro-American opportunists or settlers intruded into these former hinterland areas. The small, often aggregate, Native "contingent communities" (see Bernard and Robinson 2018) that emerged from such negotiations carved out niches in new or even traditional lands from which they had been temporarily displaced in the wake of fatal engagements with disease or later settlers. Thus, study of colonial-era Indigenous sites outside the direct sphere of colonial outposts has much to offer in terms of understanding the indirect effects of colonialism. In addition, the choices Native people made and the practices they sustained during this time frequently undergird the identity and sovereignty of the Indigenous communities of today (Hull and Douglass 2018; Nelson 2019).

While archaeological study of Native life in these distant areas is crucial to understanding the indirect colonial experience of Indigenous peoples, the archaeological record in such areas poses particular challenges for identifying sites that date to the colonial era. In this case, in contrast to the practice of misattributing Indigenous occupation to non-Native people (e.g., Panich and Schneider 2019, this volume), colonial-era Native components in hinterland areas of the colonial domain are unlikely to be recognized as such and instead are attributed to precolonial use (see Jordan, this volume). This misattribution is due in part to the fact that evidence of colonial-era occupation exists as a thin veneer of primarily or exclusively traditional (rather than introduced) cultural debris in sites that also contain more robust archaeological deposits from earlier periods. Non-Native "index artifacts" such as glass beads may have only been available well after the long arm of colonialism had begun to draw Native peoples into direct colonial entanglements. This means that researchers cannot rely on the presence of such items to recognize colonial-era site components in hinterland zones.

In addition, the problem of recognizing Indigenous site components of indirect or direct colonial engagements in hinterland areas is exacerbated in California and elsewhere in North America by traditional Native land-use strategies. Colonial-era components may be ephemeral at residential sites that seasonally mobile hunter-gatherers used periodically over millennia (see also Laluk, this volume). While post-fieldwork analyses such as radiocarbon or obsidian hydration dating can help archaeologists determine that a site or a site component dates to the colonial era (Panich and Schneider 2019, 656), archaeologists working in hinterland areas need to develop frameworks and protocols for identifying Indigenous colonial-era sites in the field that are appropriate for—and perhaps even specific to—the particular region under study (see Panich and Schneider 2019, 662; Russell, this volume).

The relatively short duration of site use, the common colonial-era practice of reusing sites that were episodically occupied in the more distant past, and the fine temporal scale required for archaeological study of cultural practices in the wake of colonialism necessitate a multifaceted approach in areas that were at significant distance from permanent colonial presence. Fortunately, the rich ethnohistoric, ethnographic, and archaeological records of California, at least, support a systematic approach to this issue. This research strategy entails (1) creative and exhaustive examination of diverse data sources, including documents, images, and material evidence before undertaking fieldwork to identify specific colonial-era sites in an area and to develop regionally specific archaeological expectations for colonial-era Indigenous occupation in general; (2) innovative archaeological approaches to inferring site formation, establishing chronology, and identifying artifacts and features that can reveal colonial-era components; and (3) an iterative analytical method that feeds data back into the identification process and builds on often-subtle differences between components that date before and after the first effects of colonialism were felt. While the full suite of potential data sources supporting this strategy for site identification and investigation may not be available in all areas of North America, this study illustrates this strategy with examples from the Yosemite area of the central Sierra Nevada of California (Figure 8.1) to demonstrate the efficacy of developing regionally specific criteria for the identification and analysis of colonial-era Native sites in areas at significant distance from permanent colonial occupation. If archaeologists are attentive to the potential indirect effects of colonialism on Indigenous people in hinterland areas, they can more readily recognize sites or components that relate to Native life during the colonial era and later periods through a systematic approach that incorporates a broad suite of archaeological and nonarchaeological methods and data.

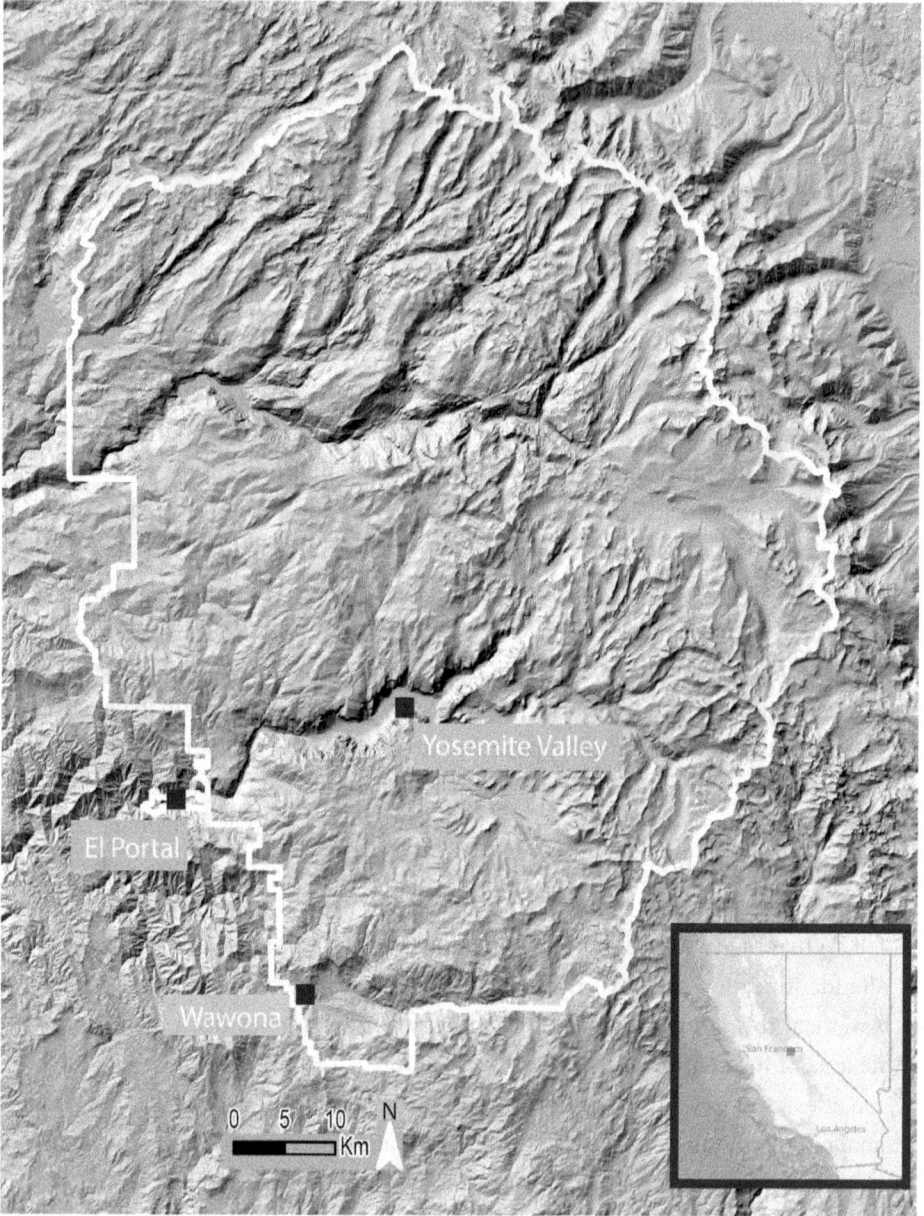

Figure 8.1. Map of Yosemite National Park noting locations referenced in text. Base image prepared by Adam Fleenor.

Site-Specific Interpretations and General Expectations from Diverse Data Sources

Archaeologists with an interest in Indigenous life during the colonial era are certainly aware of the potential utility of historic written records and images for identifying sites of Native occupation dating to this period. Use of such methods by archaeologists can be traced back at least to the direct historical approach of the 1920s (see Steward 1942), although research goals at that time were somewhat different than today. Galloway (1999, 2006) and others (Mason 2006) have provided guidance on methods for the appropriate use of historical records and Native oral history in the archaeological study of colonialism. Consistent with the direct historical approach, the bulk of this effort has focused on identifying archaeological remnants of specific villages mentioned in texts or depicted in images. For example, exact site locations may be deduced based on descriptions of terrain; proximity to identifiable natural features such as bodies of water, islands, mountains, or distinctive geological formations; spatial relationships to other groups for whom colonial-era cultural geography is already clearly understood; or all of these lines of evidence together. Moreover, specific images that can be tied to a location through these or other methods may allow researchers to recognize the size, layout, major constituents, or feature locations within a particular village instead of simply identifying the site location.

Use of ethnohistorical texts, historical visual items, early ethnographic sources, oral histories, and archaeological records in concert, however, also has significant potential to support the development of regionally specific expectations—as opposed to site-specific conclusions—about the typical location, nature, and constituents of Indigenous sites of the colonial era (see also Kretzler, this volume). Development of such expectations is especially important for study in hinterland areas as archaeologists consider if and how precolonial and postcolonial site components may differ from each other (e.g., Jordan, this volume). For example, drawing on Native oral history, ethnohistoric records, ethnographic observations, and archaeological data from various areas of North America, Hull (2009, 156–177) has enumerated several expectations for the indirect effects of colonialism on Indigenous people related to introduced disease. These expectations can inform field identification of post-1492 Indigenous sites in hinterland areas where such fatal diseases were known or were believed to have spread before Native encountered non-Native people face to face.

By choice or by chance, cultural consequences for individuals, households, or entire groups resulting from demographic collapse in the wake of fatal epidemics include the aggregation or emigration of survivors, creolization or hybridity in material culture, ethnogenesis, changes in external relations and regional interaction, decreasing cultural diversity as a result of the founder effect, and despecialization and simplification of social structures (Hull 2009, 156–177). The material manifestations of these processes will differ by region based on the epidemiology of the disease within the population and the practices that existed before catastrophic depopulation, so archaeological expectations based on such processes must be regionally specific and the pre-1492 archaeological record must be well understood. Nonetheless, some broad similarities between regions in terms of material consequences emerge from cross-cultural analysis (Hull 2009). For example, predictions for the Yosemite area that may pertain elsewhere include the following:

- the use of natural features such as rock shelters rather than constructed dwellings when a group initially reoccupied an area after temporary abandonment
- a reduction in village size and number (e.g., Jordan, this volume)
- focused habitation in especially productive zones
- separate villages or neighborhoods within villages when a group formed contingent communities through emigration (see Bernard and Robinson 2018; Kretzler, this volume)
- material assertion of group identity in pluralistic Native communities
- potential blending of cultural traditions within multiethnic Native households
- shifts in the type and abundance of nonlocal goods such as lithic materials acquired through exchange
- a temporary decline in the skills needed to produce particular items as capable practitioners were lost to disease
- cessation of practices of specialists and concomitant disappearance of the paraphernalia pertaining thereto

As these examples demonstrate, a series of expectations that encompass individual and group choice or chance that had material consequences may provide foci for fieldwork or site detection.

Beyond these broad expectations, expectations for potential site formation and constituents at a smaller scale can be derived through examination of historic photographs and other images. For example, such study may be useful in determining the spatial arrangements of typical villages, including the number of, layout of, and distances between structures, hearths, and work areas. Historical images may also indicate differences between villages given the season of use, types of activities undertaken, or implements used on site. Images may indicate the presence of camp dogs or the pursuit of particular practices that are important for taphonomic processes (see also Laluk, this volume) and thus for the interpretation of remains. While the specific village depicted may remain unknown, textual and visual data can be used to derive expectations about general site location and intrasite use, just as ethnoarchaeology and general ethnographic analogies are used to establish archaeological expectations and infer formation and structure for sites dating to the more distant past. Such data can also prompt the development of appropriate archaeological survey or excavation strategies for identifying sites or features within sites (see below).

As Hull (2009, Chapter 2) has detailed, ethnohistoric sources for the Yosemite area date back to initial Euro-American incursions into Yosemite Valley in 1851 (Figure 8.1). They include Indigenous oral histories; ethnohistoric accounts of miners, military men, travelers, and innkeepers; and paintings, photographs, and other images of Native villages. The Yosemite area record is especially rich in images, given the allure of the landscape for artists such as Albert Bierstadt, Thomas Hill, and William Keith (Ogden 1993). Likewise, renowned photographers including Eadweard Muybridge and Carleton Watkins produced images ranging from small stereographs to oversize glass, or "mammoth" plates that captured natural views and the daily life of Native or non-Native people. The dramatic topography of Yosemite Valley in particular provides a backdrop that facilitates the location of specific sites in the image view.

Systematic ethnographic study of Yosemite Native people began in the early 1900s with the work of naturalist C. Hart Merriam, followed shortly thereafter by the efforts of anthropologist Samuel Barrett (Barrett 1908, 1919; Merriam 1907, 1910, 1917). These references complement observations of early Yosemite visitors (Powers [1877] 1976) and residents (Clark [1907] 1987), who produced early ethnographies. Some of the ethnographic information Merriam collected remains unpublished, but one particularly important published report provides the names and locational information for thirty-seven village or camp sites in Yosemite Valley and several additional sites downstream along the Merced River (Merriam 1917).

While Merriam's (1917) work has been consistently referenced in archaeological study of post-1850 Indigenous life in Yosemite (McCarthy 1999, 448), realization of the full potential of other historic textual and visual records has lagged. For example, Lafayette Bunnell's (1990) account of the Mariposa Battalion's foray into Yosemite Valley in 1851 includes information about village locations and size, features such as dwellings and food caches, and traditional and non-Native tools, gear, and foods. Importantly, this book also records Native oral history regarding population collapse due to disease, which archaeological and other data now date to the 1790s, preceding direct interaction with non-Native people (Hull 2009). The memoir of Belgian miner Jean-Nicolas Perlot (1985), which details his life mining the streams of the south-central Sierra Nevada from 1852 to 1857, includes similar information. Prominent early innkeepers such as Galen Clark ([1907] 1987) and James Hutchings (1888) often made notes about Yosemite Indian life during the late 1800s, while visitor accounts and intimate photographs of this period include both portraits and scenes of Native campsites that document houses, utensils, and people at work (see also Clark [1907] 1987, 29). Bates and Lee (1990), who enumerate several of these observations in their study of changing basketry traditions, note that Indigenous settlements were often unobtrusive or were simply unseen, evidently reflecting the marginalization of Native people as non-Native settlement increased.

What specific information can be gleaned from these sources to facilitate identification and enhance interpretation of archaeological deposits dating to the colonial era and later periods of American hegemony in the Yosemite area? One example in Perlot's (1985, 188) particularly rich and sympathetic account of the Native people he interacted with during his time prospecting in the Merced River area is his mention of a "camp [consisting] of three villages, whose huts, scattered as if at random, resembled enormous beehives." In 1854, Perlot was led to this village by two Native men, one of whom was the son of the village chief. While specific geographic data are compromised somewhat in the published English version of Perlot's memoir since the editor omitted details because he believed that such information would "add little to the narrative, or to the historical record" (Lamar 1985, xiii), information is sufficient to infer that Perlot was referring to a village in present-day El Portal (see Figure 8.1)—likely site CA-MRP-250/H. Naturalist C. Hart Merriam (1917) recorded this village location at the turn of the twentieth century with the Miwuk name Po-ko-nó. At that time, Merriam noted that the site included "a number of circular depressions marking the sites of former bark houses" (quoted in Hull and Acevedo 2015, 19).

Situated on three adjacent knolls that may correspond to the three villages of Perlot, CA-MRP-250/H was subject to archaeological investigations for compliance work in the early 1980s, including excavation within one of several apparent house pit depressions (Baumler and Carpenter 1982). This investigation resulted in the identification of a compact house floor and recovery of a Green River knife blade, a metal buckle, glass beads, and other items consistent with occupation in the 1850s. Subsequent archaeological excavations at CA-MRP-250/H (Burton et al. 2004; Riley 1987) focused on other site areas and the authors did not attribute additional items of non-Native manufacture found in these areas (other than a few glass beads) to Indigenous use, despite Baumler and Carpenter's (1982) results. As is typical for sites occupied by residentially mobile hunter-gatherers (see also Laluk, this volume), the circa 1850s component exists as a sparse, shallow deposit on a site that reveals episodic use in various areas dating back at least to 1200 BCE and perhaps as early 6000 BCE (Baumler and Carpenter 1982; Hull and Acevedo 2015; Riley 1987).

Since Perlot's (1985) memoir was unknown at the time the original archaeological work was undertaken at CA-MRP-250/H, the post-1492 Native component was originally recognized based primarily on the presence of artifacts of non-Native manufacture, evidently affirming affiliation with Merriam's (1917) Po-ko-nó and consistent with the memories of Maria Lebrado (Bates and Wells 1981, 5; Baumler and Carpenter 1982, 24). However, the juxtaposition of the new textual and material evidence that is now possible makes this site especially important as a source of archaeological data on the Gold Rush experience of Yosemite Native people. Perlot's account provides the names of some of the Indigenous inhabitants and insight into their struggles, such as their intimate knowledge of the treaty they had signed, which Perlot (1985, 189) noted "the *old man* knew from memory" (emphasis in original). This detailed ethnohistoric picture allows us to understand and appreciate even more deeply what the material record reveals. Moreover,

Perlot's identification of "three villages" may indicate an aggregate village or contingent community. This suggests not only the potential for addressing important questions pertaining to Indigenous experience of Euro-American colonialism and later American hegemony but also the need to develop an appropriate field strategy for obtaining relevant data in any future study of late Native occupation at this site.

Another example of specific site identification through sources other than material remains is a Yosemite Valley summer village depicted in images produced in 1873 by both painter Albert Bierstadt and photographer Eadweard Muybridge. In particular, Muybridge's ten photographs of this village in his "Indians of California" stereograph series provide an intimate view of the spaces, dwellings, sweatbaths, baskets, domestic tools, clothing, and activities of Native men, women, and children, revealing an exceptionally detailed portrait of daily life at this time. Based on broader views of the site both Bierstadt and Muybridge produced, the exact location of the village in Yosemite Valley has been confirmed through repeat photography (Figure 8.2). Work currently underway that juxtaposes historic and modern photographs may ultimately make possible virtual placement of the dwellings and other structures on the site using GIS. In this case, however, it seems that archaeological data will not be available to complement the visual records, since the village was located on a sand bar along the Merced River from which all archaeological traces have been erased by seasonal flooding and deposition. Still, these data prompt us to consider why Indigenous people chose this location and how such a seasonal camp related spatially and socially to non-Native development and to more permanent Native villages that were present in Yosemite Valley in the 1870s. This example is also important because it demonstrates habitation on a landform that is not typically anticipated to have been used for occupation by Indigenous people given expectations based on the extant archaeological record. The use of historic photographs to identify colonial-era and later Indigenous sites can challenge biases based on the pre-1492 archaeological record and opens our eyes to potentially marginalized settlement after Euro-American incursion and displacement of Indigenous people (see Jordan, this volume; Kretzler, this volume). As Panich and Schneider (2019, 664) suggest, developing such methods can "more fully capture the various ways that Indigenous people used ancestral sites after the arrival of Europeans—potentially unobtrusive patterns that have often gone unrecorded in existing regional site inventories."

Figure 8.2. Comparison of Albert Bierstadt's *Indians in Council, California* (1872, *top*) with photograph of same location in 2019 (*bottom*). Bierstadt image courtesy of Smithsonian American Art Museum, Gift of Marvin J. and Shirley F. Sonosky in memory of Harryette Cohn; 2019 photograph by Kathleen L. Hull.

A third example of the use of diverse data sources in Yosemite Valley pertains to site CA-MRP-62, a rock shelter that Hull (2009) initially identified as a potential colonial-era site based on the ethnographic work of C. Hart Merriam. Merriam (1917) recorded this locale as the village of He-le'-jah, given information he received in the early 1900s. Equally important, however, is that habitation in a rock shelter is consistent with general expectations for Indigenous reoccupation of Yosemite Valley following self-imposed exile in the wake of catastrophic depopulation in the 1790s (Hull 2009, 213). Archaeological investigations carried out at this site about twenty years ago revealed the presence of several glass beads and horse bones that confirmed use of the site around 1820. In addition, a shallow, tray-like feature made up of one to two layers of parallel strips of cedar bark and a surrounding "rim" of cedar and pine bark was discovered within the rock shelter. Some of the ends of these cedar strips exhibited axe cuts, indicating manufacture with the aid of metal tools, and small fragments of non-Native textiles including blue denim, a coarse navy blue cotton, and a finer tan cotton with a faded red floral design were found in and around the feature. The association of heavy textiles such as denim with this feature may indicate use of the fabric as a lining or covering of some type, or perhaps a wrapping or sack to contain vegetal material within the feature. In any case, this feature clearly relates to Indigenous use of the site after entanglements with Euro-Americans and ready access to non-Native goods. Thus, the ability to initially identify this site through documentary data, assess its potential to date to the period of interest based on general expectations derived through cross-cultural ethnohistoric research, and confirm affiliation of post-1850 use through material evidence led to the discovery of a feature dating to mid-nineteenth century Indigenous life that had never before been identified in the Yosemite area.

Pursuing Innovative Archaeological Approaches to Identify Sites

Once potential Indigenous sites that date after 1492 have been identified through documents, other media, material evidence, or some combination of sources, additional detailed analyses of archaeological data present at such sites can lead to recognition of particular traits or subtle practices indicative of colonial-era, or later, Indigenous occupation, consistent with Panich and Schneider's (2019, 662) call to "expand the kinds of material evidence used to mark Indigenous use or residence." As the examples above highlight, potential components at sites in colonial hinterland areas that are initially identified through site-specific data or conformity to general expectations based on knowledge of the indirect effects of colonialism must always be confirmed through archaeological field and laboratory methods. Development of such methods must be sensitive to the nature of the archaeological record in a region and, to the greatest extent possible, must take advantage of the particular strengths of that record. Methods must be suited to the processes of site formation, must confirm chronology at the finest scale possible, and must allow for derivation of data on daily life sufficient to address a range of issues, including the specific indirect effects of colonialism.

To assess site formation, site-specific field studies undertaken to examine colonial-era Indigenous experience require the application of archaeological field methods that are different from those that are commonly used to sample deposits to assess integrity and data potential as part of compliance studies. Specifically, broad areal excavation is appropriate for research issues relating to colonial-era entanglements (see Lightfoot 1995), as this strategy facilitates intrasite spatial analysis—including identification of features suggested by documentary or visual sources—and subsequent intersite assemblage comparisons that lead to better understandings of Indigenous persistence. As Lightfoot (1995, 209) has discussed (see also Hull 2009, 47), the typical compliance focus of excavation on a relatively small number of, deep, noncontiguous 1-by-1-meter units to define site boundaries and sample all site components does not provide a spatially coherent dataset for interpreting the context of use of the items recovered. Fortunately, colonial-era and later Indigenous deposits are often present at or very near the surface, so excavation over extensive areas is often feasible. For example, excavation of a contiguous 1-by-9-meter transect to a maximum of 20 centimeters deep from the front to the back of the CA-MRP-62 rock shelter enabled me to identify both the tray feature noted above and the hearth at the dripline where most of the glass beads and other cultural materials were found (Hull 2009, 194). It is unlikely that both of these features would have been identified through more limited excavation. The broad excavation also enabled me to consider the spatial arrangement of these features and other cultural debris observed at the site.

As Panich and Schneider (2019) have noted, colonial-era occupation can often be confirmed after completing fieldwork through various absolute dating methods instead of relying on the presence of non-Native goods. Radiocarbon assays or obsidian hydration dating or both may be possible depending on the types of cultural materials present, although the statistical error associated with both methods means that it is not always possible to provide the fine-grained chronological information that is generally desired. In addition, source-specific differences in the rate of obsidian hydration and variations in environmental factors such as temperature that affect hydration rate may make this technique more—or less—effective in a given area (Friedman and Smith 1960; Mazer et al. 1991). For example, reliance on an obsidian that hydrates especially slowly or dating deposits in high-elevation sites that have a lower effective hydration temperature may preclude use of this technique for identifying colonial-era deposits. The rates of hydration typical for the obsidians Indigenous people used in central California, however, indicate that obsidian artifacts relating to colonial-era use tend to exhibit less than 1.2 microns of hydration (e.g., Hull 2009; Panich et al. 2018). Since hydration rims that are less than approximately 0.7 microns generally cannot be discerned via standard microscopic techniques used for hydration dating (Hull 2009, 126), colonial-era and later components are most readily identified by the presence of a high proportion of artifacts with no visible hydration that lack evidence of damage by fire or other factors that might remove hydration rims (Hull 2009; Silliman 2005).

Additional chronological data may be provided through reference to general material expectations for indirect effects of colonialism, detailed laboratory analysis of artifacts from likely colonial-era components, and rigorous comparison of individual artifacts and assemblages from such components with those of pre-1492 components. Such methods can help researchers identify "index artifacts" of Indigenous manufacture during the colonial era rather than objects of non-Native manufacture or materials. General expectations for evidence of the effects of catastrophic depopulation include potential changes in the artifact assemblage diversity, a decline in the technical expertise necessary to produce tools, and despecialization in social life that would have material manifestations in the archaeological record. Thus, laboratory methods designed to identify differences between pre- and post-1492 assemblages must include detailed technological (rather than simply functional or stylistic) analysis of lithic, bone, ceramic, or other tools. For example, technological analysis of flaked-stone tools should be sufficient to identify manufacturing errors such as overshot damage or perverse fractures from notching failures on bifaces, exhaustive use of materials through bipolar reduction given the possible disruptions in traditional exchange systems, and changes in the sequence of reduction (e.g., blank types, basal thinning) or final finishing of tools (e.g., serration, notching for hafting) that reflect different production traditions that were introduced to or replaced local traditions as Native people relocated in the wake of demographic collapse. Likewise, instrumental methods of tracing source materials (e.g., X-ray fluorescence analysis) are required to identify changes in the source and quantity of exotic materials because of deteriorating traditional exchange systems or demographic shifts that disrupted trade. While the range of source materials may be the same, the relative abundance of different materials may have shifted significantly as external relations deteriorated or movement was restricted. Technological data that complement geochemical provenance data can be used to infer potential shifts in the form in which materials were acquired and subsequently used.

In the Yosemite area, such data have been used to further refine chronologies of Indigenous colonial-era and later occupation and to identify temporal markers that can be used to recognize colonial-era components at sites that evidently lack other material indicators of post-1492 Native use. For example, decades of obsidian hydration research in the central Sierra Nevada now allows archaeologists to confidently conclude that the latest Native lithic use is represented in components with only, or a high percentage of, specimens with no visible hydration band (Hull 2009). As noted above, this observation is consistent with data that are emerging from throughout central California. The only exception is if there is evidence to suggest that post-depositional thermal damage from hearths or wildfires likely removed hydration rims, thereby resulting in a similar abundance of specimens with no visible hydration.

As another example, the archaeological excavations at CA-MRP-62 noted above revealed the presence of several serrate Desert Side-notched projectile points in addition to glass beads, horse bones, axe-cut bark, and woven textile fragments. While Desert Side-notched points are common in the Sierra Nevada and are a well-known temporal marker for post-1200 CE Indigenous presence in this region and elsewhere in east-central California (Baumhoff and Byrne 1959; Justice 2002, 379–388), the relatively high percentage of specimens with serrate edges at CA-MRP-62 suggests that this trait relates specifically to colonial-era Native life (Hull 2009). Importantly, subsequent review of regional archaeological literature (Hull 2004) confirmed the temporal association of serrate Desert Side-notched points with nineteenth-century Indigenous occupation in Yosemite. This trait apparently represents the fusion of an existing point style with a tradition of point serration that was likely introduced as Native people were displaced into the Sierra Nevada and the adjoining foothills as the Spanish colonial presence in central California expanded.

A third example of a potential trait that is primarily related to post-1800 occupation in the Yosemite area is the use of bedrock milling slicks for processing vegetal food. While dating of the onset of bedrock milling technology in the Sierra Nevada remains elusive, it appears that initial use of bedrock mortars dates no later than circa 1300 CE in the central and southern Sierra Nevada (Stevens et al. 2019). However, as Hull (2007) has discussed (see also Hull and Acevedo 2015), geographic differences exist in the distribution of bedrock mortar cups that are more than 9.5 centimeters deep and bedrock milling slicks. Ethnographic data suggest that each of these technologies relates to the milling of seeds rather than acorns (McCarthy 1985). Thus, the differential distribution of slicks and deep mortars may relate to group-specific milling preferences. In the Yosemite area, milling slicks are more common than deep mortars in areas north of Wawona (see Figure 8.1), and Hull (2009, 188; Hull and Acevedo 2015) has suggested that this may relate to frequent intermarriage between Yosemite Native men and Mono Paiute women after many people of the Yosemite region temporarily relocated to the east side of the mountains due to catastrophic depopulation in the late 1700s. That is, milling stones and manos were the traditional tools Paiute women used to process vegetal materials, so the prevalence of bedrock milling slicks in the Yosemite area may relate to the influx of Paiute women and the legacy of their descendants after the Native people reoccupied their land in Yosemite in the 1800s. Thus, the presence or abundance of such features at a given site may serve as a chronological indicator of post-1800 occupation in the region.

Geochemical data for a random sample of obsidian debitage from the component that dates to the early 1800s at CA-MRP-62 also underscore differences between pre- and post-1492 components in Yosemite in the relative representation of eastern California obsidians. Specifically, Mono Craters obsidian is most common at CA-MRP-62 (where it makes up approximately 53 percent of the late component debitage sample; Hull 2009, Table 6), whereas Casa Diablo obsidian dominates debitage assemblages from sites in Yosemite Valley that date to the more distant past (Hull 2009, 204–205; Hull and Roper 1999). Since the domes and flows that make up the Mono Craters source did not form until after circa 1345 CE (Sieh and Bursik 1986) and this locale is closer to Yosemite Valley than any other obsidian source, the higher proportion of Mono Craters obsidian at CA-MRP-62 is not unexpected (Hull 2002). Nonetheless, this assemblage characteristic may be added to the emerging suite of traits that serve to identify colonial-era Indigenous occupation in this region. While the Native tradition of scavenging obsidian from earlier deposits on the western slope of the Sierra Nevada (Hull and Roper 1999) complicates simplistic conclusions based on geochemical analysis alone, the potential for obsidian geochemistry to contribute to recognition of colonial-era Indigenous use argues for the routine incorporation of such techniques in archaeological studies that seek to identify such components in this region and perhaps in other regions. Significantly, edge-modified glass has only rarely been identified in Yosemite sites (see McCarthy 1999, 448), and no glass or ceramic projectile points have ever been recovered. Moreover, this pattern is consistent with the data from the Owens Valley to the east of the Sierra Nevada (see McGuire 1992) but contrasts markedly with archaeological results from some foothill areas both north and south of Yosemite. For example, projectile points of bottle glass have been found at both Hidden Reservoir on the Fresno River and at New Melones Reservoir on the Stanislaus River (see Moratto 1984, 325; 1999). The apparent rejection of non-Native material for projectile manufacture in Yosemite may reflect the fact that Native people continued to access traditional lithic materials such as obsidian or that foreign raw materials were not readily available or desirable as a replacement (see also Bamforth 1993). While not sufficient on its own to unequivocally identify colonial-era Indigenous use, a relatively high proportion of Mono Craters obsidian in a debitage assemblage coupled with a significant number of obsidian specimens with no visible hydration should prompt a closer look for other indicators of potential colonial-era Indigenous use at sites in Yosemite and elsewhere in eastern California.

As these examples demonstrate, recognizing new index artifacts of colonial-era Indigenous occupation can be accomplished only with knowledge of and reference to the unique histories and the specific nature of the archaeological record in an area. Details about Indigenous life derived through analysis of ethnohistoric documentary, visual records, and Native oral history (Kretzler, this volume) provide clues about the types of archaeological data that may be relevant to this task. In hinterland areas, in particular, archaeologists cannot rely on presence of non-Native goods to identify relevant site components, especially because Native people in some areas evidently avoided incorporating non-Native materials into traditional technologies even when those materials were available. As Lightfoot (1995) has emphasized, however, using fine-grained archaeological data to identify post-1492 Native use is possible only if there is a good understanding of the archaeological record of earlier periods. That level of knowledge enables researchers to make detailed comparisons and identify subtle differences that might otherwise go unnoticed or unappreciated.

Iterative Feedback

A final crucial step in identifying post-1492 Indigenous sites or site components is feeding the full suite of archaeological data from sites known to date to the colonial era or later back into the site identification process. This iterative practice helps build new or bolster emerging chronological indicators and identify new sites based on often-subtle differences between pre- and post-1492 components. Once a researcher has recognized Indigenous sites, components, assemblages, or artifact characteristics that can be confidently dated to the eighteenth or nineteenth centuries based on documentary or material evidence, they need to look for such data at other sites that might provide further material attributes that date to particular eras after 1492. For example, since Hull (2009) first associated prevalent use of serrate Desert Side-notched projectile points with post-1850 occupation in Yosemite, serrate Desert series points have been identified at several additional sites, both in existing collections and through subsequent compliance investigations (e.g., Curtis 2012).

In this sense, the research strategy outlined here echoes the direct historical approach of a previous generation of archaeological work. However, instead of using sites relating to Native use after 1492 CE that have been identified through this method as a jumping-off point to trace the culture history of a group further back in time, the material evidence at such sites might be used to define narrow slices of time after the indirect or direct effects of colonialism to trace Indigenous practice and persistence from the time Euro-American incursion began in the Americas.

Discussion and Conclusions

As Panich and Schneider (2019, 662) note, "Accounting for a broader range of Indigenous experiences under colonialism requires that . . . archaeologists have a thorough understanding of the culture-historical developments in the areas they work, including the possibilities of postcontact Indigenous presence." This includes understanding the potential for and likely consequences of the indirect effects of colonialism in hinterland areas. Regional knowledge is also key to developing strategies and carrying out the studies that are needed to identify Indigenous sites or components of this period. This chapter has focused on how diverse archaeological and non-archaeological methods and data can be used to help archaeologists recognize specific sites or develop general expectations that have potential material manifestations in the archaeological record. Such expectations can, in turn, inform field and laboratory methods both to enhance potential identification of relevant deposits and to identify morphological and technological changes in implements or the proportional representation of tools or materials in assemblages that have their roots in demographic shifts in the wake of disease.

While the discussion here has illustrated this approach through examples from the Yosemite area, similar aspects of site location, formation, structure, and constituents might serve equally well in other geographic or temporal contexts where non-Native artifacts might not be as useful for recognizing colonial-era and later Indigenous sites. The potential now exists to define research strategies that explicitly address the research potential of components that represent Indigenous occupation in the colonial era and later, including protocols for conducting archival research before fieldwork is undertaken, appropriate archaeological survey and excavation methods, and analytical techniques suited to the archaeological materials that are likely to be present. Moreover, such methods can and should be incorporated into regional research designs that guide agency and consultant compliance work so that sufficient and appropriate fieldwork is undertaken to assess site significance. Archaeologists need to think creatively and in very detailed ways, searching for often-subtle differences in the archaeological record in kind or quantity that can facilitate recognition of post-1492 Indigenous habitation and use. Through such methods, archaeologists can make visible what heretofore has often been considered invisible for this critical period in Indigenous people's negotiation of their lives, their identities, and their sovereignty in the wake of colonialism.

References Cited

Bamforth, Douglas. 1993. Stone Tools, Steel Tools: Contact Period Household Technology at Helo. In *Ethnohistory and Archaeology: Approaches to Postcontact Change in the Americas*, edited by J. Daniel Rogers and Samuel M. Wilson, 49–72. New York: Plenum Press.

Barrett, Samuel A. 1908. The Geography and Dialects of the Miwok Indians. *University of California Publications in American Archaeology and Ethnology* 6(2): 333–368.

———. 1919. Myths of the Southern Sierra Miwok. *University of California Publications in American Archaeology and Ethnology* 16(1): 1–28.

Bates, Craig D., and Martha J. Lee. 1990. *Tradition and Innovation: A Basket History of the Indians of the Yosemite-Mono Lake Region*. Yosemite, CA: Yosemite Association.

Bates, Craig D., and Karen P. Wells. 1981. *Late Aboriginal and Early Anglo Occupation of El Portal, Yosemite National Park, California*. Tucson, AZ: USDI National Park Service, Western Archeological and Conservation Center.

Baumhoff, Martin A., and J. S. Byrne. 1959. Desert Side-Notched Points as a Time Marker in California. *University of California Archaeological Survey Reports* 48: 32–65. Berkeley.

Baumler, Mark F., and Scott L. Carpenter. 1982. *Archeological Investigations in the Central Sierra Nevada: The 1981 El Portal Project*. Publications in Anthropology No. 20. Tucson, AZ: USDI National Park Service, Western Archeological and Conservation Center.

Bernard, Julienne, and David W. Robinson. 2018. Contingent Communities in a Region of Refuge. In *Forging Communities in Colonial Alta California*, edited by K. L. Hull and J. G. Douglass, 113–132. Tucson: University of Arizona Press.

Bunnell, Lafayette Houghton. 1990. *1990 Discovery of the Yosemite and the Indian War of 1851 which Led to That Event*. Yosemite Association, Yosemite. Reprint of 4th edition. Los Angeles, CA: G. W. Gerlicher.

Burton, Jeffery F., Lynne M. Bucher, and Danielle Desruisseax. 2004. *Archeology along the Merced River: Test Excavations at Three Sites at El Portal Yosemite National Park, California*. Yosemite Research Center Publications in Anthropology 26. Yosemite, CA: USDI National Park Service, Yosemite Research Center.

Clark, Galen. (1907) 1987. *Indians of the Yosemite Valley and Vicinity*. Walnut Creek, CA: Diablo Books.

Curtis, David L. 2012. *Archeological Survey for the 2011 Wilderness Restoration Program, Yosemite National Park, California*. Yosemite, CA: USDI, National Park Service, Branch of Anthropology, Division of Resources Management and Science.

Friedman, Irving, and Robert L. Smith. 1960. A New Dating Method Using Obsidian: Part 1, the Development of the Method. *American Antiquity* 25: 476–522.

Galloway, Patricia. 1999. The Archaeology of Ethnohistorical Narrative. In *Columbian Consequences*, vol. 3, *The Spanish Borderlands in Pan-American Perspective*, edited by David Hurst Thomas, 453–469. Washington, DC: Smithsonian Institution Press.

———. 2006. *Practicing Ethnohistory: Mining Archives, Hearing Testimony, Constructing Narrative*. Lincoln: University of Nebraska Press.

Hull, Kathleen L. 2002. The Temporal Significance of Mono Craters Obsidian and Pumice Exploitation. Paper presented at the 28th Biennial Great Basin Anthropological Conference, Elko, NV.

———. 2004. Emergent Cultural Traditions in the Central Sierra Nevada Foothills. *Society for California Archaeology Proceedings* 17: 113–118.

———. 2007. The Sierra Nevada: Archaeology in the Range of Light. In *California Prehistory: Colonization, Culture, and Complexity*, edited by T. Jones and K. Klar, 177–190. Walnut Creek, CA: AltaMira Press.

———. 2009. *Pestilence and Persistence: Yosemite Indian Demography and Culture in Colonial California*. Berkeley: University of California Press.

Hull, Kathleen L., and Shannon Acevedo. 2015. *Archeological and Anthropological Synthesis for the El Portal Administrative Site, Yosemite National Park*. University of California, Merced. Submitted to USDI National Park Service, Yosemite National Park, CA.

Hull, Kathleen L., and John G. Douglass, eds. 2018. *Forging Communities in Colonial Alta California*. Tucson: University of Arizona Press.

Hull, Kathleen L., and C. Kristina Roper. 1999. Obsidian Studies. In *Archeological Synthesis and Research Design, Yosemite National Park, California*, by Kathleen L. Hull and Michael J. Moratto, 297–355. Yosemite Research Center Publications in Anthropology 21. Yosemite, CA: USDI National Park Service Yosemite Research Center.

Hunter, Ryan, Stephen W. Silliman, and David B. Langdon. 2014. Shellfish Collection and Community Connections in Eighteenth-Century Native New England. *American Antiquity* 79: 712–729.

Hutchings, James M. 1888. *In the Heart of the Sierras*. Oakland, CA: Pacific Press Publishing House.

Justice, Noel D. 2002. *Stone Age Spear and Arrow Points for California and the Great Basin*. Bloomington: Indiana University Press.

Lamar, Howard R. 1985. Editor's Preface and Acknowledgments. In *Gold Seeker: Adventures of a Belgian Argonaut during the Gold Rush Years*, by Jean-Nicolas Perlot, xiii–xiv. New Haven, CT: Yale University Press.

Liebmann, Matthew. 2012. *Revolt: An Archaeological History of Pueblo Resistance and Revitalization in 17th Century New Mexico*. Tucson: University of Arizona Press.

Lightfoot, Kent G. 1995. Culture Contact Studies: Redefining the Relationship between Prehistoric and Historical Archaeology. *American Antiquity* 60: 199–217.

Mason, Ronald J. 2006. *Inconstant Companions: Archaeology and North American Indian Oral Tradition*. Tuscaloosa: University of Alabama Press.

Mazer, J. J., C. M. Stevenson, W. L. Ebert, and J. K. Bates. 1991. The Experimental Hydration of Obsidian as a Function of Relative Humidity and Temperature. *American Antiquity* 56: 504–513.

McCarthy, Helen. 1985. Ethnographic Background. In *Cultural Resources of the Crane Valley*

Hydroelectric Project Area, Madera County, California. Vol. 1, Ethnographic, Historic, and Archaeological Overviews and Archaeological Survey, edited by Susan K. Goldberg, 43–70. INFOTEC Research, Inc., Sonora, CA. Submitted to Pacific Gas and Electric Company, San Francisco, CA.

———. 1999. Historical Context for Native American Historical Archeology. In Archeological Synthesis and Research Design, Yosemite National Park, California, by Kathleen L. Hull and Michael J. Moratto, 411–456. Yosemite Research Center Publications in Anthropology 21. Yosemite, CA: USDI National Park Service Yosemite Research Center.

McGuire, Kelly R. 1992. Post-Contact Paiute Culture Change in the Inyo-Mono Region of Eastern California. Paper presented at the Twenty-Third Biennial Great Basin Anthropological Conference, Boise, ID.

Merriam, C. Hart. 1907. Distribution and Classification of the Mewan Stock of California. American Anthropologist 9: 338–357.

———. 1910. The Dawn of the World: Myths and Weird Tales Told by the Mewan Indians of California. Cleveland, OH: Arthur H. Clark Company.

———. 1917. Indian Villages and Camp Sites in Yosemite Valley. Sierra Club Bulletin 10(2): 202–209.

Moratto, Michael J. 1984. California Archaeology. Academic Press, New York.

———. 1999. Cultural Chronology, 1: Regional Context. In Archeological Synthesis and Research Design, Yosemite National Park, California, by Kathleen L. Hull and Michael J. Moratto, 65–120. Yosemite Research Center Publications in Anthropology 21. Yosemite, CA: USDI National Park Service Yosemite Research Center.

Nelson, Peter A. 2019. Indigenous Refusal of Settler Colonialism in Nineteenth-Century Central California. In Indigenous Persistence in the Colonized Americas: Material and Documentary Perspectives on Entanglement, edited by Heather Law Pezzarossi, and Russell N. Sheptak, 169–186. Albuquerque: University of New Mexico Press.

Odgen, Kate Nearpass. 1993. Sublime Vistas and Scenic Backdrops: Nineteenth-Century Painters and Photographers in Yosemite. In Yosemite and Sequoia: A Century of California National Parks, edited by Richard J. Orsi, Alfred Runte, and Marlene Smith-Baranzini, 49–67. Berkeley: University of California Press.

Panich, Lee M. 2013. Archaeologies of Persistence: Reconsidering the Legacies of Colonialism in Native North America. American Antiquity 78: 105–122.

———. 2020. Narratives of Persistence: Indigenous Negotiations of Colonialism in Alta and Baja California. Tucson: University of Arizona Press.

Panich, Lee M., Ben Griffin, and Tsim D. Schneider. 2018. Native Acquisition of Obsidian in Colonial-Era Central California: Implications from Mission San José. Journal of Anthropological Archaeology 50: 1–11.

Panich, Lee M., and Tsim D. Schneider. 2019. Categorical Denial: Evaluating Post-1492 Indigenous Erasure in the Paper 2 Trail of American Archaeology. American Antiquity 84: 651–668.

———, eds. 2014. Indigenous Landscapes and Spanish Missions: New Perspectives from Archaeology and Ethnohistory. Tucson: University of Arizona Press.

Perlot, Jean-Nicolas. 1985. Gold Seeker: Adventures of a Belgian Argonaut during the Gold Rush Years. Translated by Helen Harding Bretnor. New Haven, CT: Yale University Press.

Powers, Stephen. (1877) 1976. Tribes of California. Berkeley: University of California Press.

Riley, Lynn M. 1987. Archeological Investigations in the Merced River Canyon: Report of the 1983

El Portal Archeological Project. Yosemite Research Center Publications in Anthropology 3. Yosemite, CA: USDI National Park Service, Yosemite Research Center.

Sieh, Kerry, and Marcus Bursik. 1986. Most Recent Eruption of the Mono Craters, Eastern Central California. *Journal of Geophysical Research* 91(B12): 12539–12571.

Silliman, Stephen. 2005. Obsidian Studies and the Archaeology of 19th-Century California. *Journal of Field Archaeology* 30: 75–94.

Stevens, Nathan E., Adrian R. Whitaker, and Jeffrey S. Rosenthal. 2019. Bedrock Mortars as Indicators of Territorial Behavior in the Sierra Nevada. *Quaternary International* 518: 57–58.

Steward, Julian. 1942. The Direct Historical Approach to Archaeology. *American Antiquity* 7: 337–343.

Wilcox, Michael V. 2009. *The Pueblo Revolt and the Mythology of Conquest.* Berkeley: University of California Press.

9

Looking at the World
through Rose-Colored Flaked Glass

HANNAH RUSSELL

Archaeological practice is deeply enmeshed in western forms of knowledge production (Atalay 2006; Cutajar 2008). Yet much of the gaze of American archaeology falls on Indigenous cultures, landscapes, places, and materials.[1] Problematically, much of standard American archaeological practice has divorced cultural places and materials from the Indigenous experience and especially from descendent communities, their recent histories, and their very deep histories (Steeves 2015b; Watkins 2000). As Paulette Steeves writes, "Impacts of cleaved and disrupted connections to the land across time and place enforced through Western knowledge production are intimately tied to archaeological denial of the deep Indigenous past; enforcing embedded erasure and Indigenous ownership of the past and present."[2] She continues, "For Indigenous people there is no separation between the past and the present, all time and all history are crucial to culture and wellbeing. Rupturing connections between the present and the past, as archaeology has done, has been a very violent and destructive historic event."[3] Reparations for that violence within archaeology will take time, self-reflection, a great deal of collaboration, and an expansion of how we collect, think about, identify, and interact with the cultural materials and places of Indigenous peoples across all archaeological professions. Above all, we must commit to recognizing and dismantling the harm we do.

Societal, institutional, and disciplinary biases permeate archaeological method and theory. Undoubtedly as a result of western biases in our archaeological epistemologies and methodologies, many Indigenous and other non-western cultural heritages, places, and materials have fallen on blind eyes, resulting in a failure to consistently recognize, validate, document, and value those places and things. These issues weigh particularly heavy on the compliance archaeology sector (see Beaudoin, this volume).

I am a white archaeologist in compliance archaeology (cultural resource management) contending with my own limitations and privileges while navigating the privilege and limitations of archaeology generally.[4] As others have pointed out, the work of owning our own privileges is critical to deconstructing the colonialist overtones of our industry so that we can learn from and work collaboratively with descendent communities for better and more thoughtful cultural preservation, stewardship, and management (McDavid 2007). Despite important advances in archaeological practice toward the multiple evidence base approach, decolonialist narratives, and traditional knowledges, understanding the effects of archaeological bias continues to be a work in progress that is the topic of debate. This volume is specifically focused on how these substantial and ongoing archaeological biases adversely influence the identification and documentation of post-1492 Indigenous cultural expressions. I address this topic from a compliance archaeology perspective in the United States, focusing specifically on such routine aspects of fieldwork as site recording practices.

Archaeological site forms, a primary mechanism for collecting site data are a staple in the compliance archaeology toolkit. As a tool based in western objectivism and the long history of colonialized archaeology, site forms are rife with institutionalized bias and reflect and enable the biases of archaeologists as they record sites, creating a closed circuit that facilitates and perpetuates bias and the collection of bad data (Beaudoin 2016; Panich and Schneider 2019).[5] This is especially true since site forms seek to collect data about a site's cultural materials, which are predominately divided into "prehistoric" and "historic" material classes on these forms.

Postcontact Indigenous sites or site components can include culturally ambiguous artifact types as a result of the integration of "nontraditional" materials that don't fit neatly into a site form's artifact classes of prehistoric (the domain of Indigenous peoples) and historic (the domain of non-Indigenous peoples). This is amplified when nontraditional materials were manipulated or repurposed in traditional and adaptive ways, leading some field archaeologists to inaccurately disregard important cultural signatures that challenge their preconceived biases about postcontact Indigenous archaeology. Flaked glass is an example of this phenomenon, as I will illustrate in greater detail below.

Compliance Archaeology, the Business of Section 106, and Site Form Determinism

Compliance archaeology is the most prolific, most regulated, and most regimented form of professional archaeology in the United States. In Utah in 2019, for example, the Utah State Historic Preservation Office (SHPO) issued 973 compliance archaeology project numbers (Deb Miller, personal communication 2020). As of March 2020, 184 were available to archaeologists with access to Utah SHPO's online database and the University of Utah Marriot Library database. A review of these 184 reports shows that these projects included nearly 32,000 acres of pedestrian archaeological survey and 700 recorded or updated archaeological sites. While Utah has a high density of sites and a high percentage of public lands, this snapshot illustrates the prevalence of National Historic Preservation Act (NHPA) Section 106 compliance archaeology projects.[6]

The volume of work performed in the compliance sector demonstrates the impact of compliance archaeology on the archaeological canon, but compliance archaeology is also incredibly consequential. Section 106 projects frequently provide the foundation for more in-depth archaeological research for all professional archaeological sectors. As a frontline regulation for the preservation and stewardship of historic properties, the Section 106 compliance archaeology process is tethered to undertakings that want to break ground for the successful completion of projects such as a housing complex, a mining operation, or an ecological restoration project. If compliance archaeologists make a bad National Register of Historic Places (NRHP) eligibility recommendation or miss a component or quality of a non-eligible site, that site and the information it contains may very well be lost forever to a pipeline or a parking lot.[7] Even sites that are not NRHP eligible contribute to the story of the cultural landscape. It is partly because of the potentially irreversible ramifications of compliance archaeology that this sector of the discipline is as regulated and regimented as it is. The qualifications of professionals are vetted, nearly every project goes through at least two layers of review, compliance archaeology projects typically need to be permitted, methodologies are standardized, and site forms and final reports are formulaic. The process is streamlined.

It is important to remember that private sector compliance archaeology is a business that relies on competitive bidding, building and maintaining strong and positive client and agency relationships, and managing profit margins and budgets. For field crews, the practicalities of archaeological business mean hitting survey acreage totals and site recording numbers. Further, the preparation of compliance archaeological reports and final draft site forms is constrained by time limits and lack of availability to resources that academic archaeologists can access more easily.

Archaeological fieldwork is hard. It requires long, physically demanding days and contending with biting bugs and critters, high temperatures above 100 degrees or below 32 degrees Fahrenheit, extreme and sometimes sudden weather, and challenging terrain. On top of the expectation that field crews will be especially hardy (and let's be honest, the bragging rights that go with such hardiness), they are also required to have specialized knowledge of the natural and cultural landscape, cultural features and materials, technology (both modern and archaeological), regulations, deep time, and modern and historic land use. In addition, there is much repetition and formulaic workflow, especially when recording sites. When recording the most common site types in Utah, field crews can easily record between three and six sites a day, which means that they are spending no more than a few hours at a site, during which time they must define the boundary of the site, fill out the site form, identify and record artifacts and features, map the site, and photograph the site, including any features or notable artifacts. This repetitive work is often done in strained situations: the weather might be extreme, crews might not have good rapport, a crew chief or project director might dislike certain site types or cultural materials, to give a few examples. Nevertheless, the vast majority of work done by compliance archaeologists is good. It is undertaken with consideration, enthusiasm, experience, knowledge, true interest in the field, and care for cultural stewardship. The practical challenges of fieldwork can compound the process and circumstances that make the recognition and consideration of nuance and anomaly (such as identifying a potential postcontact Indigenous presence at a site) much more difficult.

Site forms can aggravate the difficulty of identifying archaeological nuance and anomaly. Before delving too deeply into how site forms can complicate the site recording process, it is important to discuss their functionality and management value. Site forms standardize the site recording process. They tell those completing them which data points are most valued for management, consideration, interpretation, and consensus on the archaeological site. Without a standardized set of data points to collect, the management of archaeological sites would be impossible.

So how do site forms complicate recording sites with nuance, especially sites that fall outside of the standard precontact-postcontact paradigm? Site forms are deterministic. They are not all-knowing or comprehensive. They are (primarily) designed by archaeologists who have their own agendas, cultural and archaeological understandings, theoretical bents, preferred terminologies, priorities, and professional and academic biases. The data points from a site, as the site recorders understand and interpret them, either fit into the predetermined categories on a site form or they don't. If they do not fit, the data can easily be lost to the form or to the measurable metrics on the form. In statistical research and survey methodology studies, these elements of form design are known to influence response effect, or the variability in responses as a result of both the survey (form) design and the respondents' (site recorders') understanding, biases, and values (Bradburn 1983; Tourangeau et al. 2000, 2). While response effect can happen in many ways, essentially it is contingent on the development of the form and the quality of the data entered into it.

Site recording taps into our own attitudes about cultural and archaeological expressions.[8] If a site's cultural expression is aligned with the site recorder's culture and the valued data to be collected on the form is aligned with that culture, then all the elements of site recordation are in harmony (see Fischoff 1991; Tourangeau et al. 2000). Conversely, if one of those elements is discordant with the others (i.e., the site form doesn't expressly account for postcontact Indigenous sites, features, or materials or the site recorder is distrustful of potentially postcontact Indigenous cultural expressions), then the potential for losing data is much greater.

While site forms are a standard tool for managing archaeological sites, they are not without the capacity to do harm. Psychological survey research has been extensively used to develop the questions the US Census Bureau asks and the questions on standardized academic tests. Like an archaeological site form, both are examples of surveys intended to collect information about the lives of people.[9] The consequences of an adverse response effect in federal censuses and standardized testing is huge. These surveys affect funding for communities and the futures of students in classrooms and academic institutions. Without careful consideration of how the survey instruments are developed, censuses and standardized tests can lead to the absence of certain groups from the public record and from institutions of higher education, especially of Black people, Indigenous people, people of color, and women. The archaeological site form can lead to that same kind of erasure from the archaeological record (e.g., Ferris 2014; Silliman 2014; Steeves 2015b; Vizenor 2008; Wilcox 2014).

While site forms play a role in perpetuating biases against postcontact Indigenous archaeological documentation, response effect in archaeological data collection is shaped by the attitudes, beliefs, and understandings of the respondents (i.e., the site recorders). Bias is difficult to quantify, and the thing being discriminated against is easy to dismiss. There are probably no words spoken in archaeology with as much frequency and cynicism—and with as little merit—as "I don't like it." In my career, I have heard this line spoken about the antiquity of a can scatter, overly large flakes, flaked glass, and any number of subjective and biased field and lab calls related to material culture. There are real consequences to dismissing what we don't like at first glance. When we are dismissive of what challenges us, not only do we run the risk of making a bad National Register eligibility call, which has immediate im- plications, we also end up being dismissive of groups of people and activities that are poorly represented in the historical and archaeological records (see also Scheidecker et al., this volume). Skepticism in science is healthy. When skepticism veers into cynicism, though, it becomes a problem that causes real harm. We need to push ourselves beyond our cynical biases to be able to criti- cally quantify the things we "don't like" at first glance. No form of qualitative or quantitative research would ever accept "I don't like it" as a sound research result. Across all archaeological disciplines, this is terminology that needs to be dropped from our professional lexicon.

Traditional Knowledge, Indigenous Continuance, and the Historical Archaeological Record

The practice of archaeology is methodology informed by theory, even within the structure of contract archaeology. Increasingly, as this volume indicates, archaeologists are considering the adoption of non-Indigenous materials, knowledge, and technologies in postcontact Indigenous cultural contexts. Silliman (2005) and Scheiber and Finley (2010) have discussed these issues in terms of culture change and continuity and technological transitions. Lightfoot and Martinez (1995) discuss them in terms of creolization or syncretization. Still others discuss postcontact Indigenous peoples' adoption of mass-produced goods and technologies in terms of acculturation, an issue that has been discussed at great length elsewhere (Panich and Schneider 2019; Silliman 2005). In more recent years, Silliman has advanced the idea of survivance, a term coined by Gerald Vizenor (2008), who rooted the idea in the active presence of Indigenous people in defiance of victimization at the hands of colonialist powers. Silliman (2014) has expanded the term to include Indigenous agency and choice, especially in the face of struggle. Ethnographer Rodney Frey and the Coeur d'Alene Tribe have also used the ideas of empathetic adaptability and adaptive traditionalism, concepts rooted in Indigenous agency and sovereignty that are consistent with the frameworks of traditional knowledge and traditional ecological knowledge. These theoretical concepts draw upon the principles of multivocality, the multiple evidence base approach, and adaptive co-management (Frey n.d., 2017; Russell 2014).

Adaptability is a defining tradition of Indigeneity. Berkes (1999, 15), for example, notes that change is integral to Indigenous ways of knowing. Hunn (1993, 13) similarly notes that as tradition is passed down from one generation to the next, "new ideas and techniques may be incorporated into a given tradition, but they fit into a complex fabric of existing traditional practices and understandings. Thus traditions are enduring adaptions."

While the concept of adaptive traditionalism is particularly relevant to postcontact Indigenous contexts, it could also apply to trading obsidian or shell beads, adopting horticulture, or embracing Clovis technology, which spread across the continent. Native American culture change as a result of direct and indirect interactions with non-Indigenous people was rapid and extreme and had devastating and heartbreaking consequences. Native peoples' adaptive use of European, Euro-American, Asian, or African American materials during after contact, however, was not fundamentally incompatible with Indigenous ways of knowing and living, nor was it inconsistent with the exchange of ideas, technologies, and materials among differing Indigenous groups during that period.

In post-1492 archaeological contexts in parts of Utah, examples of adaptive traditionalism include Ute rock-marking styles that integrate elements of older rock-marking styles in the region, including elements similar to Ancestral Puebloan rock markings (Cole 1990, 223). Other examples include the adoption of Plains-style teepees or buffalo hunting (Cuch 2016). The exchange of ideas, technologies, and materials was just as integral to Indigenous traditionalism after 1492 as it had been before 1492. While indirect or direct contact with non-Indigenous people had a particularly significant impact on Indigenous peoples, their incorporation of guns, metal, glass, cotton and wool, and horses into their existing cultural frameworks is not fundamentally different than their addition of other Indigenous materials. A historic Ute site with teepee poles and tin can fragments is still Ute (see also Scheiber, this volume). After all, European and Euro-American trade with Indigenous peoples would not have been effective if Indigenous peoples were not open to and interested in trade goods that were useful or interesting. Furthermore, Indigenous peoples actively traded European-derived goods after contact.

Cultural Keystoneness and Flaked Glass

Many scholars, including those in this volume, advocate for the expansion of post-1492 archaeological study beyond trait lists and index artifacts to include a range of source materials such as historical accounts and documents, ethnographies, and collaboration with descendent communities (Panich and Schneider 2019; see also Cowie and Teeman, this volume; Hull, this volume). While interdisciplinary, collaborative, and multifaceted research does much to improve our field, incorporation of this level of research into contract archaeology can be difficult to achieve and can vary depending on the place and the project. Time is an especially constant and limiting factor for compliance archaeologists. Additionally, the existence and availability of historical ethnographic data that includes maps or discussions of Indigenous localities is common in some places but uncommon in other areas (including Utah). The applicability of such ethnographic data, even where it exists, may not correlate well with an Area of Potential Effect for a compliance archaeology project.[10] And while modern ethnographic study is a common component of the cultural heritage management industry, archaeologists do not always have access to knowledge derived from compliance-driven ethnography due in no small part to concerns about confidentiality regarding traditional knowledge (Bengston 2019). Finally, interactions between Indigenous leaders and knowledge holders with contract archaeologists varies from state to state and from region to region. In Utah, involvement between compliance archaeologists and Indigenous descendent communities before or during fieldwork, especially at the survey level, is uncommon.

Where the multiple evidence base approach for identifying postcontact Indigenous sites is not possible, especially within the fast-paced world of contract archaeology, the idea of the index artifact can be flipped on its head. Although archaeological sites are recorded to the terms of the site form, sometimes a single artifact can make a person stop and reevaluate what the materials encountered on a site might suggest, and who the site might correlate to. The process is similar to slipping on a pair of rose-colored glasses for a change in perspective.

In this sense, the idea of the keystone or "keystoneness" is helpful. In architecture, a keystone is the stone at the apex of an arch that distributes force equally down the sides of an arch to give it structural integrity. Generally speaking, an arch won't stand without a keystone. In ecology, keystone species are species that especially influence the function and diversity of an ecosystem. Their presence or absence in their environments have a disproportionate effect on the health of their ecosystem (Cagua et al. 2019). For ecologists, the abundance or absence of a keystone species or the health of a keystone community or of certain individuals may trigger research questions about the health of an ecosystem. Metaphorically, a keystone is the piece that locks the whole together.

Transferring that concept to archaeology, a cultural keystone can indicate significant contexts and information that can prompt archaeologists to ask new questions and consider new ways of interacting with cultural materials and places. Like keystone species, cultural keystones uniquely inform us about the archaeological environment and challenge us to reconsider our biases or our archaeological understanding. Diagnostic artifacts or features have keystoneness because they help bridge a gap in archaeological knowledge about a site, but by and large what we seek to know from diagnostics is culturally who is associated with the site or material in question and when that was the case. Keystone artifacts, features, and sites bridge gaps in knowledge about the archaeological environment and in our understanding of the cultural landscape. This knowledge, in turn, shapes how we interact with that environment. Keystone artifacts challenge us to ask new questions and reconsider our preconceived notions. As a keystone, postcontact Indigenous archaeology is located at the apex of a bridge where one side represents precontact Indigenous history and material culture and the other represents living Indigenous peoples. As many researchers have noted (e.g., Ferguson 1996; McGuire 1992; Swindler et al. 1997), the two sides have been largely disconnected. For westerners in cultural heritage preservation, postcontact Indigenous archaeology extends the arc of Indigenous history from deep history to now. When archaeological materials (e.g., flaked glass) or features suggest postcontact Indigenous presence, new questions can be asked that ideally will result in an improved, more considerate archaeology that can mitigate or prevent harm and acknowledge the agency and identity of historic Indigenous peoples.

In the consideration of the Indigenous use of glass as a flintknapping material or any other artifact or feature type, it is imperative to remember that there is no catch-all artifact, feature, or archaeological quality that defines Indigeneity or postcontact Indigenous material culture. The material expressions of postcontact Indigenous peoples depend on the culture of the Indigenous peoples whose homeland the archaeological research is conducted on, the agency of individuals or small groups, the effects of European-derived diseases on Native populations, the policies and values of Euro-American settlers, the time period, the population density of historic non-Indigenous people in a place, the interactions between postcontact Indigenous groups, and any number of other variables. The ways colonial Spain dealt with Native American populations in the Southwest and California, for instance, were very different from Mormon policies in Utah. As Beaudoin (this volume) notes in his discussion on searching for signifiers, context matters.

To be sure, flaked glass is not a particularly common artifact type. The paucity of flaked glass on the landscape can be attributed to any number of possible conclusions: Indigenous populations declined in the post-1492 period, glass never fully replaced traditional lithic sources, not all Indigenous peoples adopted glass as a flintknapping material or perhaps some used it infrequently, and the most obvious Indigenous glass artifacts may be and may have been most at risk of surface collection. Further, in some historic contexts, glass was flintknapped by non-Indigenous peoples in the United States

(Clark 1981; Wilkie 1996). In historical and ethnographic records, however, the evidence of adaptive use of glass is clear (Bethard 1981; Martindale and Jurakic 2006; Mason 1893).

Even though Indigenous peoples in the United States adopted glass as a flintknapping material, the vast majority of scholarship on Indigenous flaked glass and flintknapping focuses on other parts of the world (Cooper and Bowdler 1998; Foghlu et al. 2016; Pallo and Borrazzo 2017). While those studies are informative about the global effects of colonialism and, to an extent, about technology, Indigenous use of flaked glass in the United States hasn't received the same level of diagnostic technological or cultural study as glass beads have (see, for example, *Beads: Journal of the Society of Bead Researchers*). Some exceptions include Martindale and Jurakic's (2006) reporting and experimentation on expedient glass tool use at a Tsimshian village and Shackley's (2011) analysis of glass tools created by Ishi (see also Hull, this volume). In the context of contract archaeology, which relies heavily on in-field macroanalysis of artifacts, some useful tools from the literature can inform on how to record potential flaked glass.

In 2008, Clemente Conte and Romero (2008, 252) conducted a study of glass to compare use wear on unmodified and modified glass edges. They did experiments in which they compared glass used to scrape wood and hides with trampled glass. The experimental glass pieces were then analyzed with magnification as great as 500x. The results indicated that the vast majority of broken and trampled glass does not produce edges with the appearance of flaking or use wear. When microflake scars are produced through breakage and trampling, five contiguous flake scars can result that appear to have been retouched. A high-powered microscope is necessary to distinguish the patterning of anthropogenic use wear from the pattern trampling creates.

Wilkie (1996, 37) recorded thirty-five glass tools from an African American cabin in Louisiana that dates from the 1840s through the 1930s. Wilkie's analysis of the tools used historic bottle terminology to describe the morphology of the tools in relation to the source material (the bottle or jar); lithic analysis in order to discuss edge angle, modification, and use wear (41–42); and historical and ethnographic accounts. In Wilkie's sample, wear indicates tool use and function and the use and function of the glass tools were consistent with the ethnographic data.

Well-funded academic or late-phase contract archaeological studies have the luxury of thorough and experimental analysis on use wear, but as Young and Bamforth's (1990, 406) experiment with macroanalysis of use wear indicates, macroanalysis is not particularly effective. In fact, their experiment indicated that macroanalysis was correct only 25 percent of the time and that "most archaeologists will identify similar classes of flaked-stone artifacts as used, but . . . these identifications very often will be inaccurate and not representative of the full range of tasks that prehistoric people actually carried out."

Compliance archaeologists can take practical lessons from the works of Clemente Conte and Romero, Wilkie, and Young and Bamforth. From Clemente Conte and Romero, glass flakes and flake scars are not the norm for broken and trampled glass. The lesson I draw from their study is to be circumspect, but not cynical, in identifying flaked glass. From Wilkie, we learn that the standardization of bottle morphology terminology, including terms for the interior and exterior of the glass vessel and the longitudinal (y) axis of the vessel and latitudinal (x) axis of the vessel, will aid in the identification of culturally modified glass. Lastly, from Young and Bamforth, we learn that macroanalysis is not an adequate methodology for categorically dismissing potential glass flakes and flaked-glass tools during survey-level compliance archaeological site documentation Another point of note: When Terry Knight (2019), a Ute Mountain Ute tribal historic preservation officer, extemporaneously presented at the 2019 Utah Professional Archaeological Council, he intimated that flakes and debitage are not trash; rather, they are useful and have meaning. Moving forward, when we discuss flakes, both lithic and glass, we should be careful to not call them trash or dismiss them as such.

Site 42GR3923

Site 42GR3923 is located in the Cisco Desert in eastern Utah on the ancestral homelands of the Paiute Indian Tribe of Utah, the Ute Indian Tribe, the Ute Mountain Ute Tribe, the Southern Ute Indian Tribe, the Hopi Tribe, the Navajo Nation, the Pueblo of San Ildefonso, the Pueblo of Zuni, the Pueblo of Zia, the Pueblo of Acoma, the Pueblo of Laguna, the Santa Clara Pueblo, and the Pueblo of Jemez. The site is located on Bureau of Land Management lands in the Moab Field Office in a dynamic archaeological landscape that spans from the Book Cliffs in the north to the Colorado River in the southwest. The archaeological landscape of the Cisco Desert ranges from Archaic to Fremont camps. It includes Ute camps; a nineteenth-century narrow-gauge railroad grade with associated historic trash scatters that indicate the construction, use, and dismantling of the short-lived railroad; historic cattle and sheep grazing camps; mining camps; and Civilian Conservation Corps landscape modifications to control erosion (Stavish and Russell 2007).

Site 42GR3923, which was recorded for a compliance archaeology project in 2007, includes a modest lithic scatter on and around the elevated narrow-gauge grade of the Denver and Rio Grande Western Railroad that dates to the 1880s. Recorded surface materials were limited to fifty-two pieces of lithic debitage and two midstage biface fragments. My first impression of the site was that the construction of the railroad displaced the cultural material of a precontact site and in so doing likely destroyed any integrity the lithic scatter may have had. In the process of fleshing out the site during recordation, however, one aqua glass flake measuring 2.5 centimeters was identified.

Finding this one complete primary glass flake, which was likely removed from a bottle base and had a clear point of impact, a bulb of percussion, and radial lines, made the railroad grade, which is the highest point on the landscape for miles around, part of the lithic scatter site. The site interpretation incorporated questions about the adaptive use of glass as a flintknapping material, especially in the context of the much harder locally occurring chert sources that provided the source material for the other lithic artifacts; about postcontact Indigenous interactions with Euro-Americans and nineteenth-century industrialization, including possible employment on railroad development; and about post-reservation traditional use of the landscape. Importantly, finding the glass flake influenced the recommendation of significance. Location, setting, and even feeling elements of integrity remained intact and the site was recommended eligible under Criterion D of the NRHP. The Bureau of Land Management and the Utah SHPO concurred with this recommendation.[11] While no other diagnostic artifacts were present on the site, the standard interpretation of the site without the glass flake would have been that the site was precontact. The presence of the glass flake provided a key that changed how I interpreted the site and enabled me to see the possibility of postcontact Indigenous use and participation at the site and on the landscape.

Site 42BE3107

Site 42BE3107 is located on the eastern edge of the Basin and Range Province in western Utah on the ancestral homelands of the bands of the Paiute Indian

Tribe of Utah and the Hopi Tribe. The site is located on private land in the San Francisco Mountains at the head of a steep mountain drainage. The archaeology of the San Francisco Mountains is largely defined by the San Francisco mining district, which primarily extracted silver and boomed from the 1870s through the 1920s. During its heyday, the mines of the San Francisco Mountains brought over 6,000 people to the towns and camps of the mines.

The archaeological indication of Indigenous use of the San Francisco Mountains is much subtler than the large-scale mining sites throughout the mountain range. During several cultural heritage inventories, only one lithic scatter site and five isolated finds of lithic materials that ranged from singular obsidian flakes to a small diffuse scatter of six flakes were identified and recorded. Although no other archaeological indicators of Indigenous peoples were encountered, local history and landscape names indicate the postcontact presence of Indigenous peoples in the area. Some of the flakes found during survey were located on historic mining sites. Because the artifacts are made from nonlocal material and are generally indicative of tool retouch and because of the substantial depth of Indigenous history in the area, it is very likely that the flakes have no association with the nineteenth- to early twentieth-century mining sites they coincide with. The majority of the lithic artifacts encountered were obsidian and were likely derived from regional volcanic mountain ranges that the San Francisco Mountains are not part of. Notably, no good lithic material for tool manufacture is located in the mountain range.

The archaeological landscape suggests that Indigenous peoples came to the San Francisco Mountains despite the notable lack of lithic materials and water and the absence of longer-term occupation by Indigenous people, probably to procure game and plants and other necessities. Without obsidian hydration, none of the Indigenous archaeological materials we encountered were indicative of any particular time period.

Site 42BE3107 was originally recorded in 2007 as a Euro-American mining site that dates from the 1870s to the 1920s and includes mine adits, an ore chute, a rail system, a trash scatter (with a notable lack of recorded glass artifacts), and small masonry architectural features. During the 2007 recording, the site was recommended eligible under Criteria A and D of the NRHP. The Utah SHPO concurred with the eligibility recommendation (Bassett 2008). The site was updated in 2018 during a compliance archaeology project. During the site update in 2018, a colorless glass scraper was found on a west-facing ridge with clear views of the valley below near a mine adit and rail (Figure 9.1). The scraper was made from the body of a colorless glass vessel and measures 5.5 by 2.6 by 0.5 centimeters and is unifacially flaked along one longitudinal side on the exterior side of the bottle. There are nine contiguous flake scars along the length of the longitudinal edge with the appearance of microflaking all along the flaked edge (Russell 2018).

The presence of the scraper may suggest historic Paiute presence at the site and in the greater San Francisco Mountain area during or after the time of the mining boom. If so, the tool may suggest the presence of a new material source for flintknapping purposes, since there are no locally available materials in the mountain range. If that's the case, the scraper may suggest the perpetuation of Paiute seasonal rounds in the mountain range after the establishment of local reservations. The scraper may also suggest that Paiute or members of other nonlocal Indigenous groups were employed in the mines

Figure 9.1. Colorless glass scraper from Site 42BE3107. Photograph by Hannah Russell.

during the boom (Hattori 1975). These scenarios may not be the truth of the scraper, but its presence opens a number of avenues of inquiry about possible Indigenous experiences in a mining district during the late nineteenth to early twentieth centuries.

Conclusion

The material culture of postcontact Native Americans is poorly understood and inadequately documented. Western objectivist regimented experimentation, experiment repetition, classification systems, and consistent terminologies that are so abundant for precontact and non-Native historic archaeological contexts have not been applied to the archaeology of Indigenous peoples after 1492 with the same rigor or consistency. Neither have the ethnographies that touch on so much of modern Native life. Additionally, the construction of modern archaeological professions has largely excluded Indigenous narratives once Europeans reached American shores, leaving the postcontact Indigenous landscape underprotected and underdocumented. Our understanding, management, and consideration of that landscape is vastly inadequate. This is especially the case in the business of cultural heritage management, which is rooted in the language set forth in NHPA of 1966 and the objectivist ideas of processualism that dominated the anthropological and archaeological theoretical landscape for so long. Over half a century later, we are still contending with the colonialist overtones and impacts of the persistent industry standard of "prehistory" or "history." One of the most common questions I am asked when I tell people that I am an archaeologist is "What are you looking for?" Many in this volume discuss methods for identifying post-1492 archaeological sites for study, but contract archaeologists need to be able to identify, as best as we are able, what falls within our survey areas, which means that our need to identify and reckon with the reasons why we fail to see those sites is all the greater.

Western terminology, methodologies, and theories have divided what is Indigenous history, when it started and when it ends, and who has access to and ownership of it. As Steeves (2015a, iv) writes, this is a violence that archaeologists commit against Indigenous people. That is a hard pill to swallow. However, by facing that truth, we can start making reparations for the damage we have done. In compliance archaeology, that means discarding the biases we recognize and listening to Indigenous knowledge holders and critical theory stakeholders to find the biases we are not yet aware of. In the private sector of compliance archaeology, we can be more considerate regarding how we word the data we collect on site forms, how we organize that data, and which sources we cite and what language we use in our reports. We should advocate for multivocality, increased reverence for Indigenous knowledge, greater collaboration, and the multiple evidence base approach where appropriate and available. By opening our eyes and slipping on a pair of metaphorical rose-colored glasses to change our points of view, we can be better partners in the stewardship and management of the cultural heritage we have the pleasure and privilege to work with.

Acknowledgments

I could not have written this chapter without the help of a number of wonderful people who were willing to talk with me and share their experiences and expertise. Sometimes a conversation, even one via email or a Twitter thread, can be remarkably eye opening. Thanks to Greg Nunn, Sean Gantt, Charles Hutcheson, Rodney Frey, Deb Miller, and Savanna Agardy and to William Frey with the Metropolitan Policy Program at the Brookings Institution and Courtney Kennedy at the Pew Research Center for helping me through the new-to-me world of survey research. Thanks to Lee Panich and Tsim Schneider for organizing the conversations and this edited volume that brought all this research together. Thank you to the Moab Field Office of the Bureau of Land Management for permission to include a discussion of Site 42GR3923 in this chapter, and finally, thanks to Laura Martin, Mary Petrich-Guy, and Ashley Morton for reading previous drafts and offering helpful edits and points of consideration.

Notes

1. The terms western and Indigenous are used here consistently with Atalay's use in "Indigenous Archaeology as Decolonizing Practice." As she writes, the terms "denote very broad, general groups of people and communities . . . [with] a great deal of complexity and diversity of views . . . I do not intend to insinuate that either term refers to a monolithic, homogenous group with rigid and clearly defined epistemologies and worldviews, but rather each includes a great deal of diversity" (2006, 303). Further, the use of the term Indigenous in the context

of this chapter refers specifically to Indigenous groups within the geopolitical boundary of the United States.

2. Paulette Steeves, Twitter post, January 26, 2020, 8:24 a.m., https://twitter.com/PauletteSteeves, accessed January 26, 2020. See also Steeves (2015a).

3. Paulette Steeves, Twitter post, January 26, 2020, 8:28 a.m., https://twitter.com/PauletteSteeves, accessed January 26, 2020. See also Steeves (2015a); and Cowie and Teeman (this volume).

4. I prefer the terms contract archaeology, compliance archaeology, or cultural heritage management over cultural resource management. The term "resources" in particular, is steeped in western capitalism and is antithetical to cultural and natural elements and qualities of the landscape and to the efforts of this work, even as an archaeologist in the business of archaeology. Deconstructing colonialist narratives at the most basic level means consideration of the language we use.

5. Bad data is information or missing information that lead to incorrect or problematic results and can include no data, unrelated data, missing data, data inconsistencies, unstructured data, and misrepresentations (Hatt 2018) among other things.

6. The National Historic Preservation Act (NRHP) (1966), and specifically Section 106 of the NRHP, is a defining piece of legislation for compliance archaeology that states that the effect of "undertakings" (construction projects that involve Federal Agency money, lands, or permissions) on "historic properties" (sites, places, landscapes, or objects that are eligible to or listed on the National Register of Historic Places) must be taken into account prior to the approval of the undertaking. This work typically falls to private sector compliance archaeologists who work with agencies. See the National Historic Preservation Act of 1966 and National Register Bulletin 15: How to Apply the National Register Criteria (1995) for a list of the four criteria and the seven elements of integrity used to determine NRHP eligibility.

7. Because undertakings are expected to avoid adverse effects to historic properties, compliance archaeology projects survey for and record archaeological sites and materials and assess those cultural elements for NRHP eligibility.

8. In social psychology, attitude refers to our "enduring evaluation of something . . . a person, a product, or a social group" (Stangor et al. 2011, 168).

9. Psychological survey refers to the development of survey as a tool for collecting information informed by "Social psychological study of attitudes, stereotypes, and prejudice" (Converse 1987) to minimize the collection of bad data or to be able to interpret data in a way that accounts (as best as possible) for variability in interpretation. Both response effect and attitude research are aspects of the extensive study of psychological survey.

10. An Area of Potential Effect is an area that is to be surveyed to satisfy the conditions of Section 106 so that an undertaking won't impact historic properties.

11. See Note 4.

References Cited

Atalay, Sonya. 2006. Indigenous Archaeology as Decolonizing Practice. *American Indian Quarterly* 30(3 & 4): 280–310.

Bassett, Everett. 2008. *San Francisco Abandoned Mine Reclamation Project.* Transcon Environmental. Submitted to Utah Division of Oil Gas and Mines. On file at the Utah State Historic Preservation Office. Salt Lake City.

Beaudoin, Matthew A. 2016. Archaeologists Colonizing Canada: The Effects of Unquestioned Categories. *Archaeologies: Journal of the World Archaeological Congress* 12(1): 7–37.

Bengston, Ginny. 2019. The Status of Great Basin Ethnographic CRM Studies and Reports since 1990. In *Cultural Resource Management in the Great Basin, 1986–2016*, edited by Alice M. Baldrica, Patricia A. DeBunch, and Don D. Fowler, 36–40. Salt Lake City: University of Utah Press.

Berkes, Fikret. 1999. *Sacred Ecology*. London: Routledge.

Bethard, Kenneth Randall. 1981. A Projectile Point Typology for Archaeological Site CA-BUT-301: An Exogene Cave in the Northern Sierra Foothills. Master's thesis, California State University, Sacramento.

Bradburn, Norman M. 1983. Response Effect. In *Handbook of Survey Research*, edited by Peter H. Rossi, James D. Write, and Andy B. Anderson 289–328. New York: Academic Press.

Cagua, Edgar Fernando, Kate L. Wootton, and Daniel B. Stouffer. 2019. Keystoneness, Centrality, and the Structural Controllability of Ecological Networks. *Journal of Ecology* 12(1): 1–12.

Converse, Jean M. 1987. *Survey Research in the United States: Roots and Emergence, 1890–1960*. Berkley: University of California Press.

Clark, J. 1981. Glass Scrapers from Historic North America. *Lithic Technology* 10(2 & 3): 31–34.

Clemente Conte, Ignacio, and Facundo Romero. 2008. Microware Analysis of Retouched Glass Fragments from Fortlet Minana, Azul, Argentina, 1860–1863. *International Journal of Historical Archaeology* 12(3): 248–262.

Cole, Sally. 1990. *Legacy on Stone: Rock Art of the Colorado Plateau and Four Corners Region*. Boulder, CO: Johnson Publishing.

Cooper, Zarine, and Samdra Bowdler. 1998. Flaked Glass Tools from the Andaman Islands and Australia. *Asian Perspectives* 37(1): 74–83.

Cuch, Forrest S. 2016. "Forrest S. Cuch—A Discussion about Utah's Utes." Presentation at Brigham Young University, Charles Redd Center for Western Studies, Provo, Utah. YouTube video, https://www.youtube.com/watch?v=FHzp-v_KvSQ.

Cutajar, JosAnn. 2008. Knowledge and Post-Colonial Pedagogy. *Mediterranean Journal of Educational Studies* 13(2): 27–47.

Ferguson, T. J. 1996. Native Americans and the Practice of Archaeology. *Annual Review of Anthropology* 25: 63–79.

Ferris, Neal. 2014. Being Iroquoian, Being Iroquois: A Thousand-Year Heritage of Becoming. In *Rethinking Colonial Pasts through Archaeology*, edited by Neal Ferris, Rodney Harrison, and Michael V. Wilcox 371–396. Oxford: Oxford University Press.

Fischoff, B. 1991. Value Elicitation: Is There Anything in There? *American Psychologist* 46(8): 835–847.

Foghlu, Billy O., Daryl Lloyd Wesley, Sally Brockwell, and Helen Cooke. 2016. Implications for Culture Contact History from a Glass Artefact on a Diingwulung Earth Mound in Weipa. *Queensland Archaeological Research* 19(1): 1–22.

Frey, Rodney. 2017. *Carry Forth the Stories: An Ethnographer's Journey into Native Oral Tradition*. Pullman: Washington State University Press.

———. N.d. Huckleberries: Stories from the American Indian Experience. Manuscript on file, Department of Anthropology & Sociology, University of Idaho, Moscow, ID.

Hatt, Bertil. 2018. What Does Bad Data Look Like? *Medium.com*, August 31. Accessed October 14, 2020. https://medium.com/@bertil_hatt/what-does-bad-data-look-like-91dc2a7bcb7a.

Hattori, Eugene M. 1975. *Northern Paiutes on the Comstock: Archaeology and Ethnohistory of* an American Indian Population in Virginia City, Nevada. Occasional Paper, No. 3. Carson City: Nevada State Museum.

Hunn, Eugene. 1993. What Is Traditional Ecological Knowledge? In *Traditional Ecological Knowledge: Wisdom for Sustainable Development*, edited by Nancy M. Williams and Graham Baines, 13–15. Canberra: Centre for Resource and Environmental Studies, Australian National University.

Knight, Terry. 2019. Ute Mountain Ute Perspectives on the Bears Ears Landscape. Paper presented at the 2019 Utah Professional Archaeological Council Meeting, Moab, Utah.

Lightfoot, Kent G., and Antoinette Martinez. 1995. Frontiers and Boundaries in Archaeological Perspectives. *Annual Review of Anthropology* 24: 471–492.

Martindale, Andrew, and Irena Jurakic. 2006. Identifying Expedient Glass Tools from a Post-Contact Tsimshian Village Using Low Power (10–100X) Magnification. *Journal of Archaeological Science* 33: 414–427.

Mason, Otis T. 1893. *North American Bows, Arrows, and Quivers*. Washington, DC: Government Printing Office.

McDavid, Carol. 2007. Beyond Strategy and Good Intentions: Archaeology, Race, and White Privilege. In *Archaeology as a Tool of Civic Engagement*, edited by Barbara J. Little and Paul A. Shackel, 67–88. Lanham, MD: AltaMira Press.

McGuire, Randall H. 1992. Archaeology and the First Americans. *American Anthropologist* 94(4): 816–836.

Pallo, Maria Cecilia, and Karen Borrazzo. 2017. The Archaeology of Contact in Southern Patagonia: Some Issues to be Resolved in the Southwestern Forest. *Arts and Humanities Open Access Journal* 1(4): 00023.

Panich, Lee M., and Tsim D. Schneider. 2019. Categorical Denial: Evaluating Post-1492 Indigenous Erasure in the Trail of American Archaeology. *American Antiquity* 84(4): 651–668.

Russell, Hannah. 2014. Archaeological Investigations and Comparison of Historical Spokane Indian Sites On and Off the Spokane Reservation. Master's thesis, University of Idaho, Moscow.

———. 2018. Cultural Resource Inventory of Volantis Resources Corp.'s Proposed Eight Precious Metal Drill Locations, Water Tank Storage Sites, Helicopter Pad, and Access Routes In Beaver County, Utah. Cottonwood Archaeology. Submitted to Utah State Historic Preservation Office. On file at the Utah State Historic Preservation Office, Salt Lake City.

Scheiber, Laura L., and Judson Byrd Finley. 2010. Mountain Shoshone Technological Transitions across the Great Divide. In *Across the Great Divide: Continuity and Change in Native North American Societies, 1400–1900*, edited by Laura L. Scheiber and Mark D. Mitchel 128–148. Tucson: University of Arizona Press.

Shackley, Steven M. 2011. The Stone Tool Technology of Ishi and the Yana of North Central California: Inferences for Hunter-Gatherer Cultural Identity in Historic California. *American Anthropologist* 102(4): 693–712.

Silliman, Stephen W. 2005. Culture Contact or Colonialism? Challenges in the Archaeology of Native North America. *American Antiquity* 70(1): 55–74.

———. 2014. Archaeologies of Indigenous Survivance and Residence: Navigating Colonial and Scholarly Dualities. In *Rethinking Colonial Pasts through Archaeology*, edited by Neal Ferris, Rodney Harrison, and Michael V. Wilcox, 57–75. Oxford: Oxford University Press.

Stangor, Charles, Rajiv Jhangiani, and Hammond Tarry. 2011. *Principles of Social Psychology*. 1st international ed. N.p.: n.p.

Stavish, Patricia, and Hannah Russell. 2007. *Cultural Resource Inventory of Running Foxes Pe-*

troleum's 2D Cisco Seismic, Grand County Utah. Montgomery Archaeological Consultants. Submitted to Bureau of Land Management. On file at the Utah State Historic Preservation Office, Salt Lake City.

Steeves, Paulette. 2015a. Decolonizing Indigenous Histories, Pleistocene Archaeology Sites of the Western Hemisphere. PhD diss., Binghamton University, Binghamton, NY.

———. 2015b. Academia, Archaeology, CRM, and Tribal Historic Preservation. *Archaeologies: Journal of the World Archaeological Congress* 11(1): 121–141.

Swindler, Nina, Kurt E. Dogonske, Roger Anyon, and Alan S. Downer, eds. 1997. *Native Americans and Archaeologists: Stepping Stones to Common Ground.* Walnut Creek, CA: AltaMira Press.

Tourangeau, Roger, Lance J. Rips, and Kenneth Rasinski. 2000. *The Psychology of Survey Response.* New York: Cambridge University Press.

Vizenor, Gerald. 2008. Aesthetics of Survivance Literary Theory and Practice. In *Survivance: Narrative of Native Presence,* edited by Gerald Vizenor 1–23. Lincoln: University of Nebraska Press.

Watkins, Joe. 2000. *Indigenous Archaeology: American Indian Values and Scientific Practice.* Walnut Creek, CA: AltaMira Press.

Wilcox, Michael V. 2014. Indigenous Archaeology and the Pueblo Revolt of 1680: Social Mobility and Boundary Maintenance in Colonial Contexts. In *Rethinking Colonial Pasts Through Archaeology,* edited by Neal Ferris, Rodney Harrison, and Michael V. Wilcox 150–172. Oxford: Oxford University Press.

Wilkie, Laurie A. 1996. Glass-Knapping at a Louisiana Plantation: African-American Tools? *Historical Archaeology* 30(4): 37–49.

Young, Donald and Douglas B. Bamforth. 1990. On the Macroscopic Identification of Used Flakes. *American Antiquity* 55(2): 403–409.

10

Home and Homeland in the Land Beyond the Mountains

LAURA L. SCHEIBER

This chapter presents innovative methodologies for exploring nineteenth- and twentieth-century Indigenous histories in the Rocky Mountains and the western Great Plains. Archaeologists across the United States are developing methodologies for defining Native sites in colonial settings and offering new insights into Native innovation, investment, and invisibility (Hull, this volume; Jordan, this volume; Lightfoot and Gonzalez 2018; Trabert, this volume). This research incorporates material diagnostics, dating techniques, and rich historical documentation (Panich and Schneider 2019). In situations where these avenues are not available, other data sources can be combined to creatively restore Indigenous contributions to recent history (Martin 2016; Newton 2018; Russell, this volume; Scheiber and Finley 2010b).

Permanent Euro-American settlement did not occur in the western United States until after a long period of cultural entanglement between Native residents and newcomers (Scheiber and Burnett 2020). The region's past is often severed in two, with the Native story ending as the settler story begins. This practice leads to a false impression that the two are mutually exclusive, that they overlap only briefly, or worse, that Indigenous communities no longer exist (see also Dickson and Steinmetz, this volume). The narrative presented here is neither the final chapter of Indigenous presence nor the first chapter in settler occupation but instead seeks to weave the two together.

Using a case study of a location that is synonymous with the Wild West, the town co-founded by William F. "Buffalo Bill" Cody, this research combines sources from oral and local histories, biographies, newspapers, landscape metaphors, photography, ethnography, and archaeology to reveal deep engagements with placemaking by multiple stakeholders over time. The methodology for this research is not wholly systematic or wholly interpretive; it combines both approaches. The project started as an investigation of the archaeology of everyday hunter-gatherer campsites (i.e., tipi rings) in an area rich in local history. When I could not obtain permission from the landowner to study the archaeological features themselves, those features prompted me to find innovative ways to envision a much broader biography of place. This scaffolding approach is consciously interdisciplinary, multivocal, and embedded with Indigenous symbolism. Being denied access to the archaeological sites led to a deeper introspection about Indigenous presence and persistence in the nineteenth and twentieth centuries and an opportunity to reconnect contemporary people and places.

Cody, Wyoming, is a gateway to Yellowstone National Park, one of the most popular travel destinations in the United States. Here, dividing lines between the Old West and the New West remain fluid and intertwined, and the seeping of the past into the present (or the merging of the two) is readily evident. Tourists visit Cody on their way to see geysers, hot springs, and mud pots, buffalo, grizzlies, and wolves. They enjoy the nightly old-time gunfight outside the historic Irma Hotel (which Buffalo Bill built in 1902) and shop in stores filled with Native-themed souvenirs. It is an anachronistic playground of cowboys and Indians.

This homage to the past is not new. Promoting (and constructing) the West started almost immediately after the American Indian Wars, in events at which former rivals and friends assumed new roles as entertainers and fought in staged re-creations of actual historic events. Buffalo Bill's Wild West is well known for these exhibitions; employees of that show performed for thousands of visitors around the world in the period 1883 to 1916. The region is famous for colorful stories of how mountain men, cowboys, and outlaws triumphed over hostile Indians and an untamed wilderness in pursuit of Manifest Destiny (Woods 1997). Early encounters among Natives and newcomers form the foundation of these stories. However, discussions of cross-cultural interactions and transformations within the settler colonial context are largely absent.

In order to highlight Native presence in colonized spaces, in this chapter I first establish a place-based Apsáalooke (Crow) social geography. I trace Indigenous history through the nineteenth century, then I argue that the Crow played a critical role in the development of a sustainable tourist economy in the twentieth century, transforming a small American ranching community into a destination that attracts millions of visitors each year. Finally, I demonstrate how tangible reminders of the past can be useful heuristic tools for conceptualizing intangible cultural heritage today.

Situating Crow Country

It is commonly said that Apsáalooke (Crow) Country is in exactly the right place (Medicine Crow 2000, 24) (Figure 10.1). In 1873, Chief Blackfoot described the Crow homeland as a lodge held down by rocks with four poles that extend in four directions across significant portions of Wyoming and Montana (Nabokov 1967, xvii). For Crow people, place rather than time defines their world view. Therefore, knowing when events occurred is not as important as recalling where they occurred. This concept is essential for understanding Apsáalooke placemaking.[1] Sometimes Crow places refer to physical attributes; other times, they refer to stories or past events (Nabokov and Loendorf 2004). This conceptualization of place is not unusual among Native North American communities (Basso 1996).

The research presented here is tethered to the Bighorn Basin portion of Crow Country, an intermontane basin in the Rocky Mountains that represents one of the four poles of the Crow homeland. The Crow have a rich oral history about the basin, which they call Ammitaalasshé (West End of the Lodge). Crow men whom Edward Curtis (1909, 80, 114) interviewed in the early twentieth century also referred to it as the Land Beyond the Mountains. Focusing on Crow Country in the Bighorn Basin reintroduces connections that often stop in the nineteenth century at the Montana state line and reservation boundaries (see also Dickson and Steinmetz, this volume).

Mention of the Crow in twentieth-century Wyoming history is often limited to discussions of Native peoples as remnants of the past, inserted into and just as quickly withdrawn from the larger story of American colonization of the West (Calloway 1991). It is a story about the destiny of immigrants, not one of situated landscapes with Indian inhabitants. The settler practice of renaming places and landmarks further rendered the Indian invisible (Wolfe 2006). The Indian presence today seems intangible at best. Contemporary residents, some of whom are fifth-generation descendants of settlers, are gen-

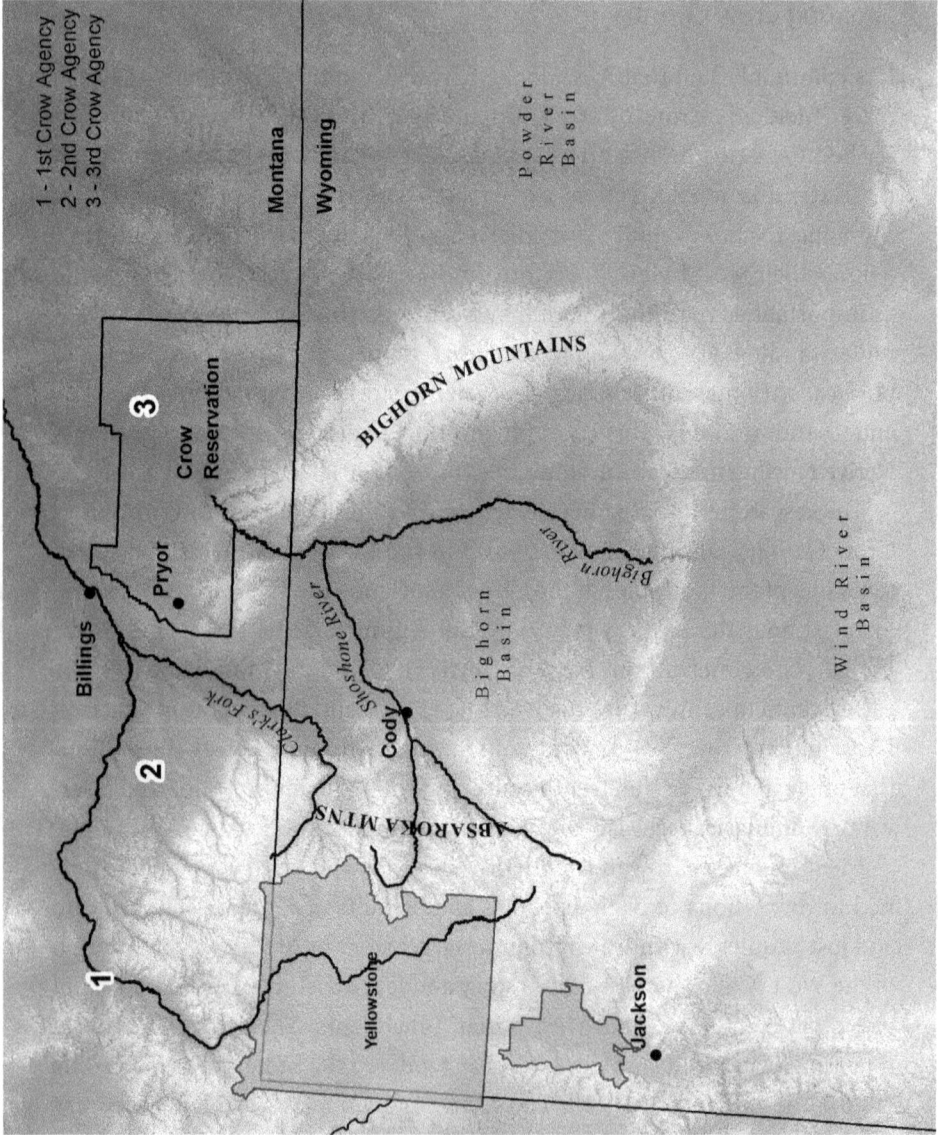

Figure 10.1. Map of study area, including locations of the three Crow agencies. Illustration by Rebecca Nathan and Laura Scheiber, using an ESRI ArcGIS basemap.

1 - 1st Crow Agency
2 - 2nd Crow Agency
3 - 3rd Crow Agency

Billings

Pryor

Crow Reservation

Montana

Wyoming

BIGHORN MOUNTAINS

Powder River Basin

Clark's Fork

Shoshone River

ABSAROKA MTNS

Cody

Bighorn Basin

Bighorn River

Wind River Basin

Yellowstone

Jackson

erally unfamiliar with recent Native history (Keller 2014). For the most part, the Apsáalooke and Native peoples more generally are invisible to modern inhabitants. The perception is that they live a long way away.

This separation is not so clear among Crow people, as the reservation border is just an hour's drive north of Cody. Connections to the area have continued through the tradition of retelling stories about people and places to younger generations. Elders shared stories that grandparents and great-grandparents who were familiar with the Bighorn Basin told them (Bauerle 2003; Grant Bulltail, personal communication 2017; Elias Goes Ahead, personal communication 2010; Keller 2014; McCleary 2001; Henry "Sarge" Old Horn, personal communication 2010). Prominent landforms and features retain their Crow place-names in these stories.

The Shoshone River is one of the basin's most defining natural features. From deep in the mountains, two forks meet just west of Cody at what is now the Buffalo Bill Dam and Reservoir, where they join to flow through a deep gorge between Cedar and Rattlesnake Mountains. The Crow name for this canyon is Bilíaliche (Like a Tipi's Doorway), a symbolic representation of home. The river is characterized by a strong sulfuric smell, which earned it the name of Aashilitshia (the Stinking Water). The odor is due to hydrothermal activity that also left hot springs, steam vents, sink holes, boiling tar springs, and travertine terraces, most of which are largely dormant today or were inundated by the dam. The Shoshone River hot springs are located just downstream from the canyon. Freshwater and thermal springs are highly significant in Crow culture. They are powerful places where people fast, heal, and pray and where underground spirits sometimes live (Linderman 1930, 299–307; T. McCleary et al. 1996, 45–69; Nabokov and Loendorf 2004, 54). Crow healers still collect spring water for medicinal purposes (Jonathan Pretty on Top, personal communication 2015).

Stories Told in Stone

Mobile Indigenous groups on the northwestern Plains left evidence of their campsites as rings of rocks that held down the bases of tipi (sometimes referred to as tepee) homes. These surface features number in the thousands (Scheiber 1993). Many of these sites were reoccupied and reused for generations; they now appear as palimpsests on the modern landscape. In

1908, the Crow scout Curley testified to the US Senate, "The soil you see is not ordinary soil; it is the dust of the blood, the flesh, and bones of our ancestors. . . . You will have to dig down through the surface before you can find nature's earth, as the upper portion is Crow" (US Congress 1908, 774–775). Tipi rings represent this intergenerational commitment to place through time (see also Laluk, this volume). They provide windows into the daily lives of past occupants, bearing witness to social and economic organization, household dynamics, camp life, group identity, and cosmology (Oetelaar 2016; Reher 1983; Scheiber 1993). Conversations with Apsáalooke tribal members have made some archaeologists aware of the cultural importance of tipi rings (Scheiber and Finley 2010a). The Crow term for a tipi ring is *annáshe* (place where a lodge has been). Their word for the past is *biiaakashisshipée*, translated as "when we weighed down our lodges with stones." In other words, the way people refer to the past is intimately connected to the stone rings that were left behind hundreds or thousands of years ago. Further, the conceptualization of the Apsáalooke homeland as extending in four directions is represented by the four-pole foundation of the Crow tipi held down by stones. The term Chief Blackfoot used to describe this homeland is *iichiia shoopé*, which literally translates as four base poles. What this means is that every stone circle, or tipi's footprint, preserves within it not just the home but the metaphorical homeland, another direct and meaningful connection to the past.

The Crow were mobile hunter-gatherers whose lives are often described in terms of movement. Evidence of their homes is a reminder that Crow connection to place did not just mean traveling to and from somewhere else but also meant residence and persistence (see also Laluk, this volume). The fact that these sites could be from multiple time periods is not important to the Crow: past events are anchored to place, and place drives the narrative. Whether or not the stone rings on the ground today once weighed down a Crow tipi or someone else's is not critical. As Curley stated, the top layer of the earth on Crow land belongs to the Crow. These rings are thus not without history or context.

Hundreds of tipi rings were once present along the Shoshone River. Many of these features are long gone, victims of modern land development. The dozens of rings overlooking the river near Trail Creek, named for a well-traveled Native trail connecting the mountains and basins, are a rare exception (Rol-

Figure 10.2. Trail Creek tipi rings with the Tipi's Doorway and Cody C in the background. Photograph by Laura L. Scheiber.

linson 1948, 192) (Figure 10.2). A gravel road cuts through the site, leading to hot springs at the river's edge. Few objects remain on the ground surface: tiny flakes, fragments of rusted cans, a Coca-Cola bottle base. If other items were left behind, they have been systematically collected by generations of towns-people who (usually) left only the tipi stones behind (Frost 1942). These foot-prints of former homes are a tangible connection to the past.

During the winter of 1807–1808, fur trader Manuel Lisa hired John Col-ter and George Drouillard (both formerly of the Lewis and Clark Corps of Discovery) to contact the Crow about new trading opportunities. Each man encountered Crow families camping along the forks of the Stinking Water, living in tipis undoubtedly held down with stones. Colter, a fourth-gener-ation Virginian, is celebrated as the first white person to visit the Yellow-stone region. He described thermal springs, bubbling tar, and geysers at the Stinking Water, which came to be known as Colter's Hell (Victor 1871, 80). Drouillard, the son of a Shawnee mother and a French Canadian father, was a skilled interpreter from the Upper Great Lakes. The Crow told him they preferred camping along the Stinking Water because local grasses provided excellent winter pasture for horses (Skarsten 1964, map inset). Drouillard and Colter later presented William Clark with geographic details that were used to create the first widely distributed American map of the West. In recognition of its unique contribution to the past, Colter's Hell was listed on the National Register of Historic Places in 1973. The significance of the area for Indigenous inhabitants was partly responsible for the success of the nomination.[2]

The romanticized vision of intrepid mountain men crossing uncharted country in the dead of winter is part of the allure of the frontier story. But the Crow who met those men were already culturally entangled with other nations. Their parents and grandparents regularly traveled east to Hidatsa and Mandan villages in the middle Missouri area to exchange dried meat and bison robes for corn, beans, and native tobacco (Ewers 1968). They had witnessed the effects of European/Euro-American expansion in the eighteenth century through the introduction of horses, infectious diseases, firearms, and new trade items. The Crow cultivated their role as intermediaries in the context of a culture that relied on horses (Calloway 1986; Medicine Crow 2000; Nabokov and Loendorf 2004, 44–45), as the written accounts of early trappers and traders document (Hamilton 1910, 244–247; Leforge 1974, 101–103; Leonard 1839, 83–85).

Crow oral histories also feature the Land Beyond the Mountains and frequently refer to memorable landmarks such as the Stinking Water and Heart Mountain (a prominent isolated butte where people fasted and prayed). Plenty Coups, Plainfeather, Comes Up Red, Blackfoot, Holds the Enemy, Two Leggings, Pretty Shield, and Hunts to Die all shared a connection to Ammitaalasshé.[3] The Crow were not the only Indigenous residents. Many of their stories describe encounters with other Tribes, such as the Shoshone, Blackfeet, Lakota, Cheyenne, Bannock, Nez Perce, and Arapaho.[4] Crow people left visual reminders of their personal achievements in battle as biographical rock art (Keyser and Poetschat 2009; McCleary 2016).

The Fort Laramie Treaty of 1851 established Crow tribal boundaries in what is now northern Wyoming and southern Montana, following Chief Blackfoot's reference to the four-pole tipi. This boundary was drastically reduced to a fifth of its size less than two decades later at the Fort Laramie Treaty of 1868. Increasing conflict with traditional enemies that pushed farther west, pressure from prospectors and settlers, and Sioux (Teton Lakota) attacks on the United States in Crow territory all attributed to this reduction in land (Hoxie 1995). Non-Indian settlers soon arrived in the newly formed Wyoming Territory.

In 1869, the US government established the first Crow Indian agency at Mission Creek near present-day Livingston, Montana, 172 kilometers northwest of the confluence of the two forks of the Stinking Water. Yellowstone National Park was created in 1872, further separating Native people from resources and significant places. In efforts to present Yellowstone as a pristine landscape unaltered and untainted by humans, early officials effectively eliminated Native presence from written history (Nabokov and Loendorf 2004). Band leaders farmed intermittently near the agency, seeking safety from attacks and escape from smallpox epidemics (Hoxie 1995). However, they did not abandon their southern and western territories, even after gold, silver, and coal attracted miners and settlers. Chief Blackfoot highlighted this in his 1873 testimony. "This summer we intend to go to Heart Mountain to get skins for our lodges. . . . We understood Heart Mountain and Stinking Water were in the Crow reservation, but you say it is not. Above the canyons they have been digging gold; now the whites want to take Heart Mountain, and we do not understand it" (quoted in Wright 1874, 498–499).

In 1875, the government moved the Crow Indian agency east to a location near present-day Absarokee, Montana (just 115 kilometers north of Cody). This was a response to pressure from prospectors and politicians and because the farmland and camping shelter in the Stillwater Valley were better (Brown 1961). The Crow collected rations and supplies there, but they traveled elsewhere to hunt and to avoid increased attacks by Lakota hunting bands who were actively fighting over the Black Hills. This situation reached a crisis when Custer's 7th Cavalry and their Crow and Arikara scouts were defeated by the Lakota, Cheyenne, and Arapaho at the Battle of the Little Bighorn on June 25, 1876. The battle occurred on the Crow Reservation.

Meanwhile, white ranchers such as Judge William Carter, John Chapman, and Otto Franc established large cattle-grazing operations on the open range of the Bighorn Basin (Edgar and Turnell 1987). Victor Arland and John Corbett arrived in Wyoming Territory in 1880. They opened a series of trading posts, the first of which was at Trail Creek, not far from the hot springs and from Crow campsites.

The government moved the Crow Indian agency a third time in 1884 to its present location on the Little Bighorn River, 174 kilometers northeast of present-day Cody. The last move was motivated by rancher lobbyists' expectations that they would gain the western part of the reservation. (This hope was largely unrealized.) Crow seasonal mobility practices faced numerous challenges. Buffalo herds dwindled in size and then disappeared, and food shortages led to dependency on government rations. The increased presence of white settlers and domesticated livestock contributed to changes in the cultural and physical landscapes. Finally, tribal members faced penalties for leaving the reservation without written permission (Bradley 1970).

Letters, diaries, and memoirs written by Euro-American cattle ranchers and their families suggest that despite hardships, dozens of Crow families were present in the Bighorn Basin in the 1880s. Hostile and racist encounters certainly occurred between Natives and settlers, but written descriptions are usually friendly. From trading-post owner Victor Arland, a French immigrant, we learn that in the early 1880s the Crow came to the basin to hunt and to trade animal furs for supplies, especially in the winter and spring.[5] They also bet on horse races, played poker, and drank whiskey (Deane 1996, 54–55). The Crow remember Victor Arland, whom they called Úuxe (The Deer), as the man who introduced them to honey. It was at Arland's trading post that a Crow couple asked for "mosquito sugar," a term that is still the Crow translation for honey today (Grant Bulltail, personal communication 2017). A number of Crow families spent the winter of 1884 at Arland's frontier town, which consisted of a store, a saloon, a dance hall, and a brothel (Nichter 2012). Tom Osborne recalled that the cowboys taught the Native women to square dance while the Native men bargained for cigarettes.[6]

In the summer of 1884, Mahlon and Nancy Frost and their children left southern Minnesota in covered wagons to cross the Plains. In Montana they met Chief Plenty Coups, the last hereditary chief of the Crow Tribe, who lived on the western side of the reservation in a two-story house in the community of Pryor. The Frosts ultimately settled near Crow camps on the South Fork of the Stinking River. Their four-year-old son Ned spent his first several winters in Wyoming playing with only Crow children (Frost and Frost 1984). Ned later recalled, "The old Teepee circles that we see along the bench near DeMaris springs were, in those days, sometimes occupied by many Indian lodges. Late in the fall the Indians would come in to kill their winter supply of meat."[7] Homesteader A. C. Newton found tipi poles left behind above the springs, at Rattlesnake Mountain, and at Trail Creek (Sanzenbacher 1957). Although the wooden poles are long gone, some of the rings are still there today.

The Bighorn Basin was a place of refuge for Crow during the early reservation period. Food shortage was a common theme in settler accounts (Ruskowsky 2008, 108; Woods 1997, 210). In the fall of 1885, Jim Winn noted that the seventy-five Crow families who were camping in the southern part of the basin were likely killing the ranch's cattle (Woods 1997, 111). The winter of 1886–1887 was particularly harsh. Thousands of cattle died of exposure and starvation. In February 1887, the temperatures hovered below 0 degrees Fahrenheit and deep snow prevented people and animals from getting to food reserves. The weather was so bad that some Crow dug up dead cattle for food.[8] In the spring, Crow families had difficulty leaving the basin because so many of their horses had died of exposure (Lindsay 1932, 133).

The Crow in these stories were nomadic equestrians who saw the arrival of cattle and the disappearance of buffalo. They traded animal furs, gambled and danced and bet on horse races, and rode to agencies for inadequate food rations. They hunted and camped along the riverbanks, visited the hot springs, fasted at Heart Mountain, and stole horses from their enemies. Evidence of Crow seasonal settlement stops after Wyoming became a state in 1890. Crow presence was rarely recorded by either settler or Indigenous communities after that time. The Crow of the early twentieth century experienced disease and depopulation, social disruption and oppression, high infant mortality, racism, forced attendance at boarding schools, ineffective government leadership, land losses, and the banning of Native language and religious practices (Bradley 1970; Hoxie 1995; Voget 1984). Most Apsáalooke who were interviewed in the early twentieth century chose not to discuss their lives after the buffalo days (Linderman 1930, 311; Nabokov 1967, ix).

Performers, Promoters, and the Wild West

The turn of the twentieth century marked a transition from resident to visitor for the Crow. The visible transformation from Indian country to cowboy country was complete on the Cody landscape. In 1901, *The Cody Enter-*

prise reported that "a band of Crow Indians, numbering about thirty, passed through Cody last Monday on their way to visit the Shoshones."[9] The Crows were no longer residents; they were "passing through."

The hot springs at Colter's Hell were long recognized for their healing properties. In the mid-1880s, entrepreneur Charles DeMaris "discovered" the mineral springs of the Stinking Water and promoted the water's therapeutic qualities at his hotel and bathhouse through the sale of bottled spring water.[10] Town founders considered the Bighorn Basin to be ideal for promoting tourism and they devoted considerable efforts to increasing the attractiveness of the region (Bonner 2007). In 1895 they laid the plat for "Cody City" on top of former Indian campsites near the hot springs. They soon relocated the town several kilometers east to its present location, where it was incorporated in 1901. The Buffalo Bill Dam and Reservoir, which controls the flow of the Shoshone River and provides irrigation and drinking water across the basin through a series of canals and reservoirs, was completed in 1910 (Bonner 2007).

The growth of American settlements is often presented as a process that was devoid of Native people, but this depiction is not entirely accurate (see also Russell, this volume). Crow families returned to newly founded towns as entertainers and participants in commemorations of "past" Indian lifeways. They rode in parades at county fairs, danced for tourists on hotel porches and at guest ranches, cut ribbons at park openings, and performed in reenactments of military battles (Kensel 2010, 119–121; Mellis 2003, 55–61; Nabokov and Loendorf 2004, 44).

Chief Plenty Coups and other Crow leaders were instrumental in negotiating the terms by which the railroad to reach Cody could pass through the Crow Reservation. The Chicago, Burlington, & Quincy Railroad, which ran from Toluca, Montana, to Cody operated from 1901 until 1911. Due to a steep grade and frequent mechanical issues, the trains on this line frequently fell behind schedule (Wasden 1973, 236). The Crow believe that the trains ran late because the Awakkulé, or Earth Holders (aka Little People), deliberately slowed them down.[11]

Buffalo Bill maintained friendships with Lakota from the Wild West show, some of whom joined him in Cody (Bonner 2007). His relationships with the nearby Crow, including Plenty Coups, who lived just 106 kilometers north of Cody, are less well documented. The prominent imagery of the Wild West does not emphasize that the Crows allied with the American government; they fought alongside US soldiers, not against them. Native people rode in parades alongside Buffalo Bill wearing full regalia to represent the past. In 1913, when Prince Albert I of Monaco became the first reigning European monarch to visit the United States, several dozen Crow men and their families participated in the celebration.[12] During an extravagant parade, Prince Albert and Chief Plenty Coups dramatically exchanged gifts as symbolic rulers. They both later visited the DeMaris Hot Springs (possibly together), an indication of the significance and importance of the springs in the twentieth century.[13]

Town leaders continued to capitalize on Buffalo Bill's name recognition even after he died suddenly in 1917. By the 1920s, tourists traveled to Cody to stay at guest ranches, ride horses, camp in the mountains, and watch cowboy-and-Indian performances, all part of a constructed Old West experience (Nicholas 2006). Hundreds of Crow people participated in these events, despite the fact that Indian agents limited Crow participation in summer fairs and rodeos because such events took them away from farm production and assimilation activities (Mellis 2003, 57). Novelist and local newspaper editor Caroline Lockhart and Cody area businessmen created the annual Cody Stampede, which featured parades, rodeos, and a town extravaganza that was held over the Fourth of July holiday (a tradition that continues today). The participation of Lockhart's Crow friends made the event extremely successful. It was easier for Native community members to obtain permission to leave the reservation during the national holiday (Clayton 2007; Elias Goes Ahead, personal communication 2010).

The Stampede Rodeo in the 1920s included more than a dozen Indian-only competitive events for both men and women.[14] Newspapers across the country heavily promoted the Crow presence.[15] Cody residents and businesses personally funded these trips. They paid for travel, food, and lodging (often at their own homes).[16] Crow men such as Simon Bull-Tail saw these invitations as opportunities to introduce their children to Cody and to obtain important resources such as eagle feathers.[17]

Crow participation in Cody events was mutually beneficial to both parties. The Crow presence increased tourist dollars, while Crow participants received compensation and opportunities to compete for prize money. Participating in commemorative events allowed the Crow to return to culturally significant places during a period when they otherwise were not allowed and/or encouraged to leave the reservation. They could also practice banned or discouraged activities, such as speaking their language, dancing, socializing, traveling, and collecting medicinal plants. These appearances further shaped the myth of the glory days of the Old West that was being written onto an increasingly changing post-frontier world. In the context of these performances, men and women like William Cody, Caroline Lockhart, and Ned Frost created possibilities for Native peoples like Plenty Coups and Simon Bull-Tail to return to places of personal and cultural importance (Medicine Crow 2000, 39). While inequality and exploitation was inevitable in these arrangements, dismissing the benefits for the Crow removes their active manipulation of the cowboy-and-Indian theme to their advantage (Mellis 2003). Both settlers and Natives in Cody realized that wearing certain clothing and adopting certain mannerisms was what made these events economically successful and made Cody "western" (Clayton 2007; Nicholas 2006).

Plenty Coups often visited the Frosts when he was in town. Ned Frost was a professional outfitter and businessman. His wife Mary operated a curios store, where she bought and sold Native-made items. Sometimes Ned drove Plenty Coups across the river to visit the hot springs. During one of these trips, they stopped at the tipi rings, where Plenty Coups identified the circle of stones where his tipi had stood sixty years before (Frost and Frost 1984, 78; M. Frost 1942). We do not know the exact ring that Plenty Coups identified at the site, but all tipi rings represent Crow home and homeland.

Connecting the Past and Present

Since the early 1900s, Cody has advertised itself as a gateway to Yellowstone. It is located only 87 kilometers from the park along the North Fork of the Shoshone River. From 1903 to 1925, all motorized vehicles on the Cody Road to Yellowstone passed the hot springs and the tipi rings. By 1924, nearly 60,000 visitors were traveling though Cody every year on their way to the park (Nicholas 2006, 46). Yellowstone pamphlets listed a trip to the DeMaris Springs and Tepee Rings as one of the "Ten Interesting Side Trips while visiting Cody." About the same time, Cody high school students used rocks (likely from the rings) to create a giant letter C on the hill next to the site, a sign of civic pride that was visible from downtown. Incoming high school seniors are now responsible for repainting the C every year; it used to be part of the initiation of the freshman class.[18]

Vehicle traffic across the site ultimately impacted the tipi rings. In 1942, Mary Frost wrote:

> Vandals do so much harm. Only last summer a very sweet old lady showed me, with great pride, two large gray stones from the tepee rings she was taking home to Kansas for her rock garden. . . . We are in the heart of the tourist country, and if precautions are not taken in the near future, our tepee rings that have been used and left to us by a fast disappearing people will also be gone, along with another link to the past. (Frost 1942, 52–53)

As Frost denounced the impact of tourism on archaeological sites in Cody, the Crow struggled with poverty, poor health care, and unemployment (Hoxie 1991; Nabokov 1988; Voget 1984). They were not, however, a "fast disappearing people." The population was rebounding. Hundreds of Crow men served in World War II (Bauerle 2003; Medicine Crow 2000). The children and grandchildren of those who had known Buffalo Bill and Caroline Lockhart continued to perform in Cody. During the 1941 Stampede Rodeo, when Aloysius Holds-the-Enemy died after he was thrown from his horse during the first race of the show, the editor of the *Cody Enterprise* wrote that "it was the passing of a great and true friend of Cody, whose relations with our town and people were not purely mercenary. He has done far more for us than money could ever buy."[19]

The Wyoming State Historical Society commemorated the 150th anniversary of Colter's journey in 1957 by reenacting his trek through Wyoming. Ned Frost led a tour to the tipi rings dressed in fringed buckskin clothing.[20] The Historical Society invited Arapaho and Shoshone from Wyoming's Wind River Reservation to participate in the pageant. "They pitched their tepees near the old tepee rings on the bench above the Shoshone River where their forefathers had camped for generations" (Dominick and Chivers 2004, 132). The organizers clearly saw the stone circles as an important connection to the past. Mountain man rendezvous clubs camped on top of old Indian encampments at Trail Creek at least through the 1980s (Cook et al. 1996, 161; Ruskowsky 2008). Local historian Bob Edgar founded Old Trail Town in 1967 over the abandoned plat of the original Cody City for the purpose of collecting and preserving neglected historic structures. The cabins of both Victor Arland and Curley are there today.[21]

During the middle of the twentieth century, thousands of people swam at the hot springs, crossing the river via a new suspension bridge. The restaurant was relocated in the late 1960s, and floods permanently damaged the swimming-pool building in the early 1980s (Cook et al. 1996, 157). The loss of the structure and the later loss of the bridge did not deter townspeople from meeting at the hot springs, where baptisms were as common as beer busts.

In 1985, archaeologists officially recorded part of the tipi ring site that is on federally managed land owned by the Bureau of Reclamation as part of Section 106 compliance for a power-line survey. The site was outside the impact corridor, and it was only briefly inspected. The report states, "As this site is a well-preserved example of a poorly documented site type in this environmental context, it is recommended that it be carefully mapped and examined for diagnostic cultural materials."[22] That task was never completed, partly because the greatest density of tipi rings at the site extends onto private land. The exact number of features and the spatial organization of the site remain unknown. Stone circle sites more broadly are often poorly documented because they are a common site type with limited deposition and artifacts (Scheiber 1993). However, archaeologists are currently revisiting their importance and investigating their potential for addressing the large-scale social dynamics of hunter-gatherer populations (Ortman et al. in press), and the site is officially considered eligible for nomination to the National Register of Historic Places.

In the New West (the land of ski resorts, microbreweries, covered-wagon espresso kiosks, and low taxes), wealthy outsiders regularly purchase second homes (Clayton 2008, 179; Sheridan 2007). Billionaires like Bill Gates and Kanye West are the latest celebrities who have been drawn to Cody.[23] In 1993, a New York businessman purchased several thousand acres that includes the tipi rings, hot springs, and trails to the mountains.[24] He subsequently removed public access, an action that angered many Cody residents, who for years had swum at the springs, driven all-terrain vehicles up the mountain, walked their dogs along the river, and picked up artifacts. They considered that land to be a common resource for everyone's enjoyment and they shared a collective sense of ownership and stewardship. The landowner cleaned up debris left from decades of unsupervised recreational use and built a modern private pool at the thermal springs.

This cycle is reminiscent of the one cattle ranchers started in the 1870s. Their descendants now are in the position that former Indigenous residents were, indignant that outsiders tell them where they can be and what belongs to them. The county road reopened after a decade-long battle between the landowner and the city. However, no trespassing signs warn visitors not to leave the road; a locked gate blocks the two-track gravel road; and a strict no-access policy is enforced. Exclusion is the current price of conservation. People can no longer drive over the rings, remove what is left of tiny artifacts, or carry away tipi ring rocks to Midwest flower gardens. Perhaps developing an inclusive site biography will lead to more comprehensive stewardship strategies in the future.

Conclusion

Crow history is place history, a history of cultural and natural features that have literally witnessed the passing of time as dynamic living landscapes. Indigenous people such as the Crow pried rocks from riverbanks to serve as footprints of their tipi homes. They met the first Euro-American trappers and traders and settlers such as George Drouillard, Victor Arland, and Charles DeMaris (all of whom shared an underappreciated French heritage). These Crow encampments represent the place where Plenty Coups played in long-gone geysers, camped and swam in the mineral springs, tracked down horse thieves, and visited with men such as Prince Albert of Monaco, Buffalo Bill Cody, and Ned Frost. The tipi rings were used to promote Colter's Hell and Yellowstone tourism. They became part of commemorations and reenactments. And they are now part of conversations about private versus public lands in a new era of wealthy exclusionism. The history here includes multiple stakeholders and descendant communities.

Crow history is also Apsáalooke history, the history of the people who helped craft sustainable heritage tourism over the last century and who remain connected to Ammitaalasshé through the stories their grandparents handed down to them about the land, the people, and ways to live a good life, but also through stories of traders and cowboys, of the Cody Stampede and dances and rodeos and parades and powwows. Personal relationships between settlers and Natives shaped a lasting western legacy that paradoxically is built on the image of a vanishing Indian. However, these relationships also created opportunities for Crow people to practice traditions that were not always available to them in their reservation homes and are memorialized (literally) in the footprints of their old homes.

This case study offers a hybrid methodology for reinserting Indigenous presence in colonized spaces by combining disparate sources to connect threads of the past. These data demonstrate ongoing multiethnic entanglement, persistence, and innovation that do not appear when archaeologists use conventional methodologies and recording techniques. Some archaeologists marginalize the interpretive potential of tipi ring sites because they lack temporal control. However, Indigenous landscapes are not products of western concepts of time. Restoring the Indigenous past, present, and future to the Bighorn Basin, the Land Beyond the Mountains, begins by acknowledging this fundamental difference.

Acknowledgments

I am extremely grateful for the enthusiastic participation of Cody residents and Crow tribal members, especially the entire Two Leggins family, Mary Keller, Sue Simpson, Hunter Old Elk, and Mack Frost. The Buffalo Bill Center for the West, the Cody Institute for Western Area Studies, the Wyoming Historical Society, the Wyoming Council for the Humanities, the Heart Mountain Ranch Nature Conservancy, and the National Park Foundation provided financial and logistical support. Timothy McCleary, Grant Bulltail, Lawrence Loendorf, Elias Goes Ahead, Patrick Hill, and Burdick Two Leggins clarified Crow place-names, history, and culture. Staff at the McCracken Research Library at the Buffalo Bill Center of the West, the Park County Archives (Cody, Wyoming), and Little Big Horn College graciously tracked down countless unpublished resources. Finally, I thank the organizers of and contributors to this volume and the external reviewers for their feedback and inspiration.

Notes

1. Timothy McCleary, Timothy Bernardis, and Vida Falls Down, "The Chief Plenty Coups House and Sacred Spring," 1996, manuscript on file, Little Big Horn College Library, Crow Agency, Montana; Waller (2015).

2. Ned Frost, "Colter's Hell, Cody, Park County, Wyoming, National Register #73001937," National Register of Historic Places Nomination Form, United States Department of the Interior, National Park Service, Washington, DC, August 14, 1973.

3. "Cowboys Group Has Cody Meet," *Billings Gazette*, August 17, 1940, 2. See also Curtis (1909, 70, 86, 114); Linderman (1930, 100–101); Medicine Crow (2000, 38–39); Nabokov (1967, 39, 74, 109); and Wright (1874, 489–499).

4. "The Recent Battle of Stinking Water," *Colorado Banner*, February 8, 1850, 7. See also Beckwourth (1856); Curtis (1909, 86–91); and Linderman 1932, 114).

5. Letters from Victor Arland to Camille Dadant, Victor Arland Collection, MS 002.01.07, MS 002.01.15, MS 002.01.16, MS 002.01,29, McCracken Research Library, Buffalo Bill Center of the West, Cody, Wyoming.

6. Tom Osborne Memoirs, Park County Archives, Cody, Wyoming.

7. "Ned Frost Vividly Relates Tales of Hunting with Gun and Camera," from the files of the Cody Business and Professional Women's Club, 1935, 1. Ned Frost Collection, Park County Archives. See also Dominick and Chivers 2004, 114.

8. Journal #1 of Otto Franc Von Lichtenstein from the Pitchfork Ranch, entry for February 4, 1887, Count Otto Franc Von Lichtenstein Collection, MS 010.02.01.14, McCracken Research Library.

9. "Local Short Stories," *Cody Enterprise*, July 18, 1901, 3.

10. "City and County," *Billings Gazette*, May 11, 1886, 4.

11. Stuart W. Conner, "Crow Conversations with Conner," 202, 1993, manuscript on file, Little Big Horn College Library, Crow Agency, Montana; Patrick Hill, personal communication 2017.

12. "Prince of Monaco Presents Rifle to Chief Plenty Coos," *Park County Enterprise*, September 17, 1913, 8.

13. "Distinguished Guests at DeMaris Springs," *Park County Enterprise*, September 20, 1913, 1.

14. "Buffalo Bill's Town Prepares for Stampede," *Billings Gazette*, June 28, 1928, 1.

15. Lon Smith, "Up in Buffalo Bill's Country," *Los Angeles Times*, May 11, 1924, 5–6.

16. "City and County," *Billings Gazette*, July 2, 1950, B1; Alta Booth Dunn, "Crow Indians Guests of Honor at Cody Stampede," *Casper-Star-Tribune*, December 31, 1922, M3.

17. "Are You Spoiling for a Good Time? Then Come to Cody Stampede Ball," *Park County Enterprise*, November 30, 1921, 1.

18. Cody High School Bronc Yearbook, 1940, 19, Park County Archives.

19. Breck Moran, "Al Holds-the-Enemy Is Gone to the Kanawha of Kanawhas," newspaper clipping from July 1941, Hazel People's Scrapbook, Crow Indian Collection, Park County Archives.

20. Jack Richard Photograph Collection, MS 089, McCracken Research Library. .

21. Dewey Vanderhoff, "Bob Edgar," *Powell Tribune*, April 27, 2012.

22. John C. Acklen, "Wyoming Cultural Property Form, 48PA898," Buffalo Bill Powerline Survey (outside survey area) for the Wyoming Area Power Authority and Bureau of Reclamation, conducted by Mariah Associates, October 3, 1985.

23. Elliot Ross, "Kanye, Out West," *New York Times*, February 23, 2020.

24. Ruffin Prevost, "Park County Reopens Road to Foot of Rattlesnake Mountain," *Billings Gazette*, September 13, 2007, 1A, 9A.

References Cited

Basso, Keith H. 1996. *Wisdom Sits in Places: Landscape and Language among the Western Apache*. Albuquerque: University of New Mexico Press.

Bauerle, Phenocia, ed. 2003. *The Way of the Warrior: Stories of the Crow People*. Lincoln: University of Nebraska Press.

Beckwourth, James P. 1856. *The Life and Adventures of James P. Beckwourth, Mountaineer, Scout, and Pioneer, and Chief of the Crow Nation of Indians*. New York: Harper and Brothers.

Bonner, Robert E. 2007. *William F. Cody's Wyoming Empire: The Buffalo Bill Nobody Knows*. Norman: University of Oklahoma Press.

Bradley, Charles Crane. 1970. After the Buffalo Days: Documents on the Crow Indians from the 1880s to the 1920s. Master's thesis, Montana State University, Bozeman.

Brown, Mark H. 1961. *The Plainsmen of the Yellowstone: A History of the Yellowstone Basin*. Lincoln: University of Nebraska Press.

Calloway, Colin G. 1986. The Only Way Open to Us: The Crow Struggle for Survival in the Nineteenth Century. *North Dakota History* 53: 24–34. 1991.

———. 1991. Indian History in Wyoming. *Annals of Wyoming* 63: 125–130.

Clayton, John. 2007. *The Cowboy Girl: The Life of Caroline Lockhart*. Lincoln: University of Nebraska Press.

———. 2008. When Cowboys Became Capitalists and the West Became New. *Drumlummon Views* (Fall): 173–182.

Cook, Jeannie, Lynn Johnson Houze, Bob Edgar, and Paul Fees. 1996. *Buffalo Bill's Town in the Rockies: A Pictorial History of Cody, Wyoming*. Virginia Beach, VA: Donning.

Curtis, Edward S. 1909. *The North American Indian*. Vol. 4, *The Apsaroke, or Crows, The Hidatsa*. Seattle, WA: E. S. Curtis.

Deane, John W. 1996. *The Major of Meeteetse: The Autobiography of John W. Deane*. Worland, WY: Serlkay.

Dominick, DeWitt, and Mary Dominick Chivers. 2004. *Doctor Dewey: Stories from the Life and Career of Dr. DeWitt Dominick of Cody, Wyoming*. Cody, WY: WordsWorth.

Edgar, Bob, and Jack Turnell. 1987. *Brand of a Legend*. Basin, WY: Basin Republican Rustler.

Ewers, John C. 1968. *Indian Life on the Upper Missouri*. Norman: University of Oklahoma Press.

Frost, Dick, and Mary Frost. 1984. *Tracks, Trails, and Tales*. Cody, WY: D. Frost.

Frost, Mary. 1942. Mysteries of the Past. *Annals of Wyoming* 14: 51–55.

Hamilton, William T. 1910. Trapping Expedition, 1848–9. *Contributions to the Historical Society of Montana* 7: 231–252.

Hoxie, Frederick E. 1991. Searching for Structure: Reconstructing Crow Family Life during the Reservation Era. *American Indian Quarterly* 15: 287–309.

———. 1995. *Parading through History: The Making of the Crow Nation in America, 1805–1935*. New York: Cambridge University Press.

Keller, Mary L. 2014. Indigenous Studies and "the Sacred." *American Indian Quarterly* 38: 82–109.

Kensel, W. Hudson. 2010. *Dude Ranching in Yellowstone Country: Larry Larom and Valley Ranch, 1915–1969*. Norman: University of Oklahoma.

Keyser, James D., and George Poetschat. 2009. *Crow Rock Art in the Bighorn Basin: Petroglyphs at No Water, Wyoming.* Oregon Archaeological Society Publication 20. Portland: Oregon Archaeological Society Press.

Leforge, Thomas. 1974. *Memoirs of a White Crow Indian.* Lincoln: University of Nebraska Press.

Leonard, Zenas. 1839. *Narrative of the Adventures of Zenas Leonard.* Clearfield, PA: D. W. Moore.

Lightfoot, Kent G., and Sara L. Gonzalez. 2018. The Study of Sustained Colonialism: An Example from the Kashaya Pomo Homeland in Northern California. *American Antiquity* 83: 427–443.

Linderman, Frank B. 1930. *Plenty-Coups: Chief of the Crows.* Lincoln: University of Nebraska Press.

———. 1932. *Pretty-Shield: Medicine Woman of the Crows.* Lincoln: University of Nebraska Press.

Lindsay, Charles. 1932. The Big Horn Basin. *The University Studies of the University of Nebraska* 28–29: 1–274.

Martin, Curtis. 2016. *Ephemeral Bounty: Wickiups, Trade Goods, and the Final Years of the Autonomous Ute.* Salt Lake City: University of Utah Press.

McCleary, Carrie Moran. 2001. Crow Landscapes not Forgotten: Project Preserves Traditional Names. *Indian Country Today,* 3 January. Accessed December 3, 2015.

McCleary, Timothy. 2016. *Crow Indian Rock Art: Indigenous Perspectives and Interpretations.* New York: Routledge.

Medicine Crow, Joseph. 2000. *From the Heart of the Crow Country.* Lincoln: University of Nebraska Press.

Mellis, Allison Fuss. 2003. *Riding Buffaloes and Broncos: Rodeo and Native Traditions in the Northern Great Plains.* Norman: University of Oklahoma Press.

Nabokov, Peter. 1967. *Two Leggings: The Making of a Crow Warrior.* New York: Thomas Y. Crowell.

———. 1988. Cultivating Themselves: The Inter-Play of Crow Indian Religion and History. PhD diss., University of California, Berkeley.

Nabokov, Peter, and Lawrence L. Loendorf. 2004. *Restoring a Presence: American Indians and Yellowstone National Park.* Norman: University of Oklahoma Press.

Newton, Cody. 2018. Equestrian Hunter-Gatherers and the Animal Trade of the Western Great Plains and Adjacent Rocky Mountains, 1800–1860. PhD diss., University of Colorado, Boulder.

Nicholas, Liza J. 2006. *Becoming Western: Stories of Culture and Identity in the Cowboy State.* University of Nebraska Press, Lincoln.

Nichter, Daniel A. 2012. French Influences in the History of Wyoming from La Salle to Arland. Master's thesis, University of Wyoming, Laramie.

Oetelaar, Gerald A. 2016. Places on the Blackfoot Homeland: Markers of Cosmology, Social Relationships and History. In *Marking the Land: Hunter-Gatherer Creation of Meaning in Their Environment,* edited by William A Lovis and Robert Whallon, 45–66. New York: Routledge.

Ortman, Scott, Laura L. Scheiber, and Zachary Cooper. In press. Scaling Analysis of Prehistoric Wyoming Camp Sites: Implications for Hunter-Gatherer Social Dynamics. In *Intra-Site Spatial Analysis of Mobile Peoples: Analytical Approaches to Reconstructing Occupation History,* edited by Amy E. Clark and Joseph A. M. Gingerich. University of Utah Press, Salt Lake City.

Panich, Lee M., and Tsim D. Schneider. 2019. Categorical Denial: Evaluating Post-1492 Indigenous Erasure in the Paper Trail of American Archaeology. *American Antiquity* 84: 651–668.

Reher, Charles A. 1983. Analysis of Spatial Structure in Stone Circle Sites. In *From Microcosm to Macrocosm: Advances in Tipi Ring Investigation and Interpretation*, edited by Leslie B. Davis, 193–222. Lincoln, NE: Augstums Pr. Service.

Rollinson, John K. 1948. *Wyoming Cattle Trails*. Caldwell, ID: Caxton.

Ruskowsky, Nancy Heyl. 2008. *Two Dot Ranch: A Biography of Place*. Greybull, WY: Pronghorn.

Sanzenbacher, Dorothea A. 1957. *Trail Creek Ranch. Park County Wyoming*. Cody, WY: D. A. Sanzenbacher.

Scheiber, Laura L. 1993. Prehistoric Domestic Architecture on the Northwestern High Plains: A Temporal Analysis of Stone Circles in Wyoming. Master's thesis, University of Wyoming, Laramie.

Scheiber, Laura L., and Katherine L. Burnett. 2020. Writing Histories at Êngkahonovita *Ogwêvi*: Multicultural Entanglement at Red Canyon, Wyoming, USA. *Antiquity* 94(378): 1592–1613.

Scheiber, Laura L., and Judson Byrd Finley. 2010a. Domestic Campsites and Cyber Landscapes in the Rocky Mountains. *Antiquity* 84(323): 114–130.

———. 2010b. Mountain Shoshone Technological Transitions across the Great Divide. In *Across a Great Divide: Change and Continuity in Native North America, 1400–1900*, edited by Laura L. Scheiber and Mark D. Mitchell, 128–148. Tucson: University of Arizona Press.

Sheridan, Thomas E. 2007. Embattled Ranches, Endangered Species, and Urban Sprawl: The Political Ecology of the New American West. *Annual Review of Anthropology* 36: 121–138.

Skarsten, M. O. 1964. *George Drouillard: Hunter and Interpreter for Lewis and Clark and Fur Trader, 1807–1810*. Spokane, WA: Arthur H. Clark.

US Congress. Senate. 1908. *A Company for Breeding Horses on the Crow Indian Reservation, Montana and the Survey and Allotment of Indian Lands within the Limit of the Crow Indian Reservation, Montana. Hearings Before the Committee on Indian Affairs, United States Senate on the Bill S. 2087 and on the Bill S. 2963*. Washington, DC: Government Printing Office.

Victor, Frances Fuller. 1871. *The River of the West: Life and Adventure in the Rocky Mountains and Oregon*. Hartford, CT: Columbian Books.

Voget, Fred W. 1984. *The Shoshoni-Crow Sun Dance*. Norman: University of Oklahoma.

Waller, Nicholas. 2015. Exactly in the Right Place: Ways of Making and Maintaining a Crow Landscape. PhD diss., School of Global Studies, University of Gothenburg.

Wasden, David J. 1973. *From Beaver to Oil: A Century in the Development of the Big Horn Basin*. Cheyenne, WY: Pioneer.

Wolfe, Patrick. 2006. Settler Colonialism and the Elimination of the Native. *Journal of Genocide Research* 8: 387–409.

Woods, Lawrence M. 1997. *Wyoming's Big Horn Basin to 1901: A Late Frontier*. Spokane, WA: Arthur H. Clark.

Wright, James. 1874. Report of the Commission to Negotiate with the Crow Tribe of Indians. In *Annual Report of the Commissioner of Indian Affairs to the Secretary of the Interior for the Year 1873*, edited by Edward P. Smith, 481–511. Washington, DC: Government Printing Office.

11

Seeking Indigenous Trade Networks of the Midcontinent through Glass Beads from *La Belle* (41MG86)

HEATHER WALDER

In colonial contexts of North America, Indigenous peoples' acquisition, trade, and exchange of manufactured items occurred in a wide range of contexts and was often driven by social factors rather than by technology (Allender 2018; Forde 2017; Legg et al. 2019; Michelaki et al. 2015). The presence of European-made material culture in "colonial spaces" need not represent discontinuity of Indigenous practices, interaction networks, or power structures (Beaudoin 2019; Blair 2016; Ferris et al. 2014, 11–13; Silliman 2010; Witgen 2012). Likewise, as this volume contends, dominant theoretical and methodological considerations in archaeology can obscure the agency, identity, and presence of postcontact Indigenous communities (Panich and Schneider 2019).

This chapter investigates Native American exchange relationships in North America's western Great Lakes region using a rather unlikely source of evidence: glass trade beads excavated from a French ship that sank off the coast of what is now Texas in 1686 (Bruseth et al. 2017). The recipes used to produce the glass beads packed onto the ship *La Belle*, which was equipped to trade with local communities on the Mississippi Delta, provide insight into exchange networks and social connections of Indigenous communities of the Great Lakes region. René Robert Cavelier, Sieur de La Salle, a French explorer who led the *La Belle* expedition, provides a connection between these artifacts and geographic areas. La Salle's prior travels across the Great Lakes and on the upper Mississippi River laid the framework for his final, unsuccessful attempt to establish a colony at the mouth of that river.

Most of the 770,000 glass trade beads recovered from the *La Belle* shipwreck are common types that are widely found across seventeenth-century archaeological sites in North America (Perttula and Glascock 2017; Walthall 2015). In the Great Lakes region, these sites are associated with Potawatomi, Menominee, Kaskaskia, Ojibwe, Meskwaki, Wendat, and other Indigenous communities. Nondestructive analysis of the chemical compositions of beads and the recipes used to make them provides opportunities to identify similarities in glass recipe that extend beyond visual differences. Comparative analysis of the *La Belle* shipwreck assemblage with other bead assemblages can be used to connect recipes for glass beads from sites in the Great Lakes to those of beads that French trade networks delivered to North America. While individual glass trade beads from *La Belle* and from archaeological sites in the Great Lakes are not compositionally identical, they have close similarities and fit the same glass recipe subgroups.

Examining base glass and trace elements in these glass recipes clarifies how Indigenous peoples incorporated European-made glass beads into their own economic and social networks in the Great Lakes region. The excavators of *La Belle* suggest the ship's beads may have come from an Italian glasshouse, citing a historical text that mentions trade in "Venetian pearls" (Bruseth and Turner 2005, 87), but their European provenience remains unconfirmed. A recent typological and chemical study of glass beads from *La Belle* also asserted the need for comparative information from French, Venetian, and other European glasshouses (Perttula and Glascock 2017, 523). Identifying the chemical elements present in glass beads clarifies the methods used in various beadmaking centers and patterns of European production (Dussubeiux and Karklins 2016; Karklins and Bonneau 2019; Loewen 2019). This step is necessary for tracing these objects across their "global itineraries" as they become integrated into Native North American social and economic value systems (Blair 2015). This project contextualizes Indigenous communities as active participants in both regional exchange and in the global trade networks of seventeenth-century colonial enterprises.

The Great Lakes region has been visualized as a Native New World of socially structured and dynamic connections among sovereign Indigenous nations, such as Dakota and Anishinaabeg communities who actively resisted colonial authority by blatantly trading with illicit French traders (*coureurs de bois*) and accepted gifts from the French on their own terms (Witgen

2012, 257–261). Highlighting the presence of Indigenous value systems and exchange relationships in colonial contexts makes it possible to identify previously unrecognized links among the diverse and dynamically interacting Indigenous communities of the Great Lakes region in the seventeenth century. This work applies an innovative archaeometric method to examine an artifact category (glass beads) that, like other "diagnostic" trade items, is often overinterpreted as a marker of Indigenous and colonial interactions and relationships (Hull, this volume; Walder and Yann 2018).

Why Glass Trade Beads?

This chapter examines glass trade beads not as objects of colonial encounters but as evidence of Indigenous agency. Although past acculturation-based paradigms (e.g., Quimby 1966) placed undue emphasis on glass beads as diagnostic markers of colonial encounters to the detriment of the study of "less flashy" material categories (Jordan, this volume), beads can represent cultural resiliency and innovation. For example, Plains and western Great Lakes communities reworked beads into pendants through a technologically sophisticated process of remelting (Billeck 2016; Schultz and Walder 2016; Walder 2013a). These pendants were often included in funerary assemblages, a sign of their social significance (Howard 1972). Others have commented on the material and color symbolism of glass beads in Indigenous contexts (Hamell 1983; Panich 2014; Ross 1997; Turgeon 2001), the rapid incorporation of glass beads in robust precolonial trade networks (Grover 2016), and the importance of beads as adornment that indicate identity (Loren 2010; White 2008).

Glass beads are critical tools for tracing intercultural interactions, population movements, and other regional-scale activities of Indigenous communities of the midcontinent. A glass bead or other manufactured item does not mean "a European was here," especially when it is found alone or with an otherwise "precontact" material assemblage (Russell, this volume). Communities connected by down-the-line trade within extant precolonial exchange networks are an overlooked aspect of the archaeology of this period, and these so-called protohistoric sites can be easily missed (Brown and Sasso 2001; Grover 2016; McLeester and Schurr 2020). Manufactured items may occur in small quantities at sites that are distant from known European trading centers of the era, especially in the western Great Lakes region. The goal of my documentation of glass bead recipes from a French trade ship is to learn how Indigenous peoples of the midcontinent who were connected to Great Lakes trade networks obtained glass beads and exchanged them internally. Bead recipes are markers that connect otherwise unassociated archaeological sites to distinct Indigenous communities.

Historical Background

French explorers, traders, and missionaries were some of the first Europeans to visit the interior and western Great Lakes region in the seventeenth century. They brought glass beads and other gifts to foster new relationships with peoples they encountered. In 1679, René Robert Cavelier (Sieur de La Salle) traveled through the Great Lakes and stopped at the islands of Wisconsin's Door Peninsula, including Rock Island (Mason 1986, 17). La Salle and other early explorers relied heavily on Native guides and contacts to help them develop alliances and trading relationships and for guide them in unfamiliar territory (White 1991, 28, 35). These missions were not always successful. For example, archaeologists continue to search for La Salle's ill-fated trade ship *Le Griffon,* which sank somewhere in Lake Michigan between Green Bay and Michilimackinac on September 18, 1679 (Quimby 1966, 45–62). La Salle, who was not aboard, continued to explore the interior of North America, eventually traversing the Mississippi River and entering the Gulf of Mexico on April 9, 1682, then returning to France via Quebec in 1683 (Bruseth et al. 2017, 4–5).

In 1684, La Salle departed from France in command of four ships, including a barque christened *La Belle* (Bruseth and Turner 2005). *La Belle* was fully stocked with trade items necessary for establishing a strategic French colony near the mouth of the Mississippi River so France could control interior North American trade routes (Bruseth and Turner 2005, 20). Problems with navigation caused the explorers to overshoot their destination, and in 1686, *La Belle* ran aground and eventually sank in Matagorda Bay off the southern coast of Texas. The surviving sailors and colonists established Fort St. Louis (41VT4) approximately 50 miles inland. They occupied the site from 1685 to 1689. Spanish colonizers later took over the settlement and constructed the Presidio Nuestra Señora de Loreto de la Bahía, which they operated from 1721 to 1730 (Bruseth et al. 2004; Perttula 2006).

In 1996 and 1997 a massive, publicly funded archaeology project constructed a dry cofferdam around the wreck, which was formally designated the La Salle Shipwreck Site (41MG86). Meticulous excavation provided a unique opportunity to study a French colonial-era ship stocked for the Americas. The excavations revealed that *La Belle* carried cannons, woodworking tools, ceramic jars, axes, iconographic rings, pins, needles, and an entire box of glass trade beads strung to be easily divided and exchanged (Bruseth et al. 2017). There also may have been another barrel containing beads that was accidentally blown open during preliminary excavations (Bruseth and Turner 2005, 87). The glass beads La Salle brought with him for the new colony at the mouth of the Mississippi may have come from the same European glass workshops that provided beads for his earlier expeditions in the Great Lakes.

Research Goals and Assumptions

The goal of analyzing glass beads from *La Belle* is not simply to document French colonial trade goods but rather to compare the recipes used to create them to those of a dataset obtained from archaeological sites associated with Indigenous communities of the Great Lakes (Walder 2013b, 2015, 2018). The primary research question is: Are the glass beads recovered from *La Belle* compositionally similar to those from any sites in the Great Lakes region that La Salle may have visited? If so, how can such compositional similarity illuminate Indigenous trade networks and interactions? Can social networks or exchange relationships be inferred? Additional questions connecting beads from *La Belle* and the associated onshore colonial settlements are likewise considered.

Several assumptions underlay my reasoning for examining glass trade beads as a method of tracing Indigenous connections. One is that the procurement of beads for trade in La Salle's final mission was similar to how beads were obtained for earlier journeys. Another is that glass workshops continued to produce beads of similar types and recipes over the decade in question. A third is that the data from beads recovered from *La Belle* can serve as a general proxy for beads brought by French traders in the latter part of the seventeenth century, not specifically beads traded by La Salle himself. In this case, the compositional similarities of beads can highlight trade connections between sites with limited other known affiliations in the historical or archaeological record, linking well-established points to sites with less clear connections in the midcontinent.

Methods and Materials

Analytical Methods

Glass beads are visually classified using a descriptive typology based on color, shape, and manufacturing processes (Karklins 1982; Kidd and Kidd 1970). The method used to discern the composition of the glass, laser ablation-inductively coupled plasma-mass spectrometry (LA-ICP-MS), is minimally invasive. Laure Dussubieux, lab manager of the Elemental Analysis Facility at the Field Museum of Chicago, supervised the analyses. A laser removes material from four sampling areas less than 100 microns (0.1 mm) in diameter. The sampled material is then ionized, using a Varian (now Bruker) inductively coupled plasma-mass spectrometer (ICP-MS) connected to a NewWave UP213 laser. At this facility, the detection limits of the LA-ICP-MS range from 10 parts per billion to 1 part per million for most elements. Accuracy ranges from ±5 percent to ±10 percent, depending on the elements and their concentrations. See Dussubieux et al. (2009) for additional details on the methods and performance of this technique.

Concentrations for major elements, including silica, are calculated with the assumption that in glass the sum of their concentrations in weight percent equals 100 percent (Gratuze 2013). For all major elements, compositional results are presented in oxide weights, while minor and trace elements are presented in parts per million. Exploratory multivariate statistical analyses using IBM SPSS 26.0 (including hierarchical cluster analyses with nearest neighbor and Ward's method) and principal component analysis were used to identify patterns of elements that could be further explored using bivariate scatterplots (see Walder 2015, 752–760; bivariate approach after Hancock et al. 2008).

Samples Analyzed

Eighty-three glass samples were analyzed. These included all major bead types recovered from the shipwreck (n = 67 glass samples, from 65 beads) and a limited subset (n = 16) beads from the associated Fort St. Louis and slightly later Spanish presidio (Table 11.1). Beads were selected from all major

Table 11.1. Analysis of glass bead samples from *La Belle,* Fort Saint Louis (FSL), and Presidio Nuestra Señora de Loreto de la Bahía

Chemical subgroup and approximate dates of circulation in Great Lakes trade	Color	Variety, *La Belle* nomenclature	N from Great Lakes subgroup	N from *La Belle*	N from FSL French	N from Spanish Presidio
Cobalt-colored Mg-low-P (before 1700)	Blue	Variety 1, Variety 8	219	47	5 (SL_02, 03, 04, 05, 13)	1 (SL_09)
Cobalt-colored P-low-Mg (after 1700)	Blue	n/a	101	0	0	1 (SL_11)
Cobalt +antimony Mg-low-P (post-1670, before 1700)	Blue	Variety 1	55	5	2 (SL_01, 07)	1 (SL_12)
Cobalt +antimony P-low-Mg (after 1700)	Blue	n/a	23	0	0	1 (SL_10)
Copper-colored Mg-low-P (before 1700)	Blue	n/a	127	0	1 (SL_06)	0
Copper-colored P-low-Mg (after 1700)	Blue	n/a	104	0	1 (SL_08)	0
Manganese-colored black (dates unknown)	Black	Variety 2	13	5	2 (SL_14, 15)	0
Antimony-opacified white (after 1670)	White	Variety 3	18	5	1 (SL_16)	0
Antimony-opacified white (after 1670)	White	Variety 4 (compound beads)	1	1	0	0
Antimony-opacified blue (after 1670)	Blue	Variety 4 (compound beads)	4	4	0	0

Note: The glass samples are sorted by compositional subgroup as delineated for Upper Great Lakes sites (Walder 2018).

shipboard contexts of *La Belle* and from features or areas with clear French or Spanish associations onshore.

The most common glass bead type recovered from *La Belle* is a cobalt blue translucent seed bead, Variety 1 in the *La Belle* project's nomenclature. A total of forty-seven beads of this type were analyzed from the shipwreck. When these beads were first uncovered, some of them were still on strings, possibly as packaged from the glassmaker. The blue coloration varies and was described as light, medium, and dark, but most fall into the IIa55/56 Kidd and

Kidd type. Notably, beads classified as Variety 1 have several different glass compositions, as described below. Other bead types analyzed included both black and white seed beads (respectively, Variety 2, n = 5; and Variety 3, n = 5). The white beads from *La Belle* had a translucent outer layer around a white inner core (best described as Kidd and Kidd compound type IVa13). Only the translucent outer layer was sampled. The Fort St. Louis white bead (SL_16) is a simple IIa14 type.

Monochrome beads are common across early French colonial sites in North America. However, one type from the shipwreck *La Belle*, a blue-white-blue compound bead of Kidd and Kidd type IVa16 (Variety 4), is not reported in Great Lakes archaeological assemblages. Five glass analyses from three beads of this type were obtained by sampling individual glass layers (three samples of blue outer layers from three beads and one sample each from the white middle and the blue core of one bead).

Results: Tracing Interactions and Trade Routes using Glass Bead Recipes

Beads from *La Belle* and associated onshore sites in Texas and the Great Lakes region (Table 11.1) were made of soda-lime glass; they are classified according to recipe subgroups (Walder 2018). These subgroups correspond to colorants, opacifiers, and other glass ingredients and indicate chronological shifts in European glass bead production technology. The approximate dates of subgroups based on known occupation periods of Great Lakes sites (Table 11.2) fit well with the chronology of *La Belle,* French Fort St. Louis, and the Spanish presidio. Within subgroups, the glass recipes for individual beads are generally most similar to those of beads of the same type recovered at the same archaeological site. However, comparisons between sites can provide data that are useful for identifying patterns within subgroups. The findings for each compositional subgroup are discussed individually.

Navy Blue, Cobalt-Colored Beads

The forty-seven monochrome translucent cobalt blue "seed" beads type IIa55/56, or Variety 1, from *La Belle* came from several different contexts on the ship: Box 1 and Box 4 from the aft hold, and Cask 26 from the main hold (Perttula and Glascock 2017). The recipes of these beads fit a broad Great

Lakes compositional subgroup, cobalt-colored magnesium low-phosphorus (Mg-low-P). This subgroup dates before 1700. It contains 219 beads that include the forty-seven from *La Belle*, five from Fort St. Louis, and one from the Spanish presidio (SL_09). Notably, the Mg-low-P beads from onshore contexts in Texas were compositionally distinct from the shipwreck beads (Walder 2015, 758–760). This is not unexpected, since presumably some cargo boxes were transported ashore while others sank with the ship. The differences in the recipes for beads from Fort St. Louis and those from *La Belle* are minimal and could reflect different batches of beads or beads from slightly different glass workshop sources that were stored in different cargo containers. A single bead (SL_011) from a Spanish presidio feature onshore fit a later cobalt-colored phosphorus low-magnesium (P-low-Mg) subgroup that dates after 1700, as was expected.

Within the cobalt-colored Mg-low-P pre-1700 subgroup, beads from *La Belle* were compared to beads from archaeological sites associated with Indigenous communities across the Great Lakes. Elevated levels of trace elements niobium (Nb), molybdenum (Mo), and hafnium (Hf) were the major source of recipe variation in beads from sites dated to approximately 1650 or earlier (Figure 11.1). This indicates that beads from *La Belle* were *least* similar to beads from Hanson, Red Banks, New Lenox, Goose Lake Outlet #3, and the Cadotte sites, all of which are Great Lakes sites that could date as early as 1625–1650. This temporally significant finding eliminates the possibility that beads from the supplier La Salle used for *La Belle's* cargo were available at those earlier sites. The finding of a slightly different composition in beads from likely early- to-mid seventeenth century sites corroborates their dates of occupation during a period when historical records of Indigenous communities in the western Great Lakes region are minimal. Three beads (MM_001, MM_007, and GG_16) with the early seventeenth-century glass recipe of elevated niobium/molybdenum/hafnium come from mid- to late seventeenth-century contexts at Marquette Mission and Gillett Grove; these are interpreted as curated beads.

Of the remaining twenty mid- to late seventeenth-century Great Lakes archaeological sites with beads in the cobalt-colored Mg-Low-P subgroup (Table 11.2, in bold print), several are places where La Salle may have stopped to trade with Indigenous communities. La Salle's travels in 1679–1682 took him across Lake Huron, past the Cloudman site on Drummond Island, and

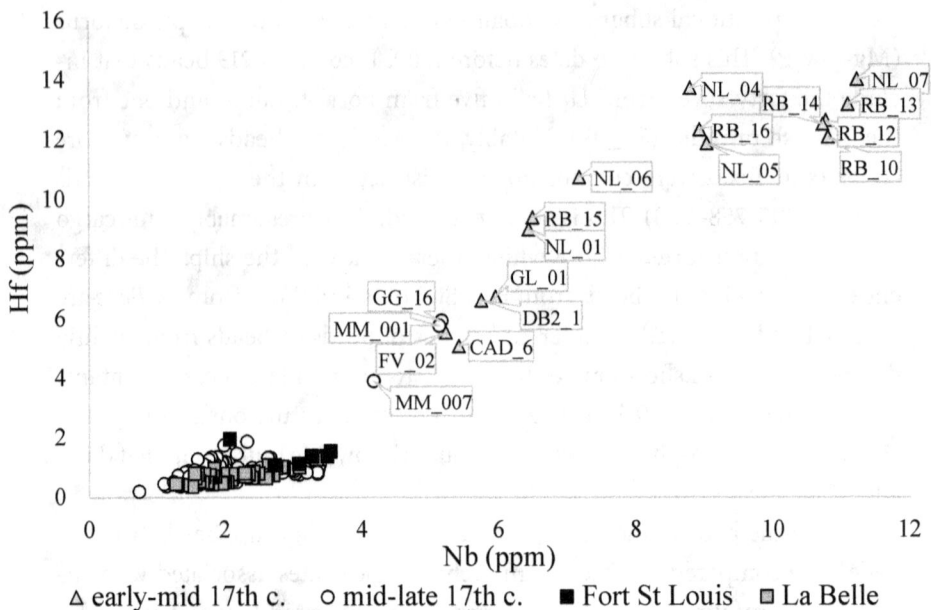

Figure 11.1. Biplots of trace elements niobium (Nb) and hafnium (Hf) illustrating a temporal difference in beads from early- to mid-seventeenth century sites in the Great Lakes (labeled by sample ID) and later sites, including *La Belle* and Fort St. Louis.

through the Straits of Mackinac in Michigan, which includes the Marquette Mission, Gros Cap, and the later Fort Michilimackinac sites. Notably, the single bead (CM_13) sampled from Fort Michilimackinac from outside the fortification walls is the only bead of the pre-1700 recipe analyzed from that site. All others fit the post-1700 recipe. The recipe and context of CM_13 likely reflect the presence of the local Odawa community and their interactions with European traders prior to the construction of the French fort in 1714.

La Salle likely also stopped at Rock Island, off the Door Peninsula of Wisconsin (Mason 1986, 2015), a well-known place for people to rendezvous, socialize, and exchange goods and information. Archaeological evidence of palisade construction there in the mid-seventeenth century coincides with an intertribal alliance against Iroquoian intrusions at a place historically called A'otonatindie (Mason 2015). Most European-made trade items excavated at Rock Island are associated with a later Potawatomi occupation (Period 3) documented from approximately 1670 to 1730 (Mason 1986). La Salle's sub-

Table 11.2. Archaeological sites of the Great Lakes region and their affiliated communities

Site	Site number	County and State	Occupation Dates (AD)	Historically Linked Communities
Arrowsmith	11ML6	McLean Co., IL	ca. 1730	Meskwaki
Bell	47WN9	Winnebago Co., WI	ca.1680–1730	Meskwaki
Cadotte	47AS13	Ashland Co., WI	ca. 1625–1660	Multiethnic
Carcajou Point	47JE2	Jefferson Co., WI	17th–18th century?	Ho-Chunk (?)
Chickadee	47OU251	Outagamie Co., WI	c. 1670–1730	Meskwaki (?)
Cloudman	20CH6	Chippewa Co., MI	Early 17th C.?	Odawa
Doty Island Village	47WN30	Winnebago Co., WI	ca. 1680–1712?	Meskwaki?
Farley Village	21HU2	Houston Co., MN	Mid-±to late 17th century?	Oneota/Ioway
Fort Michilimackinac	20EM52	Emmet Co., MI	1715–1781	Metis/French
Fort St. Joseph	20BE23	Berrien Co., MI	1691–1781	Metis/French
Gillett Grove	13CY2	Clay Co., IA	17th century	Oneota/Ioway
Goose Lake Outlet #3	20MQ140	Marquette Co., MI	ca. AD 1630–1650	Odawa/Ojibwe(?)
Gros Cap	20MK6	Mackinac Co. MI	17th century	Wendat/Tionontate(?)
Hanson	47DR185	Door Co., WI	ca. 1625–1650	Eastern Great Lakes (?)
Iliniwek Village	23CK116	Clark Co., MO	ca. 1640–1683	Illinois
Marina	47AS24	Ashland Co., WI	ca. 1715–1775	Ojibwe/various
Marquette Mission	20MK82	Mackinac Co. MI	ca. 1670–1701	Wendat/Tionontate
Milford	13DK1	Dickinson Co., IA	17th century	Oneota/Ioway
Mormon Print Shop	20CX59	Charlevoix Co., MI	17th century?	Indeterminate
New Lenox	11WI213	Will Co., IL	ca. 1625–1650	Illinois
Peshtigo Point	47MT165	Marinette Co., WI	17th century	Menominee?
Red Banks	47BR437	Brown Co., WI	ca. 1625–1650	Menominee, Ho-Chunk, Potawatomi?
Rock Island Period 2	47DR128	Door Co., WI	ca. 1650	Huron-Petun-Odawa (proto-Wyandotte)
Rock Island Period 3	47DR128	Door Co., WI	ca. 1670–1730	Potawatomi
Rock Island Period 4	47DR128	Door Co., WI	ca. 1760	Odawa
Zimmerman	11LS13	La Salle Co., IL	ca. 1650–1690	Illinois

Note: Names of sites that yielded cobalt-colored Mg-low-P beads that are similar to those from *La Belle* are in boldface.

sequent travels through the Upper Mississippi watershed led to interactions with Illinois (Peoria and Kaskaskia) communities, likely resulting in deposition of some beads of the cobalt-colored Mg-low-P pre-1700 subgroup at the Zimmerman and Iliniwek Village sites. However, other European explorers may have had access to beads of this composition, which might explain their widespread distribution across the landscape. Down-the-line exchange and redistribution of beads acquired from La Salle and other traders further complicate the possibility of tracing beads specifically traded to Indigenous communities by La Salle's party.

To delineate beads from the Great Lakes region that are compositionally most similar to beads from *La Belle* in the cobalt-colored Mg-low-P subgroup, bivariate splitting removed the early seventeenth-century (niobium/molybdenum/hafnium) group. In the remaining dataset, elements responsible for some minimal recipe variation within the group include aluminum (Al), iron (Fe), titanium (Ti) and arsenic (As) (Figure 11.2), although other elements also contribute. Beads from *La Belle* are compositionally most similar first to one another and then to individual beads from the Cloudman site (n = 6) on Drummond Island in northern Lake Huron (Kooiman and Walder 2019); Rock Island Periods 3b and 4 (n = 4) off the Door Peninsula in Wisconsin (Mason 1986); Marquette Mission (n = 8) at St. Ignace on the Straits of Mackinac (Branstner 1992); and the Bell site (n = 2) in eastern Wisconsin (Behm 2008). These beads are identified by sample ID in Figure 11.2.

Except for the Bell site, all of these sites are located along probable routes of La Salle's travel in the Great Lakes. Bell is a palisaded Meskwaki site near Lake Winnebago, Wisconsin, that was well connected to French trade networks via the Fox River, but it was not directly on La Salle's likely path. In 1682, La Salle likely passed another Meskwaki village on Doty Island at the north end of Lake Winnebago (Behm 2008, 17). The two beads from Bell therefore may be examples of down-the-line exchange within Meskwaki trading networks.

Blue, Cobalt-Colored Antimony-Opacified Beads

Other Variety 1 blue beads analyzed were types IIa46/47. These were not translucent but were opacified with antimony. A single bead of this type from the Spanish presidio area (SL_10) matches a post-1700 recipe subgroup (P-low-Mg) in the Great Lakes and is similar in composition to twenty-two

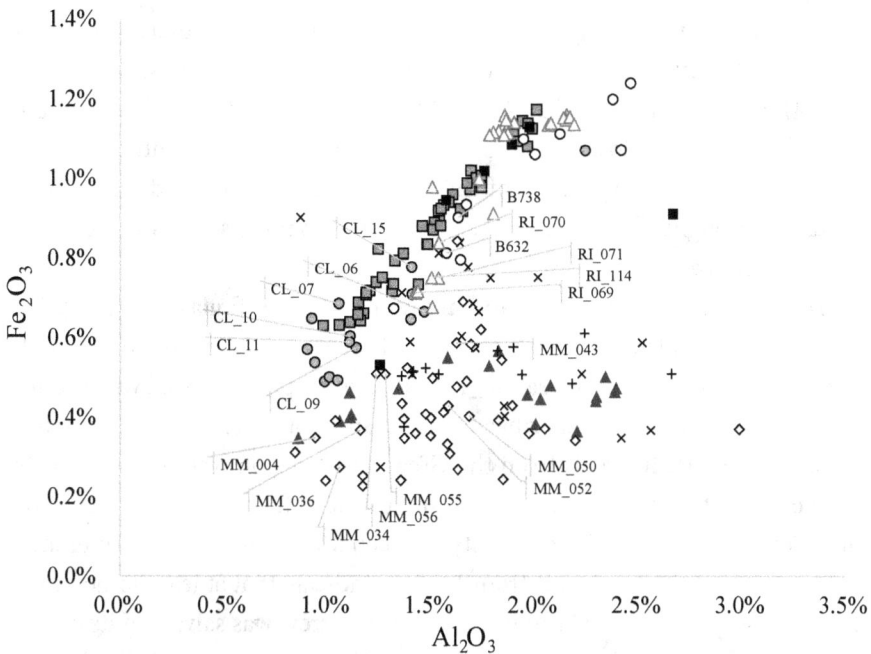

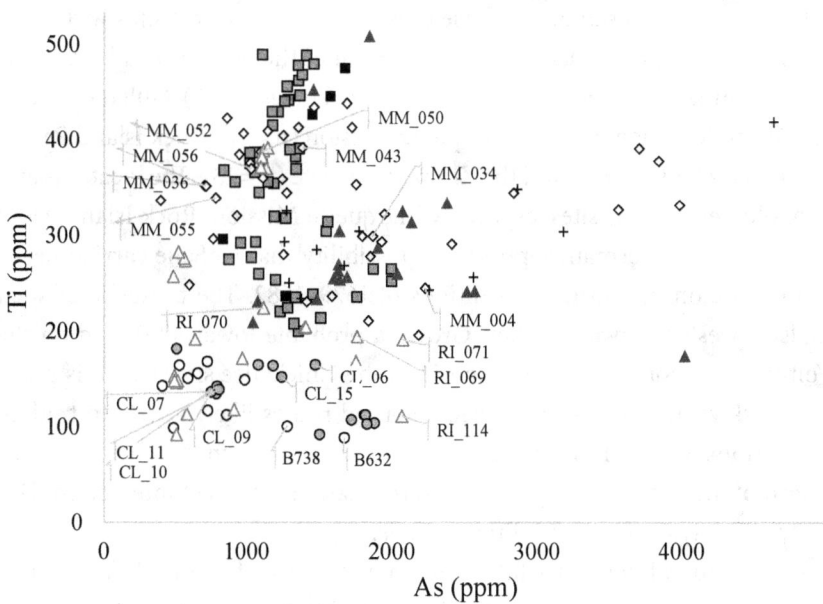

Figure 11.2. Comparison of similar beads from *La Belle* (gray squares), Fort St. Louis (black squares), and key seventeenth-century sites of the Great Lakes region (see legend), with biplots of important chemical elements found in glass. *Top*: Aluminum oxide (Al_2O_3) versus ferric oxide (Fe_2O_3); *Bottom*: Arsenic (As) versus titanium (Ti). Labeled points are sample IDs for beads most like those from *La Belle*.

sampled beads from early to mid-eighteenth-century sites there, including Fort Michilimackinac (n = 7), Doty Island Village (n = 1), Doty Island Mahler (n = 4), Rock Island Period 3b (ca. 1700–1730; n = 1) and Period 4 (ca. 1760, n = 10), and Fort St. Joseph (n = 5). Presidio bead SL_10 is slightly higher in lead and antimony than most of the Great Lakes samples and was almost certainly brought to the presidio area by later Spanish settlers rather than French colonizers.

The earlier, pre-1700 cobalt-and-antimony Mg-low-P glass subgroup includes five beads from *La Belle,* two from Fort St. Louis (SL_01 and SL_07), and one from the presidio area (SL_12). SL_12 is a type IIa40 bead with higher levels of antimony than other beads in this subgroup. Recipes of antimony-opacified type IIa40 beads from the Great Lakes region were more variable than other antimony-opacified types, and the bead from the presidio may be an older, curated bead. The similarity between SL_01 and SL_07 from French colony site and the five beads from *La Belle* indicate that at least some beads from the ship likely were brought ashore as the crew was salvaging its cargo.

These five cobalt-and-antimony Mg-low-P beads from *La Belle* also are similar to fifty-five beads from the Great Lakes region that were produced after 1670 but before 1700. I arrived at this date range after comparing the glass recipes in this sample to those of beads at Great Lakes sites with well-established occupation dates (Walder 2018). Sites that yielded beads with this recipe include Chickadee (n = 2), Doty Island Village (n = 1), Gillett Grove (n = 1), Iliniwek Village (n = 15), Marquette Mission (n = 11), Rock Island Period 3a (ca. 1670–1700; n = 4), and the Zimmerman site (n = 13). The locations and chronologies of these sites, especially Marquette Mission, Rock Island, Doty Island, and Zimmerman, support the possibility that La Salle carried beads of this type on his earlier expeditions of 1679–1682. The presence of such beads in western Iowa at Gillett Grove (a probable Ioway site), and on the Wolf River in northeastern Wisconsin at the Chickadee site (which is probably Meskwaki), north of La Salle's recorded routes likely attests to trading connections among Indigenous communities and down-the-line exchange instead of indicating that these sites were locations of direct interaction with La Salle's party or with other French traders.

A compound blue-and-white bead type recovered from *La Belle* (Variety 4) that is not identified in Great Lakes assemblages fits Kidd and Kidd type IVa16. This type constitutes approximately 4 percent (n = 31,552) of all of the beads from *La Belle* (Perttula and Glascock 2017), but it was not recovered at Fort St. Louis. The white layer is glass with a relatively high silica content (83.5 percent) that was opacified by antimony, while the blue layers are similar to other cobalt-colored soda-lime glass seed beads. However, elevated antimony levels also are present in the blue glass, indicating either overlap in these layers during production or inadvertent sampling of some antimony-opacified white glass during analysis. In general, the type IVa16 beads are compositionally similar to those beads in a antimony-opacified, Mg-low-P group produced from around 1670 to 1700 (Walder 2018), an appropriate timeframe for beads from *La Belle*.

Similar IVa16 beads have been excavated on St. Croix Island, Maine (Bradley 2012, 158), and from the Coosa River Valley of Alabama and across the Southeast (Little 2010, 223–225) from sites that date from the late sixteenth century to the early- to mid-seventeenth century. The fact that this bead type was present on *La Belle* but not in Great Lakes assemblages may indicate that La Salle sourced his beads from a different supplier or that the supplier had newly obtained these blue-white-blue compound beads in their inventory when La Salle was stocking his cargo for the colony mission several years later. This further indicates that we should not expect to see beads that are compositionally identical to those from *La Belle* at Great Lakes archaeological sites.

Copper-Colored Blue Beads

Beads can also be colored blue by using copper instead of cobalt. Such beads exhibit the same recipe distinctions before and after 1700 as the cobalt-colored beads discussed above. While copper-colored beads are common across Great Lakes assemblages, none were identified in the sample of glass beads from *La Belle*. One copper-colored bead from Fort St. Louis (SL_06) fits the pre-1700 Mg-low-P subgroup. In the Great Lakes region, beads of this subgroup (n = 126) were recovered from a wide geographic and temporal range of seventeenth-century sites, including Arrowsmith (n = 1, probably curated), Bell (n = 4), Chickadee (n = 6), Doty Island Village (n = 1), Doty Island Mahler (n = 1), Gillett Grove (n = 5), Iliniwek Village (n = 23), Marina (n = 2), Marquette Mission (n = 40), Mormon Print Shop (n = 2), New Lenox (n = 3), Norge Village (n = 1), Peshtigo Point (n = 4), Red Banks (n = 2), Rock Island Period 3a (n = 2), Fort St. Joseph (n = 3), and Zimmerman (n = 26).

One bead from the post-1700 copper-colored P-low-Mg subgroup also comes from Fort St. Louis (SL_08), but none of the beads in this subgroup came from the ship. This bead may be an intrusion from the Spanish occupation of the presidio site. In the Great Lakes region, the post-1700 subgroup contained beads (n = 102) from a range of sites and components that dated to the early- to mid-eighteenth century, including Cadotte (n = 1, possibly curated or intrusive), Fort Michilimackinac (n = 25), Fort St. Joseph (n = 16), Doty Island Village (n = 3), Doty Island Mahler (n = 6), Marina (n = 7), and Rock Island Periods 2–4 (n = 44).

Since no copper-colored blue glass beads are directly associated with *La Belle*, it is difficult to connect this glass recipe to Indigenous interactions and trade networks that specifically link to La Salle's earlier travels, but the existence of the Mg-low-P and P-low-Mg subgroups in these beads from Great Lakes sites highlights the widespread change in glass recipes at approximately 1700. This shift is itself useful for assigning dates to Indigenous-affiliated sites with limited archaeological evidence for the period of occupation and deposition. Such sites may yield only a few glass beads, a probable result of down-the-line exchange networks or Indigenous population movements that preceded the arrival of Europeans (Walder 2018).

Black and White Beads from La Belle

A few black beads and a few white beads from *La Belle* were analyzed for future comparisons. There is no current comparative Great Lakes dataset for these, although some "dark blue" beads (n = 13) from the Great Lakes dataset (Walder 2015) yielded high levels of manganese, a colorant used for black glass. Black beads colored with manganese recovered from Fort St. Louis (n = 2) are generally similar than those sampled from *La Belle* (n = 5), but the composition is not identical to beads from *La Belle*.

Five white beads from *La Belle* and one from Fort St. Louis were sampled. Much more antimony was detected in the latter bead (SL_16; antimony = 54,238 parts per million) than those from the shipwreck (170–430 parts per million). This is because LA-ICP-MS sampling analyzed the opaque white, antimony-rich core of the bead from Fort St. Louis but a clear glass outer layer of beads from the shipwreck. Such layering is documented on other white beads (Shugar and O'Connor 2008). No outer layer of clear glass is evident on the Fort St. Louis bead, so it either came from a different source or degraded due to taphonomic processes that did not affect beads from the shipwreck in the same way. Further studies of black and white beads in the Great Lakes region would provide a useful dataset to compare to samples from *La Belle*.

Discussion: Using Glass Beads to Investigate Indigenous Presence

The LA-ICP-MS analyses of glass bead recipes presented here contribute to a growing list of methodological advances in archaeology that can correct for biases in reporting and interpretation that have long been part of this discipline (Holland-Lulewicz et al. 2020; Kooiman and Walder 2019; McLeester and Schurr 2020; Panich and Schneider 2019; Supernant 2017). Analysis of glass beads from colonial contexts across North America is making it possible to characterize long-standing trade and exchange relationships of Indigenous communities as they integrated foreign materials into existing frameworks of interaction. Beads from *La Belle* fit the general Mg-low-P Great Lakes recipe subgroup, but within that subgroup they were most similar first to each other. This demonstrates that although glass beads produced in the same European workshops and supplied to traders were relatively similar, we can expect ranges of variation across batches of beads produced a few years apart.

Differences between beads from *La Belle* and the associated Fort St. Louis colony illustrate the range of expected differences in glass recipes between French colonial contexts. In Variety 1, the IIa55/56 cobalt-colored Mg-low-P subgroup, the blue beads analyzed were very similar but minor compositional differences between beads from the shipwreck and the two onshore contexts were identified. The boxes and casks that remained on *La Belle* were of course not the ones that were taken ashore, and different cargo boxes might have contained beads produced in different workshops or batches. This finding is useful for understanding similarities between beads from *La Belle* and from sites in the Great Lakes region associated with Indigenous communities that may have interacted with La Salle. In this case, degree of difference seems most critical. The recipe differences observed between beads from *La Belle* and from Fort St. Louis suggest that similar variations are inevitable among batches of beads distributed through Indigenous trade networks in the Great Lakes region. Identical bead recipes should not be expected between beads from *La Belle* and beads from sites associated with La Salle's earlier Great Lakes explorations.

In general, beads from the French-associated contexts of Fort St. Louis are distinct from those in the Spanish presidio contexts. The presidio beads fit the post-1700 glass recipe (P-low-Mg) subgroups found in the Great Lakes, although one bead of type IIa40 (SL_12) may be a curated artifact. In the eighteenth century, French and Spanish traders could have obtained beads from the same European same glasshouses or from workshops that used comparable recipes. If that were the case, we can expect general similarities between the recipes for beads from the presidio and those from early eighteenth-century Great Lakes sites. During this period, bead production was increasing, a greater volume of trade items was becoming available, and colonial interactions intensified. Given these factors, glass recipes are less useful as a proxy for Indigenous trade networks and interactions in the eighteenth century than they are for earlier periods. However, the single white bead high in antimony and the post-1700 recipes from the presidio context indicate ongoing resupply there during the Spanish occupation. These glass recipe subgroups could be traced across local Aranama and Kawankawa (a collective term for local coastal Indigenous peoples) archaeological sites in the western Gulf Coast region (Walter and Hester 2014) to clarify dates of occupation, potential trading connections, population movements, and interactions.

Using only compositional similarities between Mg-low-P bead subgroups from *La Belle* and the Great Lakes, it is not possible to trace the specific paths of Indigenous trade networks or to corroborate La Salle's historically documented route because La Salle and other contemporary explorers of the Great Lakes region may have been obtaining beads from the same glasshouse(s). Most glass trade beads sampled from *La Belle* fit the Co-colored Mg-low-P recipe subgroup, which is compositionally quite homogeneous and widely distributed across the Great Lakes region. The Co-colored, Sb-opacified Mg-low-P beads sampled from *La Belle* are another glass recipe that also fits a compositional subgroup of beads from Great Lakes sites along La Salle's route. However, since beads were likely redistributed among Native communities throughout eastern North America via intertribal exchange, down-the-line trade, and other means, widespread distribution of these common and apparently popular glass bead types has led to compositional variability among and within bead assemblages.

Nevertheless, down-the-line exchange and redistribution are evident within the homogeneous Mg-low-P subgroup. A few beads that are considered to be most similar to those from *La Belle* come from sites that are not directly associated with La Salle's earlier routes through the western Great Lakes. These include two beads from the Bell site, which was affiliated with a Meskwaki community that was well connected to French trade networks via the Fox River but that La Salle did not visit, according to historical accounts (Behm 2008, 17). Participation in Indigenous exchange networks is also evidenced by cobalt-and-antimony Mg-low-P beads recovered at the Meskwaki-affiliated Chickadee site in northeastern Wisconsin and at the Ioway-affiliated Gillette Grove site in western Iowa.

Conversely, although analyzed beads from the Rock Island, Doty Island, Cloudman, Marquette Mission, Zimmerman, and Iliniwek Village are most similar to glass beads of the same type and recipe subgroups as the beads from *La Belle* and although these sites are located along La Salle's probable route, it is impossible to specify how Indigenous people obtained these beads. Given that both Rock Island and the Straits of Mackinac (where Marquette Mission is located) were both well-known rendezvous points for multiple Indigenous communities, the gifting and redistribution of trade items was a likely activity at both of those sites.

Analysis of glass bead compositions offers another line of evidence for identifying tribal affiliations or cultural connections of archaeological sites that have limited or no colonial documentation or oral histories that link them to known communities. Identifying the niobium/molybdenum/hafnium subset of cobalt-colored Mg-low-P beads distinguishes blue glass beads produced circa 1625–1650. These beads are visually indistinguishable from beads of the same type made later. This recipe is not present in beads from *La Belle* and occurs in beads from western Great Lakes sites that predate both the shipwreck and the arrival of nearly all French explorers. Thus, this subset demonstrates Indigenous participation in trade networks that included European-made materials before any significant presence of European people in the western Great Lakes. Similarly, the single bead with the pre-1700 recipe from outside Fort Michilimackinac attests to the material presence of an Odawa community that inhabited the Straits of Mackinac in the late seventeenth century. They are mentioned in historical documents but are poorly represented in the excavated artifacts from the site. This illustrates a long-standing bias in archaeological research objectives at Fort Michilimackinac.

Excavation efforts there have almost exclusively focused on the French and British colonial structures within the fortification walls.

Finally, curation of beads and items with beadwork such as clothing, adornments, or containers is a human element to consider in studies of glass recipes. Evidence of this practice was observed in instances when earlier recipe types were identified in a few beads from archaeological contexts associated with later occupations. The practice of curation implies that an object has value, usefulness, or significance over years, if not decades. While accessing the particular meaning of individual curated beads (or the items to which they were formerly affixed) is unlikely, identifying the hidden presence of these curated beads raises new research questions related to memory, continuity of meaning, and the symbolic significance of glass beads among various Indigenous communities throughout colonial eras.

The analysis of glass trade beads from *La Belle* and from French and Spanish contexts associated with colonial activities on shore near the shipwreck provided new insight into the timing of archaeological components and the glass recipe similarities of trade beads that circulated in the Great Lakes region during the late seventeenth and early eighteenth centuries. Ongoing typological and compositional analyses should provide further comparable datasets, enabling archaeologists to clarify the nature of Indigenous exchange networks across the eastern North America. This work offers an innovative approach to the archaeology of Ho-Chunk, Potawatomi, Menominee, Meskwaki, Wendat, and other Indigenous groups during a period of significant population movement, trade, and colonial disruptions. As archaeometric analyses of historic-era materials becomes more common, they can contribute to collaborative research undertaken with descendant communities. A project that directly addresses research questions of the Huron-Wendat First Nation in Quebec (Walder and Noël in press) employs glass recipe analysis as a tool for investigating previously hidden or overlooked paths of their historical Wendat movements across the Great Lakes region. Minimally invasive glass recipe analyses offer the opportunity to identify regional-scale connections among postcontact Indigenous communities, especially those from periods for which texts and material evidence are limited, and in cases where historical biases in archaeological practice and theory have overlooked their presence.

Acknowledgments

Complete compositional analysis results for all samples analyzed in this project are available for open research access and long-term archiving at the Digital Archaeological Record, https://www.tdar.org/, tDAR ID: 398989. Bradford M. Jones and James E. Bruseth of the Texas Historical Commission permitted and facilitated analyses of beads from *La Belle* and the onshore sites as part of my dissertation research. That work was funded with a National Science Foundation Doctoral Dissertation Improvement Grant (BCS-1321751). My dissertation advisor and NSF PI, Sissel Schroeder, provided significant guidance throughout my doctoral studies. Continued access to scholarly resources at the University of Wisconsin-La Crosse has made this publication possible. I appreciate the helpful suggestions of two peer reviewers of this chapter and thank Tsim Schneider and Lee Panich for their thoughtful editorial comments while coordinating this well-organized volume. I dedicate my chapter to my much-loved dog Dudley, who passed away as this manuscript was being prepared.

References Cited

Allender, Mark. 2018. Glass Beads and Spanish Shipwrecks: A New Look at Sixteenth-Century European Contact on the Florida Gulf Coast. *Historical Archaeology* 52(4): 824–843.

Beaudoin, Matthew A. 2019. *Challenging Colonial Narratives: Nineteenth-Century Great Lakes Archaeology*. Tucson: University of Arizona Press.

Behm, Jeffery A. 2008. The Meskwaki in Eastern Wisconsin: Ethnohistory and Archaeology. *Wisconsin Archeologist* 89(1 & 2): 7–85.

Billeck, Bill. 2016. Ethnographic and Historical Evidence for Glass Pendant Function in the Plains. *Plains Anthropologist* 61(240): 410–424.

Blair, Elliot H. 2015. Glass Beads and Global Itineraries. In *Things in Motion: Object Itineraries in Archaeological Practice*, edited by Rosemary Joyce and Susan Gillespie, 81–99. Santa Fe: School for Advanced Research Press.

———. 2016. "Glass Beads and Constellations of Practice." In *Knowledge in Motion: Constellations of Learning across Time and Place*, edited by Andrew P. Roddick and Ann B. Stahl, 97–125. Tucson: University of Arizona Press.

Bradley, James W. 2012. Glass Beads. In *St. Croix Island International Historic Site, Calais, Maine: History, Archaeology, and Interpretation*, edited by S. Pendery, 157–169. Occasional Publications in Maine Archaeology. Augusta: Maine State Museum, Maine Historic Preservation Commission.

Branstner, Susan M. 1992. Tionontate Huron Occupation at the Marquette Mission. In *Calumet and Fleur-de-Lys: Archaeology of Indian and French Contact in the Midcontinent*, edited by J. A. Walthall and T. E. Emerson, 177–201. Washington, DC: Smithsonian Institution Press.

Brown, James A., and R. F. Sasso. 2001. Prelude to History on the Eastern Prairies. In *Societies in Eclipse: Archaeology of the Eastern Woodland Indians A.D. 1400–1700*, edited by D. Brose, W. Cowan, and R. C. Mainfort, 205–228. Washington, DC: Smithsonian Institution Press.

Bruseth, James E., Amy Borgens, Bradford M. Jones, and Eric D. Ray, eds. 2017. *La Belle: The Archaeology of a Seventeenth-Century Vessel of New World Colonization*. College Station: Texas A&M University Press.

Bruseth, James E., Jeffrey J. Durst, Tiffany Osburn, Kathleen Gilmore, Kay Hindes, Nancy Reese, Barbara Meissner, and Mike Davis. 2004. A Clash of Two Cultures: Presidio La Bahía on the Texas Coast as a Deterrent to French Incursion. *Historical Archaeology* 38(3): 78–93.

Bruseth, James E., and Toni S. Turner. 2005. *From a Watery Grave: The Discovery and Excavation of La Salle's shipwreck, La Belle*. College Station: Texas A&M University Press.

Dussubieux, Laure, and Karlis Karklins. 2016. Glass Bead Production in Europe during the 17th Century: Elemental Analysis of Glass Material Found in London and Amsterdam. *Journal of Archaeological Science: Reports* 5: 574–589.

Dussubieux, Laure, Peter Robertshaw, and Michael D. Glascock. 2009. LA-ICP-MS Analysis of African Glass Beads: Laboratory Inter-Comparison with an Emphasis on the Impact of Corrosion on Data Interpretation. *International Journal of Mass Spectrometry* 284(1–3): 152–161.

Ferris, Neal, Rodney Harrison, and Matthew A. Beaudoin. 2014. Introduction: Rethinking Colonial Pasts through the Archaeology of the Colonized. In *Rethinking Colonial Pasts Through Archaeology*, edited by N. Ferris, R. Harrison and M. V. Wilcox, 1–34. Oxford: Oxford University Press.

Forde, Jamie E. 2017. Volcanic Glass and Iron Nails: Networks of Exchange and Material Entanglements at Late Prehispanic and Early Colonial Achiutla, Oaxaca, Mexico. *International Journal of Historical Archaeology* 21(2): 485–511.

Gratuze, Bernard. 2013. Glass Characterisation Using Laser Ablation Inductively Coupled Plasma Mass Spectrometry Methods. In *Modern Methods for Analysing Archaeological and Historical Glass*, edited by Koen Janssens, 201–234. West Sussex, UK: John Wiley & Sons.

Grover, Margan Allyn. 2016. Late Precontact and Protohistoric Glass Beads of Alaska. *Arctic Anthropology* 53(2): 69–80.

Hamell, George R. 1983. Trading in Metaphors: The Magic of Beads, Another Perspective upon Indian-European Contact in Northeastern North America. In *Proceedings of the 1982 Glass Trade Bead Conference*, edited by Charles F. Hayes, 5–28, Rochester, NY: Research Division, Rochester Museum & Science Center.

Hancock, Ronald G. V., K. E. Hancock, and J. K. Hancock. 2008. Thoughts on the Utility of a Bivariate-Splitting Approach to Olmec Ceramic Data Interpretation. *Archaeometry* 50(4): 710–726.

Holland-Lulewicz, Jacob, Victor D. Thompson, James Wettstaed, and Mark Williams. 2020. Enduring Traditions and the (Im)materiality of Early Colonial Encounters in the Southeastern United States. *American Antiquity* 85(4): 694–714.

Howard, James H. 1972. Arikara Native-Made Glass Pendants: Their Probable Function. *American Antiquity* 37(1): 93–97.

Karklins, Karlis. 1982. *Glass Beads: The Levin Catalogue of Mid-19th Century Beads: A Sample*

Book of 19th-Century Venetian Beads: Guide to the Description and Classification of Glass Beads. Hull, Quebec: Canadian Government Publishing Centre, Supply and Services Canada.

Karklins, Karlis, and Adelphine Bonneau. 2019. Evidence of Early 17th-Century Glass Bead-making in and around Rouen, France. *BEADS: Journal of the Society of Bead Researchers* 31: 3–8.

Kidd, Kenneth E., and Martha A. Kidd. 1970. A Classification System for Glass Beads for the Use of Field Archaeologists. In *Canadian Historic Sites: Occasional Papers in Archaeology and History.* Vol. 1. Ottawa: Department of Indian Affairs and Northern Development.

Kooiman, Susan M., and Heather Walder. 2019. Reconsidering the Chronology: Carbonized Food Residue, Accelerator Mass Spectrometry Dates, and Compositional Analysis of a Curated Collection from the Upper Great Lakes. *American Antiquity* 84(3): 495–515.

Legg, James B., Dennis B. Blanton, Charles R. Cobb, Steven D. Smith, Brad R. Lieb, and Edmond A. Boudreaux. 2019. An Appraisal of the Indigenous Acquisition of Contact-Era European Metal Objects in Southeastern North America. *International Journal of Historical Archaeology* 23(1): 81–102.

Little, Keith J. 2010. Sixteenth-Century Glass Bead Chronology in Southeastern North America. *Southeastern Archaeology* 29(1): 222–232.

Loewen, Brad. 2019. Glass and Enamel Beadmaking in Normandy, circa 1590–1635. *BEADS: Journal of the Society of Bead Researchers* 31: 9–20.

Loren, Diana DiPaolo. 2010. *The Archaeology of Clothing and Bodily Adornment in Colonial America.* Gainesville: University Press of Florida.

Mason, Ronald J. 1986. *Rock Island Historical Indian Archaeology in the Northern Lake Michigan Basin.* MCJA Special Paper No. 6. Kent: Kent State University Press.

———. 2015. The Search for A,otonatendïe. *Midcontinental Journal of Archaeology* 40(2): 116–133.

McLeester, Madeleine, and Mark R. Schurr. 2020. Uncovering Huber Lifeways: An Overview of Findings from Four Years of Excavations at the Huber Phase Middle Grant Creek Site (11WI2739) in Northern Illinois. *Midcontinental Journal of Archaeology* 45(2): 102–129.

Michelaki, Kostalena, Ronald G. V. Hancock, Gary Warrick, Dean Knight, Ruth H. Whitehead, and Ronald M. Farquhar. 2015. Using Regional Chemical Comparisons of European Copper to Examine its Trade to and among Indigenous Groups in Late 16th and Early 17th Century Canada: A Case Study from Nova Scotia and Ontario. *Journal of Archaeological Science: Reports* 4: 285–292.

Panich, Lee M. 2014. Native American Consumption of Shell and Glass Beads at Mission Santa Clara de Asís. *American Antiquity* 79(4): 730–748.

Panich, Lee M., and Tsim D. Schneider. 2019. Categorical Denial: Evaluating Post-1492 Indigenous Erasure in the Paper Trail of American Archaeology. *American Antiquity* 84(4): 651–668.

Perttula, Timothy K. 2006. *The Glass Beads and Sundry Other Beads from Fort St. Louis (41VT4), Victoria County, Texas.* Austin: Texas Historical Commission.

Perttula, Timothy K., and Michael D. Glascock. 2017. Glass Beads. In *La Belle: The Archaeology of a Seventeenth-Century Vessel of New World Colonization,* edited by J. E. Bruseth, A. Borgens, B. M. Jones and E. D. Ray, 509–530. College Station: Texas A&M University Press.

Quimby, George I. 1966. *Indian Culture and European Trade Goods.* Madison: University of Wisconsin Press.

Ross, Lester A. 1997. Glass and Ceramic Trade Beads from the Native Alaskan Neighborhood. In *The Archaeology and Ethnohistory of Fort Ross*, vol. 2, *The Native Alaskan Neighborhood: A Multiethnic Community at Colony Ross*, edited by Kent Lightfoot, Ann Schiff, and Thomas Wake, 179–212. Contributions of the University of California Archaeological Research Facility No. 55. Berkeley: Archaeological Research Facility, University of California at Berkeley.

Schultz, Sarah, and Heather Walder. 2016. Technologies of Refired Glass Pendant Production: Experimental Replication Results. *Wisconsin Archeologist* 97(2): 29–47.

Shugar, Aaron, and Ariel O'Connor. 2008. The Analysis of the 18th Century Glass Trade Beads from Fort Niagara: Insight into Compositional Variation and Manufacturing Techniques. *Northeast Historical Archaeology* 37(1): 58–68.

Silliman, Stephen. 2010. Indigenous Traces in Colonial Spaces. *Journal of Social Archaeology* 10(1): 28–58.

Supernant, Kisha. 2017. Modeling Métis Mobility? Evaluating Least Cost Paths and Indigenous Landscapes in the Canadian West. *Journal of Archaeological Science* 84: 63–73.

Turgeon, Laurier. 2001. Material Culture and Cross Cultural Consumption: French Beads in North America 1500–1700. *Studies in the Decorative Arts* 9: 85–107.

Walder, Heather. 2013a. Laser Ablation-Inductively Coupled Plasma-Mass Spectrometry (LA-ICP-MS) Analysis of Refired Glass Pendants from the North American Upper Great Lakes. In *Archaeological Chemistry VIII*, edited by R. A. Armitage and J. H. Burton, 365–396. Vol. 1147 of the American Chemical Society Symposium Series. New York: Oxford University Press.

———. 2013b. Stylistic and Chemical Investigation of Turquoise-Blue Glass Artifacts from the Contact Era of Wisconsin. *Midcontinental Journal of Archaeology* 38(1): 119–142.

———. 2015. "... A Thousand Beads to Each Nation": Exchange, Interactions, and Technological Practices in the Upper Great Lakes c. 1630–1730. PhD diss., University of Wisconsin, Madison.

———. 2018. Small Beads, Big Picture: Chronology, Exchange, and Population Movement Assessed through Compositional Analyses of Blue Glass Beads from the Upper Great Lakes. *Historical Archaeology* 52(2): 301–331.

Walder, Heather, and Stéphane Noël. In press. Compositional Analysis of Glass Beads from Huron-Wendat Contexts at the Notre-Dame-de-Lorette Mission Site, Quebec. *Canadian Journal of Archaeology* 45(2).

Walder, Heather, and Jessica Yann. 2018. Resilience and Survivance: Frameworks for Discussing Intercultural Interactions. In *Encounters, Exchange, Entanglement: Intercultural Interactions throughout the Western Great Lakes*, edited by H. Walder and J. Yann, 1–18. Midcontinental Journal of Archaeology Occasional Papers, Volume 2. https://www.midwestarchaeology.org/mcja/occasional-papers.

Walter, Tamara L., and Thomas R. Hester. 2014. "Countless heathens": Native Americans and the Spanish Missions of Southern Texas and Northeastern Coahuila. In *Indigenous Landscapes and Spanish Missions: New Perspectives from Archaeology and Ethnohistory*, edited by Lee M. Panich and Tsim D. Schneider, 93–113. Tucson: University of Arizona Press.

Walthall, John A. 2015. Seventeenth-Century Glass Trade Beads from La Salle's Fort St. Louis and the Grand Village of the Kaskaskia. *Midcontinental Journal of Archaeology* 40(3): 257–281.

White, Carolyn L. 2008. Personal Adornment and Interlaced Identities at the Sherburne Site, Portsmouth, New Hampshire. *Historical Archaeology* 42(2): 17–37.

White, Richard. 1991. *The Middle Ground: Indians, Empires, and Republics in the Great Lakes Region, 1650–1815*. Cambridge: Cambridge University Press.

Witgen, Michael J. 2012. *An Infinity of Nations: How the Native New World Shaped Early North America*. Philadelphia: University of Pennsylvania Press.

12

Small and Under-Recorded Sites as Evidence for Gayogohó:nǫ' (Cayuga) and Onöndowa'ga:' (Seneca) Regional Settlement Expansion, circa 1640–1690

KURT A. JORDAN

The archaeology of Haudenosaunee (Six Nations Iroquois) sites in what is now termed upstate New York understandably has focused on town sites. Towns of three to four hectares (8–10 acres) housing as many as 2,000 people were a key part of Haudenosaunee settlement patterns by the sixteenth century (Engelbrecht 2003). These towns, comprised of bark-covered multifamily longhouses and often surrounded by defensive wooden palisades, were inhabited for spans of ten to forty years before planned relocation. Given this number of person-years of occupation, town sites are highly visible archaeologically and have attracted the interest of archaeologists, antiquarians, and looters since the early years of Euro-American settlement (Houghton 1912; Huey 1997). These large towns often were accompanied by smaller satellite villages of 500 or fewer inhabitants, frequently within a day's walk or less from the principal towns (Jordan 2010, 2013). Archaeologists working in Haudenosaunee territory have created models for the relocations of individual Haudenosaunee communities through space and time, and the comparatively short use lives of individual sites allows for detailed diachronic reconstruction of changes in subsistence, settlement, and cultural practices (e.g., Jordan and Gerard-Little 2019). After European colonization of lands to the east and south of Haudenosaunee territory, these towns and local satellites were the bulwark of Haudenosaunee political, economic, and spatial autonomy.

Emphasis on these large, impressive sites has its downside. Smaller sites have not often been targeted for investigation as they are simply not as rewarding as the towns in terms of artifacts and analyzable data (for exceptions, see Abel 2000; Rieth 2008; Rossen 2015). Further, large-scale cultural resource management survey has been rare in the region, perhaps due to the relatively stagnant (or declining) upstate economy. While it is widely recognized that Haudenosaunee people were extremely mobile and made use of the full expanse of their territories for hunting, gathering, fishing, travel, military expeditions, trade, and diplomacy (Parmenter 2010), most reconstructions of Haudenosaunee activities outside the towns are based on historical documents and ethnographic accounts. These sources offer very limited spatial and temporal coverage.

The detailed attention paid to creating town occupation sequences in areas where sites are well preserved also has diverted attention away from other parts of Haudenosaunee territory where more sporadic occupations took place. Site destruction, especially in urban areas before US historic preservation laws were passed, further obscures the full extent of past landscape use. These factors have resulted in the erasure of aspects of the Indigenous past from both scholarly and popular consciousness, a fact that has repercussions for present-day Haudenosaunee communities.

In this chapter, I attempt to counter these tendencies by concentrating on evidence from small and underreported sites dating to a fifty-year window in post-Columbian Haudenosaunee history. During the course of twenty-five years of research in Haudenosaunee archaeology, I noticed that diagnostic post-Columbian artifacts recovered at smaller sites tended to date to the mid- to late seventeenth century. I suggest that this pattern is not the accidental product of a small sample, but rather reflects a distinct Haudenosaunee land-use pattern that took advantage of particular political-economic conditions.

This pattern was hard to spot, lurking within confusing, often multi-component, Indigenous sites. Some data come from professionally excavated and reported sites where collections are extant and accessible, while other instances rely on non-archaeologists' written descriptions of sites that have been destroyed and assemblages scattered. With the exception of a few seventeenth- and eighteenth-century specialists, I expect that many archaeologists likely would have passed over this evidence (see also Russell, this volume; Scheidecker, this volume). Materials from seventeenth-century Haudenosaunee sites include a mix of locally sourced products, and goods obtained from both European and Indigenous trade partners (see also Dickson and Steinmetz, this volume; Scheiber, this volume). While certain diagnostic artifacts, such as Christian-themed medals and rings and glass beads, are widely recognized as hallmarks of the era, other material classes actually deriving from post-Columbian Indigenous sites might receive erroneous classification as "prehistoric" artifacts (such as lithic debitage or faunal remains processed with Indigenous methods) or "historic" settler material (such as iron tools or white clay pipe fragments). Thus seventeenth-century sites may be misinterpreted as multicomponent or the extent of seventeenth-century occupation may be minimized due to mistaken assumptions about the time period of certain classes of material.

I use examples from Gayogohó:nǫ' (the self-name for Cayuga) and Onöndowa'ga:' (the self-name for Seneca) territories to argue that seventeenth-century Haudenosaunee nations intensified their use of space within their homelands (Figure 12.1). They did so with smaller settlements and agricultural endeavors in a way that scholars have not previously recognized and that were largely unnoted in the documentary record. I propose that this expansion was related to a high point in Haudenosaunee political-economic power and prosperity. Territorial intensification was a strategy autonomous Haudenosaunee nations used to increase economic returns, minimize labor, and shorten travel time. While I discuss only five sites in this essay, I suspect that the pattern I have identified holds much more broadly.

Securing an expanded body of evidence to test this claim would be difficult, given that New York State site records suffer from the same classificatory problems that Panich and Schneider (2019) have identified in records for post-Columbian sites in California (particularly heterogeneous uses of the problematic term "protohistoric"). This issue is exacerbated by the extremely balkanized nature of site recordkeeping in New York, where at least eight different institutions keep their own site files and efforts to centralize this information are only in preliminary stages (Nancy Herter, personal communication 2020).[1] While Panich and Schneider's (2019) comprehensive study and reanalysis of site records from Marin County, California—which were undertaken to obtain a full inventory of known sites with post-Columbian Indigenous occupations—provides some hope for this type of reassessment, it required a significant commitment of labor. The process would be even more difficult in New York State, where in-person visits to multiple repositories would be needed to view their paper records. Even then, the researcher would still be at the mercy of the thor-

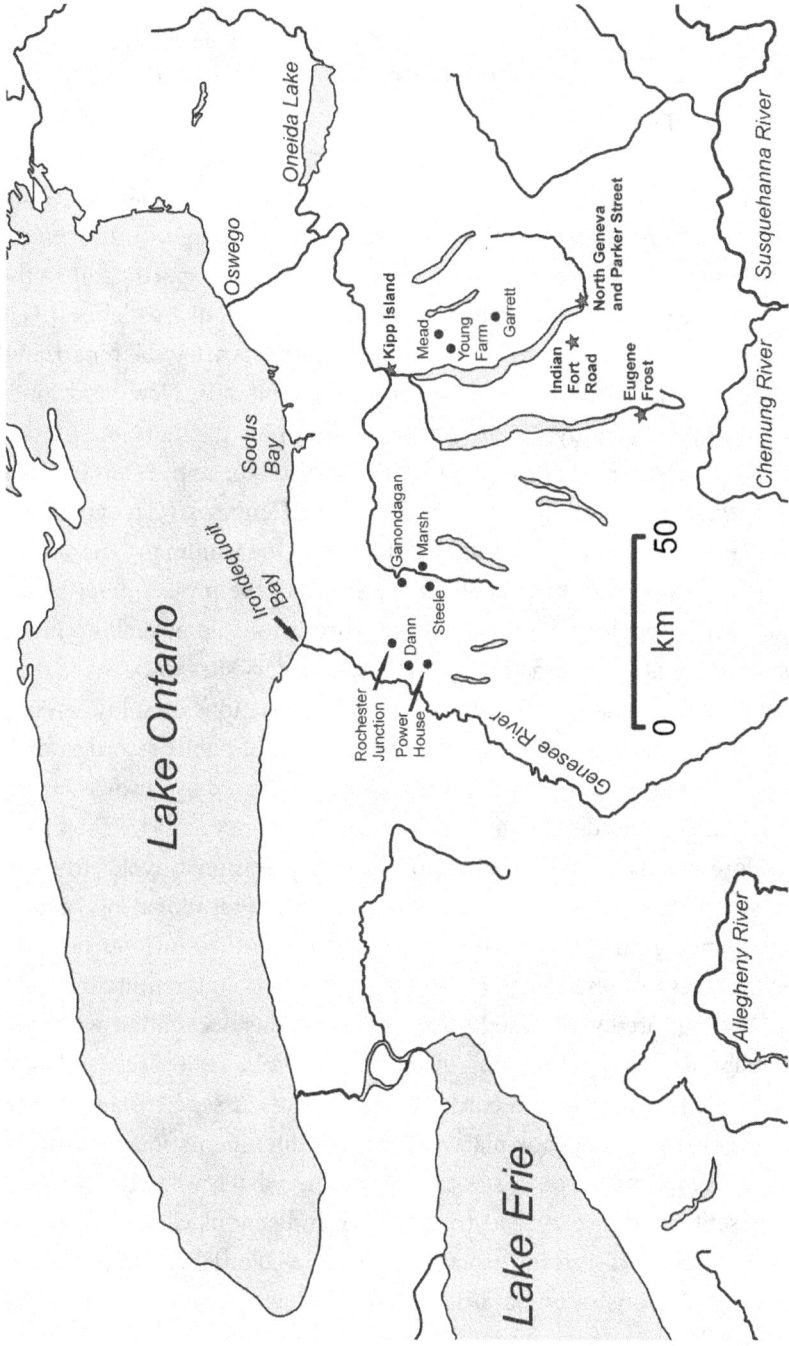

Figure 12.1. Gayogo̱hó:nǫ' (Cayuga) and Onöndowa'ga:' (Seneca) regional expansion sites and principal towns, circa 1640–1690. Stars mark regional intensification sites; circles represent large principal towns. Map by Kurt A. Jordan.

oughness of recorders of site data and individual interpretations of the various temporal and cultural labels their institutions used.

This project arose within the course of long-term collaborative engagement with Haudenosaunee partners (see Jordan and Gerard-Little 2019, 41). Onöndowa'ga:' partners gave me guidance on field methods during my excavation projects at the White Springs (ca. 1688–1715) and Townley-Read (ca. 1715–1754) sites and on the selection of the White Springs site for study. Scholarships from Cornell University's American Indian and Indigenous Studies Program enabled eighteen Indigenous students to participate in the White Springs project at no cost. The projects resulted in a collaboratively designed website[2] and all artifacts from these projects are to be repatriated to the Seneca-Iroquois National Museum in Salamanca, New York, once study is complete (Beduya 2020). I am grateful to my partners and guides, especially Christine Abrams, David George-Shongo, and Peter Jemison (Onöndowa'ga:'); Sachem Sam George and Steve Henhawk (Gayogǫhó:nǫ'); Michael Galban (Mono Lake Paiute/Washoe); and Joe Stahlman (Tuscarora).

A few words need to be said about the ethics of the project described in this chapter, particularly because I discuss three probable or definite Indigenous cemetery sites. Information about these cemetery sites was derived from preexisting paper materials; I did not conduct excavations or study physical collections. The existence of these sites was a matter of public record prior to my research; all three were mostly or completely destroyed by Euro-American road-building and residential construction sixty or more years ago. Their locations are presented here with an intentional lack of precision to avoid attracting further settler attention. I have passed along more exact locational information to descendant community leaders that they can use for their own purposes.

The histories of these cemetery sites present a troubling reminder of how settlers have ignored and erased traces of Indigenous occupation with little concern about even documenting their actions (Wolfe 2006; see also Laluk, this volume). The minimally recorded burial sites discussed here suggest that many other desecrations took place without any documentation whatsoever. This study provides a lesson to settler populations: what is written down does not represent the full story, and treatment of Indigenous cemeteries represents a particularly disturbing aspect of American colonialism. In particular, this research demonstrates that Ithaca, New York, was far from *terra nullius*, as it usually has been portrayed.

For Indigenous people, knowledge of this sort of desecration is all too well known, but the locations of ancestral places often are not. Both the Gayogo̱ hó:nǫ' and Onöndowa'ga:' were pushed out of the Finger Lakes region by the early nineteenth century. Onöndowa'ga:' reservations are now in far western New York State at Allegany, Cattaraugus, and Tonawanda and in Oklahoma. The Gayogo̱hó:nǫ' have not had an official reservation in New York since 1807 and large-scale efforts to return did not begin until 2003 (Levitt 2018). Present-day Gayogo̱hó:nǫ' and Onöndowa'ga:' persons acknowledge that much knowledge about the Finger Lakes region has been lost to community memory. Scholarly studies like this one can help communities recover ties to ancestral places that can then be revisited and pondered and respects can be paid.

Regional Settlement Expansion

The middle and late seventeenth century was a peak period in the military, diplomatic, and economic power of the Haudenosaunee Confederacy (Jordan 2010, 2013; Parmenter 2010). The Haudenosaunee had either defeated or were in the process of defeating many rival Indigenous groups on their borders (including the Mahicans, Wenros, Wendats [Hurons], Petuns, Attawandaron [Neutrals], Eries, and Susquehannocks) and European colonies were distant. Many groups and individuals from defeated nations had been incorporated within Haudenosaunee territories, providing the demographic boost needed to reverse losses from European-borne diseases and warfare. Documentary evidence indicates thriving trade with European colonists that centered on the exchange of beaver pelts for trade goods. Archaeologically, this prosperity is reflected in the enormous quantities of gun parts and marine-shell wampum beads on Haudenosaunee sites of this period (Ceci 1989; Wray 1973, 1985). While this trade did not protect Haudenosaunee populations from intermittent danger or occasional violence, the overall tenor of the period was much more positive than negative.

During this era, the Haudenosaunee made notable changes in how they used space. Table 12.1 presents a shorthand distinction between local, regional, and extraregional spaces using a framework I have developed elsewhere. This heuristic estimates the travel time between sites and acts as a proxy for the likely ease of social connection among Haudenosaunee com-

Table 12.1. Schema for the Haudenosaunee use of space

Local space	Within a 20-kilometer radius, easy pedestrian access, steady communications likely took place
Regional space	Within an 80-kilometer radius, one-way travel times of two days or less
Extraregional space	Beyond an 80-kilometer radius, distance would have impeded (but not eliminated) regular communication

Note: Previously presented in Jordan (2008, 2013).

munities. While this effort could be made more precise through the use of locally specific GIS-based movement models, concentric circles of 20 kilometers and 80 kilometers around a particular site provide a quick and visually simple way of estimating access. Local sites were at a distance where interaction was not demanding, whereas special effort was needed to connect sites that were farther apart at regional or extraregional distances.[3]

In the 1640–1690 period, the local core of the Haudenosaunee settlement system remained quite consistent with that of earlier times. Each of the five nations had one or more principal towns, often alongside smaller satellite villages within the local (walking-distance) zone. But during this period, the Haudenosaunee also established what I have termed extraregional satellite communities—in effect, colonies—at greater distances from the homeland (Jordan 2013). Seven settlements that the French knew collectively as the Iroquois du Nord were founded on the north shore of Lake Ontario in the period 1665–1670 (Konrad 1981). Other satellites were established relatively close to French settlements in the St. Lawrence Valley starting in the 1660s, and still others were established in the Susquehanna Valley in the 1680s. Documentary sources make clear that all satellites maintained connections to the homeland, sharing information and at times people (Parmenter 2010).

In this chapter, I suggest that Haudenosaunee extraregional expansion had a regional counterpart. I claim that Haudenosaunee people—or at least the western Gayogǫhó:nǫ' and Onǫndowa'ga:' Nations—expanded use of their homeland regions in places distant from principal towns and satellites. These occupations differed in character from the small sites that were used for resource procurement, travel stopovers, and other short-term uses that

are an enduring feature of the archaeology of the Haudenosaunee homeland. Regional expansion sites left more substantial archaeological traces
and some sites may have been occupied for lengthy periods. I draw on
several types of data accumulated in catch-as-catch-can fashion to make
this case. While I did not make a systematic study (which would likely
be difficult or impossible given the disparate nature of the evidence and
complexities of site reporting in New York State), I have run across enough
instances—without trying to do so—to suggest that I have captured a small
part of a larger pattern.

There is some, but limited, documentary support for this position. Most
Europeans who visited or resided in Haudenosaunee territory were missionaries, diplomats, or military personnel whose duties and interests concentrated on the larger settlements. Missionaries and diplomats directed their
attention to large populations and Indigenous leaders, while military missions sought sizeable towns to destroy. Although some authorities (e.g., Norris 1961, 15) assert that longer-term European residents, especially Jesuit missionaries, explored widely within Haudenosaunee lands, they were often the
only Europeans for miles, and in the seventeenth century they often feared
for their lives (e.g., Thwaites 1899a, 191; 1899b, 77, 115–117; 1899c, 61; 1900a,
245; 1900b, 173). Diplomats, such as the New York official Wentworth Green-
halgh in 1677 (Snow et al. 1996, 188–192), were directed by Indigenous guides
and it is likely that their visits were extensively stage managed so that they
only observed what their hosts wanted them to.

As a result, European observers did not see or record large stretches of
Haudenosaunee territory. This means that the archaeologically recognized pattern of regional settlement expansion is largely invisible in the textual record.
In a rare exception, the Sulpician René Bréhant de Galinée mentioned one such
site in his account of a 1669 diplomatic mission to Onöndowa'ga:' territory:

> On the 8th of August we arrived at an island where a Seneca Indian
> has made a sort of country house, to which he retires in summer to eat
> with his family a little Indian corn and squash that he grows there every
> year. He has concealed himself so well, that unless one knew the spot
> one would have a great deal of difficulty in finding it. They are obliged
> to conceal themselves in this way when they leave their villages, lest
> their enemies, who are always around for the purpose of surprising and
> killing them, should discover them. (Coyne 1903, 17)

While this account demonstrates that outlying settlements were not entirely free from danger, for this particular Onöndowa'ga:' family, the benefits outweighed the drawbacks. I expect they would not have remained in this isolated location had they been consistently living in fear.

Of necessity, this chapter employs a mixed-method approach. I discuss five sites in New York's Finger Lakes region (Figure 12.1): first, Indian Fort Road, where I draw on artifact collections and recent radiocarbon results; second, the Eugene Frost site, where a Cornell University crew under my direction conducted limited test excavations and examined a private collection in 2007; third, the Kipp Island site, where two museum collections described in a thesis evidence a seventeenth-century component; and finally, a pair of mostly or completely destroyed sites in the city of Ithaca that are described briefly in a 1969 local history publication, which I supplemented with manuscript work at two Ithaca repositories. It is likely that these five occupations included populations affiliated with either the Gayogohó:nǫ' or Onöndowa'ga:'.

The Sites

Indian Fort Road

Indian Fort Road is principally known as a sixteenth-century Gayogohó:nǫ' nucleated town site, approximately 2.4 hectares in size and partially or completely enclosed by a wooden palisade. The site is located on Taughannock Creek in present-day Tompkins County. In the sixteenth century, it may have housed as many as 1,800 residents. Substantial Cornell University domestic-context excavations were conducted at Indian Fort Road by David Jones in 1979–1981 and Sherene Baugher in 1992–1997 (Baugher and Clark 1998; Jones and Jones 1980; Sanft 2013, 2018). At the time, Indian Fort Road was viewed as a single-component site.

Samantha Sanft's master's thesis (2013) analyzes some previously unpublished materials from the Jones assemblage. While most of the data (including one new AMS radiocarbon date and three recalibrated conventional radiocarbon dates) pointed unambiguously to a sixteenth-century occupation during the period 1520–1560, a second new AMS date taken from a carbonized maize kernel found in Postmold 731 (Beta-350737) returned a calibrated, one-sigma date of 1650–1670. The two-sigma calibration generated two principal date ranges, 1640–1680 and 1760–1770. In her thesis, Sanft concluded that the seventeenth-century dates were the most likely. Sanft subsequently modified her interpretation, and a journal article derived from the thesis does not mention the possibility of multiple occupations (Sanft 2018, 4–5). Since that publication, new information has arisen that justifies reexamining the number of components at Indian Fort Road.

Postmold 731 lies within an array of features that suggest that one or more domestic structures had been erected in the vicinity. While most of the posts appear to relate to a sixteenth-century house, Postmold 731 was not in an obviously structural position and could date to a later reoccupation of the site. The radiocarbon date thus suggests a seventeenth-century occupation that was substantial enough for post placement, presumably involving farming because of the presence of the maize kernel.

Little material culture that is obviously diagnostic to the seventeenth century has been found at Indian Fort Road. The marine-shell and copper-based artifacts all appear to date to the sixteenth century based on morphology and manufacturing methods.[4] In 2018, Sanft reported that "no artifacts representative of either a seventeenth- or eighteenth-century occupation have been recovered from the site" (2018, 4), but recent reanalysis of photographs of a white tubular bead recovered by Baugher changed this conclusion. The bead was originally assumed to be a wampum-like marine-shell bead due to the known sixteenth-century occupation. It was photographed, repatriated to Gayogǫhó:nǫ' leaders, and presumably reburied (Sherene Baugher, personal communication 2020). Although the bead itself is no longer available for study, over twenty pictures exist. These photos were reassessed by adornment item expert Karlis Karklins (personal communication 2020), who identified the bead as glass.

Karklins classifies the bead as Kidd and Kidd (1970) variety Ia4. It is made of translucent oyster white glass with broken or unfinished ends. This bead form is significantly less common than its opaque white tubular counterpart. While single translucent white tubulars have been found at post-1690 sites (Jordan 2008:Table 5.3; Kaitlin LaGrasta, personal communication 2020), they are much more common at earlier sites. In the Gayogǫhó:nǫ' sites Adrian Mandzy reviewed, "clear white tubes" were found only at Rogers Farm and René Menard Bridge Hilltop, both satellite communities that were occupied circa 1660–1685 (Mandzy 1992, 146, 174). In Onöndowa'ga:' territory, two translucent white tubulars were reported in a small assemblage from the circa 1655–1675 Dann site (Ryan and Dewbury 2010, Table 3). The type has also been reported at sites dating to circa 1625–1660 in the Mohawk and Oneida regions (Clark 2019, 21, 31; Rumrill 1991, Table 13; Snow 1995, 289–292) and is found most commonly on Onondaga sites that date to circa 1640–1680 (Jim Bradley, personal communication 2020). The dated finds of Ia4 variety beads in Haudenosaunee territory therefore are consistent with the 1640–1680 AMS date at Indian Fort Road.

Indian Fort Road lies approximately 26 to 40 kilometers from the principal Gayogǫhó:nǫ' towns at Garrett, Mead, and Young Farm, which were sequentially occupied during 1640–1680 (DeOrio 1978). The straight-line distances do not account for the intervening presence of Cayuga Lake. The site is thus clearly in Gayogǫhó:nǫ' regional space (as defined in Table 12.1) and was quite isolated from the core Gayogǫhó:nǫ' population. While by 1640 approximately eighty years would have passed since the previous occupation—meaning the site would have been covered by good-sized trees unless it had been maintained in the interim (see Engelbrecht 2003, 104–107)—the location retained the advantages of secure access to water and productive soils that had supported a large Gayogǫhó:nǫ' population in the 1500s.

Eugene Frost

I initiated a small survey and excavation project on the property of Mr. Eugene Frost in 2007 after hearing he had recovered post-Columbian Indigenous artifacts on his farm. The site is located on Catharine Creek, a tributary of Seneca Lake, in Schuyler County. Documentary sources suggest that Frost's farm may have contained a revolutionary-era or postrevolutionary Indigenous site, both research interests of mine, and Frost was enthusiastic about attracting scholarly attention to his property. However, Cornell surface investigations, shovel testing, and test-unit excavation failed to turn up evidence from this era and the project concluded.

The team also examined Frost's private collection. It includes artifacts from multiple archaeological components that range from early Late Woodland Levanna-style projectile points to nineteenth-century American settler refuse. Of particular interest were Frost's brass metal-detector finds: a Christian-themed ring, a mouth harp, two flattened thimble fragments, and six brass buttons. The ring is what Alice Wood (1974) termed an IHS Motif 1 type (IHS refers to Latin for "Jesus Savior of Mankind"). While IHS rings have been found on

Onöndowa'ga:' sites dating to between 1640 and 1755 (Eastly 2012), the triple-ridge band decoration on the Frost site ring was most common during 1640–1687 (Wood 1974, Table 2). Herlich's (2008) study of sixty-five rings from the circa 1715–1754 Onöndowa'ga:' Townley-Read site identified three IHS rings, none of which contained the three-ridge ring band design.

The mouth harp, the thimble fragments, and the brass buttons are not precisely diagnostic and could derive from the seventeenth, eighteenth, or nineteenth centuries. Given that the 2007 excavations were not able to relocate the locus of Haudenosaunee activity originally found by Frost, it is possible that other seventeenth-century materials—both diagnostics and less flashy finds such as animal bone fragments and stone tool-making debris—may still be present on the site.

The seventeenth-century Indigenous occupation at the Frost site appears to have been small in scale, but the recovery of a Christian-themed ring diagnostic of the 1640–1687 era suggests that additional fieldwork is warranted. The Eugene Frost site is quite distant from Onöndowa'ga:' towns of this period. It is almost 80 kilometers from the easternmost principal towns of the 1640–1687 period at Dann and Ganondagan, just within the outer limits of what I have defined as "regional space."

Kipp Island

A third example of regional settlement expansion is the Kipp Island site. The island is a glacial drumlin within Montezuma Marsh in Seneca County at the north end of Cayuga Lake, an area that would have been valuable for fishing, for hunting and gathering wetland resources, and for growing domesticated crops.[5] It is multicomponent, best known for the Woodland period domestic sites and cemeteries William Ritchie excavated (Ritchie 1980; Ritchie and Funk 1973), which subsequently have been redated and reanalyzed (e.g., Hart et al. 2011).

Mandzy (1992, 133) reports on assemblages curated by the Cayuga Museum of History and the Museum of the American Indian that contain "Contact materials" reportedly recovered from Kipp Island. Mandzy's inventory consists of 61 glass beads (59 tubular in form), 21 white shell tubular wampum beads, 1 unfinished gray slate gorget, 1 beaver-tooth pendant, 1 hair comb (presumably made of antler), and an Indigenous-made ceramic smoking pipe. Based on the seriation of glass beads, Mandzy (1992, 65) places Kipp Island in the mid-seventeenth century. The preponderance of tubular beads is reminiscent of circa 1659–1666 Mohawk glass bead assemblages Rumrill (1991) categorized as the "Short, Finished-End, Tubular Bead Period." The absence of wire-wound beads from the sample also points to a pre-1700 date for the site.

The hair comb and the overall preponderance of adornment items in the seventeenth-century assemblage suggest that these items derived from a cemetery. The Kipp Island occupation thus likely was more substantial and enduring than those described at the Indian Fort Road and Eugene Frost sites. Distressingly, roughly two-thirds of Kipp Island was removed for use as fill for the construction of the New York State Thruway prior to 1954, including portions containing Indigenous sites (Ritchie 1980, 234). It is uncertain whether the part of the island with the seventeenth-century component still exists.

By straight-line distance, Kipp Island lies 35 kilometers from the Gayogohó:nǫ' principal town at the Garrett site, founded circa 1640, and 20 to 21 kilometers from the later principal towns at Mead and Young Farm. To reach any of these principal settlements, upstream water travel would have been necessary.

Sites in Ithaca, New York: North Geneva Street and Parker Street

The Ithaca area at the southern end of Cayuga Lake in Tompkins County is generally viewed as having been lightly occupied by Indigenous peoples. There are few recorded archaeological sites and hardly any extant artifact collections. Further, historic documents—particularly accounts by Moravian missionaries who passed through the area in the 1750s and 1760s—note only intermittent occupations by Native people, including refugee Delawares and Tutelos (Beauchamp 1916). Many have concluded that Indigenous occupations concentrated on the northern half of Cayuga Lake, where the soils are better for agriculture, shallower lake depths facilitate fishing, and the Seneca River (a major east-west transportation route) can be easily accessed.

A 1969 publication by Tompkins County historian Glenn Norris reinforces this impression. His account of a few archaeological sites within the city of Ithaca is brief. Norris was not an archaeologist, and his site and artifact descriptions are ambiguous at best. He mentions an Indigenous grave that was disturbed during house construction on North Geneva Street in downtown Ithaca, noting that this burial was probably located in a seasonal fishing camp (Norris 1969, 38). I initially assumed this was a pre-Columbian site, as Norris did not describe any artifacts (an example of a recording problem). In older sources, most nonspecialists (and some professionals, see Parker 1922) expected Indigenous sites to be pre-Columbian and did not specifically note typical finds such as stone tools or locally made pottery. They commented more frequently on the "modern" trade goods acquired from Europeans, since these were unexpected.

I found that my assumption was mistaken when I fortuitously discovered William Eliot Griffis's manuscript artifact inventory from a site on North Geneva Street while investigating the archives of The History Center in Tompkins County, New York.[6] Griffis clearly described the same site as Norris, who may have based his 1969 account on Griffis's document. Griffis, however, noted that multiple graves were impacted in 1901 and identified several classes of exchange goods from the site, including brass kettles of nested sizes; a glass "brandy bottle"; "necklaces" of beads (presumably glass); and "wampum disks." Griffis also mentioned recovery of a "chunk of petrified paint," "tomahawks and war hatchets," and "stone and arrow heads" that may indicate the North Geneva site was multicomponent. This site has been largely or completely destroyed by residential construction; what happened to the human remains and associated artifacts since 1901 is unknown.

While several of Griffis's identifications are imprecise or erroneous—including "wampum disk," as wampum are tubular rather than discoidal—he provides enough information to date the site much more precisely. Griffis describes three "wampum disks" as being "ornamented with the symbol of the six ellipses or emblems of the six nations (Mohawks, Oneidas, Onondagas, Cayugas, Senecas and Tuscaroras, that were confederated together in war and peace). . . . They were strung together so as to lie flat on the breast" (n.d.). This description is immediately recognizable as what archaeologists today term an "arc rosette" disk runtee. These are flat shell disks, often with incised designs on one face, that have two perforations to allow them to hang flat while strung on a necklace. These runtees range from 1.5–4.5 centimeters in diameter and have an average thickness of 0.5 centimeter (Esarey 2013, 208). The arc rosette form contains a flower-like design probably made with a drawing compass; Griffis's "six ellipses" presumably refer to the six-petal arc rosette design found on other runtees recovered in the Northeast (Esarey 2013, Figure 3.4).

Duane Esarey's 2013 dissertation inventories and dates 536 disk runtees of various styles derived from 77 sites that are preserved in museum collections across the Northeast. Esarey determined that the disk runtee form was highly diagnostic of the 1645–1710 era (2013, 208–211). The arc rosette form is even more temporally specific, as it does not appear until after 1670 (211). The 1670–1710 date for the arc rosette form means that Griffis was mistaken in interpreting the imagery as representing the Six Nations of the Haudenosaunee Confederacy, since the form predates the Tuscaroras joining the alliance as the sixth nation in the 1720s. In Gayogo̱hó:nǫ' territory, disk runtees have been found at the Garrett, Mead, and Young Farm principal towns and the Rogers Farm and Lamb satellites, all dating to circa 1640–1710, but not at earlier or later sites (2013:171; Esarey's published data do not distinguish which Gayogo̱hó:nǫ' disk runtees are of the arc rosette type).

Norris (1969, 38) also discusses a village and cemetery that had been located on a twelve-meter-high sandbank near Parker Street on Ithaca's East Hill. He cited an unpublished memoir by early Ithaca settler and physician Samuel Parker Jr.; this document is preserved in Cornell's Rare and Manuscript Collections and contains much more information than Norris's summary.[7] Parker relates that American settlers destroyed the sandbank and looted the approximately fifty graves in it in the 1830s; they took the sand for land-filling activities in the swampy flats of Ithaca. This site has almost certainly been completely destroyed by grading and residential construction, and no known artifacts or human remains from it survive. Parker clearly describes post-Columbian artifacts alongside more temporally ambiguous forms such as stone celts and "arrowheads" of unspecified material. He also notes that all interred individuals apparently were buried either in a flexed position or as rearranged secondary burials and that all burials were covered by the flat stones abundant in the Ithaca area. The apparent uniformity in the burial program reported by Parker weighs against the site being multicomponent.

Parker's description of the post-Columbian artifacts is rather sparse; he mentions copper-based kettles, "usually about ten inches [25 centimeters] in their mouth diameters, with a heavy iron band around their tops, and a stout bale. Most were . . . damaged by use or intentional destruction of their bottoms."[8] While what Parker describes is reminiscent of Basque-derived iron-banded copper kettles diagnostic of sixteenth-century trade (Fitzgerald et al.

1993), no complete Basque kettles have been found outside the St. Lawrence River Valley and they have never been found on any site in the numbers described by Parker. Additionally, most recovered Basque kettles are significantly larger than the 25-centimeter diameter Parker reported (Fitzgerald et al. 1993, Table 2). He may have been referring to iron wire reinforcements that many later brass kettle rims were folded around. Parker also identified "remnants of knives," which I take to mean metal knives, as Parker was unlikely to have identified a lithic form as a "knife."[9]

While the presence of brass kettles and iron knives is diagnostic only of an occupation dating to after 1560, the quantity of kettles suggests an occupation after 1615, when intact kettles become commonplace in the region (DeOrio 1978; Wray and Schoff 1953, 57). The mortuary patterning may provide another temporal clue: extended burial was extremely common in Gayogǫhó:nǫ' and Onöndowa'ga:' towns after about 1670 (DeOrio 1978; Wray and Graham 1960, 4), so Parker Street may have been occupied prior to that date. It is interesting that Parker does not mention glass or shell beads, which are staples at seventeenth century Indigenous sites in the region. This atypical material signature, if genuine, could mean that Parker Street represents an occupation by an incorporated foreign population brought under Gayogǫhó:nǫ' protection, similar to the settlements of incorporated Delawares and Tutelos in the Ithaca area during the eighteenth century.

North Geneva Street and Parker Street lie only about 600 meters apart, and the artifacts and mortuary patterning suggest that they may have been occupied sequentially or even contemporaneously. In tandem, they represent a fairly substantial seventeenth-century occupation by Gayogǫhó:nǫ' people or their allies. The 1670–1710 date for the North Geneva Street runtee aligns with the occupations of Gayogǫhó:nǫ' principal towns located 44 kilometers or more north of Ithaca.

Conclusions

The case for intensified use of regional space by the western Haudenosaunee Nations rests on data of quite varying quality that were collected and assessed using disparate methods and often came to light through blatant acts of colonialist desecration and erasure. Of the artifacts discussed here, sound knowledge of spatial location and context of recovery exists only for the Indian Fort Road site, and even there the tubular glass bead diagnostic of seventeenth-century occupation was repatriated and reburied before it was securely identified. The brass objects from the Eugene Frost site were recovered through metal detection by an avocational archaeologist who did not record the locations of his finds. The Kipp Island assemblage is contextualized only at the site level. The Ithaca sites—North Geneva Street and Parker Street—are clearly the most problematic as there are no extant archaeological collections and recording was done haphazardly and ambiguously. This suggests that it would be very difficult to generate a full inventory of seventeenth-century Indigenous sites (particularly small sites or those mostly or completely destroyed) to further examine the pattern outlined here. But further scouring of existing records and museum collections could locate other sites that could extend (or complicate) this model.[10]

I underscore that when the majority of the sites discussed in this essay—Kipp Island, North Geneva Street, and Parker Street—were destroyed, the full nature of their archaeological contents were not carefully recorded or preserved. These three sites likely contained Indigenous burials that were desecrated and human remains and grave goods that were dispersed. Griffis noted that "bushels of beads and arrow heads were also unearthed but [were] thought to be of little value, so were destroyed" at North Geneva Street.[11] Parker relates that several brass kettles recovered from Parker Street graves were repaired by a local coppersmith and that he had "seen such used as kitchen utensils" by Ithaca settlers (quoted in Norris 1969, 38).[12] This is certainly a form of erasure, one of the hallmarks of settler colonialism (Wolfe 2006). Such erasure leaves landscapes historically blank, enabling settlers to create new forms of memorialization, commemoration, and memory focused on themselves without acknowledging the ties Indigenous peoples had and continue to have to the exact same spaces (e.g., Barker 2018). Recovering information on these sites partly undoes such erasure and repatriation of location information enables Indigenous descendants to reconnect with the spaces—although not the remains—of their ancestors.

To summarize the findings, diagnostic artifacts and burial patterns suggest occupation dates of circa 1625–1685 for the reoccupation of the Indian Fort Road site; circa 1640–1687 at the Eugene Frost site; circa 1650–1700 for the likely cemetery on Kipp Island; circa 1670–1710 for North Geneva Street; and (perhaps) circa 1615–1670 for Parker Street. Historic documents are mute about these sites. This new information is particularly significant for the Ithaca area, since it provides evidence for fairly substantial seventeenth-century Indigenous occupations in an area that was previously considered to be a little-settled backwater.

I find it noteworthy that the evidence clusters in the period from 1640 to 1710 and that the occupations of these sites may even have overlapped. Historical evidence about the military climate in the region may help refine and narrow these occupation estimates. The French mounted a series of invasions of Haudenosaunee territory, starting with the 1684 LaBarre expedition. Although LaBarre's force returned to New France without inflicting any damage, this invasion appears to have spurred changes in the use of space in Haudenosaunee territory, as the Onöndowa'ga:' began to fortify a defensible hilltop location shortly thereafter (O'Callaghan 1855, 254, 261). The French then conducted a series of scorched-earth campaigns against the Haudenosaunee in 1687, 1693, and 1696 that affected all of the Five Nations except the Gayogohó:nǫ' (Parmenter 2010). The early part of the eighteenth century was little better, as French-sponsored western Indians continued to raid Haudenosaunee territory.

The period from 1687 to 1710 was no time to be living in small, isolated settlements like the ones I have described here. Indeed, the archaeological record suggests that even substantial satellite communities—including extraregional, regional, and local examples—were abandoned during this period and that their populations consolidated with the principal towns. Haudenosaunee settlements on the north shore of Lake Ontario were vacated by 1687. There is no archaeological evidence for satellite communities in Gayogohó:nǫ' or Onöndowa'ga:' territory between the French invasions and 1704, when documentary sources suggest that a small Onöndowa'ga:' satellite existed in the vicinity of Kendaia (Jordan 2008, 182).

I use these five sites to posit that numerous small communities were established in the hinterlands of Haudenosaunee regional territory from 1640 to the mid-1680s. While the sites I have described mostly are distant from each other, I expect that they are not the sole examples. It seems reasonable that these sites represent nodes in a network of small sites—most of which have not been discovered by archaeologists and because of their size and issues with record-keeping may never be—rather than isolated outposts.

I argue that 1640 to 1684 was an era of heightened Haudenosaunee occupation of their regional landscapes in a form and with an intensity that was not exactly paralleled at any time before and has not been since. This pattern has not been perceived by document-based historians and may in fact have developed almost completely outside the purview of European observers. While archaeologists often use small sites to mark Indigenous persistence or refuge in difficult times, I think the Haudenosaunee example signals a somewhat different motivation: an aggressive intensification of the use of regional space during a period of political and economic confidence.

Acknowledgments

I am grateful to Lee Panich and Tsim Schneider for the invitation to participate in this volume and to fellow authors for their work. Earlier versions were presented at the 2015 New York State Archaeological Association annual meeting in Watertown and the 2019 Society for American Archaeology annual meeting in Albuquerque. In addition to the guidance from Indigenous collaborators already recognized in the chapter text, I received interesting comments and suggestions from the editors and reviewers and from Tim Abel, Lisa Anselmi, Nancy Herter, Kaitlin LaGrasta, Wayne Lenig, Jon Parmenter, Jack Rossen, and Martha Sempowski. I thank Sherene Baugher, Karlis Karklins, and Samantha Sanft for their perspectives on Indian Fort Road. Mary Ann Levine and Jim Delle initially connected me to Eugene Frost, who generously gave my crew access to his property and collection. Beth Ryan analyzed the Cornell fieldwork at the Frost Site. Bob DeOrio, Charles Burgess, and Nick Perez helped me understand Gayogo̱hó:nǫ' sites and settlement dynamics. Jim Bradley provided information about iron-banded copper kettles and glass beads. Donna Eschenbrenner (History Center) and Eileen Keating, Brenda Marston, and Cheryl Whited (Cornell Rare and Manuscript Collections) facilitated my archival work.

Notes

1. These institutions include the State University of New York research centers in Albany, Binghamton, Buffalo, and Stony Brook; the New York State Museum; the state Office of Parks, Recreation, and Historic Preservation, which includes the State Historic Preservation Office; the Rochester Museum and Science Center; and the Southold Indian Museum.

2. Onöndowa'ga:' (Seneca) Haudenosaunee Archaeological Materials, circa 1688–1754,

digital collection, Cornell University Library, https://digital.library.cornell.edu/collections/seneca, accessed January 21, 2021.

3. This model assumes pedestrian travel. The Haudenosaunee did not widely adopt horses for transportation in the seventeenth century (Jordan 2008, 295–296). Modeling water-based travel is difficult because downstream travel was quicker and easier than upstream travel and because water levels varied seasonally (Little 1987).

4. While compositional analysis showed that the copper-based materials from Indian Fort Road were European alloys, the forms are most consistent with a sixteenth-century date (Sanft 2018, 9–11).

5. Gayog̱ohó:nǫ' faithkeeper Steve Henhawk notes that Montezuma Marsh was likely to have been a space of refuge after the Gayog̱ohó:nǫ' lost their New York reservation territories in the early 1800s (personal communication 2019).

6. William Elliott Griffis, "Notes on Indian Relics Found at North Geneva Street, Ithaca New York, 1901," n.d., Box V-3-3-12A, Folder 2, New York State Indians Collection, The History Center in Tompkins County, Ithaca, New York.

7. Samuel J. Parker, "A Picture of Ithaca, N.Y. as I Saw It in Childhood," 35, typescript dated 1895, Samuel J. Parker Papers, Manuscript Collection 2521, Division of Rare and Manuscript Collections, Cornell University Library, Ithaca, New York.

8. Parker, "A Picture of Ithaca, N.Y.," 35.

9. Parker, "A Picture of Ithaca, N.Y.," 34.

10. This model of regional settlement expansion may require archaeologists to rethink some sites. Take, for example, the well-documented circa 1660–1680 Gayog̱ohó:nǫ' Rogers Farm site (Mandzy 1990, 1992, 139–152; Williams-Shuker 2005). I previously described Rogers Farm as akin to a local satellite because it was "placed adjacent to major transportation corridors along which Cayugas and other Iroquois frequently passed" (Jordan 2013, 36). However, this site technically is within regional, rather than local, space compared to contemporaneous principal towns, and I neglected the fact that the upstream connection from Rogers Farm to principal would have been significantly more difficult and time consuming than the reverse trip downstream. Thus, Rogers Farm could be viewed as another example of regional settlement expansion contemporaneous with the sites discussed in this essay.

11. Griffis, "Notes on Indian Relics Found at North Geneva Street, Ithaca New York, 1901."

12. Parker, "A Picture of Ithaca, N.Y.," 36.

References Cited

Abel, Timothy J. 2000. The Plus Site: An Iroquoian Remote Camp in Upland Tompkins County, NY. *North American Archaeologist* 21(3): 181–215.

Barker, Adam J. 2018. Deathscapes of Settler Colonialism: The Necro-Settlement of Stoney Creek, Ontario, Canada. *Annals of the American Association of Geographers* 108(4): 1134–1149.

Baugher, Sherene, and Sara Clark. 1998. An Archaeological Investigation of the Indian Fort Road Site, Trumansburg, New York. Archaeology Program, Cornell University, Ithaca, New York. Submitted to New York State Office of Parks, Recreation & Historic Preservation, Albany.

Beauchamp, William M., ed. 1916. *Moravian Journals Relating to Central New York, 1745–66.* Syracuse, NY: Dehler Press.

Beduya, Jose. 2020. Artifacts from Upstate Indigenous Towns Digitized, Repatriated. *Cornell Chronicle,* September 23, 2020. Accessed January 21, 2021. https://news.cornell.edu/stories/2020/09/artifacts-upstate-indigenous-towns-digitized-repatriated.

Ceci, Lynn. 1989. Tracing Wampum's Origins. In *Proceedings of the 1986 Shell Bead Conference,* edited by Charles F. Hayes III, 63–80. Research Records no. 20. Rochester, NY: Rochester Museum and Science Center.

Clark, Douglas. 2019. Oneida Glass Trade Bead Chronology. *Chenango Chapter of the New York State Archaeological Association Bulletin* 37(2): 1–94.

Coyne, James H., ed. 1903. *Galinee's Narrative and Map.* Translated by James H. Coyne. Ontario Historical Society Papers and Records 4. Toronto: Ontario Historical Society.

DeOrio, Robert N. 1978. A Preliminary Sequence of the Historic Cayuga Nation within the Traditional Area, 1600–1740. *Beauchamp Chapter Newsletter* 9(4): n.p.

Eastly, Sarah A. 2012. A Question of Faith: Jesuit Missions to the Seneca Iroquois as Viewed through Archaeological and Textual Records. Master's thesis, Cornell University, Ithaca, New York.

Engelbrecht, William. 2003. *Iroquoia: The Development of a Native World.* Syracuse, NY: Syracuse University Press.

Esarey, Duane E. 2013. Another Kind of Beads: A Forgotten Industry of the North American Colonial Period. PhD diss., University of North Carolina, Chapel Hill.

Fitzgerald, William R., Laurier Turgeon, Ruth Holmes Whitehead, and James W. Bradley. 1993. Late Sixteenth-Century Basque Banded Copper Kettles. *Historical Archaeology* 27(1): 44–57.

Hart, John P., Lisa M. Anderson, and Robert S. Feranec. 2011. Additional Evidence for Cal. Seventh-Century A.D. Maize Consumption at the Kipp Island Site, New York. In *Current Research in New York Archaeology: A.D. 700–1300,* edited by Christina B. Rieth and John P. Hart, 27–40. New York State Museum Record 2. Albany: New York State Education Department.

Herlich, Jessica M. 2008. The Copper-Alloy Assemblage from the Seneca Iroquois TownleyRead Site, circa 1715–1754 C.E. *Bulletin: Journal of the New York State Archaeological Association* 124: 1–30.

Houghton, Frederick. 1912. The Seneca Nation from 1655 to 1687. *Bulletin of the Buffalo Society of Natural Sciences* 10(2): 363–464.

Huey, Paul. R. 1997. The Origins and Development of Historical Archaeology in New York State. *Bulletin: Journal of the New York State Archaeological Association* 113: 60–96.

Jones, David M., and Anne Jones. 1980. The Defenses at Indian Fort Road, Tompkins County, New York. *Pennsylvania Archaeologist* 50(1–2): 61–71.

Jordan, Kurt A. 2008. *The Seneca Restoration, 1715–1754: An Iroquois Local Political Economy.* Gainesville: University Press of Florida and Society for Historical Archaeology.

———. 2010. Not Just "One Site Against the World": Seneca Iroquois Intercommunity Connections and Autonomy, 1550–1779. In *Across a Great Divide: Continuity and Change in Native North American Societies, 1400–1900,* edited by Laura L. Scheiber and Mark D. Mitchell, 79–106. Tucson: University of Arizona Press.

———. 2013. Incorporation and Colonization: Postcolumbian Iroquois Satellite Communities and Processes of Indigenous Autonomy. *American Anthropologist* 115(1): 29–43.

Jordan, Kurt A. and Peregrine A. Gerard-Little. 2019. Neither Contact nor Colonial: Seneca Iroquois Local Political Economies, 1670–1754. In *Indigenous Persistence in the Colonized*

Americas, edited by Heather Law Pezzarossi and Russell N. Sheptak, 39–56. Albuquerque: University of New Mexico Press.

Kidd, Kenneth E., and Martha A. Kidd. 1970. A Classification System for Glass Beads for the Use of Field Archaeologists. *Canadian Historic Sites: Occasional Papers in Archaeology and History* 1: 45–89.

Konrad, Victor. 1981. An Iroquois Frontier: The North Shore of Lake Ontario during the Late Seventeenth Century. *Journal of Historical Geography* 7(2): 129–144.

Levitt, Emily. 2018. Taxing Neighbors: Tribal and Municipal Conflict over New York's Fiscal Borders. PhD diss., Cornell University, Ithaca, New York.

Little, Elizabeth A. 1987. Inland Waterways in the Northeast. *Midcontinental Journal of Archaeology* 12(1): 55–76.

Mandzy, Adrian Oleh. 1990. The Rogers Farm Site: A Seventeenth-Century Cayuga Site. *Bulletin: Journal of the New York State Archaeological Association* 100: 18–25.

———. 1992. History of Cayuga Acculturation: An Examination of the 17th-Century Cayuga Iroquois Archaeological Data. Master's thesis, Michigan State University, East Lansing.

Norris, W. Glenn. 1961. *Early Explorers and Travelers in Tompkins County*. Ithaca, NY: DeWitt Historical Society of Tompkins County.

———. 1969. *Old Indian Trails in Tompkins County*. Rev. ed. Ithaca, NY: Dewitt Historical Society of Tompkins County.

O'Callaghan, E. B., ed. 1855. *Documents Relative to the Colonial History of the State of New York*. Vol. 9. Albany: Weed, Parsons.

Panich, Lee M., and Tsim D. Schneider. 2019. Categorical Denial: Evaluating Post-1492 Indigenous Erasure in the Paper Trail of American Archaeology. *American Antiquity* 84(4): 651–668.

Parker, Arthur C. 1922. *The Archeological History of New York*. Bulletin of the New York State Museum 235-239. Albany: New York State Museum.

Parmenter, Jon William. 2010. *The Edge of the Woods: Iroquoia, 1534–1701*. East Lansing: Michigan State University Press.

Rieth, Christina B., ed. 2008. *Current Approaches to the Analysis and Interpretation of Small Lithic Sites in the Northeast*. Bulletin 508. Albany: New York State Museum.

Ritchie, William A. 1980. *The Archaeology of New York State*. Rev. ed. Harrison, NY: Harbor Hill Books.

Ritchie, William A., and Robert E. Funk. 1973. *Aboriginal Settlement Patterns in the Northeast*. New York State Museum and Science Service Memoir 20. Albany: University of the State of New York.

Rossen, Jack, ed. 2015. *Corey Village and the Cayuga World: Implications from Archaeology and Beyond*. Syracuse, NY: Syracuse University Press.

Rumrill, Donald A. 1991. The Mohawk Glass Trade Bead Chronology: ca. 1560–1785. *Beads: Journal of the Society of Bead Researchers* 3: 5–45.

Ryan, Beth, and Adam G. Dewbury. 2010. The Eugene Frost Collection: Artifacts from the Seneca Iroquois Dann Site, circa 1655–1675. Cornell University Archaeological Collections Documentation Project, Report No. 1. Manuscript on file, Division of Rare and Manuscript Collections, Cornell University Library, Ithaca, NY.

Sanft, Samantha M. 2013. Beads and Pendants from Indian Fort Road: An Analysis of a Sixteenth-Century Cayuga Site in Tompkins County, New York. Master's thesis, Cornell University, Ithaca, New York.

———. 2018. Beads and Pendants from Indian Fort Road: Native Cultural Continuity and Innovation in the Sixteenth-Century Haudenosaunee Homeland. *Northeast Anthropology* 85–86: 1–20.

Snow, Dean R. 1995. *Mohawk Valley Archaeology: The Sites*. Albany: Institute for Archaeological Studies, State University of New York.

Snow, Dean R., Charles T. Gehring, and William A. Starna, eds. 1996. *In Mohawk Country: Early Narratives about a Native People*. Syracuse, NY: Syracuse University Press.

Thwaites, Reuben Gold, ed. 1899a. *The Jesuit Relations and Allied Documents*. Vol. 52. Cleveland: Burrows Brothers.

———. 1899b. *The Jesuit Relations and Allied Documents*. Vol. 54. Cleveland: Burrows Brothers.

———. 1899c. *The Jesuit Relations and Allied Documents*. Vol. 56. Cleveland: Burrows Brothers.

———. 1900a. *The Jesuit Relations and Allied Documents*. Vol. 59. Cleveland: Burrows Brothers.

———. 1900b. *The Jesuit Relations and Allied Documents*. Vol. 60. Cleveland: Burrows Brothers.

Williams-Shuker, Kimberly Louise. 2005. Cayuga Iroquois Households and Gender Relations During the Contact Period: An Investigation of the Rogers Farm Site, 1660s–1680s. PhD diss., University of Pittsburgh.

Wolfe, Patrick. 2006. Settler Colonialism and the Elimination of the Native. *Journal of Genocide Research* 8(4): 387–409.

Wood, Alice S. 1974. A Catalogue of Jesuit and Ornamental Rings from Western New York State. *Historical Archaeology* 8: 83–104.

Wray, Charles F. 1973. *A Manual for Seneca Iroquois Archeology*. Honeoye Falls, NY: Cultures Primitive.

———. 1985. The Volume of Dutch Trade Goods Received by the Seneca Iroquois, 1600–1687 AD. *Bulletin KNOB* 84(2): 100–112.

Wray, Charles F., and Robert J. Graham. 1960. New Discoveries on an Old Site: The Bunce Site. *Bulletin: Journal of the New York State Archaeological Association* 18: 1–4.

Wray, Charles F., and Harry L. Schoff. 1953. A Preliminary Report on the Seneca Sequence in Western New York, 1550–1687. *Pennsylvania Archaeologist* 23: 53–63.

13

Navigating Entanglements and Mitigating Intergenerational Trauma in Two Collaborative Projects

Stewart Indian School and "Our Ancestors' Walk of Sorrow" Forced Removal Trail

SARAH E. COWIE AND DIANE L. TEEMAN

Traditional Indigenous landscapes are imbued with cultural meaning and value that are best understood by researchers from both etic and emic perspectives and through collaborative research. We, the authors, are engaged in long-term partnerships with numerous American Indian communities in the American Great Basin, including the Burns Paiute Tribe. Co-author Diane L. Teeman is enrolled in this Tribe and is the director of its Culture & Heritage Department. Together we endeavor to document and understand typically unconsidered aspects of how and why the US government forcibly removed American Indians from their ancestral homelands in the American West in the nineteenth century; how and why the government attempted to assimilate tribal children into mainstream society; and, how and why government oversight continues to regulate Indigenous heritage through federal archaeological policies that often perpetuate colonial practices. Colonialist worldviews define what has value as a "cultural resource" and what has life, presence, and agency in narrow terms compared to the definitions in many Indigenous epistemologies. The fact that who and what has personhood in cultural resource management are rarely topics of discussion cross-culturally leads to an incomplete scope for cultural resource management consideration. This lack of recognition also means that research funding opportunities for archaeology would rarely include work on these topics. Furthermore, the fact that Indigenous peoples rarely have opportunities to assert Indigenous worldviews in management discussions has led to laws, policies, implementations, and research funding distributions that do not meet the needs of tribally understood cultural landscapes and ecosystems. In addition to this lack of inclusion in cross-cultural discussions of ontology and epistemology, the paths established by law and by agency protocols for protecting culturally important places and things are inadequately revealed to Tribes because they are not agency interlocutors.

In this chapter we address two related case studies in collaborative Indigenous archaeology. Both projects were developed under a grant entitled "Governmentality and Social Capital in Tribal/Federal Relations Regarding Heritage Consultation," which funded collaborative archaeological research to explore conflicting heritage discourses on public lands. Both projects presented here featured archaeological field schools that included substantial involvement from Native students, staff, and volunteers with the goal of interrogating conflicting discourses and epistemologies about Indigenous heritages. We first describe a project that recently began on an Indigenous trail that the federal government used in the nineteenth century to forcibly remove Indigenous prisoners of war (POWs) from their homelands. Then we report on a completed project at Nevada's historic Stewart Indian School, another Indigenous landscape that the federal government later repurposed as part of its effort to assimilate Native children.

Both projects highlight concepts of entanglement, removal, and trauma. "Removal" refers to the forced removal of Indigenous peoples from their homelands, removal of children from their families in the boarding school system, removal of cultural materials from the ground through standard archaeological practices, and removal of Indigenous voices from heritage management. Removal practices are related to entanglement, both in the sense of colonial entanglements (e.g., Silliman 2005) and in the sense of analogies with research on temporality and on entangled relationships that cross space-time continuums (e.g., Bakhtin 1981; Schlosshauer 2010). The concept of trauma addresses the painful disruptions created by historical acts of removal, and the subsequent wounds of intergenerational trauma that are at times reopened by standard archaeological practices today. These three interrelated concepts—removal, entanglement, and trauma—inform archaeologies of colonized Indigenous landscapes, peoples, and heritages. It is our hope that researchers working with Indigenous landscapes will consider how they may reduce the perpetuation of colonialist domination in archaeological study. Working in a truly collaborative way with Indigenous communities may help mitigate traumas associated with tragic events and will invaluably broaden and enrich archaeologists' understandings of the research effort. When individuals holding Indigenous ways of knowing are physically present in real-time research efforts, there are opportunities to present alternative standpoints that broaden our cross-cultural understandings.

Our research design on these projects is also informed by concerns about power and the state. The United States has implemented numerous policies to control, disempower, erase, and, in some cases, exterminate Indigenous North Americans. Since their inception, the disciplines of archaeology and anthropology have been tools of the state that have worked to control Indigenous peoples and their heritage (Atalay 2010, 79; Warrick 2017, 88; Wobst 2010, 77). In North America, anthropologists historically dismissed Indigenous peoples' perspectives about their own cultures (Thomas 2000, 101). Many Indigenous groups have been silenced by their experiences with colonialism and the sociopolitical plight they faced after conquest. In addition, academic archaeologists assumed that they were experts about Indigenous communities (Deloria 1992, 595), and gatekeeper of Indigenous heritage (Colwell-Chanthaphonh et al. 2010).

We use a Foucauldian lens in our research. Foucault's (1991, 1998, 2007) ideas about knowledge, power, biopolitics, and governmentality apply to the historic events related to forced removal of Indigenous peoples, the Indian boarding school system, and the contemporary attitudes, practices, and management of Indigenous heritages. As Atalay (2006, 296) observes, sometimes it can be productive to use the "master's tools" of western scholarship to provide critiques that eventually decenter dominant western practices and create counterdiscourses in Indigenous studies. Our theoretical approach combines western and Indigenous philosophies (see also Fowles 2010). Like Panich and Schneider (this volume), we hope to directly address the need for broader processes of "undisciplining" and confronting the ignorance or "unknowing" that pervades settler colonialism in the academy and beyond. Our blended theoretical approach is helpful for navigating between our need to serve Great Basin Indigenous communities and our need to operate within systems that have oppressed those communities (see also Schneider et al., this volume). This approach could be called theoretical code-switching; it enables us to productively move between these two situations.

Perhaps most importantly, our two projects are collaborative. Collaborative archaeology endeavors to provide a space for multivocality for all the identified stakeholders that desire to participate in a project. This approach is an Indigenous archaeology, a term Watkins (2000) championed and Nicholas (2008, 1660) later defined as "an expression of archaeological theory and practice in which the discipline intersects with Indigenous values, knowledge, practices, ethics, and sensibilities, and through collaborative and community-originated or directed-projects and related critical perspectives." Indigenous archaeologies are an essential component of decolonizing archaeological practice today (Atalay 2006; see also Harris 2010; Smith 1999; Wilcox 2010). Indigenous archaeologies exist in a perpetual state of becoming. The foundational theory is that in the absence of colonialist/state control, we as human cultures hold a level of intellectual equality that facilitates consideration of epistemological difference.

"Our Ancestors' Walk of Sorrow" Forced Removal Trail Project

The more recent of these two projects began in 2016 and will be the subject of Teeman's PhD dissertation in anthropology; preliminary results are presented here. The project arose in part from the partnership between University of Nevada Reno Department of Anthropology (Cowie, a settler of European descent) and the Culture & Heritage Department Director of the Burns Paiute Tribe (Teeman, an enrolled Tribal member). The Burns Paiute Tribe has had a long-standing interest in documenting their forced removal from their ancestral homelands in the winter of 1879. The physical corridor of the removal trail is poorly documented and there are few accounts from the POWs, but their descendants now have the opportunity to change that through our collaborations. Collaborators in the project are not "informants" in the ethnographic sense; rather, they are knowledge holders and contributing research partners. Their presence as members of the research team brings a validity to the knowledge creation process that a strictly etic research performance could never attain.

Our project will identify the physical corridor used to march more than

500 Indigenous POWs from Fort Harney, Oregon, to Fort Simcoe, Washington (Figure 13.1). We endeavor to identify the metaphysical dimensions of the removal corridor as the descendants of the forced march understood them. In 1872, President Ulysses S. Grant signed an executive order that established the Malheur Indian Reservation subsequent to a treaty signed at Fort Harney. Non-Native pressure for the land led to deteriorating conditions on the reservation, and in 1879 an uprising occurred to the east among the Bannock Indians over settler infringements in Idaho that spilled into eastern Oregon (Burns Paiute Tribe 2001). Two primary first-hand accounts of the effect of the Bannock War effect on the Indigenous people of the northern Great Basin have been published (Howard 1907; Hopkins [1883] 1994). Stowell (2008) provides a recent academic study on the topic, but many questions remain. The Bannock War was short lived and poorly documented. The death of Chief Egan of the Paiute Tribe was the final blow to the uprising, and once the POWs were back at the reservation and held at Fort Harney, debate over what should happen to them began. Indian agent William V. Rinehart wrote an account of the POW removal:

> After the end of the war in the fall of 1878, the U.S. Army brought Paiute Indians from southeastern Oregon to Camp Harney, located about fifteen miles east of present-day Burns. In December of that year, the camp commander told Sarah Winnemucca, a Paiute interpreter and activist, that he had orders to remove the Paiute to the Yakama Indian Reservation 350 miles to the north. In her autobiography, Sarah wrote that she was struck with horror. "What, in this cold winter and in all this snow," she responded, "and my people have so many little children? Why they will die."
>
> Approximately 550 Paiute men, women, and children—many of whom . . . had not engaged in hostilities—traveled north for nearly a month through the snow and over two mountain ranges. The women and children traveled in wagons, but some of the men were forced to march in leg irons. Five children, one woman, and an elderly man died along the way, their bodies left alongside the road since it was too cold to bury them. . . . Rinehart complains about the exorbitant cost of the winter removal and notes that the Paiute were forced to leave Camp Harney under-equipped even though supplies were enroute from the Malheur agency. Yakama Agent James Wilbur remarked that the newly arrived

Figure 13.1. Map showing start and end points of forced march of over 500 Indigenous men, women, and children from Fort Harney in Oregon to Fort Simcoe in Washington in 1879. The march of more than 300 miles took place in rugged, snowy terrain in the month of January. Map courtesy of Christina McSherry.

Paiute were "utterly destitute" and that he was given no notice of their coming "and of course no arrangements for giving them rations." (Oregon History Project 2008)

The people who survived the march struggled for survival at Fort Simcoe. Some people escaped from their internment, but the majority of the prisoners of war were not released for half a decade. In their absence, the Malheur Reservation was returned to the public domain and surviving POWs were landless when they returned to their homelands. Descendants of the survivors of the forced march now live scattered on at least fourteen reservations and tribal communities in five western states (tribal collaborators, personal communications 2016–2018).

Collaborative Research Design for the Trail

Numerous descendant collaborators have made themselves available to the removal trail project so that they might have an opportunity to represent their Ancestors' experiences and share their own experiences of the tragedy. Project preparation began with identifying additional descendants of the forced march. In 2016–2017, Teeman contacted the tribal communities that in 1934 sent representatives to attend a General Council meeting that was held in Burns, Oregon, to discuss pursuing a Malheur Reservation court case. Teeman worked to identify whether people wanted to hear our proposal. Each tribal community determined who we should address with our project proposal and how they wanted to receive and review the proposal.

The critical initial goal for presenting the research proposal to communities was to identify whether this research would be welcomed. If any of the communities Teeman visited indicated that they did not want research conducted on the removal trail, we planned to terminate the effort. When no objections were raised, Teeman and Cowie hosted project convenings to develop a tentative working title for the trail project and achieve consensus about best cross-cultural practices for implementing the project. The project collaborators are descendants of the POW forced march and they chose by consensus the working name of the project: "Our Ancestors' Walk of Sorrow (or Sadness)." The name may be translated into Paiute at a future convening. The Paiute language is alive and holds personhood status. It hears us and knows when it is honored, so more time is needed to develop consensus on the correct translation. This is one of many reasons that collaborative research requires abundant time, patience, and sincere care.

During the fall 2017 convening, collaborators traveled along the southernmost portion of the removal trail as public land managers understood it. We also agreed on communication logistics and acceptable research options to identify whether any methods should be modified or removed from consideration. The group also supported a field school in collaborative Indigenous archaeology that was held in the summer of 2019 at the Malheur Indian Agency site near Burns, Oregon. This site is contemporary with and related to the events of the removal trail. Teeman served as the field school's instructor and all the field school students were tribal members. This project will be detailed in later publications.

One of the most obvious points of interest that emerged from our convenings and discussions during the field school is that numerous discrepancies exist between the written record as the US War Department and the Office of Indian-Affairs of the U.S. Department of the Interior chronicled it and the first-hand accounts of the forced march as asserted by the Burns Paiute Tribe. These discrepancies include how many people were involved, how many lives were lost, and the distance of the march. Even more elusive is an account of the physical route taken during this military action. Trails are often ephemeral to begin with, and detecting the presence of discreetly visited locales with little physical evidence is difficult with standard archaeological methods (see also Laluk, this volume; Scheidecker et al., this volume). This challenge is compounded by three complicating factors: processes of settler colonialism and the way the ideology of Manifest Destiny worked to erase prior Indigenous presence; non-Native researchers' historical exploitation of Native peoples' knowledge and Native peoples' subsequent hesitance to share sensitive information (see also Scheidecker et al., this volume); and the fact that earlier Native trails often became wagon roads and then highways, which means that the physical evidence of the trail was often lost/destroyed (regarding settlers' erasure and rebranding of Indigenous places, see also Bauer, this volume; Scheiber, this volume; Trabert, this volume).

Furthermore, our discussions made the need to include cross-cultural understandings and concerns even more evident. Our collaborators illuminate why it is essential that they be involved in federal and state agency management discussions of the corridor today. The metaphysical components of the corridor, the need for appropriate acknowledgement of and reverence to the Ancestors, and the traumatic experiences still present in these places complicate what it means to appropriately manage heritage matters in ways that are completely unknown to many non-Native people.

This project will eventually provide a comprehensive analysis of the retrievable quantifiable data that exists on the landscape of this event while also providing room for the more qualitative data that exists in the minds and hearts of the descendants of the POWs. Given these physical and social landscape considerations, the issue of identifying the removal trail corridor of the Our Ancestors' Walk of Sorrow Project will proceed with a considerable amount of collaborator discussion before the route can be adequately mapped with the additional tools of satellite imagery, aerial photography, and archaeological work. Together, we will also parse out practical and symbolic meanings of the military road as it was constructed and then differentiate its original use from the symbolic meaning it holds as the trail of a forced march removal.

From this effort, we will provide a more complete narrative of this traumatic event in mid-nineteenth-century American history than standard archaeological practice could achieve. This will allow us to develop culturally appropriate recommendations to federal land management agencies regarding preservation of the corridor that will be informed by both physical (archaeological) and metaphysical considerations (e.g., the loss of life along the trail and the imprint of suffering that was left on the land). In the Our Ancestors' Walk of Sorrow Project discussions, we endeavor to identify, disentangle, and represent the series of events from the perspectives of power and representation that occurred then and are perpetuated in different manifestations of settler colonialism today.

Stewart Indian School Project

The authors initially met on a collaborative Indigenous archaeology project at the Stewart Indian School in Carson City, Nevada, that began in 2012 (Cowie et al. 2019). American Indian boarding schools constitute a traumatic history for many Tribal peoples (see also Montgomery and Colwell 2019; Surface-Evans and Jones 2016). Like other Indian boarding schools in the United States, Stewart Indian School was mandated in 1890 by the Bureau of Indian Affairs and designed to force Native children to assimilate as settlers encroached on their lands (Figure 13.2).

This case study began with a partnership between archaeologists at the University of Nevada, Reno; the Tribal Historic Preservation Office (THPO) of the Washoe Tribe of Nevada and California (hereafter Washoe THPO); and the Nevada Indian Commission. As with the Our Ancestors' Walk of Sorrow Project, we reached out to numerous personal and professional connections in the region to discuss archaeological sites that could be considered for the focus of an archaeological field school in service to the wishes of tribal communities. We restricted our discussion to sites that tribal organizations thought were suitable.

After several meetings, several of which were facilitated by the Nevada Indian Commission and its Stewart Advisory Committee, consensus developed that the project would take place at the Stewart Indian School. The Nevada Indian Commission, whose office as a state agency is currently located on the grounds of the school, and the THPO for the Washoe Tribe of Nevada

Figure 13.2. Boys in military-style uniforms at Stewart Indian School, circa 1890s–1900s. Courtesy of Nevada State Museum, Carson City, Nevada Department of Tourism and Cultural Affairs.

and California, the Tribe whose ancestral homelands include the site, were particularly supportive. Numerous tribal members from regional communities explained that this would be the most appropriate site for a number of reasons. Traumatic memories of the Indian boarding school system are still painfully fresh in Native communities today. In contrast, because of processes of settler colonialism, non-Native peoples are largely ignorant of those histories and still often relegate Native peoples to ancient history. Our collaborators aimed to raise awareness of this important part of Native American history and to contribute to its preservation through that raised awareness. One aspect of the research design was the goal of gaining the attention of the media, the state legislature, and the governor's office through our physical presence at the site (located in Carson City, Nevada's state capital). Our plan was to conduct archaeology very visibly in the public eye to demonstrate the powerful and oft-heard Indigenous declaration that "We are Still Here" and to continue to care for these places despite settler colonialists' brutal attempts to erase tribal peoples and heritages throughout the world (see also Dickson and Steinmetz, this volume, Laluk, this volume, and Schneider et al., this volume). Indeed, many stakeholders pointed out that selecting Stewart Indian School for this project would benefit many Tribes, not just one. Members of numerous Tribes passed through Stewart during its 90-year history.

The Stewart Indian School opened in 1890 and operated until 1980 (for a history of the school, see Thompson-Hardin 2019). It is currently listed on the National Register of Historic Places, and the Nevada Indian Commission plans to nominate it as a National Historic Landmark. Young Native Americans from roughly 200 different Tribes in the western United States attended the school, and it has significance for numerous descendant communities today. The school was established by a mandate from the Bureau of Indian Affairs that was part of federal policies designed to force assimilation. In the earliest years, attendance was mandatory and children were literally rounded up in wagons and taken from their families (Thompson-Hardin 2019). The federal biopolitical (see Foucault 2007) policies of controlling Indigenous bodies for political purposes were readily visible. For example, children were forced to cut their hair upon their initial arrival at school in an attempt to remove all signs of Indian identity. In Great Basin communities, cutting hair was a traumatic event with deep cultural meaning. Anthropologist Julian Steward (1943, 81; Dean and Marler 2001, 35) wrote that cutting hair traditionally only occurred when a close loved one died. According to Dean and Marler (2001, 35) cutting hair is called *nadegqa'se*, which means "taking or killing oneself—where the mourners are literally sending a part of themselves to be with the dead." Other activities were required of the children that disciplined their bodies, including requiring them to march in lines and wear military uniforms. Our excavations recovered objects related to bodily discipline, such as lice combs, medicine bottles, and buttons from army clothing that reflect the oppressive efforts of settler colonialism. We recovered other objects such as soda bottles that alumni recalled enjoying with other treats (Washoe Elder Jo Ann Nevers, personal communications in Cowie et al. 2019). This reminded us that not all artifacts represent one side of a dynamic of colonial domination or resistance; children at the school may have engaged with some mass-produced items just because they enjoyed them (see also Panich and Schneider, this volume). Other items included a small number of flaked lithic and glass materials. We did not determine whether the lithics could have been flaked by the students; this uncertainty helps unsettle the problematic distinction between precontact and postcontact periods.

Like many Indian schools of this era, Stewart Indian School was designed to teach children skilled trades. This was the federal government's effort to train their minds as well as their bodies and to assimilate them as productive members of the American workforce. The federal government recognized the implications of removing children from their homelands in a state-sponsored attempt to address the so-called Indian problem (see Ruuska 2019 for more on the federal government's strategies for Indian education in Nevada). Such policies had widespread repercussions that created disrupted connections between the landscape and cultural and spiritual knowledge attached to specific places that were accessed through visitation and oral traditions. A number of scholars have described the inseparability of the natural and cultural worlds in Indigenous epistemologies and the disruptions resulting from colonialism, including Keith Basso's *Wisdom Sits in Places* (1996) and Julie Cruikshank's *Do Glaciers Listen?* (2005). It is clear that when Indigenous children were taken from their families and their homelands, their access to cultural memories and future guidance was restricted.

The removal of American Indians from their ancestral homelands occurred both at a large-scale regional community level (as in the Our Ancestors' Walk of Sorrow Project) and at the individual level (as in children who were taken to Stewart Indian School). These events have resulted in complex intergenerational trauma. This has parallel implications for the taken-for-granted practice of removing artifacts from sites during archaeological projects.

Implications of Removing Artifacts

Dissonances between federal and tribal values are the subject of ongoing research. Collaborative work can productively address conflicts among and between spirituality, ethics, and western and Indigenous knowledges. These discussions are critical for building relationships and providing space for historically suppressed voices to tell their truths. Thus, this project was designed not only to learn about a painful aspect of tribal histories at Stewart Indian School but also to interrogate colonialist policies in heritage preservation law and current archaeological practices that perpetuate the oppression of Native peoples today. Archaeological research cannot provide an accurate picture without meaningful involvement of the communities from whom cultural materials emerged.

Among other things, our collaborative project generated important conversations about the implications of removing artifacts from archaeological sites for research. On one hand, federal legislation was written to allow and encourage the scientific removal of artifacts from sites. In contrast, numerous participating tribal members discussed the importance of leaving certain artifacts in place. This became one of the most important themes that emerged from this collaborative project.

We discussed standard archaeological excavation procedures at the beginning of the project and invited participants to critique any of our practices. We developed the research design with input from our research partners and other tribal members who participated in various ways as students, staff, and interested individuals. From the beginning, the Washoe THPO stated that they prefer that certain artifacts, particularly lithics, flaked glass, and any artifacts from the precontact period be left in place. This preference contrasts with standard archaeological procedures and has important implications.

An important aspect of archaeology is the documentation of cultural items in place. Once cultural items are collected for further analysis, holding them in museums in perpetuity has also been advocated for to allow for later archaeological reexamination. To this end, the National Historic Preservation Act of 1966 (amended 1992) states that it is the policy of the federal government to "encourage owners who are undertaking archaeological excavations to . . . allow access to artifacts for research purposes."[1] For public lands, the code of federal regulations narrowly dictates the requirements for cultural items collected as part of an archaeological excavation; they must be permanently curated in a federally approved repository.

Given these legal requirements, agencies and archaeologists have limited latitude for alternative outcomes for the permanent disposition of the cultural items they excavate. Still, laws and regulations are subject to interpretation. Who determines which repositories meet federal standards? Is field examination and reburial of artifacts a viable option? Why were tribal communities not considered as potential keepers of excavated materials? Resource protection is the stated goal for much legislation, yet archaeologists, whose methods destroy the integrity of a site through excavation, have been given authority by the state to control the spoils of that destruction. Meanwhile, the Indigenous people that have affiliations to these same cultural items and landscapes are not given equal consideration. What would our cultural resource management legislation look like if Indigenous communities had been part of legislation development discussions? A lack of diversity in the discussion of cultural resource management laws led to laws that protect western scientific interests and silence tribal interests that don't coincide with the interests of archaeologists. One such example of this quandary is given by the Washoe tribal historic preservation officer:

> If all the artifacts are removed from the landscape, then we have nothing to show that we were ever there. That is why it so important to leave archeological materials, lithics etc; in place. It is our story and we want to maintain that connection to the landscape. Nobody should have the right to erase history by the removal of material evidence. (Darrel Cruz, tribal historic preservation officer, Washoe Tribe of Nevada and California, personal communication, March 31, 2014)

Such considerations are rarely if ever discussed in archaeological discourse. They are an example of an inadequate recognition of cross-cultural considerations that could have been avoided had tribal communities been part of the rule-making process. Current federal policies also uncloak the underlying institutionalized racism that continues to guide how knowledge is produced and whose voices are part of that knowledge production.

It is important to remember the diversity of tribal peoples and the different perspectives that may arise in the management and categorization of artifacts. Current problematic dichotomies of Native and non-Native or prehistoric and historic are two examples. For example, the Washoe THPO made an important distinction between flaked and nonflaked material, but not every Tribe would. Other communities, including many Paiute peoples, emphasize the difference between an object's origin material and the type of modification that was made to it and the metaphysical discussion of whether something that is changed in form continues to have a consistent essence. This applies to archaeological sites, too, since a site's essence is made up of all of its parts. It makes little difference if the parts (e.g., artifacts, soils, water, and such) are moved around on a site as long as they are moved about with care. In many Paiute perspectives, a site still has integrity if the items are moved about on the land. In fact, they have agency to move about on their own or with the help of other beings in their community. These values can be worked into treatment plans for archaeological mitigation (see also Laluk, this volume, for a discussion of Ndee recommendations of avoidance, leaving artifacts in situ, and developing tribally approved treatment plans).

As others in this volume have rightly pointed out, imposing a stark contrast between prehistoric and historic or Native and non-Native artifacts is highly problematic (e.g., Panich and Schneider, this volume; Russel, this volume). Likewise, as Kretzler (this volume) observes, "artifacts" might be better understood as personal belongings. This conceptualization powerfully blurs past and present and acknowledges the continued presence of important ties.

Much work is needed to unsettle and undiscipline archaeology's problematic dichotomies, and it will be important to consider Tribes' variable metaphysical understandings of life, time, power, and land. Each Indigenous community has their own conceptualizations of how to classify things the Ancestors left on the landscape. Archaeologists can honor communities' knowledge and sovereignty by classifying artifacts based on individual communities' own epistemological-ontological frameworks as best we can with the current federal legislation.

Many Native American Tribes have deep relationships with their homelands and hold a deep respect for the power of place that is distinctive for those communities and places. For example, for most Numic-speaking Tribes, the term for such power or energy is *puha*. Anthropologist Alex Carroll and her colleagues (2004, 129) explain that *puha* "pervades all manifestations of the physical world and concentrates in certain people, places, and objects to higher degrees than in others." They explain that object deposition in specific locations serves to reciprocate *puha* by both attempting to "harness" and "lend" power at a particular place (Carroll et al. 2004, 131). Citing work by Jay Miller (1983, 79–80), they further describe *puha* "as a cosmic force that, together with the life force, forms the fabric of the universe; . . . it constantly flows through a web-like structure that connects all things and beings, human or otherwise, that make up the universe." From this exchange, even ordinary places can become imbued with additional *puha* through ceremony and maintaining a relationship to the location (Carroll et al. 2004, 132–3; see also Basso 1996).

Perhaps the most memorable of all the lessons from the Stewart Indian School project for archaeological students was the understanding that in essence, *an archaeological project that disturbs the earth may adhere to federal and state regulations but still risk disrupting the very fabric of the Universe.* An experience from the Stewart Indian School illustrates this potentiality. During opening discussions for the first day of school, as the Indigenous students were preparing themselves, it was suggested that we offer prayer as a group. Having no objections, the tribal Elder in our group led prayer. During this time, he explained the need to prepare oneself for the work we were beginning because disturbing the Earth and seeking out those things left behind by the Ancestors was a form of "breaking through time" (Mark Johnson, personal communication 2013).

Mark's prayer asked for protection and understanding as we proceeded with the effort and considered the tragedies of its dark past and asked for protection in the present to make way for a stronger future. When we returned the following day, we found a large dead owl near the place where we had convened the morning before. In some people's cultural understanding, owls are messengers that warn of impending illness or death. We never knew what caused the owl to die in that location, but the following day after Mark was absent from fieldwork, we learned that he was hospitalized and recovering from a stroke. We cannot prove that the events were interconnected, but it was startling for all participants and caused us each to reevaluate our behavior and connectedness to one another as we worked. After discussion among the tribal members on the project, we sent medicine and prayers to Mark and adhered to the protocols those tribal members used to protect themselves. We also provided offerings to the spirits of the children who had lived and died and remain in that place.

Removal, Entanglement, and Mitigating Trauma

Indigenous sciences and spiritualties may be inextricable from larger understandings of the environment and the cosmos. Mark Johnson's description of archaeological excavation as "breaking through time" is reminiscent of *puha*, the force that connects everything and everyone in the Universe. These concepts do not need validation from other fields; Indigenous knowledges stand on their own right. However, it is worth considering what practitioners in other fields can learn from similar conceptualizations of interconnected time and space. Other disciplines have also observed the entanglements of people, places, objects, and experiences that are co-present beyond time and place.

For example, linguist and literary theorist Mikhail Bakhtin describes the connection between space and time as a chronotope ("literally, time space"), where time is a fourth dimension of space. In literary applications, time, "as it were, thickens, takes on flesh, becomes, artistically visible; likewise, space becomes charged and responsive to the movements of time, plot and history" (Bakhtin 1981, 84). Bakhtin likens this phenomenon to Einstein's theory of relativity "almost as a metaphor (almost, but not entirely)" (84).

Indeed, the assertion that sensitive objects have powerful relationships across time and space is, at least on the surface, similar to recent research in quantum mechanics. Physicists have successfully entangled particles whose relationships to each other cross time-space continuums. This phenomenon, which Einstein originally described as "spooky action at a distance," is known as a quantum nonlocality (Crull 2018). Quantum entanglement at this stage of research may be best understood as an analogy rather than as an actual mechanism for the connective power many Indigenous communities describe (although, like Bakhtin, we may hedge our bets here). Research to date has only produced very short relationships under highly controlled circumstances before the "death" of the quantum entanglement, and researchers continue to seek longer-lasting coherence (e.g., Almeida et al. 2007; Schlosshauer 2010). Currently, there are no known examples anywhere near the time scale of the archaeological record.

However, the fact that quantum entanglement *happens at all* suggests that conversations are warranted between physicists, archaeologists, and Indigenous knowledge holders. Researchers in archaeology and Indigenous studies are beginning to investigate the implications of alternative temporalities for heritage research. For example, Shannon Lee Dawdy (2010, 762) encourages archaeologists to explore "new possibilities that come from willfully collapsing archaeological and ethnographic time." This bears similarities to work by geographer Vanessa Watts (Mohawk and Anishinaabe), who asserts the agency of nonhumans in the world and the importance of phenomenologically experiencing Indigenous "place-thought" as a way to access the "precolonial mind" (Watts 2013). Recognition of such ontological and epistemological differences offers potential practical applications for future productive considerations of place-time in tribal consultation (e.g., Richland 2018).

Much has been said here about the pain of *removal*, so we must briefly address the possibility that *returning* can heal. Healing also occurs when sites, situations, and ecosystems are brought back to a greater level of completeness. From the cultural perspective of the Burns Paiute, a disruption occurs when one or more components or beings in a community are unceremoniously removed. This upsets the previous homeostasis among the mingled *puha* of beings present in a location. The removed item(s) and the associated landscape and ecosystem are disrupted when the dynamic is modified by addition or removal. This has become most evident with the removal and loss of presence of Indigenous peoples in these landscape interactions. Our returned presence is needed on the landscape for the landscape to heal. Our presence is needed in and on our cultural landscapes to return the ecosystem to a place of homeostasis.

When Indigenous peoples return to their ancestral homelands, when alumni of the boarding schools visit the Stewart Indian School, when archaeologists return (or repatriate) artifacts and human remains, there are opportunities for healing, but not without a great deal of pain along the way. Many of our collaborative research meetings paused for weeping, as collaborators connected past and present events of intergenerational traumas. However, like other researchers who are exploring the potential for healing that can come from revisiting places and repatriating remains (e.g., Colwell 2019; Schaepe et al. 2017), it is our hope that the pain of return is outweighed by strengthened connections and emancipated truths.

In conclusion, we are grateful that Mark Johnson and other participants at the Stewart Indian School have contributed essays for a multivocal edited volume on Stewart Indian School (Cowie et al. 2019). We also anticipate similar multi-authored publications for the Our Ancestors' Walk of Sorrow Project. It is clear that the acts of removing communities from their traditional homelands, removing children from their communities, removing artifacts from sites, and removing voice from the people who experience these actions have similar traumatic implications. These four acts of removal are driven by similar processes of governmentality and biopolitics and are embedded historical-colonial and modern-colonial power imbalances. Thus far, most archaeologists and the agencies for whom they work are privileging legislative power that regulates archaeological work. In doing so, they ignore other kinds of power that are critical not only to tribal sovereignty but perhaps also to connectedness across space and time.

Both case studies demonstrate that governmentality, biopolitics, legislative processes, and knowledge production act similarly on landscapes, human bodies, and artifacts. In collaborative archaeology, living community members with blood and other ties to these landscapes are contributing tribal knowledge and oral history as research partners. Through such partnerships, our work groups have developed a more complete picture of our shared histories. Holistic approaches to understanding the past also may help mitigate the intergenerational trauma and historical grief that accompanies many such landscapes of conflict.

Acknowledgments

Thanks to the Washoe Tribal Historic Preservation Office, Nevada Indian Commission, Burns Paiute Tribe's Culture & Heritage Department, and numerous students and tribal communities who participated in these projects. The research reported here was funded under awards (#W911NF1210205 and #W911NF1610150) from the U.S. Army Research Office/Army Research Laboratory. The views expressed are those of the authors and should not be attributed to the Army Research Office/Army Research Laboratory. Our analysis has benefited greatly from conversations with Jenanne Ferguson, Paul White, Timur Tscherbul, Ted Howard, and Lonnie Teeman. Thanks also to Christina McSherry for producing the map in this chapter and for her collaborative work on the Malheur Indian Agency project. Previous versions of this chapter were presented at meetings of the Society for Historical Archaeology, the American Anthropological Association, and the Japanese-American-German Frontiers of Science Symposium sponsored by the National Academy of Sciences. We are grateful to Tsim Schneider and Lee Panich for welcoming us to this inspiring volume. Their comments and those of the peer reviewers provided welcome suggestions for improvement and expansion of this chapter. Errors or misinterpretations are the sole responsibility of the authors.

Note

1. "National Historic Preservation Act of 1966 as Amended through 1992," Public Law 102-575, accessed April 20, 2020, https://www.nps.gov/history/local-law/nhpa1966.htm.

References Cited

Almeida, M. P., F. de Melo, M. Hor-Meyll, A. Salles, S. P. Walborn, P. H. Souto Ribeiro, and L. Davidovich. 2007. Environment-Induced Sudden Death of Entanglement. *Science* 316(8824): 579–582.

Atalay, Sonya. 2006. Indigenous Archaeology as Decolonizing Practice. *American Indian Quarterly* 30(3 & 4): 280–310.

———. 2010. Indigenous Archaeology as Decolonizing Practice. In *Indigenous Archaeologies: A Reader on Decolonization*, edited by Margaret M. Bruchac, Siobhan M Hart, and Hans Martin Wobst, 79–85. Walnut Creek, CA: Left Coast Press.

Bakhtin, M. M. 1981. *The Dialogic Imagination: Four Essays by M. M. Bakhtin*. Edited by Michael Holquist. Translated by Caryl Emerson and Michael Holquist. Austin: University of Texas Press.

Basso, Keith. 1996. *Wisdom Sits in Places: Landscape and Language among the Western Apache*. Albuquerque: University of New Mexico Press.

Burns Paiute Tribe. 2001. Wadatika Ma Ne Pu Neen. Manuscript on file at the Burns Paiute Tribe's Culture & Heritage Department, Burns, Oregon.

Carroll, Alex K., M. Nieves Zedeño, and Richard W. Stoffle. 2004. Landscapes of the Ghost Dance: A Cartography of Numic Ritual. *Journal of Archaeological Method and Theory* 11(2): 127–156.

Colwell, Chip. 2019. Can Repatriation Heal the Wounds of History? *The Public Historian* 41(1): 90–110.

Colwell-Chanthaphonh, Chip, T. J. Ferguson, Dorothy Lippert, Randall McGuire, George P. Nicholas, Joe E. Watkins, and Larry J. Zimmerman. 2010. The Premise and Promise of Indigenous Archaeology. *American Antiquity* 75(2): 228–238.

Cowie, Sarah E., Diane L. Teeman, and Christopher C. LeBlanc, eds. 2019. *Collaborative Archaeology at the Stewart Indian School*. Reno: University of Nevada Press.

Cruikshank, Julie. 2005. *Do Glaciers Listen? Local Knowledge, Colonial Encounters, and Social Imagination*. Vancouver: University of British Columbia Press.

Crull, Elise. 2018. You Thought Quantum Mechanics Was Weird: Check Out Entangled Time. *Aeon*. Last modified February 2, 2018. Accessed October 25, 2020. https://aeon.co/ideas/you-thought-quantum-mechanics-was-weird-check-out-entangled-time.

Dawdy, Shannon Lee. 2010. Clockpunk Anthropology and the Ruins of Modernity. *Current Anthropology* 51(6): 761–793.

Dean, Patricia A., and Clayton F. Marler. 2001. Shoshone Spirituality and Enhancing Archaeological Interpretation in Southeast Idaho. *SAA Archaeological Record* (March): 34–36.

Deloria, Vine, Jr. 1992. Indians, Archaeologists, and the Future. *American Antiquity* 57(4): 595–598.

Foucault, Michel. 1991. Governmentality. In *The Foucault Effect: Studies in Governmentality*, 87–104. edited by Graham Burchell, Colin Gordon, and Peter Miller. Chicago: University of Chicago Press.

———. 1998. *The History of Sexuality: The Will to Knowledge*. London: Penguin.

———. 2007. *Security, Territory, Population: Lectures at the College de France, 1977–1978*. Edited by Michel Senellart. New York: Palgrave Macmillan.

Fowles, Severin. 2010. The Southwest School of Landscape Archaeology. *Annual Review of Anthropology* 39: 453–468.

Harris, Heather. 2010. Indigenous Worldviews and Ways of Knowing as Theoretical and Methodological Foundations behind Archaeological Theory and Method. In *Indigenous Archaeologies: A Reader on Decolonization*, edited by Margaret M. Bruchac, Siobhan M Hart, and Hans Martin Wobst, 63–68. Walnut Creek, CA: Left Coast Press.

Hopkins, Sarah Winnemucca. (1883) 1994. *Life among the Paiutes: Their Wrongs and Claims,* Reno: University of Nevada Press.

Howard, Oliver Otis. 1907. *My Life and Experiences among our Hostile Indians: A Record of Personal Observations, Adventures, and Campaigns among the Indians of the Great West, with Some Account of Their Life, Habits, Traits, Religion, Ceremonies, Dress, Savage Instincts, and Customs in Peace and War.* Hartford, CT: Worthington & Company.

Miller, Jay. 1983. Basin Religion and Theology: A Comparative Study of Power (*Puha*). *Journal of California and Great Basin Anthropology* 5: 66–86.

Montgomery, Lindsay M., and Chip Colwell. 2019. *Objects of Survivance: A Material History of the American Indian School Experience.* Denver: Denver Museum of Nature & Science and Denver University.

Nicholas, George P. 2008. Native People and Archaeology. In *Encyclopedia of Archaeology,* Vol. 3, edited by Deborah Pearsall, 1660–1669. New York: Academic Press.

Oregon History Project. 2008. Report by W. V. Rinehart, 1879. Accessed December 22, 2008. https://www.oregonhistoryproject.org/articles/historical-records/report-by-wv-rinehart-1879/#.YKvnMo2Slyw.

Richland, Justin B. 2018. Jurisdictions of Significance: Narrating Time-Space in a Hopi-US Tribal Consultation. *American Ethnologist* 45(2): 268–280.

Ruuska, Alex K. 2019. Indian Education in Nevada (1890–2015): A Legacy of Change. In *Collaborative Archaeology at Stewart Indian School,* edited by Sarah E. Cowie, Diane L. Teeman, and Christopher C. LeBlanc, 68–106. Reno: University of Nevada Press.

Schaepe, David M., Bill Angelbeck, David Snook, and John R. Welch. 2017. Archaeology as Therapy: Connecting Belongings, Knowledge, Time, Place, and Well-Being (with Comments and Reply). *Current Anthropology* 58(4): 502–533.

Schlosshauer, Maximilian. 2010. *Decoherence and the Quantum-to-Classical Transition.* Berlin: Springer.

Silliman, Stephen W. 2005. Culture Contact or Colonialism? Challenges in the Archaeology of Native North America. *American Antiquity* 70(1): 55–74.

Smith, Linda Tuhiwai. 1999. *Decolonizing Methodologies: Research and Indigenous Peoples.* London: Zed Books.

Steward, Julian. 1943. Culture Element Distributions: XII Nevada Shoshoni. *Anthropological Records* 8(3): 263–292.

Stowell, Susan. 2008. *The Wada-Tika of the Former Malheur Reservation.* PhD diss., University of California, Davis.

Surface-Evans, Sarah L., and Sarah J. Jones. 2020. Discourses of the Haunted: An Intersubjective Approach to Archaeology at the Mount Pleasant Indian Industrial Boarding School. *Archeological Papers of the American Anthropological Association* 31(1): 110–121.

Thomas, David Hurst. 2000. *Skull Wars.* New York: Basic Books.

Thompson-Hardin, Bonnie. 2019. History and Daily Life at the Stewart Campus. In *Collaborative Archaeology at Stewart Indian School,* edited by Sarah E. Cowie, Diane L. Teeman, and Christopher C. LeBlanc, 107–128. Reno: University of Nevada Press.

Warrick, Gary. 2017. Control of Indigenous Archaeological Heritage in Ontario, Canada. *Archaeologies* 13(1): 88–109.

Watkins, Joe E. 2000. *Indigenous Archaeology: American Indian Values and Scientific Practice.* Walnut Creek, CA: AltaMira Press.

Watts, Vanessa. 2013. Indigenous Place-Thought & Agency amongst Humans and Non-Humans (First Woman and Sky Woman Go on a European World Tour!). *Decolonization: Indigeneity, Education & Society* 2(1): 20–34.

Wilcox, Michael. 2010. Saving Indigenous Peoples from Ourselves: Separate but Equal Archaeology Is Not Scientific Archaeology. *American Antiquity* 75(2): 221–227.

Wobst, H. Martin. 2010. Power to the (Indigenous) Past and Present! Or: The Theory and Method behind Archaeological Theory and Method. In *Indigenous Archaeologies: A Reader on Decolonization,* edited by Margaret M. Bruchac, Siobhan M Hart, and Hans Martin Wobst, 76–78. Walnut Creek, CA: Left Coast Press.

14

Conclusion

Perspectives on Presence from a Sovereign (and Very Much Present) Native American Community

TSIM D. SCHNEIDER, PETER A. NELSON,
AND NICK TIPON

> darkness is my homeland
> my origin, my grave—
> all the history I need.

—Deborah A. Miranda (Ohlone Costanoan Esselen Nation)

Over the past three decades, archaeological studies of colonialism have redefined the concepts, spatial and temporal parameters, and field and laboratory methods deployed to account for transformations and continuities in Indigenous societies around the world. We live and work in California, where Indigenous peoples confronted and continue to grapple with the consequences of a unique and highly destructive barrage of Spanish, Russian, Mexican, and American colonial programs. To understand this colonial legacy, archaeological advances there include expanded long-term views of resilient Indigenous societies making do with the sustained impacts of colonial structures (Lightfoot 1995; Lightfoot and Gonzalez 2018); recentering efforts that foreground Indigenous refusals, homeland, and place (Nelson 2020; Schneider 2010); and a sharpened focus on the agency, ethnogenesis, persistence, and survivance of Indigenous peoples and identities (Acebo and Martinez 2018; Brown et al. 2018; Panich 2020; Silliman 2004; Voss 2008). As the contributors to this edited volume amply demonstrate, the "presence" concept may be situated within this longer thread of intellectual inquiry and archaeological thought. Case studies in *Archaeologies of Indigenous Presence* also call into question taken-for-granted recording efforts, chronological models, and terminology that can effectively reinstate narratives of cultural loss among North America's Indigenous peoples—a pattern we explore more below as part of a much-needed process of undisciplining archaeology.

This conclusion serves a second purpose. In addition to spotlighting the shared themes that connect across chapters and penetrate the seemingly isolated realms of Tribal historic preservation, cultural resource management, and academic research and teaching, we introduce another analytic. "Presence" is also an inviolable frame of mind interlaced with the numerous and varied histories and identities of Indigenous peoples of the North American continent, some of whom are featured (as authors and/or the focus of research) in this edited volume. In this sense, the presence theme offers an intellectual frame for studying and interpreting the places and materials associated with postcontact Indigenous communities. It is also woven into the daily lives, conversations, and work of modern Tribal communities. Just as a shopworn term like "resistance" receives new meaning and power when reinterpreted through resilient traditions of mobility, refuge experiences, and Indigenous peoples' rebukes of imposed colonial spatial and social norms (Schneider 2015), presence takes on a similar sense of urgency and relevance when examined from the perspective of living and dynamic Indigenous communities, Tribal governments, and heritage protectors. The presencing efforts captured in this book thus bring abstract archaeological concepts in line with the ongoing efforts of Native American communities who continue to defy legacies of colonialism in the day-to-day and counteract absenting narratives scholars and the public rehash in the present. The sovereign and federally recognized Tribe of Coast Miwok and Southern Pomo people, also known as the Federated Indians of Graton Rancheria (FIGR), our community, is a case in point.

Connecting Themes and Different Directions

Sonya Atalay's (2006) call for a decolonized archaeology jump-started the important work of recentering Indigenous peoples and epistemologies in project planning, implementation, interpretation, publication, teaching, and relationship-building in American archaeology. In addition to injecting archaeology with an improved dose of ethics, Atalay and others pursuing decolonial, community-based, and Indigenous archaeological research ushered in much-needed refinements to the practice of archaeology including, fundamentally, foregrounding the perspectives of Indigenous peoples and their experiences and knowledge in the study of colonialism. This is a work in progress, and recent discussions of decolonial archaeology are examining the possibilities of even broader structural changes within institutional merit review systems and the legal frameworks that guide academic and cultural resource management archaeology.

For more equitable and relevant forms of archaeological practice, Schneider and Hayes (2020) posit that decentering and decolonization might further require archaeologists to set aside core concepts as part of a process of "undisciplining," or embracing the theoretical toolkits of other disciplines (e.g., settler colonial studies or critical Indigenous studies) and taking seriously such tenets of knowledge production as reciprocity, relationality, responsibility, and redistribution (Harris and Wasilewski 2004). An "undisciplined" archaeology, an umbrella concept for our discussion, pairs well with the self-critical style presented throughout this edited volume. Case studies show that careful scrutiny and modification of even the most banal practices in archaeology—recording, dating, and applying labels to pieces of the past— hold the potential to push archaeology beyond the conventional yardsticks for advancing the field (e.g., a new model, a refined chronology, an improved typology, a winning grant application or a successful bid, a published article or report, etc.). The presence theme moves this conversation about an undisciplined archaeology into different and perhaps deeper and choppier—but not uncharted—waters. It receives added heft and momentum when it is oriented around other critical conversations about the role of listening, empathy and the heart, and effective archaeologies.

In what might be the most surprisingly simple and chillingly important message from archaeologists in recent years, Schmidt and Kehoe (2019) discuss the crucial role of careful listening in archaeology and the role of patience that emerges from epistemic humility. Epistemic humility refers to an awareness of the limits of one's own knowledge and the ability to acquire knowledge; it also can mean acting in accordance with one's recognized epistemic limitations (Satta 2018). For archaeologists, this means acknowledging and "subjugating" the limitations of western science and critically reflecting on the "questions that we routinely ask" (Schmidt and Kehoe 2019, 14). As Beaudoin (this volume) demonstrates, for example, in the absence of evidence for Indigenous presence, knowledge shared by a Native participant in an archaeological project at the Livingston (Caradoc) Academy in Ontario, Canada, revealed a less obvious social history of Indigenous presence at this place. Buildings, nineteenth-century railroad grades (Russell, this volume), twentieth-century tourist resorts (Scheiber, this volume), and even small sites that have previously been regarded as marginal can lead to new interpretations about Indigenous peoples' assertions of authority that may have been missed in widely read local histories written by European colonizers (Jordan, this volume). In still another example, Walder (this volume) creatively observes that glass beads "need not represent discontinuity" or the disappearance of Native people from postcontact landscapes, but can instead reflect the opposite: unexpected and intact social connections between active and diverse Native groups.

Listening to the pleas of "we are still here" and more can help further dismantle a rigid archaeological sense of space and time. "We fear we will be subject to what archaeologists *think* they know," Dickson and Steinmetz (this volume, emphasis added) write. They continue: being open to the possibility that "'our' history is 'their' history too," can help Tribes and archaeologists craft research designs, narratives, and compliance documents that transcend reservation boundaries, areas of potential effect, and even the arbitrary prehistoric/historic divide. For those who might still scoff at such a seemingly elementary reminder (listen!), to do the opposite—to barrel along in pursuit of objective truths irrespective of the voices that might protest or even augment archaeological work—undermines any hope for an ethical and decolonized field. As Laluk (this volume) argues, that mentality also risks ignoring living communities who still possess relevant knowledge about even the most imperceptible messages from the past.

Acknowledging Indigenous presence requires adjustments to the vocabulary and tools of archaeology. It also demands empathy and care. "As producers of public knowledge about Indian histories and cultures," Janet Spector (1993, 128) once wrote optimistically, "archaeologists and historians could play a positive role in breaking through . . . barriers to empathy." Commenting specifically on such "cultural collisions" as the mistreatment of Native cemeteries, seizures of land, "silences and offenses" in classrooms and in the media, and cultural appropriation, these forms of settler violence persist in the present. Archaeologists have not found a route under, over, or around the formidable barriers Spector identified. Many are, however, succeeding in broadening the scope and space of collaborative and decolonial archaeological research to include "heart-centered practice" that involves love, healing, and reconciliation (Lyons and Supernant 2020, 5), as chapters in this book also demonstrate. For Cowie and Teeman (this volume), collaborative study of the Walk of Sorrow and the Stewart Indian School provide opportunities to retell histories of erasure, assimilation, and dispossession and to create, first and foremost, healing spaces for "suppressed voices to tell their truths." As other chapters also detail, rich and unbroken bonds between heart and homeland underwrite presence. For Crow people, "place drives the narrative," not time, as Scheiber (this volume) observes. And what clearer statements of place, heart, and healing can be made than the Confederated Tribes of Grand Ronde selection of their own powwow grounds for archaeological study (Kretzler, this volume), the Malheur Reservation's approval of research on a trail of forced removal and painful history (Cowie and Teeman, this volume), the harnessing of oral histories to reappraise "jumbles of historic objects" and seemingly inhospitable wetland as vital sources of Seminole identity and pride (Scheidecker et al., this volume), enduring Ndee relationships to hard-to-detect sites (Laluk, this volume), the Washoe Tribe of Nevada's collaboration at Stewart Indian School (Cowie and Teeman, this volume), and the recording of Civilian Conservation Corp-Indian Division sites by the Confederated Tribes of the Umatilla Indian Reservation (Dickson and Steinmetz, this volume) as meaningful loci of Indigenous history and resilience?

A third area of convergence evident in this volume pertains to the development of relevant research designs. Overlapping with archaeologies that listen, care, and heal, effective archaeologies are those in which scholars inspect the processes of knowledge production that "enlarge or constrain understanding, with implications for how we imagine future possibilities and our discipline's value beyond funding-agency 'impacts'" (Stahl 2020, 38). In this vein, we're seeing greater attentiveness to community needs and the power of "doing" archaeology together (Hodgetts and Kelvin 2020, 102; see also Backhouse et al. 2017; Bollwerk et al. 2015; Cowie et al. 2019; Martindale and Lyons 2014; Reetz and Quackenbush 2016). Archaeologists are designing projects grounded in pragmatism and bearing witness (Hauser et al. 2018; Mrozowski 2012), embracing novel publishing platforms for communicating information to community partners and to the broader public (Atalay et al. 2016–2017; Hull and Douglas 2020), and "braiding" Indigenous storywork into archaeological research designs to mobilize knowledge and enhance science literacy (Atalay 2020; see also Scheidecker et al., this volume). As case studies in this volume further illustrate, effective archaeologies also act with sensitivity to terms and concepts, choice of methods, and decisions about interpretation. We wonder how Indigenous histories across North America might be amplified if archaeologists made the effort, as Jordan (this volume) shows, to locate and study "less flashy" and "hard to spot" materials and "small" sites? Following Hull (this volume), what underutilized archives and creative interrogations can help counter the "pernicious effects" that conceal postcontact Native American presence in other places and regions? How can archaeologists help dismantle inaccurate settler narratives that appropriate ("rebrand") Indigenous places and isolate Indigenous histories, as Trabert (this volume) examines in Kansas and Oklahoma? Turning to an even more prosaic pattern, what if we stopped calling stuff "trash," as Russell (this volume) explores through the example of modified glass objects, and instead paused to rethink the intellectual baggage that enables kneejerk assumptions about the archaeological record (see also Jordan, this volume)? Better still, by incorporating culturally relevant concepts such as *puha* (Cowie and Teeman, this volume), *gózhó* (Laluk, this volume), and "belongings" (Kretzler, this volume), how might archaeologists continue cultivating greater appreciation for robust, enduring, and always-present Indigenous epistemologies? Taking up the challenge of doing something differently, chapters in this volume present promising examples of an ethical, enriched, and decolonial archaeology that centers Indigenous presence within the ambit of archaeological research and heritage preservation.

Further Perspective on Presence

"We are still here" is a constant and widely shared refrain spoken by First Nations and Indigenous peoples throughout North America to remind settler peoples and governments about Indigenous histories, priorities, and presence (see also Dickson and Steinmetz, this volume). Presence is something that factors deeply in the daily lives and histories of our community of Graton Rancheria. Current FIGR chair Greg Sarris reflected on the presence theme many years ago in a pamphlet accompanying a 1993 exhibit titled "We Are Still Here" produced in cooperation with the Bolinas Museum (Smith 1993). He wrote for that pamphlet before FIGR was restored as a recognized Tribe on December 27, 2000. Offering context for family photographs on display in the museum, the photographs and exhibit guide helped situate the depredations of Spanish, Mexican, Russian, and American colonial invasions within the longer arc of Coast Miwok and Southern Pomo presence and celebration:

> We are still curing ourselves. We are still keeping ourselves healthy and happy. We are giving ourselves a new beginning, new life. We are doing nothing short of the miraculous. We are alive. (Sarris 1993, 3)

As archaeologists and citizens of FIGR who also recognize that we speak from our individual perspectives and do not speak on behalf of or for our entire community we conclude this volume by reflecting on the theme of Indigenous presence in American archaeology. Drawing inspiration from our community's history and future, we comment on the presence theme as it relates directly to the daily work of Tribal historic preservation, government-to-government consultations, research, and teaching.

For readers unfamiliar with the advent and growth of Indigenous archaeology, it might at first appear strange to see the book's lead author now turn around and kick the tires of the edited volume he helped create. This is one example of the fine line that archaeologists who are Indigenous regularly walk in their research and writing. It is a precarious passageway: on the one hand, doing work that is relevant and beneficial to our communities and, on the other hand, participating in and striving to advance a discipline and system of knowledge with a long history of devaluing or excluding Indigenous peoples and knowledge. This tension can also be quite productive (e.g., Nicholas 2018) and can encourage the kind of critical self-reflection that is the lifeblood of disciplinary improvement theoretically and methodologically.

For example, one area of persistent concern reflected in several chapters (e.g., Kretzler, this volume; Laluk, this volume; Trabert, this volume) and discussed elsewhere (e.g., Martinez 2012, 358–360) is the discipline's tendency to talk to itself, as reflected in the prescriptive roles and unquestioned—and sometimes demeaning—terminology taken as a given in the daily grind of archaeology (see also Panich and Schneider 2019). Put simply: "words matter" (Dickson and Steinmetz, this volume). The ingrained positivist influence in American archaeology is reflected by the uncritical use of technical jargon and other terminology that can form barriers to effective communication between Tribes and non-Native archaeologists. It may also be seen in the assumed authoritative role of the archaeologist as an objective observer whose task is to "reveal the past, to discover or, at least approximate the truth. Within that viewpoint, power is unproblematic, irrelevant to the construction of the narrative" (Trouillot 1995, 5).

Recognizing that most Indigenous peoples would disagree that their cultures and histories were ever buried (and required discovery by an archaeologist) and acknowledging fraught power relationships—specifically, archaeology's legacy of excavating Indigenous sites, materials, and bodies—a word like "unearth" seems more appropriate for discussing the history of silencing Native voices in archaeology. "Unearth" takes on new meaning when Indigenous peoples are primary participants in the reveal and not the object of discovery. Recentering draws out and makes visible neglected or unsaid examples of Indigenous presence *in the practice of archaeology*. And just as archaeologists are not the only ones with the power to unmask and interpret "hidden" histories, Indigenous people also deploy silences of their own (e.g., Basso 1970). Thus, "presence" is a concept that is symbolic of the fine line that Indigenous people, including archaeologists who are Indigenous, walk every day. We confront and combat "edgeless" histories of colonial violence that creep into and haunt our communities in the present (King 2019), and we work to unmoor conventional discourse and seek out new terrain for listening, learning, and teaching anew how our people fought and continue to fight for their existence.

"We are still here . . . and we've been here all along!"

Refracting the core themes of unknowing, conceptual and practical advances, and presence (see Panich and Schneider, this volume) through the workings of the current and multifaceted Tribe of Graton Rancheria, we present three additional variations of the presence theme. First, Coast Miwok and Southern Pomo people have a long history of asserting their presence and advocating their values within and beyond the boundaries of conventional archaeological practice. In fact, as Bruchac (2018, 188) shows, a long line of Native American informants and Indigenous anthropologists engaged in archaeological and ethnographic research frequently "called the steps of the dance." The "We are still here" statement could therefore be amended to read: "We are still here . . . and we've been here all along!" The presence of Tribal cultural resource management within FIGR predates the modern consolidation of Coast Miwok and Southern Pomo peoples of Marshall, Bodega, Tomales, and Sebastopol onto a 15.45-acre reservation in 1920. Our families have been caring for ancestors and lands since time immemorial in the broadest sense of cultural resource management. This care for ancestors is carried forward to our modern institutions of cultural resource management, the Sacred Sites Protection Committee and the Tribal Heritage Preservation Office (THPO), even though colonialism and the presence of settlers in our Tribal lands pose many new challenges for the preservation and protection of our ancestors and cultural heritage.

Southern Pomo and Coast Miwok people follow protocols to protect the deceased and the living alike. The most important of these protocols is avoidance, or leaving something in situ, a protocol that is written into Tribal treatment plans today (see also Laluk, this volume). This protocol mandates that impacts to ancestors and cultural resources should be avoided as much as possible, although these impacts accelerated dramatically with the urbanization and development of the San Francisco Bay Area beginning in the late nineteenth century. In the past, a deceased relative and all of their possessions would be buried, burned, or retired in some way and their names would not have been spoken after that. This protocol was practiced by Coast Miwok people living at the community of 'Echcha Tamal (Echa-Tamal) in the late 1800s. It later hindered Coast Miwok people's claim in a dispute about the ownership of the lands (the 86,000-acre Rancho Nicasio) upon which Native people were still living. In one of the court cases that followed, Coast Miwok representatives had to explain why they could not produce the title to the massive land grant the Mexican government awarded them in the 1830s. The daughter of the recently deceased headman of 'Echcha Tamal had burned all of his possessions, including the title to Rancho Nicasio because it held his signature (Dietz 1976).

Our elders recall having to watch in the early 1900s as University of California researchers ignored living Coast Miwok people—whom anthropologists were busily writing off as culturally "extinct"—and took boats across Tamal Liwa (Tomales Bay) to excavate and exhume ancestors from sites in the area known as Kuluppi Tamal (Point Reyes peninsula, now part of Point Reyes National Seashore). A little farther north, some of our families near Kanwin Tamal (Bodega Bay) would keep watch over sites at night and shoot their guns at lanterns that strayed too close to them. Other elders also vividly recall traveling under cover of darkness to archaeological excavations to collect the exposed and disinterred remains of loved ones for private reburial elsewhere. Many local museums throughout Marin and Sonoma Counties, larger regional repositories (e.g., the Phoebe A. Hearst Museum of Anthropology at the University of California, Berkeley), national archives such as the Smithsonian Institution in Washington, DC, and other museum collections around the world (e.g., the British Museum in London and the Kunstkamera in St. Petersburg) possess plundered Coast Miwok and Southern Pomo belongings from an era of no or few laws or protections that would have given Native American people the legal right to protect their ancestors and cultural resources.

Since these early times, the practice of our cultural resource management has continually evolved and adapted to new laws, protections, and situations. Similar to most other Tribes, we have a highly developed genealogy of our families because the US government required proof of relationship to our base roll as a prerequisite for enrollment as a citizen of our Tribe. We have also adapted and responded to the demand for our presence and have borne witness to development and impacts to our sites through archaeology by providing Tribal monitoring services for these projects despite decades of institutional racism and other unseen barriers to a respectful and equal working relationship with governments and institutions. Although the terms of our involvement and authority over procedures within these projects have changed through the years, our core values of avoidance, minimal impact, and protection of our ancestors and cultural heritage remain. The impacts of archaeology are enormous, yet at times, archaeology has also proved useful in environmental restoration projects and the revitalization of traditional cultural and ecological knowledge about specific areas within our Tribal territory (Nelson 2017).

"We are still here . . . and we're dynamic!"

Second, our connection to the land, bodies of water, cultural places, and natural resources should not be misinterpreted as a timeless, unbending relationship. Our presence is active and lived. In this sense, "We are still here" could be altered to read: "We are still here . . . and we're dynamic!" For an example of this dynamism, we need look no further than the dissertation projects completed by Nelson (2017) and Schneider (2010). As FIGR citizens, Nelson and Schneider share common ground. They were born and raised outside their Tribal community, and they learned about their traditional knowledge, epistemologies, ontologies, and protocols in order to perform the work they both proposed. In fact, many FIGR citizens have had similar experiences, and we continue to have similar experiences of struggling to regain traditional knowledge because of a long legacy of settler colonialism. In addition to the impacts of colonial missions, ranchos, and assorted mercantile enterprises attributed to Spanish, Mexican, Russian, and American colonialism and imperialism, World War II fractured our community. Many men went to war and their family members who stayed behind moved away from the consolidated communities of Coast Miwok and Southern Pomo peoples at Tomales Bay, Bodega Bay, and the original Graton Rancheria to urban settings such as Santa Rosa, Vallejo, and Richmond, where they sought work in wartime industries. After World War II, the Graton Rancheria was wrongfully stripped of its federal recognition through the California Rancheria Termination Act of 1958. It did not regain federal status until the year 2000. For these reasons, the last three decades since the 1993 "We Are Still Here" exhibit at the Bolinas Museum have been a time of accelerated restoration and cultural revitalization.

Nelson and Schneider's research projects, which began in the first decade of the new millennium, were timely opportunities for FIGR citizens to learn about the thought processes and techniques of archaeology and about its power and limitations and the need for Tribal input and participation. Inspired by the advent of Indigenous archaeology in the late 1990s and early 2000s, Nelson and Schneider pursued collaborative and community-based participatory research that was radically different from the noncollaborative frameworks most of the archaeology of the twentieth century used throughout Graton's traditional lands. Nelson and Schneider engaged the Tribal community in questions about protocols around archaeology and Tribal cultural heritage management and they asked research questions about their ancestors' experiences of working at missions and ranchos while simultaneously maintaining ties to traditional sites. Their work also provided the Tribe with additional information about the precontact environment and how Coast Miwok and Southern Pomo ancestors experienced and managed their homeland and home waters.

Although Nelson and Schneider are citizens of the same Tribe and they both investigate aspects of our community's colonial past, their experiences of engaging in research with their Tribe differ because of changes in the larger social and political landscape. Key among the changes that were happening were a changing Tribal political climate and shifting attitudes toward archaeology that can be traced to less collaborative members of the archaeological profession working in our territory; the establishment of Graton's THPO; increasing Tribal capacity to engage with archaeological research projects; and growing support for archaeological research that supports Tribal environmental, cultural, and historical restoration efforts. Approved and supported by FIGR's Sacred Sites Protection Committee, Schneider (2010) researched ancient shellmounds as colonial-era refuge sites in the San Francisco Bay region and dismantled the widely held assumptions that colonized Indigenous peoples either lost touch with their homelands or disappeared entirely. The archaeological research Peter Nelson (2017) directed at Tolay Lake Regional Park followed a different approval process that involved the Sacred Sites Protection Committee and the new THPO. Work commenced after Nelson restructured the project's research design to align with the Tribe's newly formalized goals for the management and interpretation of Tolay cultural and natural heritage. Ultimately, Nelson was appointed chair of the Sacred Sites Protection Committee, and he became a consulting Tribal archaeologist to aid the THPO in a more official capacity during consultations and site visits, thereby providing important leverage for FIGR to advance their authority in assessing and protecting Coast Miwok and Southern Pomo cultural heritage. These two examples of Indigenous archaeology reflect a present and dynamic community.

"We are still here . . . and we'll still be here!"

Third, while foregrounding presence in archaeological practice and discourse is important, teaching presence is equally critical. Once more, we can adjust "we are still here" to acknowledge Indigenous peoples as future oriented: "We are still here . . . and we'll still be here!" From our classrooms to archaeological field sites and from laboratories to office hours where we mentor and advise students, learning environments are spaces and opportunities where we can reinforce messaging about the persistence and presence of the Indigenous peoples we partner with and learn from. Teaching and education within FIGR have a long tradition that reaches back to time immemorial. It is preserved in the traditional ecological and cultural knowledge of our ancestors and of elders such as Tom Smith and Maria Copa (see Collier and Thalman 1996), and this knowledge will be carried forward by our living relatives and youth who learn from their elders and from the cultural programs our Tribe provides.

In the context of training in western scholarship, our relatives David Peri and Greg Sarris achieved doctorates and had very productive careers in Native American Studies and Native American literature. David Peri, who passed in 2000, was apprenticed by Alfred Kroeber and served as professor of Native American Studies at Sonoma State University, and Greg Sarris began his career as a professor of English at UCLA in 1989. Sarris is now a professor in the Native American Studies department at Sonoma State University while also serving as FIGR's chair. Sarris, Peri, and many other scholars and teachers in our community who work outside academe, such as Kathleen Smith, who has published with Heyday Books (e.g., Smith 2014; and see Smith 1993), laid the groundwork for a younger generation of Coast Miwok and Southern Pomo scholars in our community. In addition to Sarris, there are currently four other tenure-track or tenured professors in our Tribe as well as primary school teachers and a robust internal program of support for Tribal citizens pursuing higher education that will no doubt result in even more educators and scholars hailing from Graton Rancheria. This strong tradition of scholarship and professionalism in academics and education in our community is a reflection of the high esteem California Indians have for education (see Soza War Soldier 2018).

In the field of archaeology, Peter Nelson and Tsim Schneider have had the opportunity to teach and mentor students in the laboratory, in the field, and in courses offered in anthropology and American Indian Studies programs. They have also relished opportunities to build capacity within their community and to share their knowledge with fellow FIGR citizens in talks and hands-on archaeological monitoring workshops in different places throughout Graton homeland. In addition to drawing examples from their Tribe's history, Nelson and Schneider also open their classrooms to—and share our knowledge with—Indigenous communities whose lands their universities occupy (i.e., the Muwekma Ohlone Tribe and Verona Band descendants for University of California, Berkeley and the Amah Mutsun Tribal Band for University of California, Santa Cruz). For Schneider, courses titled "California Archaeology" and "California Pasts" (an upper-division course for students who are not anthropology majors) provide especially rewarding experiences in teaching the methods and theories that drive twenty-first century research in the region and, more important, showcase Indigenous peoples as living communities and not as extinct cultures or hindrances to the conduct of archaeological science. Teaching from experience matters. Teaching from the perspective of a community and culture that anthropologists have tried to erase and archaeologists have maligned but that is still very much present moves us closer to social justice.

We have always been present, even when our ancestors had to go into hiding and even when aspects of our culture went dormant. Even then, as Deborah Miranda's (1999, 98) poetry at the outset of this chapter suggests, darkness, uncertainty, and silence still provided spaces for us to see and practice our culture. We are highlighting our presence now so that it will be visible to those who did not recognize these histories in the past and for those who do not know these histories now because of aggressive attempts by settlers over the past two centuries to make us disappear from view. From the beginning of our revitalization effort in the 1990s to the restoration of our federal recognition, very few non-Tribal people knew we existed. We needed the "We are still here" exhibit to shout our presence to the world and challenge the settler colonial project of removing us from our land, literally and figuratively. As Patrick Wolfe (1999, 2006) argued, settler colonialism is a structure, not an event, so the decolonizing project of reasserting rights to our land and reclaiming our presence and visibility within this land will probably never be finished. But that is our task. It is exciting to see all of the new ways we can assert our presence, moving from visibility to cultivating partnerships with governmental agencies and academic researchers to help restore our traditional lands, preserve our cultural traditions, and create a better world for ourselves and everyone around us.

Conclusion

Archaeologies of Indigenous Presence makes a strong case for improved and enhanced attention to some of the most mundane yet critical aspects of archaeological research on postcontact Indigenous history. Many Native American communities have long viewed archaeology with skepticism, if not disdain. The reasons are varied, but they center on the fact that outsiders who focused on the interpretation of material belongings from a different point of view sought to define our culture. That outsider view largely favors objective truths over Indigenous epistemologies. Great strides have been made in recent years to dismantle many of the obstacles that inhibit epistemic humility and the interpretive flexibility needed to understand long-term Indigenous histories, particularly from the point of view of Indigenous people. Tribes and archaeologists are working together to explore and advance new perspectives on persistent social identities and dynamic communities. They are rethinking where and how Indigenous peoples confronted and survived colonial invasion. Researchers in academia, cultural resource management, and Tribal historic preservation are using a slew of new technologies and statistical methods, and they are creatively combining analytical methods that were previously separated by an arbitrary division between prehistoric and historical archaeology in novel ways. And yet despite these important advances and growing momentum for a decolonized archaeology, the case studies and lessons presented in this volume suggest that a deeper accounting of Indigenous presence is foiled by even the most routine aspects of archaeology, including recording and reporting practices, assigning dates to materials and sites, and applying insensitive terminology. Contributors to *Archaeologies of Indigenous Presence* offer a route forward and inspiration for seeing and foregrounding the presence of Native peoples. We have survived and are not extinct. We are still here and we are eager to tell the stories of how our ancestors adapted to their changing world and how their lives changed in response to it.

References Cited

Acebo, Nathan, and Desireé Reneé Martinez. 2018. Leaving the Master's Tools: Shifting Toward an Analytic of Survival in California Archaeology. *Proceedings of the Society for California Archaeology* 32: 144–152.

Atalay, Sonya. 2006. Indigenous Archaeology as Decolonizing Practice. *American Indian Quarterly* 30(3 & 4): 280–310.

———. 2020. Indigenous Science for a World in Crisis. *Public Archaeology*. Published online July 30. DOI: 10.1080/14655187.2020.1781492.

Atalay, Sonya, Jen Shannon, and John G. Swogger. 2016–2017. Journeys to Complete the Work: Stories about Repatriations and Changing the Way We Bring Native American Ancestors Home. *NAGPRA Comics*, Issue 1. Accessed April 28, 2020. https://nagpracomics.weebly.com.

Backhouse, Paul N., Brent R. Weisman, and Mary Beth Rosebrough, eds. 2017. *We Come for Good: Archaeology and Tribal Historic Preservation at the Seminole Tribe of Florida.* Gainesville: University Press of Florida.

Basso, Keith H. 1970. "To Give Up on Words": Silence in Western Apache Culture. *Southwestern Journal of Anthropology* 26(3): 213–230.

Bollwerk, Elizabeth, Robert Connolly, and Carol McDavid. 2015. Co-Creation and Public Archaeology. *Advances in Archaeological Practice* 3(3): 178–187.

Brown, Kaitlin, Jan Timbrook, and Dana N. Bardolph. 2018. "A Song of Resilience": Exploring Communities of Practice in Chumash Basket Weaving in Southern California. *Journal of California and Great Basin Anthropology* 38(2): 143–162.

Bruchac, Margaret M. 2018. *Savage Kin: Indigenous Informants and American Anthropologists.* Tucson: University of Arizona Press.

Collier, Mary E. T., and Sylvia B. Thalman, eds. 1996. *Interviews with Tom Smith and Maria Copa: Isabel Kelly's Ethnographic Notes on the Coast Miwok Indians of Marin and Southern Sonoma Counties, California.* Miwok Archaeological Preserve of Marin Occasional Paper, no. 6. Miwok Archaeological Preserve of Marin, San Rafael, California.

Cowie, Sarah E., Diane L. Teeman, and Christopher C. LeBlanc, eds. 2019. *Collaborative Archaeology at Stewart Indian School.* Reno: University of Nevada Press.

Dietz, Stephen Alan. 1976. *Echa-Tamal:* A Study of Coast Miwok Acculturation. Master's thesis, San Francisco State University, San Francisco.

Harris, La Donna, and Jacqueline Wasilewski. 2004. Indigeneity, an Alternative Worldview: Four R's (Relationship, Responsibility, Reciprocity, Redistribution) vs. Two P's (Power and Profit). Sharing the Journey towards Conscious Evolution. *Systems Research and Behavioral Science* 21: 489–503.

Hauser, Mark W., Whitney Battle-Baptiste, Koji Lau-Ozawa, Barbara L. Voss, Reinhard Bernbeck, Susan Pollock, Randall H. McGuire, Uzma Z. Rizvi, Christopher Hernandez, and Sonya Atalay. 2018. Archaeology as Bearing Witness. *American Anthropologist* 120(3): 535–548.

Hodgetts, Lisa, and Laura Kelvin. 2020. At the Heart of the Ikaahuk Archaeology Project. In *Archaeologies of the Heart*, edited by Kisha Supernant, Jane Eva Baxter, Natasha Lyons, and Sonya Atalay, 97–115. Cham: Springer Nature Switzerland AG.

Hull, Kathleen L., and John G. Douglas. 2020. Conceptualizing Community to Connect Past and Present: Making the Case in *Forging Communities in Colonial Alta California. SAA Archaeological Record* 20(2): 12–14, 19–20.

King, Tiffany Lethabo. 2019. *The Black Shoals: Offshore Formations of Black and Native Studies.* Durham, NC: Duke University Press.

Lightfoot, Kent G. 1995. Culture Contact Studies: Redefining the Relationship between Prehistoric and Historical Archaeology. *American Antiquity* 60(2): 199–217.

Lightfoot, Kent G., and Sarah L. Gonzalez. 2018. The Study of Sustained Colonialism: An Example from the Kashaya Pomo Homeland in Northern California. *American Antiquity* 83(3): 427–443.

Lyons, Natasha, and Kisha Supernant. 2020. Introduction to an Archaeology of the Heart. In *Archaeologies of the Heart*, edited by Kisha Supernant, Jane Eva Baxter, Natasha Lyons, and Sonya Atalay, 1–19. Springer Nature Switzerland AG, Cham.

Martindale, Andrew, and Natasha Lyons (eds.). 2014. Special Section: Community-Oriented Archaeology. *Canadian Journal of Archaeology* 38: 425–433.

Martinez, Desireé Reneé. 2012. A Land of Many Archaeologists: Archaeology with Native Californians. In *Contemporary Issues in California Archaeology*, edited by Terry L. Jones and Jennifer E. Perry, 355–367. Walnut Creek, CA: Left Coast Press.

Miranda, Deborah A. 1999. *Indian Cartography*. Greenfield Center, NY: Greenfield Review Press.

Mrozowski, Stephen A. 2012. Pragmatism and the Relevancy of Archaeology for Contemporary Society. In *Archaeology in Society: Its Relevance in the Modern World*, edited by Marcy Rockman and Joe Flatman, 239–256. New York: Springer.

Nelson, Peter A. 2017. Indigenous Archaeology at Tolay Lake: Responsive Research and the Empowered Tribal Management of a Sacred Landscape. PhD diss., University of California, Berkeley.

———. 2020. Refusing Settler Epistemologies and Maintaining an Indigenous Future for Tolay Lake, Sonoma County, California. *American Indian Quarterly* 44(2): 221–242.

Nicholas, George. 2018. When Scientists "Discover" What Indigenous People Have Known for Centuries. *Smithsonian Magazine.* Accessed April 30, 2020. https://www.smithsonianmag.com/science-nature/why-science-takes-so-long-catch-up-traditional-knowledge-180968216/.

Panich, Lee M. 2020. *Narratives of Persistence: Indigenous Negotiations of Colonialism in Alta and Baja California*. Tucson: University of Arizona Press.

Panich, Lee M., and Tsim D. Schneider. 2019. Categorical Denial: Evaluating Post-1492 Indigenous Erasure in the Paper Trail of American Archaeology. *American Antiquity* 84(4): 651–668.

Reetz, Elizabeth, and William Quackenbush. 2016. Creating Collaborative Learning Opportunities for Indigenous Youth with Archaeology-Based Environmental Education. *Advances in Archaeological Practice* 4(4): 492–502.

Satta, Mark. 2018. Epistemic Humility as a Presidential Virtue. *Harvard Law & Policy Review* (blog), May 17, 2018. Accessed May 24, 2020. https://harvardlpr.com/2018/05/17/epistemic-humility-as-a-presidential-virtue/.

Sarris, Greg. 1993. Introduction. In *We Are Still Here: A Coast Miwok Exhibit*, edited by Kathleen Smith, 2–3. Bolinas, CA: Bolinas Museum.

Schmidt, Peter R., and Alice B. Kehoe. 2019. Archaeologies of the Listening: Beginning Thoughts. In *Archaeologies of Listening*, edited by Peter R. Schmidt and Alice B. Kehoe, 1–22. Gainesville: University Press of Florida.

Schneider, Tsim D. 2010. Placing Refuge: Shell Mounds and the Archaeology of Colonial Encounters in the San Francisco Bay Area, California. PhD diss., University of California, Berkeley.

———. 2015. Placing Refuge and the Archaeology of Indigenous Hinterlands in Colonial California. *American Antiquity* 80(4): 695–713.

Schneider, Tsim D., and Katherine Hayes. 2020. Epistemic Colonialism: Is it Possible to Decolonize Archaeology? *American Indian Quarterly* 44(2): 127–148.

Silliman, Stephen W. 2004. *Lost Laborers in Colonial California: Native Americans and the Archaeology of Rancho Petaluma*. Tucson: University of Arizona Press.

Smith, Kathleen. 2014. *Enough for All: Foods of My Dry Creek Pomo and Bodega Miwuk People*. Heyday, Berkeley, California.

Smith, Kathleen, ed. 1993. *We Are Still Here: A Coast Miwok Exhibit*. Booklet published in conjunction with the exhibition "We Are Still Here: A Coast Miwok Exhibit," August 22–October 3, 1993. Bolinas Museum, Bolinas, California.

Spector, Janet D. 1993. *What Does This Awl Mean? Feminist Archaeology at a Wahpeton Dakota Village*. St. Paul: Minnesota Historical Society Press.

Soza War Soldier, Rose. 2018. "Partial List of California Indian Faculty." *News from Native California*. Accessed May 7, 2020. http://newsfromnativecalifornia.com/partial-list-of-california-indian-faculty/.

Stahl, Ann Brower. 2020. Assembling "Effective Archaeologies" toward Equitable Futures. *American Anthropologist* 122(1): 37–50.

Trouillot, Michel-Rolph. 1995. *Silencing the Past: Power and the Production of History*. Boston: Beacon Press.

Contributors

PAUL N. BACKHOUSE is senior director of the Heritage and Environment Resources Office and the Tribal Historic Preservation Officer for the Seminole Tribe of Florida. Dr. Backhouse has served the Seminole Tribe of Florida for fourteen years and is the lead editor of *We Come for Good: Archaeology and Tribal Historic Preservation at the Seminole Tribe of Florida*.

MATTHEW A. BEAUDOIN is a principal and manager of Archaeological Assessments at Timmins Martelle Heritage Consultants Inc., a private cultural resources management firm based in London, Ontario, Canada. Matthew is the author of *Challenging Colonial Narratives: Nineteenth-Century Great Lakes Archaeology*.

SARAH E. COWIE is associate professor of anthropology at the University of Nevada, Reno. Her earlier work in historical archaeology resulted in the book *The Plurality of Power: An Archaeology of Industrial Capitalism*. More recently, she has turned toward collaborative archaeology and decolonizing methods and has co-edited *Collaborative Archaeology at Stewart Indian School*. Her research in archaeology has been recognized by the Society for Historical Archaeology, the National Academy of Sciences, and the White House Office of Science and Technology Policy.

CATHERINE E. DICKSON has been an archaeologist with the Confederated Tribes of the Umatilla Indian Reservation (CTUIR) Cultural Resources Protection Program since 1998. She strives to ensure that agencies consider impacts to historic properties from all eras, with a special focus on those of religious and cultural significance to the CTUIR. Catherine is the author of many cultural resource management reports, including *Weyíiletpu, Imatalamłáma, and Walúulapam Traditional Use of Powder, Burnt, and Malheur Rivers, Or-*

egon and *Consideration of National Register Districts in the Upper John Day Reservoir, Oregon and Washington.*

KATHLEEN L. HULL is professor of anthropology and heritage studies at the University of California, Merced. Her books include *Pestilence and Persistence: Yosemite Indian Demography and Culture in Colonial California* and *Forging Communities in Colonial Alta California*, the latter co-edited with John G. Douglass. Her research has also been published in several edited volumes and a variety professional journals, including *American Antiquity, California Archaeology, Journal of Anthropological Archaeology, Journal of Archaeological Science, Journal of California and Great Basin Anthropology, World Archaeology,* and the *International Journal of Historical Archaeology.*

KURT A. JORDAN is associate professor of anthropology and American Indian and Indigenous Studies at Cornell University and currently directs Cornell's American Indian and Indigenous Studies Program. He is the author of *The Seneca Restoration, 1715–1754: An Iroquois Local Political Economy* and "Incorporation and Colonization: Postcolumbian Iroquois Satellite Communities and Processes of Indigenous Autonomy" (*American Anthropologist* 2013).

IAN KRETZLER is affiliate curator of archaeology at the Burke Museum and project archaeologist at Cultural Resource Consultants, both in Seattle. He received the 2021 Society for American Archaeology Dissertation Award for "An Archaeology of Survivance on the Grand Ronde Reservation: Telling Stories of Enduring Native Presence." His work has been published in *Archaeologies, American Indian Culture and Research Journal,* and other venues.

NICHOLAS C. LALUK is a member of the White Mountain Apache Tribe located in east-central Arizona. He is assistant professor of anthropology at the University of California, Berkeley. His research goals mandate collaborative and multivocal research with tribal and Indigenous communities. His work has been published in the *Journal of Social Archaeology, Arizona Anthropologist,* and *The Oxford Handbook of Southwest Archaeology.*

MAUREEN MAHONEY is Tribal archaeologist for the Seminole Tribe of Florida Tribal Historic Preservation Office. She is the author of "*Tarakkvlkv* (Land of Palms): Bridging the Gap between Archaeology and Tribal Perspectives," a chapter in *We Come for Good: Archaeology and Tribal Historic Preservation at the Seminole Tribe of Florida*.

PETER A. NELSON is a citizen of the Federated Indians of Graton Rancheria and assistant professor of ethnic studies and environmental science, policy, and management at the University of California, Berkeley. His research has appeared in *American Indian Quarterly* and *Historical Archaeology*, among other venues.

LEE M. PANICH is associate professor of anthropology at Santa Clara University. He is the author of *Narratives of Persistence: Indigenous Negotiations of Colonialism in Alta and Baja California* and of various academic journal articles. He is the co-editor of *The Routledge Handbook of the Archaeology of Indigenous-Colonial Interaction in the Americas*, with Sara L. Gonzalez, and *Indigenous Landscapes and Spanish Missions: New Perspectives from Archaeology and Ethnohistory*, with Tsim D. Schneider.

HANNAH RUSSELL is the owner and principal investigator of Cottonwood Archaeology in Moab, Utah. Hannah's career has spanned over fifteen years in contract, academic, government, and research-based archaeologies in rural, backcountry, urban, and industrial environmental settings throughout the United States with particular emphasis on the West, especially Utah. Hannah is active in the Utah Professional Archaeological Council and with the Southeast Utah Pod of 500 Women Scientists.

LAURA L. SCHEIBER, PhD, is the owner and principal investigator of Bighorn Archaeology LLC. She is the co-editor of *Engineering Mountain Landscapes: An Anthropology of Social Investment*; *Across a Great Divide: Continuity and Change in Native North American Societies, 1400–1900*; and *Archaeological Landscapes on the High Plains*. Her research has also been published in *Antiquity*, *American Antiquity*, *Journal of Archaeological Science Reports*, *Journal of Field Archaeology*, and *Plains Anthropologist*.

DAVE W. SCHEIDECKER is research coordinator for the Seminole Tribe of Florida Tribal Historic Preservation Office. In this role, he manages the Seminole Site File and oversees historical and historical archaeological projects for the Tribe. He also designs and publishes interpretive story books (e.g., *Egmont Key: A Seminole Story*) for the Seminole Tribe and the public.

TSIM D. SCHNEIDER, a citizen of the Federated Indians of Graton Rancheria, is associate professor of anthropology at the University of California, Santa Cruz. He is the author of *The Archaeology of Refuge and Recourse: Coast Miwok Resilience and Indigenous Hinterlands in Colonial California*, and his research has been published in *American Antiquity, American Anthropologist, American Indian Quarterly*, and other venues.

SHAWN STEINMETZ, a member of the Chickasaw Nation, has worked as an archaeologist and ethnographer with the Confederated Tribes of the Umatilla Indian Reservation Cultural Resources Protection Program since 1998. He is the author of numerous cultural resource management reports, including "Cayuse, Umatilla and Walla Walla Tribes Traditional Relationship to Buffalo and Buffalo Hunting"; "Traditional Use Investigation in the Vicinity of the John Day Fossil Beds National Monument"; and "Traditional Use Investigation in the Vicinity of the Indian Creek Obsidian Source, Baker County, Oregon."

DIANE L. TEEMAN is a member of the Burns Paiute Tribe, director of the Culture & Heritage Department of the Burns Paiute Tribe, and vice chair of the Burns Paiute Tribal Council. She is currently a doctoral candidate and a faculty research assistant in the Department of Anthropology at the University of Nevada, Reno, focusing on collaborative and decolonizing methodologies in archaeology. She co-edited *Collaborative Archaeology at Stewart Indian School*. Diane has spent the last thirty-three years working toward the protection and revitalization of tribal culture and heritage in the Great Basin of the western United States.

NICK TIPON is an enrolled member and elder of the Federated Indians of Graton Rancheria. He is former chair of the Tribe's Sacred Sites Protection Committee and Tribal Education Committee. He also served as the Tribe's National Parks liaison and NAGPRA Liaison and is a former Tribal archaeological monitor. He has lectured at UC Berkeley and other local colleges on topics related to the effects of climate change on Native American cultural resources, archaeology, and curation of artifacts and the treatment of Native American cultural resources. He has also lectured at Moscow State University (Russia), the Smithsonian Museum of Natural History in Washington, DC, and the Field Museum in Chicago.

SARAH TRABERT is assistant professor of anthropology at the University of Oklahoma. She is the author of *Archaeological Narratives of the North American Great Plains: From Ancient Pasts to Historic Resettlement.*

HEATHER WALDER is lecturer in the Department of Archaeology and Anthropology at the University of Wisconsin, La Crosse, and a research associate at the Field Museum in Chicago, Illinois. She has published articles in *Historical Archaeology, American Antiquity, The Journal of Archaeological Science, Archaeometry,* and other venues. Since 2018, she has co-directed Gete Anishinaabeg Izhichigewin Community Archaeology Project, a collaborative endeavor of the Red Cliff Band of Lake Superior Chippewa and archaeologists.

Index

Page numbers in *italics* refer to illustrations and tables.

Paiute, 166, 265; collaboration with, 270–73; forced removal of, 268–70; glass scrapers, 188–89

Paiute Indian Tribe, 185, 186–87, 269

Palmer, Joel, 52–53

Palúus Village (45FR36), 65

Parker, Samuel, Jr., 256, 257

Parker Street site, 256–57, 258

Past, 174; disturbance and avoidance of, 76, 77–81; Indigenous, 56–57; in Wyoming history, 197–98

Paternalism, 126

Patriot War of East Florida, 129

Pawnee, 96

Payne, King, 129

Paynes Town, 129

Payóopayo Maqšmáqš, 53

Pecos Classification, 8

Pelúucpu (Palouse), 65

Pendants: glass bead, 219

Peoria, 228

Peri, David, 299

Pericolonialism, 7; European objects and, 103–4; Plains groups, 94–95, 102

Perishable material: Ndee, 73

Perlot, Jean-Nicolas, 158–59

Persistence, 12, 151; Ndee, 76–77, 81–82, 86

Peshtigo Point site, 231

Petuns, 247

Photographs, 134, 155

Picuris, 102

Pierced coins, 110, 115–16, 118

Place names, 102, 103, 199; Euro-American, 91–92; power of, 90–91; reclaiming, 89, 104

Places, placemaking, 12–13, 195, 247, 279, 290; Apsáalooke, 197–98, 291

Place-thought, 281

Plainfeather, 202

Plains peoples, 94; and tipi ring sites, 199–200

Plant remains: Grand Ronde, 40

Plateau people, 51. See also Confederated Tribes of the Umatilla Indian Reservation

Plenty Coups, Chief, 202, 204, 207, 208, 211

Point Reyes National Seashore, 296

Po-ko-nó (CA-MRP-250/H), 159

Population collapse: Yosemite area, 158

Postcolonial sites, 155

Potawatomi, 218, 226, 236

Power: of place, 279

Power relations, 7, 29–30, 267, 294

Pragmatism, 6, 292

Prayer: in Stewart Indian School Project, 280

Prehistory, 189; concepts of, 16, 43, 53–54; vs. history, 6, 95

Presence, 2, 294; concept of, 287–88; dynamic, 297–98; teaching, 298–300; "we are still here," 292–93, 295

Present: concept of, 174

Presidio Nuestra Señora de Loreto de la Bahía, 220; glass beads from, 222–23, 225, 228, 232

Pretty Shield, 202

Prisoners of war (POWs), 271; Paiute, 269–70; removal of, 266, 268–69

Projectile points, 82, 167, 252; Desert Side-notched, 165–66, 168

Protohistory concept, 6, 16, 244

Pryse, E. Morgan, 33

Public sphere: persistence and memory in, 12–13

Pueblos, 8, 185; and El Cuartelejo, 95–96, 102

Pueblo VI period, 8

Puha, 279, 280, 292

Radiocarbon dates, 164; Indian Fort Road, 250–51

Railroads, 143, 185–86, 206

Ranchers: and Apsáalooke, 204, 205

Rancho Nicasio, 295

Rattlesnake Mountain, 205

Recentering, 294

Reciprocity, 5, 81, 289

Rector, Elias, 129

Red Banks site: glass beads from, 225, 231

Redistribution, 289

Red River: Spanish Fort on, 100–101, 102

Red Stick Creek, 141

Refuge sites, 9; El Cuartelejo as, 95–96; San Francisco Bay area, 298

Relationality, 289

Removal, 93, 265; to Grand Ronde reservation, 26–27; of Paiute prisoners of war, 266, 269–70, 271, 272–73, 291; trauma of, 8, 276, 281–82; treaty of 1855, 52–53

Renaming: Euro-American practice of, 89–90, 91–92, 95

René Menard Bridge Hilltop site, 251

Repatriation, 16, 79, 246

Repositories, 277, 296

Research designs, 292; regional, 169–70

Reservation era, 64; seasonal movements, 58–59

Reservations, 53, 247; allotment system, 32–33; Crow, 199, 202–4; Grand Ronde, 26–27; Indigenous peoples outside, 9–10; Seminole, 127, 129–31, 136–37, 140–43; termination and restoration of, 33–34

Residence: indicators of, 117

Residential sites: colonial-era, 153

Resilience, 12, 27

Resistance, 151, 288

Respect: Ndee tenet of, 80, 81

Responsibility, 5, 289

Restoration: of Grand Ronde Reservation, 33–34

Returning: as healing, 281–82

Riley, Ramon, 75; on projectile point colors, 82, 83

Rinehart, William V., 269

Rings: IHS, 252–53

Rio Grande Pueblos: as refugees, 95–96

Ritchie, William, 253

Roasting pits, 84

Rock art: Apsáalooke, 202

Rock Island sites, 235; glass beads at, 230, 231, 232; La Salle and, 220, 226

Rock-marking styles, 181

Rock shelters, 156, 162, 163

Rocky Mountains, 195

Rodeo: Cody, 207

Rogers Farm site, 251, 256, 261n10

Rogue River people, 35

Round Valley Indian Tribes, 12

Sacred Sites Protection Committee (FIGR), 295, 298

Sampson, John, 61

Sampson, Leo, 61

San Bernardo (Longest site), 100

San Carlos Apache, 71

San Carlos Apache Tribe, 73

San Francisco Bay area, 295, 298

San Francisco Mountains, 187

Sanft, Samantha, 250

Santa Clara de Asís mission, 13

Santa Clara Pueblo, 185

Santa Clara University, 13

San Teodoro (Spanish Fort), 100–101

Sarris, Greg, 293, 299

Satellite communities: Haudenosaunee, 242, 248, 249–50, 256

Scott City (Kansas), 102

Scott County Pueblo (14SC1), 96

Scrapers: glass, 188–89

Seasonal movements, 75; Crow, 204, 205; CTUIR, 58–60

Section 106 process, 191nn6,7, 210; tribal significance, 55–57; in Utah, 176–77, 186, 187–88

Self-determination: Ndee, 74, 76

Self-reflection, 6, 80

Seminole, 126, 291; Big Cypress Reservation, 129–31; camps, 132–40, 143–44; history of, 127–29; reservations, 140–43

Seminole Tribe of Florida, 127; archaeology, 131–40; THPO, 144–45

Seminole Wars, 127, 129, 138, 144

Seneca. See Onöndowa'ga:'

Seneca-Iroquois National Museum, 246

Seneca Lake, 252

Settlement patterns, 92, 140, 242

Settlements, 160; Euro-American, 51–52, 92; on Grand Ronde Reservation, 34–35

Settler colonialism, 5, 13, 26, 111, 126, 196, 258, 297, 300; CTUIR, 51–52; disappearance and, 29–30; violence, 290–91

Seven Mile community, 82

Shasta, 35

Shellmounds: in San Francisco Bay area, 298

Sheoships, Joseph, 61

Shoshone, 202, 209

Shoshone River, 199; European trappers on, 201–2

Sierra Nevada: identifying Indigenous sites in, 11–12

Sioux (Teton Lakota), 203

Site formation, 153, 156–57, 163

Site forms, 175, 177–78

Site recording practices, 12, 178; identifying material culture, 10–11; New York State, 244, 246

Sites, 2, 8, 153; identifying, 9, 11–12, 168–69; public memory and, 12–13

Six Nations Iroquois. See Haudenosaunee

Skepticism, 179

Small sites: Haudenosaunee, 248–50

Smith, Kathleen, 299

Smith, Morgan (Bird Clan), 139; camp of, 132–33, 138, 140

Smith, Tom, 299

Smith, Victor: on projectile point colors, 82, 83

Smithsonian Institution, 296

Social geography: Apsáalooke, 196, 197–98
Soto, Hernando de, 93
Southern Plains, 90, 101; French on, 95, 97–98
Southern Pomo, 293, 294–95, 296, 297, 298, 299
Southern Tonto Apache, 71
Southern Ute Indian Tribe, 185
Sovereignty, 12, 16, 74, 76, 79
Space: and time, 280–81
Space use: Haudenosaunee Confederacy, 247–50, 259
Spanish, 73, 220; colonialism, 9, 95, 298; in Florida, 127, 129; on Plains, 89, 100–101; trade networks, 232, 234
Spanish Fort (Texas), 90, *91*, 97–98; cultural affiliation of, 100–101, 102–3
Spring, Otto, 98
Springs, 199; Apsáalooke use of, 204, 205; Euro-American control of, 206, 210–11
Stanislaus River, 167
St. Croix Island (Maine), 231
Stereotypes, 28, 126
Stevens, Isaac, 53
Stewart Advisory Committee, 273
Stewart Indian School (Nevada), 266, 282, 291; archaeological field school in, 273–75, 279–80; artifact treatment at, 276–77; collaborative partnerships, 14–15; history of, 275–76
St. Ignace, 228
St. Lawrence Valley, 248
Surveys, 84, 187; psychological, 178–79, 191n9; of Seminole camps, 133–34
Survivance, 26, 30, 180; archaeological evidence of, 40, 42; material culture of, 43–44, 117–18
Survivors: of epidemics, 156
Susquehanna Valley, 248
Susquehannocks, 247
Syncretization, 180

Tamalán, 63
Tamal Liwa (Tomales Bay), 296, 297
Tamánwit, 49, 55
Tamástslikt Cultural Institute, 57
Tampa Reservation, 127
Taos, 102
Taovayas band (Wichitas), 100, 101
Taughannock Creek, 250
Teabo, Dolly, 37
Teabo, Edward, 37

Teabo, Joseph, 36
Teaching: presence, 298–300
Technological analysis: pre- and post-1492 assemblages, 164–65
Terminal narratives, 5, 6, 151
Termination, 32, 33, 97, 297
Texas: *La Belle* wreck in, 217, 220–21
Textiles: Euro-American, 162
35GM22: cultural affiliation of, 63–64
Thoburn, Joseph, 98
THPOs. *See* Tribal Historic Preservation Offices
Tiger, Ada (Snake Clan), 142
Time, 290; Native American, 56–57; and space, 280–81
Tipi ring sites, 93, 196, 199–200, *202* ; Apsáalooke use of, 204–5; Euro-American use of, 209–11; tourism and, 208–9
Tipis, 181
Tolay Lake Regional Park, 298
Tonawanda, 247
Tonto Apache Tribe, 73
Tourism: Bighorn Basin, 206, 207; Seminole, 131, *135* ; tipi ring sites and, 208–10, 211
Townley-Read site, 246, 253
Towns: Haudenosaunee, 242, 252, 256, 257, 259
Trade, trade networks, 94, 219, 247; French, 97–98, 99, 220, 225–27, 228–33; glass beads in, 221–22, 233–36; Great Lakes, 217–19; trapper, 201–2
Trading posts, 12, 141; Big Cypress, 130–31; Crow Reservation and, 203, 204; Ferdinandina, 98, 99; French, 98, 99
Traditionalism: adaptive, 180–81
Trail Creek site, 200, 202, 205, 209, 210
Trail Creek trading post, 203
Trails, 130, 200; Paiute POW removal, 266, 268–70, 271, 272
Trappers: Western Plains, 201–2, 211
Trauma: boarding school, 8, 274, 282; intergenerational, 266–67
Treaties, 30
Treaty of 1855: removal, 52–53
Tribal Historic Preservation Offices (THPOs): FIGR, 295, 298; Seminole, 131, 133, 137, 144–45; Washoe Tribe, 273
Tsimshian, 184
Tumilaca la Chimba, 78
Tutelos, 254
Two Leggings, 202

9 780813 080185